T. S. Eliot's Parisian Year

UNIVERSITY PRESS OF FLORIDA

Florida A&M University, Tallahassee
Florida Atlantic University, Boca Raton
Florida Gulf Coast University, Ft. Myers
Florida International University, Miami
Florida State University, Tallahassee
New College of Florida, Sarasota
University of Central Florida, Orlando
University of Florida, Gainesville
University of North Florida, Jacksonville
University of South Florida, Tampa
University of West Florida, Pensacola

T. S. ELIOT'S
· PARISIAN YEAR ·

Nancy Duvall Hargrove

University Press of Florida

Gainesville · Tallahassee · Tampa · Boca Raton
Pensacola · Orlando · Miami · Jacksonville · Ft. Myers · Sarasota

Excerpts from "The Hollow Men," "Ash Wednesday," "Journey of the Magi," and "Sweeney Agonistes: Fragment of an Agon" in *Collected Poems 1909–1962* by T. S. Eliot, copyright 1936 by Houghton Mifflin Harcourt Publishing Company and renewed 1964 by T.S. Eliot, reprinted by permission of the publisher.

Excerpts from "Burnt Norton" in *Four Quartets* by T. S. Eliot, copyright 1936 by Harcourt, Inc. and renewed 1964 by T.S. Eliot, reprinted by permission of the publisher.

Excerpts from "East Coker" in *Four Quartets*, copyright 1940 by T. S. Eliot and renewed 1968 by Esme Valerie Eliot, reprinted by permission of Houghton Mifflin Harcourt Publishing Company.

Excerpts from "The Dry Salvages" in *Four Quartets*, copyright 1941 by T. S. Eliot and renewed 1969 by Esme Valerie Eliot, reprinted by permission of Houghton Mifflin Harcourt Publishing Company.

Excerpts from "Little Gidding" in *Four Quartets*, copyright 1942 by T. S. Eliot and renewed 1970 by Esme Valerie Eliot, reprinted by permission of Houghton Mifflin Harcourt Publishing Company.

Excerpts from *The Letters of T. S. Eliot, 1898–1922*, copyright © 1988 by SET Copyrights Limited, reprinted by permission of Houghton Mifflin Harcourt Publishing Company.

Excerpts from *Selected Prose of T. S. Eliot* by Frank Kermode, copyright © 1975 by Valerie Eliot, reprinted by permission of Houghton Mifflin Harcourt Publishing Company.

Excerpts from *Inventions of the March Hare: Poems 1909–1917* by T. S. Eliot, text copyright © 1996 by Valerie Eliot, reprinted by permission of Houghton Mifflin Harcourt Publishing Company.

Excerpts from "What Dante Means to Me" from *To Criticize the Critic* by T. S. Eliot. Copyright 1965 by T. S. Eliot. Copyright renewed © 1993 by Valerie Eliot. Reprinted by permission of Farrar, Straus and Giroux, LLC.

Excerpts from *To Criticise the Critic and Other Writings* by T. S. Eliot. Copyright 1965 by Valerie Eliot. Reprinted by permission of Faber and Faber Ltd/The T. S. Eliot Estate.

Excerpts from *The Letters of T. S. Eliot: Volume I: 1898–1922* ed. Valerie Eliot. Copyright by SET Copyrights Limited. Reprinted by permission of Faber and Faber Ltd/The T. S. Eliot Estate.

Excerpts from "A Commentary," *The Criterion* 13.52 (April 1934): 451–4 by T. S. Eliot. Reprinted by permission of Faber and Faber Ltd/The T. S. Eliot Estate.

First cloth printing, 2009
First paperback printing, 2010

15 14 13 12 11 10   6 5 4 3 2 1

Library of Congress Cataloging-in-Publication Data
Hargrove, Nancy Duvall.
T. S. Eliot's Parisian year / Nancy Duvall Hargrove.
p. cm.
Includes bibliographical references and index.
ISBN 978-0-8130-3401-0 (cloth)
ISBN 978-0-8130-3553-6 (paper)
1. Eliot, T. S. (Thomas Stearns), 1888–1965—Knowledge—France. 2. American poetry—French influences. 3. Poets, American—20th century—Biography. 4. Paris (France)—Intellectual life—20th century. I. Title.
PS3509.L43Z681594 2009
821.'912—dc22 [B]   2009011118

The University Press of Florida is the scholarly publishing agency for the State University System of Florida, comprising Florida A&M University, Florida Atlantic University, Florida Gulf Coast University, Florida International University, Florida State University, New College of Florida, University of Central Florida, University of Florida, University of North Florida, University of South Florida, and University of West Florida.

University Press of Florida
15 Northwest 15th Street
Gainesville, FL 32611-2079
http://www.upf.com

To My Grandchildren
Guy, Maggie, Elizabeth, Jacob, and Matthew

"Tantôt Paris était tout le passé; tantôt tout l'avenir:
et ces deux aspects se combinaient en un présent parfait."

T. S. Eliot, "What France Means to You," *La France Libre*

CONTENTS

ILLUSTRATIONS

PREFACE AND ACKNOWLEDGMENTS

In 1970 upon completion of my dissertation on Eliot's use of landscape at the University of South Carolina, my dissertation director Ashley Brown suggested that, after I revised the dissertation for publication, I should explore the overlooked year that Eliot spent in Paris, researching newspapers and journals of the day to discover the cultural, intellectual, and political events which took place in order to determine what may have influenced him. Twenty years later, after completing other research projects, I finally turned to the topic, hoping to find enough material for a paper to be delivered at an international Eliot symposium at Lund University in Sweden in 1993. I discovered a veritable gold mine of information that has occupied me for fifteen years on what has been the most intriguing and enjoyable project of my career. Since I myself, like Eliot, first went to Paris at the age of twenty-two as a graduate student, I knew firsthand the joy and wonder of discovering that marvelous city, the wish to experience as much as possible, and the hope of becoming a cosmopolitan Parisian; feelings which I believe that Eliot must have also had.

I hope that readers will be both informed and entertained by the text as well as by the illustrations of people, places, events, advertisements, fashions, cartoons, and works of art which give valuable insights into the times. Many of these illustrations are nearly one hundred years old and are reproduced from microfilm of 1910–1911 newspapers, and journals, and from old postcards; great care was taken to restore them to as pristine and clear a condition as possible, but some still bear the marks of their age. I include them nevertheless because of their valuable visual testimony to this period.

For permission to quote from Eliot's works, I am grateful to Faber and Faber LTD/The T. S. Eliot Estate, with thanks to Becky Thomas, Permissions Controller; to Harcourt, Brace, Jovanovich, with thanks to Anthony M. McDonald, Copyrights and Permissions Specialist; and to Farrar, Straus and Giroux, with thanks to Julia Sherrier, Permissions Assistant. Every effort has been made to identify, contact, and obtain permissions from all copyright holders.

Portions of the book were first published in the following books and journals, and I am grateful for permission to include that material: "The Great Parade: Cocteau, Picasso, Satie, Massine, Diaghilev—and T. S. Eliot," *Mosaic, a journal of the interdisciplinary study of literature* 31.1 (March 1998): 83–106; *Landscape as Symbol in the Poetry of T. S. Eliot*, University Press of Mississippi (1978); "Paris During Eliot's Residence in 1910–1911: A Practical Guide to the City," *Yeats Eliot Review* 24.1 (Spring 2007): 3–23; "'Un Présent Parfait': Eliot and La Vie Parisienne," *T. S. Eliot at the Turn of the Century*, ed. Marianne Thormählen, Lund University Press (1994); "T. S. Eliot," *Twentieth Century American Dramatists*, Vol. 7 of the *Dictionary of Literary Biography*, Gale/Cengage Learning (1981); "T. S. Eliot and the Classical Music Scene in Paris, 1910–1911," *Publications of the Mississippi Philological Association 2004* (2004): 10–26; "T. S. Eliot and the Dance," *Journal of Modern Literature* 21.1 (Summer 1997): 61–88; "T. S. Eliot and Opera in Paris, 1910–1911," *Yeats Eliot Review* 21.3 (Fall 2004): 2–20; "T. S. Eliot and the Parisian Theatre World, 1910–1911," *South Atlantic Review* 66.4 (Fall 2001): 1–44; "T. S. Eliot and Popular Entertainment in Paris, 1910–1911," *Journal of Popular Culture* 36.2 (Winter 2003): 77–115; "T. S. Eliot's Year Abroad, 1910–1911: The Visual Arts," *South Atlantic Review* 71.1 (Winter 2006): 89–131; and "*The Waste Land* as a Surrealist Poem," *The Comparatist* 19 (1995): 1–15, co-authored with Paul Grootkerk, who, along with the journal, has given me permission to use portions of the essay.

For help in securing the illustrations and permissions to use them, I would like to thank Barbara Mazza and Bruno Pouchin of the Agence Roger-Viollet; Tom Lisanti, Stephan Saks, Phil Karg, and Alice Standin at the New York Public Library for the Performing Arts; Gary M. Johnson at the Library of Congress; Lakshmi Mohandas at the Simon R. Guggenheim Museum; Anne Quarles of L & M Services; Marj Ochs at the University of Texas Libraries, Austin; Leslie A. Morris and Heather Cole at the Houghton Library, Harvard University; Tricia Smith of Art Resource; and Cristin O'Keefe Aptowicz of the Artists Rights Society. Alain Rivière, the nephew of Alain-Fournier, kindly gave me permission to use the photograph of Alain-Fournier, and Michel Baranger of the Association des Amis de Jacques Rivière et d'Alain-Fournier generously provided me with the 1986 *Bulletin* of that organization containing Stuart Barr's essay on Alain-Fournier's relationship with Eliot. Russ Houston and Katie Haynes of Photographic Services in the department of University Relations at Mississippi State University skillfully improved the quality of many of the old illustrations and put them into digital format.

I would also like to express my gratitude to the helpful staffs at the many libraries and museums in which I did research for the book: In Paris, the Bibliothèque nationale de France (François Mitterand, Richelieu, and the Department of Music);

the Bibliothèque de l'Opéra; the Bibliothèque Historique de la Ville de Paris; the Bibliothèque de l'Arsenal; the Musée du Louvre; the Musée d'Orsay; the Musée d'Art Moderne de la Ville de Paris; the Musée de la Mode et du Costume; the Musée de l'Histoire de France; the Musée des Arts et des Traditions Populaires; the Musée Carnavalet; the Musée Picasso; the Musée Montmartre; the Musée Montparnasse; the Musée Bourdelle, and the Musée Curies; in Cambridge, England, King's College Library, Cambridge University; in Cambridge, Massachusetts, the Houghton Library, Harvard University; in Boston, the Isabella Stewart Gardner Museum; in New York, the New York Public Library for the Performing Arts, the Museum of Modern Art, the Metropolitan Museum of Art, and the Simon R. Guggenheim Museum; in Birmingham, the Mervyn H. Sterne Library at the University of Alabama at Birmingham; and in Starkville, MS, the Mitchell Memorial Library at Mississippi State University.

Numerous Eliot scholars have contributed to the book. For many years, members of the T. S. Eliot Society heard various papers on my ongoing research on Eliot and Paris at the annual conferences, and I thank them for their many suggestions and their general good-will, especially Jewel Spears Brooker, David Chinitz, and Grover Smith. I want to extend heartfelt thanks to Cyrena Pondrom, Benjamin Lockerd, and Marianne Thormählen, who read the manuscript in whole or in part and offered me invaluable suggestions. The works of many Eliot scholars provided me with information and inspiration throughout my career, and the particular debts that I owe them are acknowledged in the text.

Robert West did a painstaking and thorough job of editing the manuscript at an early stage, while Laura West, Guy Hargrove III, and Francis Miller provided technical assistance. Marie Baran, Louise and Guy Serratrice, and Christophe Damien advised me on translations of several especially challenging French phrases and expressions. I owe a general debt of gratitude to my colleagues in the English Department at Mississippi State University for their support and encouragement. For financial support of my research for the book, I am grateful to the English Department, the College of Arts and Sciences, and the Office of Research at Mississippi State University; in the spring semester of 1999, I spent a sabbatical in Paris doing much of the research for this book in addition to various shorter research trips.

I would also like to acknowledge the role played by five Fulbright grants which gave me the ability to undertake this project. In 1963–64 a student grant to France gave me a facility with the language and a knowledge and love of France and French culture that determined to a large extent the course of my career and, in effect, laid the groundwork for this book, while a Junior Lectureship there in 1976–77 confirmed my affection for the country, its people, and its culture, an affection which I share with Eliot. On Fulbright Senior Lectureships to Belgium in 1984–1985 and to Sweden in 1992, I met international Eliot scholars and, after the grant periods ended, did research in Paris. Finally, the Distinguished Chair Award to Austria in 2005–2006—while focused primarily on teaching American Literature at the University of Vienna—allowed me the opportunity to research aspects of Eliot's 1910–1911 summer trip to Germany and Italy and to see art works, ballets, and operas that influenced him.

At the University Press of Florida, I am grateful for the expertise of the following people: Marthe Walters, assistant editor in the editorial department, Ray Brady, copy editor, and Amy Gorelick, Senior Acquisitions Editor.

Finally, I would like to thank my family for their love and support as I worked on this project over many years and in many locations: my husband Guy; my son Guy, his wife Barbara, and their children Guy, Maggie, and Elizabeth; and my daughter Meg, her husband Francis, and their children Jacob and Matthew.

INTRODUCTION

In his 1944 essay in French entitled "What France Means to You," T. S. Eliot notes that he had the "exceptional good fortune" to discover Paris during the academic year 1910–1911 (94),[1] a time when that city was the intellectual and cultural center of the world,[2] seething with a diversity of ideas, celebrating all the fine arts, and promoting both its established artists and its young, experimental ones, whose names include Pablo Picasso and Georges Braque, Igor Stravinsky and Maurice Ravel, Guillaume Apollinaire, and Marcel Proust. Intellectual figures such as Henri Bergson, Charles Maurras, Émile Durkheim, Pierre Janet, and Marie Curie proposed and expounded a host of exciting, innovative, and often conflicting views, while literary figures such as Charles Péguy, Paul Claudel, André Gide, St.-John Perse, and Alain-Fournier introduced new subject matter and experimented widely with style. Eliot remarked in "A Commentary" in the April 1934 issue of *The Criterion* that the city's "most exciting variety of ideas" contributed to his maturation (451–2). Its cultural riches were never more tantalizing than during the year of Eliot's residence, with extraordinary events such as the first exhibition of the Cubists at the Salon des Indépendants, the sensational multimedia extravaganza *Le Martyre de Saint Sébastien* [The Martyrdom of Saint Sebastian], the impressive showcase of the Beethoven Festival, the startlingly innovative ballets of the Ballets Russes with its acclaimed stars Vaslav Nijinsky and Tamara Karsavina, and the performance for the first time ever in Paris of Richard Wagner's tetralogy, *Der Ring des Nibelungen* [The Ring of the Nibelungs]. As Roger Shattuck remarks, "To a greater extent than at any time since the Renaissance, painters, writers, and musicians lived and worked together and tried their hands at each other's arts in an atmosphere of perpetual collaboration" (28). Paris was also the home of museums housing some of the world's greatest masterpieces of the past. Its stunning architecture included the 12th-century Cathédrale de Notre Dame, the recently constructed and highly controversial Tour Eiffel, and the nearly completed Basilique du Sacré Coeur, whose distinctive domes rose at the crest of Montmartre. In addition, it boasted technological advances such as the Métropolitain, automobiles, and occasionally an airplane overhead engaged in newly created competitions for distance and speed.

Into this heady and exciting atmosphere came the twenty-two-year-old American, whose experience there gave him the subjects, the tools, and the freedom to experiment that inspired his first poetic masterpiece, "The Love Song of J. Alfred Prufrock," and led to his becoming a major writer. It also provided him with ideas and techniques that would mark his drama and criticism as well as his political, religious, and social views. Its effects were extensive, long-lasting, and life-changing; as David Moody, one of a handful of Eliot scholars to have recognized the importance of the year, has noted, it was "a profoundly formative experience" (6). In the following pages, I demonstrate the myriad ways in which it influenced him, with particular emphasis on the Parisian cultural milieu.

Eliot came to Paris with a variety of goals in mind. First and foremost, he was seeking his poetic voice in French poetry. He reveals in "What France Means to You" that it was not chance that led him to Paris in 1910, explaining that, because of his reading the poetry of Charles Baudelaire, Jules Laforgue, Tristan Corbière, Arthur Rimbaud, and Stéphane Mallarmé as an undergraduate at Harvard, France had come to represent "la poésie" [poetry] to him (94), and he believed that "[t]he kind of poetry that I needed, to teach me the use of my own voice, . . . was only to be found in French" ("Yeats" 248). He even considered living permanently in Paris and writing poetry in French: "[D]uring the romantic year I spent in Paris after Harvard [,] I had . . . the idea of giving up English and trying to settle down and scrape along in Paris and gradually write French" (Hall 56). He in fact found not only his poetic voice, but subjects, techniques, and artistic beliefs as a result of the synergism of the arts, the interpenetration of artistic techniques, the daring experimentation, and the collaboration among various artists evident in the current cultural activities in Paris. Furthermore, he found inspiration in the arts and artists of the past as well as in the popular entertainments for which Paris was famous—or infamous. And he incorporated into his poetry—both immediately and later—aspects of the modern urban and technological scene observed in the French capital.

Because his serious-minded and conservative parents would have been unlikely to accept searching for his poetic voice as a legitimate reason for spending a year in Paris, he doubtless presented to them as his major purpose attending the lectures of the famous and wildly popular philosopher Henri Bergson at the Collège de France, with the argument that it would help to prepare him for a career as a professor of philosophy at Harvard. In addition to being a rationale likely to convince his parents of the necessity of spending a year in France, it would be an intellectually exciting experience for him. Another acceptable purpose which he perhaps proposed to them was the opportunity to immerse himself in French culture and literature and to gain fluency in French. Finally, a more personal purpose—one not likely mentioned to his parents but no doubt expressed to close friends such as Conrad Aiken prior to his departure and later indicated in a letter of April 1911 to his cousin Eleanor Hinckley (*Letters* 19–20)—was to become a cosmopolitan and sophisticated young man of the world.

His year in Paris provided him with a gold mine of cultural, intellectual, and personal experiences that extended his horizons in many directions and influenced him and his works in significant ways. He always looked back on it with nostalgia and acknowledged its impact upon him, describing the Paris of that time perhaps most memorably as "un présent parfait": "Tantôt Paris était tout le passé; tantôt tout l'avenir: et ces deux aspects se combinaient en un présent parfait" [On the one hand, Paris was completely the past; on the other hand, it was completely the future: and these two aspects combined to form a perfect present] ("What France" 94).

In the following pages, I re-create that "présent parfait" of 1910–1911 Paris, providing a comprehensive and detailed view of the complexities of the city, drawn from Parisian newspapers such as *Le Figaro, Comoedia, Le Matin, L'Action Française*, and *Le Petit Parisien;* from journals such as *La Nouvelle Revue Française* and *Comoedia Illustré;* from books about the city itself such as the 1907 edition of Baedeker's popular guidebook *Paris et ses environs* [Paris and its Environs]; from historical, architectural, and other types of accounts; and from books of photographs of Paris from this time period such as those by Borgé and Viasnoff, Beaumont-Maillet, the Caines, Deedes-Vincke, Gaillard, Gosling, and Kluver and Martin. In particular, I describe major cultural events that took place in Paris during the period of Eliot's residence. In each case, I suggest what influenced or may have influenced Eliot, based on biographical and textual information, and demonstrate the ways in which these influences contributed to his poetry, drama, and criticism. Because documentation of this period is limited to letters to and from Eliot,[3] his own reminiscences, and accounts by contemporaries such as Aiken and Montgomery Belgion, there are relatively few indications of what he actually saw, heard, or felt. Nevertheless, the available material amply demonstrates that he took extremely seriously the opportunity to immerse himself in all that Paris had to offer and provides insights into what was likely to have interested him. As I conducted my research, I often discovered a cultural event which struck me as one that Eliot would certainly have seen or known about, but proving it absolutely was not often possible.

Drawing on all these types of information, I describe the cultural and other events that occurred or were available, indicate what he actually attended, and, in the absence of those facts, speculate on what he was highly likely or perhaps likely to have attended. I also suggest the ways in which those events are or seem to be reflected in his works. Thus, while I must necessarily engage in some speculation, it is grounded in an in-depth knowledge of the period, of Eliot himself, and of his poetry, drama, and criticism. I also include his visits to other European locations during this year, and, in some instances, I explore the ways in which the effects of this early experience abroad extended into subsequent years and often throughout his life. My intention is to make a case for the powerful influence of the year as a whole, with a particular focus on its cultural opportunities.

In order to give as comprehensive a view as possible of Eliot's Parisian experience, I present important background information in the first two chapters. In Chapter 1, I provide an explanation of what brought him to Paris followed by a chronological overview of his year, including his arrival in October, offerings in high and popular culture in the fall, his two French friends, the opening of the university in November, Bergson's courses, intellectual and literary presences, the cultural scene in the spring, the end of the academic year, his summer trip, and his return to Paris in September prior to his departure for the United States. I also discuss the poems that were products of this period. In Chapter 2, I explore the practical elements of daily life in Paris in 1910–1911 as Eliot would have experienced them. After a compact history of the city from 1848 to 1911, I present brief accounts of domestic and international politics, the economy, buildings and landmarks, transportation, communications, electricity, sanitation, entertainment and photography, science and medicine, the status of men and women, and sports. Having established this background, I then turn to the major focus of the book, the cultural milieu of Paris and its influence on Eliot. Chapters 3 through 8 give detailed information about theatre, the visual arts, dance, opera, classical music, and popular entertainment, with descriptions of specific performances, performers, exhibitions, artists, and venues as well as indications of which Eliot attended, when known, or was likely to have attended, and how he was or may have been influenced by them. I close by demonstrating the profound and lifelong effects of Eliot's Parisian year on the man and his works.

Since this period was highly important to Eliot himself and since its exploration is crucial to the establishment of a more complete biographical and critical account of this major literary figure, it is somewhat surprising that there has not previously been an in-depth study of it in Eliot scholarship. Indeed, it has been largely overlooked, perhaps because of the limited amount of hard evidence regarding his specific activities and because such an undertaking requires a knowledge of French language and culture. However, in addition to my own essays, there are a few brief considerations of the subject. The most helpful are Belgion's essay, "Irving Babbitt and the Continent," which discusses the intellectual and literary influences that led

Eliot to Paris and those that affected him while there, and Herbert Howarth's marvelous chapter on Eliot's Parisian year in *Notes on Some Figures Behind T. S. Eliot*, which provides a fascinating glimpse into the literary and intellectual scene and includes the comment that "a whole book should be written on Eliot's debt, which is a debt of all of us, to the Paris of the five years before the Great War" (152). James E. Miller's *T. S. Eliot: The Making of an American Poet, 1888–1922* contains a chapter on this year with emphasis on Verdenal, Bergson, and Maurras, while three books with a biographical/critical focus each devote several pages to it: Peter Ackroyd's *T. S. Eliot: A Life* (39–45), A. D. Moody's *T. S. Eliot: Poet* (6–7, 22–30), and Lyndall Gordon's *T. S. Eliot: An Imperfect Life* (51–63).[4] There are also a number of studies of French literary and intellectual influences, both those encountered prior to his residence in Paris (such as Laforgue and Baudelaire) and those that developed or intensified during that time (such as Philippe, Gide, Péguy, Bergson, and Maurras, among others).[5] Because these influences have been treated extensively in Eliot scholarship, I restrict my discussion of them to a brief review in the first chapter.

Thus Eliot's sojourn in Paris during this *annus mirabilis* was indeed "un présent parfait" because of its combination of reverence for the past and excitement about the future; its lively intellectual climate; its variety of attractions from lecture halls to music halls, from theatre circles to boxing rings; its demonstration of the synergism of the arts; and its vibrant and magical atmosphere. All of these exerted a powerful influence upon his amazingly receptive, retentive, and synthesizing mind and imagination.

"UN PRÉSENT PARFAIT"

The Year in Review

In March 1910, Eliot informed his parents of his desire to spend the following academic year in Paris. In a letter dated April 3, 1910, his mother made clear her disapproval of such a venture and tried to dissuade or at least to discourage him by various tactics: "I have rather hoped you would not specialize later on French literature. I suppose you will know better in June what you want to do next year. . . . I can not bear to think of your being alone in Paris, the very words give me a chill. English speaking countries seem so different from foreign. I do not admire the French nation, and have less confidence in individuals of that race than in English" (*Letters* 13). Of course, as we know, he went anyway, either in defiance of her objections or with her reluctant acquiescence as a result of delicate negotiations or impassioned pleading. His desire to live in Paris was so strong that he somehow prevailed over this formidable force, who no doubt spoke for his father as well, and even secured their financial backing.

Eliot seems to have arrived at such a momentous and daring plan as the result of a convergence of influences in the years 1908–1910. The first, at least chronologically, was his discovery in the small library of the Harvard Union in December 1908 of the recently published second edition of Arthur Symons's 1899 book *The Symbolist Movement in Literature*, which introduced him to the French Symbolist poets, the most influential of whom was Laforgue. The book gave him striking insights into new ways of writing poetry and either instigated or fanned the flames of his passion for French poetry.[1] As he told Robert Nichols in a letter of August 8, 1917 (*Letters* 191), he was so impressed by them that he ordered from Paris the two-volume *Poètes d'Aujourd'hui* [Poets of Today] and subsequently the complete works of Laforgue, revealing later that he believed himself to be the first person in America to own the latter (Greene 20).

The "full extent of Eliot's debt to Laforgue is almost impossible to exaggerate" (46), as Erik Svarny suggests. He discusses some major characteristics that Eliot admired and emulated: the aim of being "'original at any cost'" (47); a "plethora of personae" who typically speak in a "cynical laconic tone" (47–8); the theme of the "painful failure of communication with the opposite sex" (48); and the use of *vers libre* (51). He singles out the dandy persona as being "of incalculable importance to Eliot's personal and poetic development," explaining that this male figure (as described in the mid-nineteenth century by Baudelaire) was highly interested in fashion, possessed impeccable taste and elegance, was intellectual, and evinced a detached, ironic impassivity (49–50); traits of Laforgue himself. Indeed, these traits are evident in many of the personae in poems which Eliot wrote "sous le signe de Laforgue" [under the sign or influence of Laforgue] just prior to, during, and immediately after his sojourn in Paris (qtd. in Greene 365; Svarny 47).

While Laforgue was the most influential of the Symbolist poets that he discovered through Symons, Eliot often acknowledged how powerfully the group as a whole affected and inspired him. He said, for example, that they evoked in him "wholly new feelings" with the force of "a revelation" ("The Perfect Critic" 5) that influenced the direction of his life: "I myself owe Mr. Symons a great debt: but for having read his book, I should not, in the year 1908, have heard of Laforgue or Rimbaud: I should probably not have begun to read Verlaine; and but for reading Verlaine, I should not have heard of Corbière. So the Symons book is one of those which have affected the course of my life" (rev. of Quennell 357). The most immediate effect was to convince him that he must go to their homeland to seek his own poetic voice. In "What Dante Means to Me," Eliot states that Laforgue taught him how to develop that voice: "Of Jules Laforgue, for instance, I can say that he was the first to teach me how to speak, to teach me the poetic possibilities of my own idiom of speech." He goes on to reveal that in both Laforgue and Baudelaire he saw that he could use as subject matter the urban scene:

> I think that from Baudelaire I learned first, a precedent for the poetical possibilities, never developed by any poet writing in my own language, of the more sordid aspects of the modern metropolis, of the possibility of fusion between the sordidly realistic and the phantasmagoric, the possibility of the juxtaposition of the matter-of-fact and the fantastic. From him, as from Laforgue I learned that the sort of material that I had, the sort of experience that an adolescent had had, in an industrial city in America, could be the material for poetry; and that the source of new poetry might be found in what had been regarded hitherto as the impossible, the sterile, the intractably unpoetic. (126)

Indeed, the role of Paris in their poetry must have compelled him to wish to see what he himself might make of it poetically.

Having realized that "[t]he kind of poetry that I needed, to teach me the use of my own voice, did not exist in English at all; it was only to be found in French" ("Yeats" 252), he seems to have decided by early 1910 that he must go to Paris, writing in "What France Means to You" that "[i]t was not chance that led me to Paris. For several years, France represented poetry above all, in my view. If I had not discovered Baudelaire, and all the poetry that derived from him—in particular that of Laforgue, Corbière, Rimbaud, and Mallarmé—I do not believe that I would ever have been able to write. This discovery assured me . . . that a modern language existed and that poetry in English held unexplored possibilities." He ends the essay with the statement that he fears that he has not fully conveyed the importance of Paris, of France, and of French literature and culture in his life (94).[2]

A second major influence, reinforcing Symons's book, was Irving Babbitt, professor of French literature at Harvard and author of *The Masters of Modern French Criticism* (1912), with whom Eliot took the course Literary Criticism in France in the fall of 1909 (*Letters* xx). In a speech given at Aix-en-Provence in 1947, Eliot described him as "a wise, learned and enthusiastic teacher" to whom he owed "the beginning of my acquaintance with and admiration for French prose" (Eliot Collection, King's College Library, Cambridge University). In addition, as Belgion perceptively points out, "To [Babbitt] may be attributed without protest the fostering of much of what is traditional in Eliot's understanding of both life and literature, and with equal impunity he can be said to have directed Eliot to proceed from Harvard to Paris as from the periphery to the centre" (51). Belgion reminds us that Babbitt was "a giant of American literary criticism," whose encyclopedic knowledge was conveyed with passion. Thus, when such a formidable force called for "the recovery of the disciplined sanity of the French classical spirit," it was an irresistible call for Eliot to make his way to Paris. As Belgion puts it, "at this point let fair stand the wind for France" (53–4).

A third attraction was the opportunity to deepen his knowledge of philosophy as well as French language and literature. In his sophomore year at Harvard, he took History of Ancient Philosophy and History of Modern Philosophy, and in his fourth year, having received a B.A. and begun an M.A., he took Philosophy of History: Ideals of Society, Religion, Art and Science under George Santayana (*Letters* xx). It would be intriguing to know how he came up with the idea of attending the courses of Bergson at the prestigious Collège de France in Paris. It could have been suggested to him by Babbitt or Santayana (who was himself influenced by Bergson), since Bergson's reputation had spread to America by 1907 (Douglass 11), and/or he may have seen it as a way to gain the approval of his parents, on the grounds that he could pursue a doctorate in philosophy upon returning to Harvard with the goal of becoming a professor in that subject, a career which they had in mind for him as more respectable and secure than that of a poet.[3] He himself had that ambition as well, according to a talk given in Brussels in December 1949, in which he referred to his intention at the age of twenty-five of becoming a professor of philosophy in America, after completing further studies at Oxford and at Harvard; he then remarked that his life followed a quite different course from what he had imagined, for he remained in Europe and pursued other activities (King's College Library).

As for French language and literature, it was only logical that he would plan to expand his facility with the former and his knowledge of the latter. At Harvard, he took French Prose and Poetry in his second year and Literary Criticism in France in his fourth year (*Letters* xx). His spoken French was apparently not very good when he arrived in Paris, as revealed in a letter of April 26, 1911 to his cousin Eleanor relaying the comment of the *femme de chambre* [maid] in his pension that a new American boarder "does not speak French very well yet. He speaks as Monsieur [Eliot] spoke in November" (*Letters* 18). To remedy this deficiency, he acquired as a tutor Henri-Alban Fournier (better known by his pseudonym Alain-Fournier), a twenty-four-year-old Frenchman who gave him conversation lessons in French and instigated his reading of the works of such writers as Philippe, Claudel, Gide, Péguy, and Dostoevsky (in French translation).

Finally, he must also have been drawn by the appeal of living in the most cultured, intellectual, liberal, and sophisticated place on earth in 1910 and becoming himself a cosmopolitan, polished man of the world like Laforgue and his speakers as well as Baudelaire's *flâneur* [stroller]. While Eliot already possessed to a certain degree "the urbane dandyism, the perfection of dress, manners, and accomplishments, which was the Harvard style of his time and in which he excelled" (Howarth 105), a year in Paris would allow him to cultivate these traits.

Arrival in Paris

And so he set sail in early October 1910 on his great adventure, apparently stopping in London on his way to Paris since his Baedeker guide, *London and Its Environs* (1908), is dated October the 14th, 1910 in black ink on the third page along with his name, inscribed as Thomas S. Eliot;[4] many sites are marked in pencil. He arrived in Paris soon thereafter and, like most people on their first visit, must have been impressed by its sights: the broad boulevards, the outdoor cafés, the open-air markets, the glorious parks, the Seine River, and such famous landmarks as the Tour Eiffel, the nearly-completed Basilique du Sacré Coeur, the Cathédrale de Notre Dame, and the Musée du Louvre (Figure 1). The streets were crowded with trams, autobuses, bicycles, and both open and closed cars, some driven by "emancipated women in bee-hive veils" (Horne 295), while ornate Art Nouveau entrances led to the Métropolitain's six underground rail lines. Demonstrating the city's reputation as the center of *haute couture*, Parisian women were dressed in the new fashions with straight lines, empire-style bodices, hemlines at the tops of their shoes, and large, elegant hats. As he walked along the streets, Eliot may have spotted the nearly blind Edgar Degas on his daily stroll or "the hooded silhouette of Remy de Gourmont, whose diseased face led him to shrink from social contacts," stealing furtively up the rue de Seine or the rue des Médicis (Belgion 58). Eliot later recalled that one always "had the chance of glimpsing Anatole France along the banks of the Seine" ("What France" 94). He perhaps peered into a dance hall such as the Bal Tabarin on the right bank or the Bal Bullier on the left bank, known as the dance hall of university students (Baedeker 42).

He took lodgings in the Pension Casaubon at 151 bis rue St-Jacques in the heart of the Latin Quarter. An old photograph (Figure 2) reveals that to the left of the main entrance to the building was a poultry shop, with chickens hanging from hooks in front, while to the right was a small restaurant.[5] Once settled in the pension, he could explore the area. A few steps from the pension was the busy rue Soufflot (Figure 3) with the imposing Panthéon to the right, in front of which was the recently installed (1906) large bronze statue *The Thinker* by the contemporary sculptor Auguste Rodin. To the left, several blocks down the hill was the Place Edmond-Rostand and the Jardin du Luxembourg, where children sailed boats and rolled hoops, as he reported to his niece (*Letters* 16). The Musée du Luxembourg, which housed recent works of art, had begun to depart from its nearly exclusive dedication to French artists by featuring foreign artists as well (Bonfante-Warren 32). The lively boulevard St-Michel extended to the Seine from the Place Edmond-Rostand, while a few blocks from the pension down rue St-Jacques was the Collège de France, where Bergson was to give his lectures once the university term began.

For the moment, though, Eliot could explore his new and fascinating environment. The kiosks along the boulevards and the Paris newspapers presented numerous cultural offerings that featured both established and aspiring artists in all fields. Literature was accorded great prominence, even in the most commonplace of publications, the newspaper. The leading Parisian newspaper *Le Figaro*, for example, regularly contained installments of novels by famous writers such as Rudyard Kipling and Anton Chekhov and featured on the front page poems by well-known poets such as Edmond Rostand (in the April 8, 1911 issue) as well as by young ones such as Maurice Levaillant who "won the national poetry prize last summer" (in the November 7, 1910 issue). Henri Barbusse in the opening sentences of a front-page article entitled "Poésie" in the December 12, 1910 issue of *Comoedia* enthusiastically stated, "Our time is more favorable to poetry than one would believe. I'm referring not only to dramatic poets, whose works our theatre directors choose to present more and more, but also to lyric poets. . . . A whole pléiade of new talents are appearing and promise us the noblest accomplishments." Also, an article entitled "Un poète maudit" [An accursed poet] in the November 8 issue of *Le Petit Parisien* praised efforts to raise money for a statue of Gérard de Nerval, whose life was "so eventful and whose end was so tragic" (3). At the Louvre were some of the great works of art that Eliot had studied or discovered for himself while at Harvard. Chief among those that he may have first tracked down in this immense museum were *Winged Victory, Venus de Milo,* da Vinci's *Mona Lisa,* and *The Madonna [or Virgin] of the Rocks,* to which he would refer in *The Waste Land.* One of the museum's new acquisitions, Mantegna's 1480s version of *Saint Sebastian,* may have initiated his interest in this artist.

The cultural events offered opportunities for him to become as sophisticated and cosmopolitan as his young Parisian counterparts. On October 20, for example, a front-page article in *Le Figaro* described the upcoming season at the Opéra-Comique, which would include "works by established masters such as Saint-Saëns, Debussy, and Massenet as well as those by an entire pléiade of new composers, some yet unknown, others already recognized." Among the latter, Maurice Ravel is specifically mentioned. The article ended with a flourish: "With such a program and such a gathering of artists, the Opéra-Comique's season cannot fail to be exceptionally brilliant and rich in artistic results" (2). The opportunities accorded to new talent in Paris were inspiring, so much so that Eliot had "the idea of giving up English and trying to settle down and scrape along in Paris and gradually write French" (Hall 56).

The wealth of choices during the week of October 20–27 alone would have been impressive, if not overwhelming to the young Eliot: the Opéra offered five works, including *Samson et Délila, Tannhäuser,* and *Tristan und Isolde.* The Comédie Française presented four plays and the Opéra-Comique seven works, among them *Madame Butterfly, Die Zauberflöte, Werther, Carmen,* and *Le Mariage de Télémaque.*

Lighter, low-brow types of entertainment, listed as *Spectacles et concerts* [Shows and Musical Entertainment] both in Baedeker's guidebook to Paris and in *Le Figaro* and other Parisian newspapers, appealed to a young man who, already having a taste for popular culture, found himself far from his mother's watchful eye and in a less restrictive society than St. Louis or Boston. The dazzling world of Parisian popular entertainment was vast and complex with melodramas, cabarets-artistiques, cafés-concerts, music halls, circuses, fairs, dance halls, and cinemas from which to choose. During this same week in October, according to announcements in *Le Figaro,* the Folies-Bergère presented such "attractions sensationnelles" as "Les

Flying Girls" from Heidenreich, Humpsti Bumpsti, and a skit entitled "Bob et son chien" performed by Little Willem and George Ali, the "first dog impersonator" from London's Drury Lane Theater. The Moulin Rouge featured "La Danse Noire," described as an "impassioned and brutal dance performed by Polaire and Gaston Sylvestre" (4). Additional options included the hilarious detective comedy "Arsène Lupin contre Herlock Sholmès" at the Théâtre du Châtelet, the famous comedian Fragson at the popular music hall the Alhambra, and the satirical comedy "Le Bois Sacré" [The Sacred Wood]. This last work had had its 100th performance at the Variétés the week before (*Le Figaro*, 15 October 1910: 7) and was perhaps a source for Eliot's title for his collection of essays published in 1920.

Entertainments such as these during his first weeks in Paris may be reflected in his four-part poem "Suite Clownesque," dated October 1910, which describes the acts (or turns) of a dance hall show, focusing on a comedian. The French word "Clownesque" in the title was added later in pencil, and some aspects of the show reflect a Parisian element. He may have had the poem partly on paper before his departure from the United States, its subject based on American vaudeville or music hall, and late in October added details gleaned from Parisian shows.

Finally, the sports activities described in the section *La Vie Sportive* [sports life] in *Le Figaro* included aviation, cycling, automobiling, and boxing. That last activity appears to have appealed to him immediately, for he took boxing lessons upon his return to Harvard, while he certainly had opportunities to develop an interest in aviation and automobiling through Alain-Fournier, who was quite knowledgeable about both.

Alain-Fournier

Soon after his arrival in Paris, in addition to acclimating himself to his new environment with all its tantalizing opportunities, Eliot made the acquaintance of the two young Frenchmen who were to play major roles in his Parisian year and leave an indelible mark upon him: Alain-Fournier and Jean Verdenal. Both were ideal friends for him as they were intelligent, sensitive, and highly interested in literature, music, drama, and art.

Eliot had, as E. J. H. Greene points out, the "inestimable good luck" to have Alain-Fournier (Figure 4) as his tutor and friend (10). The young Frenchman had returned to Paris in September 1909 after completing his military service and in May 1910 took a job as literary critic for the daily newspaper *Paris-Journal*, described as "the most Parisian, the most literary, and the most boulevardier of the newspapers of Paris" (Simon Arbellot, qtd. in "*Le Journal*"). There he became acquainted with Gide, Claudel, and others. Between the beginning of his employment and December 1910, he wrote 156 short articles on a wide variety of literary subjects for his column *Courrier Littéraire* [Literary News] (Gibson 196). In addition, he published both critical and creative pieces in *La Grande Revue* [The Grand Review], *L'Intransigeant* [The Uncompromising], and the sophisticated new journal *La Nouvelle Revue Française* [The New French Review], subtitled *The Monthly Review of Literature and Criticism*, which had been founded by Gide and several others and had begun publication in February 1909.[6] From 1910–1912 he also served as the personal assistant for the politician Claude Casimir-Périer (the son of a former president of France), while simultaneously working on his novel *Le Grand Meaulnes* [The Great Meaulnes], which was published serially in 1913 in *La Nouvelle Revue Française* and then as a book. A "quiet-spoken, witty, elegant young man, who spoke with real conviction of his ambition to write a great novel in the tradition of the established French masters," as Eliot was to describe him in a conversation with Robert Gibson in 1951 (199), he was killed in battle on September 22, 1914, one month after entering World War I.

His wide-ranging interests in literature and the arts were shared by his best friend and brother-in-law, twenty-four-year-old Jacques Rivière, who wrote astute reviews of cultural events as well as essays on writers and artists and creative pieces for *La Nouvelle Revue Française* beginning in February 1910. The letters which they wrote to each other between 1905 and 1914 whenever they were apart contained references to up-and-coming young writers whom they knew personally, such as Gide, Claudel, Apollinaire, and Péguy; writers of the (usually recent) past such as Baudelaire, Laforgue, and Philippe;[7] composers such as Wagner and Bach; and artists such as Rouault and Rousseau. Furthermore, they discussed a host of current cultural events such as the first exhibition of the Cubists, performances of the Ballets Russes, and the production of the play *Les Frères Karamazov* [The Brothers Karamazov], adapted for the stage by their friends Jacques Copeau and Jean Croué (Rivière and Alain-Fournier). The two also commented on automobiles and airplanes (Rivière and Alain-Fournier 353, 357, 372).

In order to supplement his income as a journalist, in 1910–1911 Alain-Fournier gave private lessons in French language and literature to two young men, one of whom was Eliot (Gibson 199). As Eliot's tutor, Alain-Fournier worked both to improve the American's facility with the language and to broaden his knowledge of French literature. As for the former, Eliot made enormous gains, both as a result of these lessons and of living in Paris, where he heard, spoke, and read French on a daily basis. While his French was poor upon arrival, it improved so much during the course of his stay that his tutor remarked in his sole surviving letter to Eliot (dated July 25, 1911 and published both in Eliot's *Letters* and in Alain-Fournier's *Lettres à sa famille et à quelques autres* [Letters to his family and some others]) that, judging by his French in a recent letter, the American scarcely had need of further instruction (*Letters* 26; *Lettres* 681).

As for literature, Alain-Fournier introduced Eliot to the works of a host of writers[8] who were to exert an enormous influence on him as well as to journals such as *La Nouvelle Revue Française, La Grande Revue*, and *Les Cahiers de la Quinzaine* [Notebooks of the Fortnight]. Furthermore, although Alain-Fournier had but recently entered the Parisian literary world, he personally knew (and perhaps literally introduced Eliot to) a number of contemporary writers. The young Frenchman also shared Eliot's passion for Baudelaire, Rimbaud, Corbière, and Laforgue. Concerning the latter, Stuart Barr suggests that it "would be surprising if the esthetics of Laforgue did not figure significantly in animated conversations between the two fervent admirers of the author of *Complaintes*" (13). They probably had animated conversations as well about articles such as those on Baudelaire by Faguet, Gide, and Rivière, appearing respectively in the September, November, and December 1910 issues of *La Nouvelle Revue Française*. Finally, Eliot had the opportunity to keep abreast of the current literary scene in England through his tutor, who read British journals such as *The Nation* and *The English Review* (Barr 13).

Among all the writers to whom Alain-Fournier introduced Eliot, the one whose works had the greatest immediate impact on him was Charles-Louis Philippe, a contemporary figure who had died the previous year. As Howarth points out, Alain-Fournier had at first disliked Philippe's 1901 novel *Bubu de Montparnasse*, which depicted the world of prostitutes and pimps in grim, seedy areas of Paris, but he came to admire it greatly (158–9). Rivière's letter of April 13, 1911 to Alain-Fournier, written just after he himself had read *Bubu*, reveals the enormous impact that the book had on both of them. Pronouncing it "very good," he commented on Philippe's courage in presenting the lives of such people, admitting that "we would never have had the courage to treat this subject, if we had even thought of it" (Rivière and Alain-Fournier 381–2). At Alain-Fournier's instigation, Eliot read *Bubu de Montparnasse* soon after arriving in Paris. He wrote in the preface to the 1932 English translation of the novel, "[It] was in the year 1910 that I first read *Bubu de Montparnasse*, when I first came to Paris. Read at an impressionable age, and under the impressive conditions, the book has always been for me, not merely the best of Charles-Louis Philippe's books, but a symbol of the Paris of that time[;] . . . to me *Bubu* stood for Paris as some of Dickens' novels stand for London" (qtd. in Ricks 405). Eliot also read Philippe's novel *Marie Donadieu* (1904), noting in a letter of September 22, 1949 to Violet Schiff that he first read it in 1911, "a period when the works of Philippe made a very deep impression upon me" (qtd. in Ricks 407). Since Philippe's *Lettres de Jeunesse* [Letters of Youth] (his correspondence with his friend Henri Vandeputte), was serialized in five installments beginning in November 1910 and concluding in May 1911 in *La Nouvelle Revue Française*, Eliot surely read and was influenced by them as well.

As noted by both Howarth and Grover Smith, striking echoes of the two novels and the letters appear in the third section of "Preludes," III, in "Rhapsody on a Windy Night," and in "The Love Song of J. Alfred Prufrock," all written during his Parisian year. Howarth suggests that the urban scenes in Eliot's poems of that year were influenced in particular by two of Philippe's letters in the December 1910 issue of *La Nouvelle Revue Française*. In Letter XXI, he describes the Paris cityscape as he looks out his window and muses about his character Marie: "It is so pleasant in the evening to smoke my pipe while thinking of Marie. I walk about my room, open the window, see the rose-colored reflection of the gas on the ceiling and the top of Notre-Dame, and think about her thoughts." In Letter XXV, he describes the Seine as "a hideous river, dirty yellow, dirty green, polluted with trash, and it has a depraved appearance like one of those decayed and well-dressed Parisian women whom I detested more than anything. While in the countryside one smells the fragrance of flowers, in Paris one smells the odor of the sewers" (qtd. in Howarth 159–60).

Smith notes that *Bubu* as well as *Marie Donadieu* supplied the subject, atmosphere, and imagery for the third of the "Preludes," alluding specifically to a passage from the former (in a translation by Lawrence Vail) describing the prostitute Berthe awakening in a hotel room:

> At noon, in the hotel room of the rue Chanoinesse, a grey and dirty light filtered through the grey curtains and dirty panes of the window . . . and there was the unmade bed where the two bodies had left their impress of brownish sweat upon the worn sheets—this bed of hotel rooms, where the bodies are dirty and the souls as well. Berthe, in her chemise, had just got up. With her narrow shoulders, her grey shirt and her unclean feet, she too seemed, in her pale yellowish slimness, to have no light. With her puffy eyes and scraggly hair, in the disorder of the room, she too was in disorder and her thoughts lay heaped confusedly in her head. (20)

The echoes are clear as Eliot's speaker imagines an inhabitant of one of the "thousand furnished rooms" (23) in a bleak urban landscape. The woman (perhaps a prostitute) spends a restless night observing the "thousand sordid images" (27) which comprise her soul flickering on the ceiling. In the morning, while sitting on the edge of her bed, curling the papers from her hair or clasping "the soles of feet / In the palms of both soiled hands" (37–8), she has a hopeless and despairing vision of the street outside. It seems indeed to be her cynical attitude which the speaker conveys in the line, "Wipe your hand across your mouth, and laugh," in the poem's closing triplet (52).

The two novels also contributed to "Rhapsody on a Windy Night," composed in March 1911, and again Smith makes astute observations about their similarities: "*Bubu de Montparnasse* provided again the atmosphere of loneliness, demimondaine sterility, and cultural desolation. Eliot's spectacle of a young man alone in a metropolis, where prostitutes solicit custom in the street, reflects approximately the world of Philippe. The memories, the sight of street-lamps in iron rows, the glimpse of a woman in a doorway, the awareness of smells—all came from the novel . . ." (23). From *Marie Donadieu*, Eliot modified the phrase "des odeurs de filles publiques mêlées à des odeurs de nourriture" (93) to "Smells of chestnuts in the streets, / And female smells in shuttered rooms" in lines 65–6 (Smith 24).

In addition to his reading of Philippe's works, Eliot no doubt was aware, or was made aware by Alain-Fournier, of a campaign to raise money for a bust of Philippe to be created by the French sculptor Émile Bourdelle and placed on his tomb. Indeed, the December 1910 issue of *La Nouvelle Revue Française* contained a list of those who had already made donations to this enterprise. Furthermore, soon after Eliot's arrival, there was at least one major lecture on Philippe's works, presented by none other than Gide, which he may have attended. His new interest in this writer would have been enriched and encouraged by the fact that Philippe was much in the public eye in Paris at the time.

Clearly Eliot's debt to Philippe (and to Alain-Fournier for introducing him to the writer) was enormous. In his preface to the 1932 English translation of *Bubu de Montparnasse*, he singled out as Philippe's strength his ability to record accurately the physical impressions of the boulevard de Montparnasse (Howarth 158), but in him he would also have seen (as did Alain-Fournier and Rivière) new possibilities for using materials from the modern metropolis, for portraying characters from the lower spectrum of the human race, and for the creation of atmosphere, mood, and color from the underside of the urban world. These were discoveries that he put to use immediately in the poems written during his Paris sojourn but also throughout the next decade of his poetic career, culminating brilliantly in *The Waste Land*.

Claudel was another writer whom Eliot began to read at Alain-Fournier's instigation, but in this case one who was very much alive. Indeed, Gide said of him in 1905, "He gives me the impression of a solidified cyclone" (qtd. in "Paul Claudel"). Alain-Fournier, as noted earlier, was acquainted with him through *Paris-Journal*. A prominent figure in the Roman Catholic Renaissance in France in the early years of the 20th century, his religious faith is a strong component of his highly intellectual and difficult works; as Wallace Fowlie notes, "Paul Claudel appears as the most demanding of contemporary poets. To be understood and followed, he requires from his reader a total spiritual submission and attention" (qtd. in "Paul Claudel"). As a diplomat, he lived in numerous countries, including the United States, China, Japan, Italy, and Brazil, returning to France for short periods, one of which was during the fall of 1910.

According to Eliot, his tutor assigned him Claudel's *Art poétique* [Poetic Art], *Connaissance de l'Est* [The East I Know], and his early plays for their lessons (Greene 136–7): "In 1910, when I had my first introduction to literary Paris, Claudel was already a great poet in the eyes of a younger generation—my own generation. He had published *Connaissance de l'Est, Art poétique*, and those plays which appeared in one volume under the general title of *L'Arbre* [The Tree]: and I am not sure that these three books do not constitute his strongest claim to immortality" (Foreword, Chiari x). *Art poétique*, a very complex and difficult essay published in 1907, is not about the art of poetry—as one might expect from its title—but rather about the poetic art of the universe; it is "an attempt to envisage the universe as a work of art, like a poem" ("Art poétique"). *Connaissance de l'Est*, published in 1900, is a collection of prose poems, almost all of which were written in China, whose purpose was to give insights into Chinese culture (Perez). This work, according to Greene, was the one that interested Eliot the most.

As for Claudel's poetic dramas, *L'Arbre* (1901) was a collection of five plays: *Tête d'Or* [Golden Head], *La Ville* [The City], *La Jeune Fille Violaine* [The Young Woman Violaine], *L'Échange* [The Exchange], and *Le Repos du Septième Jour* [The Repose of the Seventh Day]. Since Claudel's three-act drama, *L'Otage* [The Hostage], appeared serially in *La Nouvelle Revue Française* in the December 1910 and January and February 1911 issues, Alain-Fournier and Eliot were very likely to have discussed it, and Alain-Fournier probably kept him up to date on the progress of *L'Annonce Faite à Marie* [The Annunciation of Mary], a religious verse drama on which the playwright was at work[9] and which would appear serially in *La Nouvelle Revue Française* beginning in December 1911. Gibson notes that Eliot's tutor also introduced him to Claudel's religious treatise *Connaissance de Dieu et de soi-même* [Knowledge of God and oneself] (199). Finally, they probably also talked about his five-part poem "Cinq Grandes Odes" [Five Great Odes], published in 1910, which relates "the poet's inspiration and his gift of describing with words the mystery of the universe" ("Paul Claudel") and would have shown the aspiring young American poet that one could write a modern religious poem.

Eliot wrote in an obituary tribute to Claudel in 1955 that these and other works of his encountered in 1910–1911 made a great impression on his mind at that time, one which "is still very clear in my memory," and asserts that "[t]he work of this period was his best" ("Le Salut" 1). However, according to Eliot's letter of November 28, 1947 to Greene, he rarely read Claudel after this period and never with the attention that his works deserved (136–7). He also asserts in the obituary that Claudel is "not one of the writers from whom I myself have learned" and that "his type of drama is very different from anything at which I myself have arrived" ("Le Salut" 1).

Yet Howarth argues convincingly that Claudel's influence was not only immediate but long-lasting, affecting Eliot's own plays, despite Eliot's comments to the contrary. He asks rhetorically, "But could *any* incipient poet in Paris in that year, reading the *N. R. F.* in which *l'Otage* appeared serially, and studying Claudel for lessons, emerge from the process uninstructed?" (162), and answers by suggesting, "It would have been hard to sit opposite Fournier in 1910, to explore poetry with him, and to examine Claudel under his guidance, without receiving some stir from his passion" (164). He adds, "[It] is most tempting to believe that, no matter how much he resisted Claudel and declined to study his later work, he learned from him" (166). Howarth asserts that Claudel's verse form in *L'Otage* bears "a pictorial resemblance" to certain of Eliot's choruses in *The Rock* and *Murder in the Cathedral*, that Eliot's vocabulary in those two plays is "often startling, magistral, and yet right, as Claudel's is," and that Eliot's use of internal rhyme in "Ash Wednesday" and those two plays is similar to that of Claudel (164–5). Indeed, the mere fact that Claudel wrote poetic drama, often on religious subjects, must have served as inspiration for Eliot's own belief that it could be revived in the 20th century. It is significant that Eliot closes his tribute by calling Claudel "the greatest poetic dramatist of the century" ("Le Salut" 1).

Péguy was another important writer to whose works Alain-Fournier introduced Eliot, although we do not know in this case specifically which ones. In the winter of 1909–1910, Alain-Fournier and Rivière had first discovered Péguy through reading his articles in his bimonthly review *Les Cahiers de la Quinzaine*, and Alain-Fournier first met him in the early summer of 1910 when he went to his little bookshop at 8 rue de la Sorbonne to interview him for his literary column. In August 1910, he was further impressed upon reading Péguy's nostalgic account of the early days of the Affaire Dreyfus, titled *Notre Jeunesse*. Indeed, Gibson asserts that Péguy was the most important of his new contacts that year (200–3).

Much about this complex figure may have influenced Eliot both immediately and in subsequent years. Péguy was an advocate of French nationalism and an adversary of the modern emphasis on materialism. He was also an ardent but nonpracticing Roman Catholic, who, when his son became seriously ill in 1912, made the first of several pilgrimages on foot to the Cathédrale de Chartres, with Alain-Fournier accompanying him part of the way ("Charles Péguy"), thus reviving this old custom.[10] Furthermore, Bergson was Péguy's "main philosophical inspiration" (Tint 132).

Chief among Péguy's various achievements in the literary arena was the founding in 1900 of *Les Cahiers de la Quinzaine*, which served as a "tool for social and moral reform" ("Charles Péguy") and included among its contributors Anatole France, Romain Rolland, Maurice Barrès, Julien Benda, Georges Sorel, Jean Jaurès, and himself. Indeed, much of his own work first appeared in this publication. From its founding in 1900 until 1914, the journal reflected "the intellectual preoccupations of the French . . . , for there was no major political, social, and philosophical problem that was not aired in the *Cahiers* while Péguy was their editor" (Tint 118). Eliot was familiar with the journal, noting that it was published with "a cover of austere grey paper" ("What France" 94), reflecting its moral seriousness. To combat the materialism and pessimism of the times, Péguy ran a series called "Lives of Illustrious Men" to inspire a regeneration of the virtues of the past and thus "ward off barbarism" (Shrade 164), featuring as the first biography *The Life of Beethoven* by Rolland.

While he stood as a bastion of moral rectitude, he also believed in the importance of exchanging ideas, and his bookshop was a gathering place on Thursdays for a small group of intellectuals, writers, and friends to discuss the events of the day. As Kimball points out, "Controversy and contention were always in order" (7), and Tint asserts, "He wanted everything to be called into question all the time" (121). Alain-Fournier perhaps brought Eliot to these gatherings to see for himself the exciting clash of ideas and to literally introduce him to Péguy.

Alain-Fournier was particularly interested in Péguy's most famous poem, "Le Mystère de la Charité de Jeanne d'Arc" [The Mystery of the Charity of Joan of Arc], published in 1909, and his 1910 piece on the Affaire Dreyfus entitled *Notre Jeunesse* [Our Youth]. Concerning the latter, in a letter of August 11, 1910, Alain-Fournier tells Rivière that recently he had a long conversation with Péguy, who wrote a "bizarre and friendly" dedication in his copy of *Notre Jeunesse* (355), while in a letter of August 28, 1910, he reveals to his friend that he finds it "decidedly admirable," adding that Péguy uses repetition "like the choruses in Bach's *Passion*" (360). As Kimball notes, Péguy was "a passionate Dreyfusard" for whom the Affaire held "nearly cosmic significance" as "the stage upon which the soul of modern man struggled for significance." He asserts that it is "difficult for us to comprehend the riveting importance of L'Affaire in French life at the turn of the century," calling it "one of those world-defining, world-changing occurrences" whose "repercussions lasted decades" (8). Péguy's viewpoint was in direct opposition to the anti-Semitism of Charles Maurras, and thus Eliot was presented with a powerful conflict of ideologies in two figures whom he greatly admired.

Eliot's appreciation of and respect for Péguy, which began during his Paris year, are evident in his commendation of him in *The New Statesman* in 1916, two years after he was killed at the Battle of the Marne on September 5, 1914, as "one of the most illustrious of the dead who have fallen in this war" and as "a national, a symbolic figure, the incarnation of the rejuvenated French spirit" (qtd. in Kimball 2).

Another literary figure whose works Eliot read with Alain-Fournier was Gide, a prolific and wide-ranging writer both in genre and subject. He was a literary critic, novelist, poet, social crusader, and an early advocate for homosexual rights, known for his astute examination of moral issues ("André Gide"). He was one of the founders of *La Nouvelle Revue Française*, which began publication in 1909 and, by the time of Eliot's arrival, had already achieved a reputation as a major journal for recent and emerging literature and the arts; Eliot notes with admiration that in 1910 it was "still truly new" ("What France" 94), reflecting not only its recent appearance on the Parisian literary scene but also its concern with current developments. In their letters, Alain-Fournier and Rivière mention Gide in a variety of contexts (see, for example, 366, 372).

Although Eliot did not reveal which specific works of Gide he read with Alain-Fournier, Gibson says that his tutor "tried to communicate his enthusiasm for . . . *Paludes* and *La Porte étroite*" to Eliot (199). *Paludes* (1895) is a memoir which examines ironically Gide's former life before he accepted his homosexuality; Verdenal copied out its last sentence in a letter of February 5, 1912, noting that it had given him "enormous pleasure during the last few days" (*Letters* 30, 32), suggesting that the two friends probably discussed it. *La Porte étroite* (1909) treats the theme of freedom from moral and social codes. Other of Gide's early publications which Alain-Fournier may have assigned to his pupil are *Le Traité de Narcisse* (1891), centered on the mythic figure Eliot was to treat numerous times, culminating in "The Death of Saint Narcissus," which was composed some time before August 1915; *Le Prométhé Mal Enchainé* (1899), whose eagle Eliot refers to as a symbol of the artist's agony and suffering in "The Use of Poetry and the Use of Criticism" as well as in several poems (Smith 36, 141, 276); and the psychological novel *L'Immoraliste* (1902), on the destructiveness of hedonism, with an experimental dialogue between the inner and the outer narrator which is paralleled in "The Love Song of J. Alfred Prufrock." Interestingly, Gide called *La Porte étroite* the "twin" of *L'Immoraliste* ("André Gide").

Eliot must also have read and discussed with Alain-Fournier several pieces by Gide that appeared in *La Nouvelle Revue Française*. In the November 1910 issue, Gide published a stinging critique ("Baudelaire et M. Faguet") of Faguet's essay on Baudelaire that appeared in the September 1910 issue. Gide criticized the established intellectual figure for labeling Baudelaire a poet of the second order and presented a full-frontal argument to the contrary, no doubt winning the admiration of the two young men who were devoted to the father of Symbolist poetry.

As Howarth points out, Gide praised the moderate tone of voice of Baudelaire's speakers, citing Laforgue's assessment of it as a great innovation and noting Barrès's comment that *Les Fleurs du Mal* [Flowers of Evil] returned to the great classical tradition of discretion and subtlety. Howarth suggests that, if Eliot read this essay, he "must have been struck by" the latter, "which chimed with Babbitt's call to classicism, and by the whole argument, which made clear to him that Laforgue had taught him the use of his own speech—the low-pitched, understating speech of New England—by demonstrating the development to a fine point of a classical tradition" (170). He must also have admired (and later emulated) Gide's daring to attack a well-known literary critic, a professor of literature at the Sorbonne, and a member of the Académie Française.

Finally, Alain-Fournier and Eliot likely discussed two other pieces by Gide. In the December 1910 issue of *La Nouvelle Revue Française*, his "Journal sans Date" [Undated Journal], in which he presented everyday observations, contained an account of the November 3 incident at the Théâtre de l'Odéon when a young playwright named René Fauchois criticized Racine in a lecture, sparking a near-riot in the theater followed by demonstrations in the streets by the Camelots du Roi [the Hawkers of the King], a rowdy group of young men who violently defended the traditional beliefs of the political group L'Action Française (see below and Chapter 3). And in the February and March 1911 issues were installments of his novella *Isabelle*, a haunting tale of a young student who falls in love with a woman after seeing her picture in a mysterious miniature ("André Gide").

Years later, to illustrate how Paris combined the past and the future into a perfect present during his residence there in 1910–1911, Eliot described the possibility of both catching sight of the established older writer Anatole France strolling along the quais of the Seine and buying the latest book by Gide or Claudel on the very day that it was published ("What France" 94). Eliot was clearly excited at being able to purchase Gide's *Oscar Wilde*, *Isabelle*, and *Nouveaux Prétextes* [New Pretexts] or Claudel's *L'Otage* and *Le Chemin de la Croix* [The Way of the Cross], all of which appeared in 1910 and 1911, as they came hot off the press.

Eliot began a long personal and literary acquaintance with Gide in December 1921 when Gide wrote in French to ask if he would become a regular contributor to *La Nouvelle Revue Française*, informing its readers about recent developments in English literature. Gide noted that he was "an attentive reader of *The Sacred Wood*" and sent along a collection of his own writings "from which you will recognize, I hope, that my thoughts are often akin to yours" (*Letters* 490–1). Receiving the letter in Lausanne during his treatment for his fragile psychological state that fall, Eliot replied (in excellent French) that he would be interested if they could wait for his return to health and proposed a meeting with Gide in Paris in early

January 1922, expressing his hope that "I shall be able to have the pleasure of making your acquaintance one of these days." While he had not met Gide in Paris in 1910–1911, he wrote that "some of your works have been known to me for the last eleven years" (*Letters* 494–5). So clearly Eliot's reading in Paris with Alain-Fournier bore fruit that was to last a lifetime.

St.-John Perse, who was to figure significantly in Eliot's career in a variety of ways, was probably first brought to his attention by Alain-Fournier when Perse's early poem "Éloges" appeared in the June 1911 issue of *La Nouvelle Revue Française* under the pseudonym Saintléger Léger, drawn from his real name, Marie-René-Auguste-Alexis Léger. In this work with long, prose-like but musical lines, the twenty-five-year-old Léger celebrated his idyllic childhood on his family's coral island in Guadeloupe in the Antilles. Cronin suggests that, since Alain-Fournier first met him in 1911, he "perhaps reported his impressions to Eliot, a close friend. Léger [Alain-Fournier] describes as short and fattish, very tense and inclined to be solemn: an admirer of Laforgue's spare, cursive diction. In unconscious prophecy of *Anabase* [Anabasis], [he] adds that Léger would be 'even more extraordinary, more mysterious, if he were more simple'" (134–5). Cronin also reveals that Gide thought so highly of the poem that he paid for its publication (134–5).

Since Léger held a variety of posts in the Foreign Ministry and wished to protect his identity, he later adopted the pseudonym St.-John Perse, first using it for his epic poem *Anabase* (1924), one of the most original and difficult poems in European literature. Based on his experiences in the Gobi Desert, it features a strangely disembodied and impersonal speaker who is a tribal leader on a military expedition to conquer new empires ("Saint John Perse," *Poetry Portal* 2). Its style, as Cronin points out, is "almost religiously solemn" and concise, and it echoes such obscure works as the Egyptian Book of the Dead, Vedic hymns, and inscriptions from Asiatic steles. It has no rhymes, no regular meter, and "extremely long lines, hovering even in French, very close to prose." It abjures logical connections and "presents raw materials—like an archaeologist's finds—from which the reader must construct a whole civilization" (135–6).

The author of *The Waste Land* "immediately recognized the significance of so original a poem and repaid his debt to French literature by translating it" (Cronin 135–6), despite but also perhaps because of its difficulties. In the preface to his translation, Eliot describes it as "a series of images of migration, of conquest of vast spaces in Asiatic wastes, of destruction and foundation of cities and civilizations of any races or epochs of the ancient East." He argues that its "abbreviation of method" is justified since "the sequence of images coincides and concentrates into one intense impression of barbaric civilization" (10). He also praises it as "a piece of writing of the same importance as the later work of Mr. James Joyce" (12). He began work on the translation in late 1926 (Ackroyd 163), with Part I appearing in *The Criterion* in February 1928 (Cronin 136). The entire translation was published by Faber in 1930 with Eliot's preface.

Cronin calls it Eliot's most important translation (134) and argues that it influenced Eliot's later poetry, providing inspiration for imagery that is timeless and drawn from the natural world (as opposed to his earlier urban 20th-century imagery), for "a more lapidary style," and even for specific lines, such as lines 8–10 of "Journey of the Magi" (1927): "There were times we regretted / The summer palaces on slopes, the terraces; / And the silken girls bringing sherbet" (Cronin 137; Greene 136–7).[11] Eliot was indeed composing "Journey of the Magi" during the period in which he was translating *Anabase*, and, as Smith suggests, the poem's "vast oriental deserts and the camel caravans and marches" were "in Eliot's thoughts" at the time (123) and inform the situation, settings, and details of Eliot's poem. Smith also notes that Eliot took "a phrase or two" from section IV of *Anabase* for "Triumphal March" (160), but it seems to me that the basic framework of the poem as well is indebted to it.

Alain-Fournier also introduced Eliot to Dostoevsky in French translation. He and Rivière had been intensely interested in the Russian novelist since 1909, as revealed in their letters. The former, for instance, wrote to Rivière, "Since Claudel, no book has brought me back to Christianity as has *The Idiot*" (Rivière and Alain-Fournier 129). That interest reached a peak in April of 1911 with the stage adaptation of *The Brothers Karamazov*, written by their friends Copeau and Croué as the inaugural production of the Théâtre des Arts, a theater dedicated to presenting innovative dramas. It is entirely plausible that Alain-Fournier took Eliot to a performance as Copeau had given him eight tickets (Rivière and Alain-Fournier 379). Indeed, Eliot's tutor, who often met Copeau for dinner or conversation, may even have introduced the two.

So it is hardly surprising that Alain-Fournier shared his passion for the Russian novelist with his American pupil, having him read *Crime and Punishment*, *The Idiot*, and *The Brothers Karamazov* in a French translation. This was a doubly difficult undertaking for the young American, but one from which he reaped immediate benefits for his own writing, most obviously in "The Love Song of J. Alfred Prufrock." John C. Pope, in his essay "Prufrock and Raskolnikov" published in November 1945 in *American Literature*, asserts that the "reading of *Crime and Punishment* was a major experience and that in a multitude of ways it brought about a significant ordering of Eliot's creative imagination" (229). In response to that essay, Eliot wrote a letter of March 8, 1946 to Pope confirming the influence of Dostoevsky's novels at that time, which Pope includes in his subsequent essay "Prufrock and Raskolnikov Again": "During the period of my stay in Paris, Dostoevsky was very much a subject of interest amongst literary people and it was my friend and tutor, Alain Fournier [*sic*], who introduced me to this author. Under his instigation, I read [these three novels] in the French translation during the course of that winter. [They] made a very profound impression on me and I had read them all before *Prufrock* was completed." While he notes that Pope was incorrect about the date of composition of the poem and about his assumption that Eliot had read Constance Garnett's translation, the poet acknowledges that Pope had "established very conclusively the essentials of [his] case" ("Prufrock and Raskolnikov Again" 319) that *Crime and Punishment* influenced elements of the poem, such as Prufrock's comparison of himself to Lazarus rising from the dead to "tell all" ("Prufrock and Raskolnikov" 221, 225). Pope concludes that Eliot's letter "testifies generously to the prominence of Dostoevski [*sic*] in his mind during the period of composition" of "Prufrock" ("Prufrock and Raskolnikov Again" 321).

Evidence of the powerful influence of *Crime and Punishment* is found in Eliot's later works as well. Smith suggests that Svidrigaïlov's garret may have inspired the "low dry garret" of *The Waste Land* (313). However, he finds a more comprehensive influence in Eliot's grim vision of the isolated human being suffering under a heavy and inescapable burden of guilt evident in such works as "Literature and the Modern World," *Sweeney Agonistes*, and *The Family Reunion*, tracing it to Svidrigaïlov "among the dust and spiders of a rural bathhouse" and to "the image of hell imprinted on his mind as, with his pistol in his pocket, he walked the streets to the dark tower of his suicide" (117; see also 204).

Alain-Fournier also introduced Eliot to the work of his brother-in-law and close friend Rivière, alerting him to his reviews on all aspects of the arts published in nearly every issue of *La Nouvelle Revue Française* during Eliot's year in Paris and no doubt encouraging him to read some of the writers and attend some of the cultural events that were Rivière's subjects. It is not far-fetched to imagine that Eliot, perhaps in the company of Alain-Fournier and/or Verdenal, attended the last performance of *Tristan und Isolde* on November 7, 1910, if not an earlier one, especially since Rivière was writing a review of it for *La Nouvelle Revue Française*. This highly personal, intense, and dramatic review entitled "Sur le '*Tristan et Isolde*' de Wagner," which appeared in the January 1911 issue, contains phrases highly suggestive of the lines from the opera Eliot quotes in *The Waste Land*: "Monstrous masterpiece! I enter it like a black and blue night," Rivière wrote. "There is no work more deprived of hope than *Tristan*; because desire is the opposite of hope. . . . The third act opens in solitude as empty as the sea. . . . The last measures of the opera express an immense outpouring of despair" (29, 32–3). In addition to *Tristan und Isolde*, Rivière compellingly reviewed "Les Scènes Polovtsiennes du *Prince Igor*"

(January 1911); concerts of the music of Moussorgsky, whom he calls the "true voice of Russia" (February 1911); Debussy's opera *Pelléas et Mélisande* (April 1911); and *Petrouchka* by the Ballets Russes (September 1911). He also wrote essays on Baudelaire (December 1910) and Ingres (June 1911) and a nostalgic memoir of his idyllic youth entitled "Les Beaux Jours" (November 1911).

In the summer of 1911, he was preparing a collection of his writings for publication under the title *Études* [Studies] (1912), and we can see its impressive scope from the list he gave Alain-Fournier in a letter of July 20: "I have decided on the order of my book. I believe that it is rather good: Baudelaire—Ingres—Cézanne—Matisse—Rouault—Gauguin—Suarès—Claudel *Occident*—Claudel *Art Libre*—*Dardanus*—Bach—Franck—*Tristan*—*Ariane et Barbe-Bleu*—Ravel (*Rhapsodie espagnole*)—*Pelléas*—*Poèmes* de Debussy—*Prince Igor*—Moussorgsky—*Les Karamazov*—André Gide" (Rivière and Alain-Fournier 389). Here was a true Renaissance man who provided for Eliot a model of both critical and creative writing, whose range Eliot himself was to equal and surpass.

Eliot met Rivière once during that year, thanks to Alain-Fournier, who took him to Rivière's residence to ask for advice about an academic endeavor. In an essay in French entitled "Rencontre" published in *La Nouvelle Revue Française* in 1925 upon the death of Rivière from typhoid fever, Eliot recounts this visit:

> It was in 1911 that I met Jacques Rivière, for the first time. His brother-in-law, the much-mourned Alain-Fournier, took me to his home to ask his advice about a large project that I wanted to submit to the university. As a very young and unsophisticated student, I felt some discomfort in the presence of the secretary of *La Nouvelle Revue Française*. From this interview, in the course of which I obtained all the information and advice that I wanted—but which, alas, I was never able to use—I received an impression very similar to the one that I had again ten years later, when I met him for the second time. I recall a fragile form, a charming and gracious personality, and a mind so alert and enthusiastic that even then it seemed almost a threat to the delicate body which sheltered it. "I am in the process of writing a long essay on Gide," he said, referring to the essay that was published later in *Études*. When I saw him again in 1921, his mind remained the same as well as his manner; but his body seemed even more fragile, and indeed it was. (42)

To be even briefly in the presence of a young man only two years older than he who had already accomplished so much in the literary world could only have served as inspiration to Eliot, who certainly followed in his footsteps and beyond. Ten years later, when Eliot was invited by Gide to become a regular contributor to *La Nouvelle Revue Française*, Rivière was the editor (1919–1925), and Eliot's second meeting with him occurred in early January 1922 in Paris in order to make the formal arrangements (*Letters* 503). They had a cordial relationship based on mutual admiration from that time until Rivière's untimely death in 1925 at the age of thirty-nine.[12]

And finally, Alain-Fournier himself was a source of literary inspiration for Eliot. As an aspiring writer, he was already publishing in *La Grande Revue* and *La Nouvelle Revue Française*, among others. His review of the novel *Marie-Claire* in the former was reprinted in the latter in the November 1910 issue. In his moving short memoir "Portrait," which appeared in the September 1911 issue of the latter, the speaker feels remorse and regret over the suicide of a young man whom he had known during his school days. Its epigraph from Péguy reads in part, "We know what it is to feel regret, remorse, contrition . . . , emotions which are profound and ineffaceable" (309). Both the memoir and the epigraph express what will be a lasting theme throughout Eliot's work, at its most anguished in Section II of "Little Gidding," where the speaker conveys remorse for "things ill done and done to others' harm" (142). It is, as Barr suggests, highly probable that Eliot read it since he knew the journal well (15) and especially since Alain-Fournier in his letter of July 25, 1911 alerted him to its forthcoming publication: "You can read something by me ["Portrait"] in *La Nouvelle Revue Française* of the 1st September" (*Letters* 27; *Lettres* 682).

Furthermore, as Alain-Fournier was in the process of writing his novel *Le Grand Meaulnes* during the time that he was Eliot's tutor, it is highly likely that he discussed it with his pupil. Howarth notes perceptively that "the stage in which a writer is contending with his material and method is sometimes the stage at which he says the most illuminating things about it, at least if he is in the position where he is obliged to talk and teach." He points out that the novel concerns the vain attempt of the main character Meaulnes to recover the idyllic paradise of youth, the "old, noble regime," and "a pure dream," all represented by the countryside setting; he calls it "a descant, sung by the France of 1910," on Baudelaire's "Moesta et Errabunda," a haunting poem about an irretrievable "innocent paradis" which "spoke to Fournier's generation" (157). Both the poem and Alain-Fournier's novel spoke to Eliot as well, I would suggest, in their memories of a vanished idyllic youth, a motif which he uses in a number of poems, most strikingly in "Cape Ann" and in *Four Quartets*. Moreover, the novel's regret for a former regime added to other influences of Eliot's Parisian year that called for a return to tradition and monarchy.

Perhaps, however, the aspect of the novel which exerted the greatest influence on Eliot was the belief of Meaulnes that human love was either unattainable or too terrifying to be borne, with the result that he ran from it in terror—a reflection of

Alain-Fournier's own experiences of unrequited love for Yvonne de Quiévrecourt and his current tumultuous affair with Jeanne Bruneau. He could have discussed his feelings about love and about the possibility of achieving happiness with his American pupil, especially since his affair with Bruneau was quite intense at the time. If so, they must have made an impression on Eliot, for such issues concerned him for years. These beliefs may even be echoed in the opening section of "Burnt Norton," with its description of a moment of ecstasy, whether real, imagined, or longed for, followed by the comment, "human kind / Cannot bear very much reality" (40–1).

Alain-Fournier's July 25, 1911 letter to Eliot reveals the warm friendship shared by the two and the various subjects which engaged them. Opening with the salutation "Mon cher ami" [My dear friend], he mentions the success of the other young man whom he was tutoring. He then comments on Eliot's acumen in philosophy and French, and his own change from being an "internationalist" to one who "would now very willingly march against [the Germans]," a grim prophecy of the future. He expresses regret that he will be on military maneuvers in early September and thus will not be able to see Eliot in Paris before the American's departure for the United States. The letter also shows that Eliot reciprocated Alain-Fournier's introducing him to French writers by recommending works in English for his tutor to read. He tells Eliot that he is finishing "the book by Ford you gave me, . . . in which I find so much feverish emotion and heart-rending beauty," that he has recently finished Stevenson's *Catriona*, and that he is "busy reading *Typhoon* by Conrad, which you mentioned to me, and I am going to buy *Youth*." Thus, as Barr suggests, the Frenchman profited considerably from his pupil as well as vice versa (13). He closes by encouraging Eliot to keep him informed of "everything that happens to you or interests you" and, as noted earlier, tells him in a postscript of the forthcoming appearance of "Portrait" in *La Nouvelle Revue Française* (*Letters* 26–27; *Lettres* 860–62). Because of their close friendship, we can imagine with what grief Eliot learned three years later of Alain-Fournier's death in battle.

Alain-Fournier thus played a major role in Eliot's Parisian year, one far more complex than has typically been acknowledged, and his influence reverberated throughout Eliot's life and career in a variety of ways. He was a friend who shared Eliot's interests in literature and the arts, perhaps inviting or accompanying him to cultural events in Paris. As a mentor, he helped him improve his French language skills to such a point that Eliot was able to make excellent and varied use of them and he introduced him to a host of emerging writers. As a young person with whom Eliot spent many hours during a magical and exciting year in Paris, Alain-Fournier had a significant impact on his life and his literature.

Jean Verdenal

The other young Frenchman who played a major role in Eliot's Parisian year was Jean Verdenal, a twenty-year-old medical student who was a fellow boarder at the Pension Casaubon and who was intensely interested in literature and the arts as well as philosophy and politics (Figure 5). Sensitive, highly intelligent, and serious, he and Eliot became close friends and soul mates. Although some scholars—chief among them James E. Miller—have argued that their relationship was homosexual, there is simply not enough convincing evidence to accept such a conclusion.[13] Indeed, I will offer a few observations to the contrary. Throughout the seven surviving letters which Verdenal wrote to Eliot, he uses the formal "vous" and typically addresses Eliot as "mon vieux" [old pal or old chap]. Furthermore, in his second letter to Eliot, he demonstrates a sexual attraction to women in a description of prostitutes glimpsed during Bastille Day celebrations, evincing "forbidden desires" similar to those of Eliot[14] which the two may have discussed: "[T]he evening is filled with an ever-mounting sensual excitement; sweat makes the girls' hair stick to their temples; lottery wheels spin; a merry-go-round, attractively lit and alluring, also revolves, and with every jerk of the wooden horses, the whores brace their supple busts and a shapely leg can be glimpsed through the slit of a 'fashionably split skirt'; a heavy, sensuous gust flows warmly by" (*Letters* 24). In addition, Eliot openly and unselfconsciously expressed his affection for Verdenal, as well as his sense of loss at his death in World War I, in letters to his mother (who would be highly opposed to and shocked at a homosexual relationship) and to his cousin (*Letters* 17–18, 192, 433). I agree with George Watson in his essay "Quest for a Frenchman" that the homosexual explanation is objectionable "not only because it is unproven but because it is trivial" (475).

This irresolvable question seems to me to have overshadowed what is far more important about their relationship: that in Verdenal Eliot found a person with whom he could share his interests in literature, art, and music, as well as his innermost feelings and thoughts on a wide variety of issues and concerns. Their friendship, as reflected in Verdenal's letters to Eliot, in a few scattered remarks by Eliot in letters and essays, and in Eliot's four dedications to him of collections of poems (see Ricks 3–4), is amazingly similar to that of Philippe and Henri Vandeputte in *Lettres de Jeunesse*, published serially in *La Nouvelle Revue Française* from December 1910 to May 1911, which, I suspect, caused Eliot to long for and then to rejoice in such a friendship. He also had as a model the friendship of Alain-Fournier and Rivière, although in this instance Eliot would have heard rather than read about it. In Eliot's case, I would also suggest that, as many would attest who have lived abroad for a year or more, his friendship with Verdenal was enhanced by and associated with the exciting and magical qualities of living abroad in what was at the time the most vibrant city in the world.

What we know of Verdenal's personality suggests that he was an ideal young person. He was of high moral stature, as confirmed by reports of his courageous and honorable actions on the battlefield of Gallipoli. His citation from his commanding officer reads, "Verdenal, assistant medical officer, performed his duties with courage and devotion. He was killed on the 2nd May while dressing a wounded man on the field of battle" (qtd. in Watson 467). His letters reveal that he was highly intellectual and thoughtful, pondering life's great questions, his chosen ambition, his love of the arts and philosophy, his spirituality, and the modern world; pressing issues which he and Eliot had clearly discussed. Verdenal's interest in philosophy— that of Bergson in particular—is evident in numerous notes on Bergson's lectures which the Italian scholar Claudio Perinot found among his possessions (271). Verdenal may even have attended some of those lectures with Eliot. Evidence of Bergson's influence can be detected in Verdenal's philosophical musings in his letters along with one specific reference ("O action, O Bergson") in a wry, self-mocking commentary on the possibility of his taking action (*Letters* 32). Perinot also found notes of philosophical conversations with fellow lodgers Prichard and Milhaud (271), conversations of the kind that he had with Eliot as well.

The kinds of philosophical issues that he and Eliot pondered can be found in most of his letters. In his second letter to Eliot in Munich in mid-July 1911, for example, he meditates on the effects of materialism and science on the Parisian working class, suggesting that "many have repressed their good inner impulses through a desire to think rationally." The "Élite," however, aspire to what he calls "l'Idée," which often takes the form of a return to Christianity, listing the names of eight writers who exhibit this trait and saying, "We'll talk about all this *again* sometime, if you like" (italics mine). He ends this long paragraph with a desire to analyze each writer in order to decide "*how far he can influence our inner life towards the knowledge of the supreme good,*" a clear priority for him, and conveys his anticipation of Eliot's return in September in the hopes of sorting it all out (*Letters* 24). And in a letter of April 22, 1912, he ponders "the ideal," defining it as an "*inner impulse,*" with evidence of the influence of Bergson and of a young mind grappling with its meaning:

But men, as long as they exist, will be inspired by it (since it is inherent in the impulse of life itself) and it cannot be appeased by the achievement of any goal, since it existed before the goal. It is this which

1) Leads us to believe that life has a purpose

2) Makes that purpose unknowable.

And so we go forward, always further forward. (*Letters* 34)

The last sentence may be echoed in the speaker's thrice-uttered admonition in Section III of "The Dry Salvages" to "Fare forward" (143, 155, 168).

Despite his essentially serious disposition, Verdenal also had a sense of humor as seen, for example, in his good-natured ribbing of Eliot for not writing and in his mocking their serious conversations on serious subjects: "My dear friend, I am waiting impatiently to hear that you have found some notepaper in Bavaria, and to receive an example of it covered with your beautiful handwriting, before German beer has dulled your wits. . . [;] but beer is not to be despised—and so we carry on. O Reason!" (*Letters* 21).

Verdenal's political tendencies (traditional and monarchist) may also have been appealing to Eliot. Dr. Arthur Schlemmer, who had been a fellow medical student of Verdenal, stated in a letter to Watson that Verdenal "took a small interest, literary and political, in Charles Maurras and L'Action Française. He may have been inclined to be monarchist theor[et]ically, but not to take part in this extremist movement" (qtd. in Watson 469). So he underscored those tendencies already impressed on Eliot by Babbitt and others by discussing with him the theories of Maurras, but it is doubtful that he personally introduced him to the man himself or participated in meetings or demonstrations of L'Action Française.

He was serious, hard-working, and dedicated to performing well in the medical profession, as seen in his many references to studying hard and being a good physician, even though he would have preferred to follow his heart into literature or philosophy. That preference is poignantly revealed in his letter of December 26, 1912, the last which has survived. There he complains of the practicality of medicine: "The medical profession . . . is only interested in knowledge it can make use of. No good looking to it for anything other than the practical. It is to be my profession. At times, I feel exasperated at being obliged to submit to it." He proposes "to give myself an organized scheme of literary and philosophical study" (*Letters* 36). These comments suggest that Verdenal must have rejoiced to find such a friend as Eliot, who must have been equally happy to know someone to whom literature, the arts, and philosophy were so meaningful. Verdenal's interest in literature is evident in his possessing books by a host of writers, including Mallarmé, Laforgue, Verlaine, Philippe, Gide, Claudel, Baudelaire, Maeterlinck, and Schiller (Perinot 271–2; Watson 468), and in references in his letters to Eliot to Philippe, Péguy, Gide, Verlaine, Claudel, and others (*Letters* 21, 23–4, 32) and to the nature of literary criticism (*Letters* 22).

Like Alain-Fournier, Verdenal was particularly keen on Wagnerian opera, to judge from programs among Verdenal's possessions (Perinot 271) as well as from references in his letters. The two Frenchmen seem to have encouraged Eliot's interest, perhaps attending performances together of *Tristan und Isolde* in November, as suggested above, and all or part of *Der Ring des Nibelungen*, presented twice for the first time ever in Paris in June 1911. That Verdenal and Eliot had in-depth discussions about these works is clear from two of Verdenal's letters. In early July 1911, Verdenal urged Eliot to "hear something by Wagner in Munich" and told him that he had gone "the other day to the *Götterdämmerung* [The Twilight of the Gods], conducted by Nikisch [on June 29]," describing the end as "one of the highest points ever reached by man" (*Letters* 24–5). In early February 1912, after noting that he had been feeling lonely and depressed, he wrote that music sustained him: "Music goes more directly to the core of my being [than books], and I have been listening to quite a lot of it recently (still mainly Wagner). I am beginning to get the hang of *The Ring*. Each time the plot becomes clearer and the obscure passages take on a meaning. *Tristan und Isolde* is terribly moving at the first hearing and leaves you prostrate with ecstasy and thirsting to get back to it again. . . . I would be happy to know that you too are able to hear some Wagner in America, and something by Franck as well, if you get the opportunity. This is what I am most interested in at the moment" (*Letters* 31).

The two friends also shared an interest in art, particularly the modern art movements which were multiplying during the early years of the 20th Century. It is likely that they went to the first exhibition of the Cubists at the sensational Salon des Indépendants in the spring, since Alain-Fournier attended the *Jour de Vernissage* [Varnishing Day], a private viewing held for selected guests prior to the official opening of an art exhibition (Rivière and Alain-Fournier 383–4), and no doubt encouraged them to go, perhaps accompanying them himself. Verdenal comments on Cubism and Futurism in a letter of April 22, 1912, a year almost to the day from the opening: "Incidentally, Cubism has been destroyed by Futurism, which protests against museums, etc. and has a big exhibition at Bernheim's. Such are the manifestations of the new school, unless another springs up while my letter is crossing the sea" (*Letters* 34). Verdenal clearly kept up with current developments in art and comfortably shared with Eliot, through a bit of sarcastic wit, his disapproval of the speed and ease with which new movements appeared on the scene to conflict with or displace prior ones (although his fear about Cubism proved to be unfounded).

The family-run Pension Casaubon in which they boarded was the kind of place to foster the growth of a close and comfortable relationship, for it was small, friendly, and informal with cordial interactions among the boarders themselves, the owners, and even the staff. In a letter of April 26, 1911 to his cousin Eleanor, Eliot recorded in an amusing close translation the light-hearted banter of "my friend the *femme de chambre* [who] burst in to see me" upon his return from his Easter holiday in London and gave him "a store of news about everyone else in the house," revealing the easy nature of the pension. Learning from her that "M. Verdenal has taken" a larger room with a view of the garden, Eliot recounted going to inspect it and, seeing Verdenal in said garden below, throwing a lump of sugar at him to get his attention (*Letters* 17–18). And Verdenal writes on April 22, 1912 that he now occupies "the little room that was yours last year, and I like having the bed in a little recess, but the pattern of the wallpaper (do you remember it?) often gets on my nerves. Damn. It occurred to me a moment ago to send you a little piece of [it]—then I immediately realized that the idea was not mine but that I had got it from a letter by J. Laforgue, so I will abstain" (*Letters* 32).

The owners cultivated a family atmosphere, with Mme Casaubon presiding each evening at the dinner table and M. Casaubon presiding at tea in the garden. Verdenal in his letter of February 5, 1912 gave Eliot "news of the pension— everything is just the same (this evening, for the 2474th time, I shall see Madame Casaubon hold her napkin between her chin and her chest as her wrinkled hands mix the salad)" (*Letters* 32), while Watson describes a charming photograph of Verdenal having tea in the garden with the owners, "a silver teapot on the table and Monsieur Cazaubon [*sic*] himself an imposingly elegant figure in a white beard" (468). Eliot retained such warm memories of the pension, its owners, its boarders, and especially Verdenal that he stayed there during a week's holiday in Paris in December 1920, writing to his mother that "I stayed at my old pension Casaubon, you know the old people are all dead, and the grandson is now pro- prietor. . . . If I had not met with such a number of new people there Paris would be very desolate for me with pre-war memories of Jean Verdenal and the others" (*Letters* 433).

In addition to and indeed because of their shared passion for literature, art, music, and philosophy, and their conversations about life, the supreme good, and the ideal, they clearly had great admiration and affection for each other, as indi- cated in Verdenal's letters by the terms of address "Mon cher ami" [My dear friend] and "Mon vieux" [Old pal] and by several moving memories of Eliot, whom he greatly missed (see, for example, *Letters* 32, 34–5). An indication of Verdenal's desire that they could spend time together, and one which has not been mentioned in Eliot scholarship to my knowledge, is on a postcard of the Château d'Allaman in Aubonne, Switzerland which seems to be from Verdenal in the Eliot Collection of Harvard's Houghton Library, bMS Am 1691.6 (15). Dated September 7, 1912 and addressed to "T. S. Eliot Esq. at 16 Ash Street," it bears on the front a short note in

French, saying, "Things are going well, old pal. I wish so much that you were with me. Affectionately, Jean."

In his 1934 "A Commentary," Eliot, on his part, described his own nostalgic memory of Verdenal, couched in the framework of grief for his death, revealing that his Parisian year held significance because of this close friendship as well as because of its intellectual excitement: "I am willing to admit that my own retrospect is touched by a sentimental sunset, the memory of a friend coming across the Luxembourg Gardens in the late afternoon, waving a branch of lilac, a friend who was later (so far as I could find out) to be mixed with the mud of Gallipoli" (452). Eliot's dedication to Verdenal in four collections of his early poems confirms his affection for him and, in the two which include a quotation from Dante's *Purgatorio*, his sense of loss as well.[15] Eliot probably never had before and may never have had again a soul-mate, confidant, and friend with whom he had such an intellectual, spiritual, and emotional intimacy. As Lyndall Gordon suggests, "The Frenchman's most important legacy for Eliot was to offer a blend of sensibility and intellect missing in the English intellectual tradition since the seventeenth century" (*Imperfect* 53).

When Eliot left Paris in September 1911 to return to the United States, the two clearly intended to meet again, but, as fate would have it, they were never to do so. It is curious that Eliot did not go to Paris for a reunion with Verdenal in July 1914 on his way to Marburg, especially since he visited several cities in nearby Belgium. However, since Verdenal had joined the Eighteenth Infantry Regiment in March 1913, he was no doubt stationed elsewhere at the time, and, after the war broke out in early August and Eliot went to England, meeting would have been difficult, if not impossible. Verdenal served on the western front from August 2, 1914 to February 27, 1915, when he was sent east as a medical attendant in the 175th Infantry Regiment and was involved in the Anglo-French attack at Gallipoli which began on April 25, dying on the battlefield there on May 2 (Watson 467).

So, although we do not know exactly when Eliot met these two young Frenchmen, it must have been soon after his arrival in Paris, and they were to become and remain friends for this marvelous year of his life. When Eliot comments in a letter to Robert McAlmon that in Paris in 1910–1911 he "knew no one whatever, *in the literary and artistic world, as a companion*—knew them rather as spectacles, listened to, at rare occasions, but never spoken to" (McAlmon and Boyle 9; italics mine), he clearly means that he had no friends among the literary and artistic figures who were already famous (not unusual since he was, after all, only a twenty-two-year-old graduate student who had as yet gained no fame himself), but only observed them on occasion or attended their lectures, exhibitions, or performances, not that he had no friends whatever and was thus alone and lonely, as Ackroyd (43) suggests. The two young men played important roles during Eliot's year in Paris, providing him with close friends who shared his sensibilities, his passion for philosophy, literature, and the arts, and many of his character traits. To Eliot, fate must have seemed particularly cruel in that they died in battle just seven months apart in the early days of World War I.

Late Fall Activities and the Beginning of the University Term

By early November, then, we may speculate with some assurance that Eliot was settled in his pension, had met Alain-Fournier and Verdenal, was learning his way around Paris, had seen the dazzling array of literary and cultural opportunities to be had, and had already attended some of them. Amid the excitement of those activities, the opening of the university approached. An article entitled "At the Schools" in the Friday, November 4, 1910 issue of *Le Figaro* reported that "the Latin Quarter has resumed its typical appearance: white posters announcing courses of study and schedules and advising students to complete the formalities of registration cover the walls, while multi-colored posters tempt them to join diverse student associations. In short, since yesterday the Latin Quarter has come to life and the total reawakening of the university is near." The reporter, one Jacques-Pierre, went on to describe the activities of new students such as Eliot: "During the day in the halls of the Sorbonne . . . groups of new students located the rooms where they will have classes; others waited patiently for their turn to enroll at the windows of the registrar's office." Student head counts were important then as now, for the article ended by noting, "The first tabulations of enrollment figures give cause for optimism, leading us to predict an increase in the number of students over last year's figures, especially among the foreign contingent" (3), one of whom was, of course, Eliot. The increase in foreign students was attributed to "the superior instruction" in France, a testament to the "permanent prestige of our culture" and evidence that "the intellectual mastery of our country shows no signs of subsiding," according to a front-page article entitled "L'Esprit Française" in the November 7 issue of *Le Petit Parisien*.

On the front page of *Le Figaro* for November 4, a weather report divulged that rain had fallen without ceasing from morning until night and a cloudy sky covered the city with gloomy darkness, a continuation of the torrential autumn rains which threatened to cause floods similar to those of the previous January. *Le Petit Parisien* for November 5 referred to the bad weather more bluntly as "ce temps execrable" [this abominable weather] (2).

The next day, Saturday, November 5, saw the opening session of the Faculté des Lettres at 2:30 p.m. Eliot was no doubt among the crowd of students who, according to *Le Figaro*'s account, exchanged their impressions prior to the meeting. When the professors entered, the old students pointed out the most famous to the new ones. After the dean described university life and announced that a course in English entitled "French Pioneers in America" would be given by the president of the City College of New York, the professor of Greek gave enrollment statistics: 3,310 students had enrolled as opposed to 2,957 the previous year; 1,329 of these were foreigners (540 men and 789 women, among them 587 Russians, 187 Germans, 99 Americans, and 97 Britons). The dean concluded the session by proclaiming, in response certainly to the current heated debate over the role of the Sorbonne, that the ideal of this most prestigious French university was to produce students and professors capable of achieving more than their masters, to which the students responded with enthusiastic applause (3).

Amazingly, in the column right next to this account was a review of a lecture, also on Saturday, given by Gide on Philippe. According to the reviewer, the audience was "particularly attentive" as Gide showed the "marvelous evolution in Philippe's thought" from his earliest novel to his last. In the course of this "powerful, demonstrative, and impassioned lecture several people recited portions of [Philippe's] work," and the session ended with a reading of Claudel's poem "L'Adieu," whose "lyricism spread a funereal tone in the silence" (3). It is a distinct possibility that Eliot was in the audience, perhaps with Alain-Fournier. If so, it was a stunning experience, both hearing such a famous literary figure as Gide and hearing about Philippe, whose *Bubu de Montparnasse* he may already have begun to read.

Eliot must have been curious about the debate over the role of the Sorbonne, alluded to implicitly in the remarks of the dean at that opening session, and would perhaps have asked Alain-Fournier or Verdenal about it. And, in reply, he probably was first given a brief account of the history of the Université de Paris, of which it was a part. Begun in the twelfth century, by the thirteenth and fourteenth centuries it was made up of some forty to seventy colleges, the most famous of which was the Sorbonne, founded in 1257 by the theologian Robert de Sorbon for instruction in theology. In the early twentieth century, it was (and still is) one of thirteen colleges constituting the Université de Paris, housing the Faculties of Sciences and Letters, which Baedeker referred to in his 1907 guidebook as the seat or center of the university with approximately 325 instructors and professors and nearly 12,000 students (290), although the 1910–1911 edition of the *Encyclopedia Britannica*, evidently a bit behind the times, still defined it exclusively as the Faculty of Theology (Atkielski).[16]

Whether or not his friends filled him in, he would soon have become aware of the heated controversy which was raging about the role of the Sorbonne and which reached a peak of intensity during the fall semester of 1910, as indicated by the dean's allusion. A series of articles entitled "L'Esprit de la Nouvelle Sorbonne" [The Spirit of the New Sorbonne] and signed with the pseudonym Agathon (the name of the disciple of Socrates in Plato's *Symposium*) appeared every three weeks from July 23 to December 31, 1910 in *L'Opinion*, a weekly newspaper with nationalist sympathies. The articles denounced the new emphasis on the scientific method of the social sciences—particularly sociology under the influence of the powerful Durkheim—at the expense of the traditional classical studies in language and literature: "Higher education [today] values only the collection of data (index cards), work which is essentially passive, thus running the risk of extinguishing forever the individuality and enthusiasm which direct contact with great masterpieces maintains. . . . Originality, imagination, invention are scorned" (Agathon, qtd. in Debaene). In October 1910, just at the time of Eliot's arrival in Paris, a second, closely linked theme began to emerge—that this elevation of science threatened French culture and language specifically: "It is obvious that higher education no longer values our classical French culture" (Agathon, qtd. in Debaene). These articles were published as a pamphlet in 1911.[17]

Agathon was later revealed to be two young men, Henri Massis and Alfred de Tarde. Eliot indicated in his 1934 "A Commentary," which originated as a review of Massis's memoir *Évocations* but became Eliot's memoir of his Paris year, that he had read the articles at the time, but, like most others, did not know the identity (or identities, as it turned out) of the author: "I remember the appearance of M. Massis's first conspicuous piece of writing; though I was ignorant at the time, as were most people, that the 'Agathon' who attacked the New Sorbonne was a name covering the joint authorship of Henri Massis and Alfred de Tarde" (451). Eliot later became a friend of Massis, who shared the beliefs of Maurras, referring to him in the review as "our friend" (451). At the very least, this ferocious debate made Eliot consider—or reconsider—the value of the humanities as opposed to that of the social and natural sciences. Since neither Eliot's *Livret d'Étudiant* [student booklet] nor other documents have survived to tell us whether he took courses other than those of Bergson, we can only wonder if he attended the courses of Durkheim, as Morgenstern suggests, Lévy-Bruhl, Janet, or other great professors then teaching in Paris. He was clearly acquainted with their works later, as revealed in "A Commentary" (451–2), perhaps first reading some of them during his Parisian year as they were much in the public eye.

Since Bergson's courses did not begin until early December, Eliot had the rest of November free for additional exploration of the city, attending cultural events, reading the books which Alain-Fournier had doubtless begun to assign him, and writing Part I of "Portrait of a Lady" to go along with Part II, produced the previous February, fulfilling his hopes for poetic inspiration in Paris. The poem may have been influenced by Manet's *Woman with a Parrot*, as Dickey suggests (1–34), but also by contemporary paintings such as Matisse's *Woman in a Hat* and by his Bostonian and Parisian experiences. The poem's sophisticated, dispassionate young male speaker, caught in an awkward relationship with an older woman, is cast in the mold of Laforgue's speakers. Eliot must have felt a shock of recognition if he saw in the January 26, 1911 issue of *Le Figaro* the cartoon "Les Mauvaises fortunes" [Bad Luck], in which an older woman (euphemistically called "a woman of a certain age" by the French) leaning toward a young man, who is leaning back as far as possible, says, "I must tell you, sir, that I find you extremely attractive" (3). Perhaps Eliot had the cartoon in mind as he completed the poem in November 1911 at Harvard (Figure 6).

In December his choices for cultural enrichment included an exhibition of great artists of the nineteenth century, performances of *The Damnation of Faust* and *Aïda* at the Opéra, a production of *Phèdre* at the Comédie-Française, and a concert featuring "La Mort d'Isolde" by Saint-Saëns. On December 13, a gala concert in honor of Beethoven conducted by Siegfried Wagner, the son of Richard Wagner and the grandson of Franz Liszt, could well have attracted a young man enamored of the music of the father. However, he might have been disappointed since the performance received a negative (if witty) review in the next day's issue of *Le Figaro* (4).

During this month he completed the poem "Fourth Caprice in Montparnasse." It is likely that he wrote most or all of it while still at Harvard since it was one of a series begun in November 1909, its original title being "Fourth Caprice in North Cambridge." It is, however, dated December 1910, with his Paris location indicated in his canceling "North Cambridge" in the original ink title and adding "Montparnasse" in pencil (Ricks 111). Perhaps he did little more than change the title to give it a more cosmopolitan air and to reflect the significance of his living in Paris,[18] although details of a gloomy urban setting suggest the influence of Philippe's *Bubu de Montparnasse*.

Henri Bergson

For Eliot, the most important event of December had to be the beginning of Bergson's courses at the Collège de France (Figure 7), which was then referred to as "the house of Bergson" ("Henri Bergson" 1). It was only a five-minute walk from Eliot's pension down rue St-Jacques to rue des Écoles, where in front of the Collège was a bronze statue of Dante on a grassy plot and, just beyond, the main courtyard accessed through an arch bearing the motto "Docet Omnia" [Teach Everything]. The statue of Dante was inscribed with a sonnet by Philippe Dufour based on the legend that the Italian poet spent some time between 1307 and 1310 in Paris in the course of his wanderings.[19] Perhaps this statue inspired him to read the *Commedia* in Italian for the first time that year. Regardless, it was prophetic of his lifelong devotion to the Italian poet,[20] the most important and constant of his many literary influences.

The Collège de France was founded by François I in 1530 as an institution independent of the Université de Paris, with the goal of offering a more liberal curriculum than the limited theological studies then available, beginning with Hebrew and Greek and over the years expanding its courses to include Latin, mathematics, philosophy, modern languages, the sciences, psychology, and others.[21] Its two major purposes were (and still are) to be a center for research and a place of instruction in emerging knowledge: "The teaching does not deal with established knowledge but with knowledge in the making; it changes every year, in accordance with the latest research and has no pre-established pattern. . . . Thus, the Collège enjoys not only considerable freedom in teaching and research, but can also adapt to progress and the latest developments in all fields of knowledge" ("About" 1–2). Its dedication to openness and currently developing knowledge is captured in its motto, "Docet omnia," and in the words of one of its professors, Maurice Merleau-Ponty, inscribed in gold over the main hall: "Since its founding, the Collège de France has been charged with giving its students not established truths but the idea of unrestricted research" ("Étonnant Collège" 2). Its courses have always been free and open to all, with Baedeker's 1907 guidebook noting that they were attended particularly by "les adultes et des dames" [adult males and women] (291). Although awarding no degrees, it boasted a superb faculty, especially in philosophy, literature, and science ("Paris" 1017). According to Baedeker, there were forty-two "chaires" [professorships] in 1907 (291), so we may assume a similar impressive number in 1910–1911.

Bergson (Figure 8) began teaching at this most prestigious of French institutions of higher learning in 1900, engendering in the next decade a frenzy of excitement about his theories. Indeed, "a veritable vogue of Bergsonism" ("Bergson" 844) was at its peak during Eliot's residence. Leszek Kolakowski states that Bergson was "not just a famous thinker and writer; in the eyes of Europe's educated public he was clearly *the* philosopher, the intellectual spokesman *par excellence*" (1–2), and Sanford Schwartz points out that his influence extended to a variety of fields: "Bergson's ideas about art, intuition, and experience enjoyed an enormous vogue," especially in the years immediately preceding World War I (30). William Marx asserts that Bergson was "an immensely popular philosopher whose influence spread well beyond strictly philosophical circles into fashionable and cultural spheres and into high schools and crossed the English Channel and the Atlantic," remarking that his "pluridisciplinary" influence at the beginning of the twentieth century is "systematically undervalued" (41–2).

Beginning on December 9, 1910 and continuing until May 20, 1911, the famous professor of philosophy gave two courses, lecturing on Personality on Fridays at 5 p.m. and on Spinoza's *Traité de la réforme de l'entendement* [Treatise on the Reform of Understanding] on Saturdays at 4:15 p.m. (Bergson 845–6). Because of his enormous popularity, the lecture hall was always packed with a wide variety of excited listeners, from students to society women. Although Eliot's detailed notes in French (preserved in a booklet in the Eliot Collection of Harvard's Houghton Library) cover only January and February 1911, he doubtless attended every lecture from December to May, as indicated in his assertion that "to have truly experienced *la ferveur bergsonienne* one had to have gone, regularly, every week, to that lecture hall full to bursting where he gave his courses at the Collège de France." He adds that, in order to get in, one had to arrive an hour and fifteen minutes ahead of time ("What France" 94).[22] A period cartoon entitled "Bergson 'Attrac'cheun" (Figure 9) depicts a crowd of people pushing and shoving (one of whom seems to be using his umbrella as a weapon) to get into the lecture hall, with this explanation: "Everyone knows that one can be nearly crushed by the throng at the courses of M. Bergson, the latest of our immortals. But many do not know that this philosopher with the austere reputation is a merry companion. His book on Laughter is a collection of irresistible jokes. As he has spoken highly of Laughter, Laughter speaks highly of him" (Bibliothèque nationale de France).

Massis in his memoir *Évocations* gives us a good idea of the excitement engendered by Bergson during Eliot's year in Paris and provides us with a striking insight into Eliot's response to him. Indeed, in his 1934 "A Commentary," Eliot comments, "The book should be, for anybody, an interesting and valuable document upon a period; but has a more personal interest for me, inasmuch as M. Massis is my contemporary, and the period of which he writes includes the time of my own brief residence in Paris" (451). Eliot thus validates the authenticity of Massis's memories as similar to his own. Noting that "Bergson was then at the height of his glory," Massis describes the crowd gathered in the austere lecture hall:

Well before the hour when the lecture was to begin, an extraordinary crowd invaded the hall . . . [,] a curious mixture of students from the École Normale Supérieure, almost all of whom sat together in the same part of the hall; poets and artists rubbed shoulders with those who regularly frequented the Collège de France: old men wearing their military medals, ancient spinsters, and very young women with eager, harsh faces, Russian female students; society women wearing immense hats; and footmen who retained seats for those of the upper class attracted by curiosity more than by a taste for metaphysics. At 5 p.m., the Master appeared, evoking an air of reverent meditation and total silence. (90–91)

Massis goes on to describe Bergson's physical appearance and his gestures as he gave his lecture without notes.

When Eliot was attending his courses, Bergson's philosophy, which ran counter to the emphasis on the scientific and mechanistic nature of the universe so prevalent at the time, was based on several key concepts propounded in a graceful and lucid style in five major books published between 1889 and 1907: *Essai sur les données immédiates de conscience* [Time and Free Will: An Essay on the Immediate Data of Consciousness] in 1889; *Matière et mémoire* [Matter and Memory] in 1896; *Le rire* [Laughter: An Essay on the Meaning of the Comic] in 1900; *Introduction à la métaphysique* [Introduction to Metaphysics] in 1903; and *L'Évolution créatrice* [Creative Evolution] in 1907, the last considered to be his greatest work of these years. One of the major concepts was *la durée réelle*, defined as duration or real lived time, perceived by the mind as an endlessly flowing process. Another was *l'élan vital*, meaning vital spirit or energy, a creative force which continually generates new forms of life; thus, Bergson argued, evolution is "creative, not mechanistic" (Bergson 844). The third was *intuition*, directly apprehending or entering into the Other to discover its true essence and thus attaining absolute knowledge. The spiritual and humanistic values which many found in his views, in contrast to the materialistic and scientific theories of the day, engendered a return to or renewal of those values. As Bergson himself noted in a letter to a French Jesuit theologian, "The considerations exposed in my *Essai* throw light upon the very fact of liberty; those of *Matière et mémoire* permit [us] tangibly to ascertain, as I hope, the reality of the spirit; those of *L'Évolution créatrice* present creation as a fact. From all this clearly follows the notion of God both creating and free" (qtd. in "Bergson" 844).

Providing us with an insight into the kind of excitement which Bergson's ideas engendered in Eliot and indeed in all who fell under his spell at the time is Massis's powerful description of his own responses, which were shared by other young people. Using a host of superlatives, he states that Bergson's philosophy introduced them to "intoxicating novelties" during "our twentieth year," describing the "incomparable exaltation" that they felt upon discovering his ideas, which freed them from the shackles of their conventional modes of thinking. Comparing Bergson's thought to "the freshness of living water," he explained that what attracted him the most was "a truly experimental psychology which studied the interior life in all its manifestations and which ended at the reality of free will, at the distinction between spirit and matter, at a certain substantiality of the soul, to establish finally the probability of survival" (87–9).

He devotes an entire paragraph to an attempt to capture the essence of the experience: "Bergson introduced liberty into our prison of materialism—O intoxicating moment! . . . A new world opened suddenly from which sprang depths of unsuspected light. All that we thought we already knew appeared rejuvenated, renewed, in the clarity of dawn. We seemed to contemplate reality itself face to face for the first time. . . . That's what we felt when we read his books. But nothing can render the impression of the intimate and direct view, the strange shock that we felt in listening to the philosopher who offered to our youth the rarest of human spectacles, *the spectacle of creation*" (89). He then describes the experience of observing Bergson's mind in the process of creating new philosophical ideas during his lectures:

> For an hour, every Friday, at the Collège de France, a man was thinking, was creating in front of us. Through an effort of his entire being, he forced himself to recapture the original, the first, feeling and then to reconstitute it in a sort of vision in which he sought to express in multiple images, more and more precise, more and more subtle, what each one of us must find in the depths of ourselves, behind the screen of the superficial and conventional. Thus, we were able to follow, at the moment of its birth, the mysterious germinating activity of his thoughts, of the intuitions still fresh and like living streams. It is an unforgettable thing, and one which we doubtless will never see again. (89–90)

This insight into the intoxicating, indeed rapturous, experience of attending the lectures of Bergson brilliantly conveys what Eliot himself must have felt and thus helps us to understand the power of the charismatic philosopher as well as the feelings of freedom, hope, and inspiration which he instilled in his listeners.[23]

Bergson's theories exerted a powerful influence not only on students but also on a wide spectrum of figures in a variety of fields, including William James, Santayana, Péguy, T. E. Hulme, Proust, G. B. Shaw, Sorel, Debussy, Monet, and the emerging avant-garde art movements, especially those centered in Paris, as noted by Eliot in his 1934 "A Commentary": "His metaphysic was said to throw some light upon the new ways of painting, and discussion of Bergson was apt to be involved with discussion of Matisse and Picasso" (452).

Bergson's influence on Eliot was both immense and intense during his Parisian year when the young American was swept up by *la ferveur bergsonienne*, as he acknowledged numerous times. In a letter of January 21, 1953 to Shiv K. Kumar, for example, he wrote, "I was certainly very much under [Bergson's] influence during the year 1910–11, when I both attended his lectures and gave close study to the books he had then written" (qtd. in Ricks 412). Regarding the latter, he referred specifically to *Matière et mémoire* in "Lettre d'Angleterre" in the November 1923 issue of *La Nouvelle Revue Française*: "I can bear witness to the important influence that . . . *Matière et mémoire* had on my intellectual development at a particular period" (qtd. in Ricks 410). In the introduction to Josef Pieper's *Leisure, the Basis of Culture* (1952), he speculated about "a longing for the appearance [in the present] of a philosopher whose writings, lectures and personality will arouse the imagination as Bergson, for instance, aroused it forty years ago" (qtd. in Ricks 411). In his best-known statement about Bergson, he revealed, "My only conversion, by the deliberate influence of any individual, was a temporary conversion to Bergsonism" (*Sermon* 5). While the word "temporary" has often been emphasized in this comment, Eliot's choice of the religious term "conversion" to describe his response to Bergson's philosophy reveals just how powerful and all-encompassing that influence was at the time. Further insight into the nature of that experience is found in Eliot's paper on metaphysics and politics written at Harvard after his return from Paris: "Bergson . . . emphasises [*sic*] the reality of a fluid psychological world of aspect and nuance, where purposes and intentions are replaced by pure feeling. *By the seduction of his style we come to believe that the Bergsonian world is the only world . . .*" (qtd. in Ricks 409; italics mine).

The influence of Bergson's ideas can be seen in many of the poems that Eliot wrote during his Parisian year and immediately afterward. In a letter of April 19, 1945 to Eudo A. Mason, for example, Eliot wrote that, "at the time, or at least before ['The Love Song of J. Alfred Prufrock'] was finished, [I] was entirely a Bergsonian" (qtd. in Ricks 411). And even though he insisted that his conversion was only temporary, with influences such as that of Bertrand Russell subsequently turning him away from a total subscription to Bergson's theories, the effect of Bergson on Eliot's poetic principles and his own philosophy was in fact profound and long-lasting, as Le Brun and Douglass convincingly argue. Le Brun demonstrates that Eliot's "major formulations about poetry" (149) reflect Bergson's influence, while Douglass traces Eliot's views of the influence of the past on the present (33), his belief that the modern human being is quite similar underneath to his primitive ancestors (57; see also Crawford 67), and his moral and spiritual values (58, 63) to Bergson, whose style Eliot admired "as one of 'intense addiction to an intellectual passion'" (55). Indeed, Douglass states that the "practical effect Bergson had on Eliot's thinking was, finally, profound," illustrating in his study that Eliot's "vocabulary and operative principles owe a debt to Bergson" (63). These influences can be found throughout Eliot's works,[24] as in the opening passage of "Burnt Norton," which reflects the concept of *la durée réelle*:

> Time present and time past
> Are both perhaps present in time future,
> And time future contained in time past.
> If all time is eternally present
> All time is unredeemable. (1–5)

And the image of the rose garden was perhaps influenced by Bergson's use of a rose in *Essai sur les données immédiates de la conscience* to explain his theory of association, which was at odds with the current thinking (see Schwartz 24–5).

Bergson was, as Eliot wrote in his notes for his autumn 1916 Oxford University Extension Lectures in Yorkshire,[25] "the most noticed figure in Paris" in 1910–1911 (qtd. in Moody 49), a time when the city was filled with "noticeable" figures. For Eliot, and for most of Paris, he was the predominant intellectual star in a galaxy full of stars. In a now-famous and oft-quoted passage in his 1934 "A Commentary," after remarking on the stimulating intellectual atmosphere of Paris—especially for a young American who felt that his native country and England were intellectual deserts—he lists the brightest of these stars and then gives Bergson the place of honor:

> Anatole France and Remy de Gourmont still exhibited their learning, and provided types of scepticism [*sic*] for younger men to be attracted by and to repudiate; Barrès was at the height of his influence . . . . Péguy, more or less Bergsonian *and* Catholic *and* Socialist, had just become important, and the young were further distracted by Gide and Claudel. Vildrac, Romains, Duhamel, experimented with verse which seemed hopeful . . . . At the Sorbonne, Faguet was an authority to be attacked violently;[26] the sociologists, Durkheim, Lévy-Bruhl, held new doctrines; Janet was the great psychologist; at the Collège de France, Loisy [in Biblical Studies] enjoyed his somewhat scandalous distinction; and over all swung the spider-like figure of Bergson. (451–2)

Charles Maurras and L'Action Française

The other major intellectual influence on Eliot at the time was one which lasted for much of Eliot's life—that of the forceful and charismatic Charles Maurras (Figure 10), whose beliefs in tradition, order, hierarchy, authority, and clarity as well as his "fiercely and resolutely anti-Romantic" stance, like that of Eliot's Harvard mentor Babbitt (Torrens 314), had a powerful effect on Eliot. "One of the most extraordinary figures of the period" (Belgion 55), "Le Maître," as he was called by his followers, was the leader of L'Action Française, a political organization which promoted nationalism, monarchy, the Roman Catholic Church, and the Army, as well as an intolerance of the four "enemies" of his vision of France: Protestants, Jews, Freemasons, and foreigners, the latter designated by the derogatory term *métèques*. Its offices were located at 33 rue St-André-des-Arts, not far from the statue of Saint Michel on boulevard St-Michel. Its ideas were disseminated through its daily newspaper *L'Action Française*, whose subtitle proclaimed it *The Voice of Integral Nationalism*. A forceful and persuasive writer, Maurras had his own column on the front page every day in which he voiced his views, with violent attacks on his targets. In early April 1911, for instance, he mounted an assault on Jews that went on for days.

The newspaper was hawked in the streets by a large cadre of unruly young men called the Camelots du Roi, that also served as Maurras's bodyguard: "Under the moon, clutching his big stick and surrounded by a bodyguard of [the Camelots], he would tramp through the deserted streets" late at night as he went from his office near the Boulevards to his home on the Left Bank (Belgion 55). Further, brandishing lead-filled canes and bludgeons, they often instigated riots or demonstrations when they felt the beliefs of L'Action Française to be disparaged. Belgion notes, "You might be quietly sipping your *bock* [glass of beer] outside a café on the Boulevards and suddenly your neighbors scrambled away, tables were overturned, and the glass shivered and flew, as the *Camelots du Roi* retreated up the broad thoroughfare before a truncheon charge by the police" (55). While the number of members listed in the Paris area in 1909 was approximately 600, only 150 of those were active. In 1910 a "special forces unit" of the Camelots was formed, called the Commissaires de L'Action Française, and they along with the "regular forces" trained on a small island in the Seine, which the organization had purchased for this express purpose (Tannenbaum 99–101; Weber 54–5).

During Eliot's residence several such disturbances took place. Soon after his arrival, a highly publicized controversy known as the Affaire Fauchois erupted when the young playwright Fauchois criticized Jean Racine's *Iphigénie en Aulide* in a lecture preceding a performance of the play at the Théâtre Odéon on October 27, and a contingent of the Camelots violently shouted him down. At the subsequent lecture on November 3, a near-riot occurred in the theater, with police arriving to arrest some of the brawlers. Afterward, there was agitation on the streets outside, and, according to *L'Action Française*, demonstrators ran through the Latin Quarter. It may well be this specific incident which Eliot recalls in his 1934 "A Commentary":

"in 1910 I remember the *camelots* cheering the *cuirassiers* [mounted soldiers with chest armor] who were sent to disperse them, because they represented the Army, all the time that they were trying to stampede their horses" (453). While Maurras insisted in his front-page column the next day that the negative response of the Camelots to Fauchois's comments was not politically motivated, he undercut that assertion by boasting that "the brilliant youth of 1910 seems made to return to all our pure fountains [of classicism, nationalism, and tradition]." Gide in "Journal sans Date" in the December 1910 issue of *La Nouvelle Revue Française*, mentioned earlier, sarcastically questioned the validity of Maurras's "defense" of the Camelots' "ardent manifestation" at the Odéon and indeed presents evidence to the contrary, and Henri Ghéon took the incident as his subject in "L'Exemple de Racine" in the February 1911 issue of that journal.

Clearly Maurras and L'Action Française were much in the public eye.[27] Drawn by curiosity over the controversy or by interest in the ideas of Maurras gleaned from newspaper accounts, and perhaps from his new acquaintance Verdenal, Eliot could have attended on November 18 at 8:30 p.m. at 8 rue Danton the Grande Séance de Rentrée, a meeting to welcome old and new student members of L'Action Française at the beginning of the university term. Presided over by Maurras himself, the meeting featured speeches by the organization's leading figures. According to a front-page report in *L'Action Française* the next day, the hall was packed with attentive and passionate students who gave the speakers a huge ovation when they appeared, followed by "an almost religious silence" when Maurras rose to give his speech, which was delivered with "lucid passion" and demonstrated "the pure eloquence of his ideas." With his head and chest projected, he seemed to "seize the audience."

While we do not know whether Eliot attended this or similar meetings, his interest in the ideas of Maurras became intense during this year. Indeed, I would argue that he had at that time a conversion to the philosophy of Maurras as well as to that of Bergson. When he first read the works of Maurras is unclear, however. Schuchard states that he first heard of him in Babbitt's classes at Harvard (54), but he may not have actually read anything by him until his Paris year when "Le Maître" was such an exciting figure, perhaps beginning with his daily front-page columns in *L'Action Française* and then moving on to his early books. Eliot notes in his 1928 review of Leo Ward's *The Condemnation of the Action Française* that he had been reading his works for eighteen years ("*Action*" 195). He told Greene that in 1911 he read Maurras's 1905 *L'Avenir de l'Intelligence* [The Future of Intelligence] (173),[28] whose frightening description of the human mind reduced to total sterility as a result of the crass anti-intellectualism of the modern industrial world influenced *The Waste Land*, as well as other poems. "Triumphal March," for example, was drawn from a specific paragraph in the book and reflects both its images and its rhythm (Greene 93). Eliot wrote in "Lettre d'Angleterre" in the November 1923 issue of *La Nouvelle Revue Française* that this book along with Benda's *Belphégor* was an important influence on his intellectual development (620).

Eliot's debt to Maurras can be seen in many forms. In 1925 he planned to write a book about Maurras as part of a series on French writers that he had in mind upon assuming editorship of *The Criterion* (Ackroyd 153). In 1928, his devotion to Maurras is evident in a variety of ways. In his preface to *For Lancelot Andrewes*, his description of the collection's "general point of view" as "classicist in literature, royalist in politics, and anglo-catholic in religion" (vii) echoes the description of Maurras as "classique, catholique, monarchique" in the March 1913 issue of *La Nouvelle Revue Française* (Ackroyd 41). Further, he published in two installments in *The Criterion* Maurras's early essay "Prologue to an Essay on Criticism," having done the translation himself. As Torrens suggests, he must have found in it "a whole constellation of ideas representing the tradition that was dear to him" (315). And in a letter of January 27, 1928 to Maurras, he still addressed him as "Cher Monsieur et Maître" (Ackroyd 76), reflecting the title "Le Maître" by which Maurras was known in Paris during the heydays of L'Action Française. The next year, he dedicated to him the "longest and best of all his essays, the 1929 study of Dante" (Torrens 312), with the simple phrase "For Charles Maurras," followed by a quotation from his "Conseil de Dante."[29]

Asher asserts that "From beginning to end, Eliot's work, including both the poetry and prose, reveals itself to have been shaped by Maurras's advocacy of an endangered Latin tradition and all that it entailed," a statement which in itself invites criticism since Eliot's work was "shaped" by a multitude of sources. However, Ben Lockerd argues that Maurras's influence began to wane beginning in the late 1920s and early 1930s. This decline he traces to two causes: Pope Pius XI's placing some of his works on the Index and condemning L'Action Française in 1926 and the increasing influence on Eliot of the British Catholic historian Christopher Dawson, who maintained that religion is integral to culture. Lockerd points to statements critical of Maurras in Eliot's 1927 essay "The Humanism of Irving Babbitt" and in an unpublished letter of 1930 to the editor of the *Bookman* cited in Roger Kojecký's *T. S. Eliot's Social Criticism* (10–11). Although Maurras's influence on Eliot thus seems to have diminished somewhat, in 1948 he published a homage to Maurras in *Aspects de la France et du Monde* [Aspects of France and the World], in which he recalled his power and prestige in Paris in 1910–1911, noting that "Maurras, for certain of us, represented a sort of Virgil who led us to the gates of the temple"; this comparison reveals the great esteem in which Maurras was held by Eliot and other young people at that time, but also subtly indicates Maurras's lack of religious beliefs. Eliot's assertion that Maurras's "conceptions of monarchy and of hierarchy . . . [are] kin to my own, as they are to English conservatives, for whom these ideas remain intact despite the modern world" (qtd. in Asher 27) suggests that he still shared and valued those particular conceptions at midcentury, despite having by then some reservations about other elements of Maurras's beliefs. Finally, in a letter published in *Time and Tide* in 1953, Eliot defended Maurras against charges in an obituary notice that he was a Catholic Royalist and a Fascist, and, in a speech entitled "The Literature of Politics" in April 1955, published two months later by the Conservative Political Centre (Behr 71, 75), Eliot paid what would be a final tribute to him.

The Early Months of 1911

Bergson's two classes met on December 9 and 10, 16 and 17, and 23 and 24, 1910, followed by a break of nearly three weeks, resuming again on January 13, 1911 (Bergson 846). Eliot took advantage of the holiday by going to the Dordogne region in southwest France, perhaps after having visited with Verdenal's family in Pau in the Pyrenées Atlantiques. He was in Périgueux, the capital of the Dordogne, in early January, as indicated by a reference in a letter to his mother of September 3, 1919, in which he recounts a recent trip to the region. After giving her the details of his long and arduous journey by steamer and then by overnight train, he notes that he finally arrived at 7:30 a.m. in Périgueux, "where I last was in January 1911" (*Letters* 328). On that first visit in 1911, he no doubt saw a number of the town's famous sites: the medieval section; the Roman ruins; the 12th century church Église St-Étienne; the Cathédrale St-Front (by the architect who designed the Basilique du Sacré-Coeur, which was nearing completion during Eliot's year in Paris); one or more of the four impressive châteaux; and the Musée du Périgord, one of the best prehistory museums in France. He likely sampled the delicacies of the town: truffles, *foie gras*, and pies called *pâtes de Périgueux*. In the surrounding area, his interest in primitive cultures perhaps led him to visit some of the caves, such as the Grotte de Rouffignac with over 250 prehistoric drawings and the Abri du Cap Blanc with its paintings of horses, bison, and deer over 14,000 years old ("Périgueux" 1–2; "Périgueux France" 1–2). The Dordogne remained a favorite of his throughout his life.

While for Eliot the fall of 1910 was rich in opportunities and experiences that stimulated, informed, entertained, and challenged him in all arenas, concluding with his trip to the south of France during the Christmas and New Year's break, a rather bleak account of the year 1910 appeared on the front page of the December 31, 1910 issue of *Le Figaro*. After summarizing the year's disputes, strikes, and other disasters and characterizing it as "terrible" and "disappointing," the writer concluded, "Thus a year which began with the promise and hope of tranquility ends in agitation. To this disappointment, for which human folly is responsible, the elements of nature have added others, conspiring against us yet again. Cyclones, floods, and shipwrecks have cruelly tested us. [The only positive development has been] the advances in aviation, . . . as if the genius of man had sworn to respond to our betrayal by water through the conquest of air." This negative view was also evident in a cartoon entitled "Une Entrée en scene" [A Stage Entrance] in the December 30 issue (Figure 11), in which a reluctant actress representing the year 1911 is urged by the stage manager to go on stage as the audience waits expectantly: "Go on, my little 1911; don't have stage-fright like that! The year that you're replacing was so abominable that you won't have any trouble being better!" (3).

Despite this assurance, 1911 began grimly as continuing rains caused the Seine to flood in January, reflected in a cartoon on the front page of the January 10, 1911 issue of *Le Matin* entitled "Paris: Port of Mud," in which a couple walking gingerly through the mud wonder if the description of Paris as "a lake of mud" will change to that of Paris as "a seaport" as a result. *La grippe* [the flu] spared few in February, and winter threatened to continue throughout the spring with ice covering the bare black trees as late as April 21 (Rivière and Alain-Fournier 383). Yet to Eliot the new year could only have seemed full of promise upon his return to Paris from the Dordogne for the resumption of Bergson's courses on January 13. Added to the intellectual stimulation of the philosopher's lectures, of conversations with Verdenal, Alain-Fournier, and others, of the many conflicting but exciting and challenging ideas and theories in circulation, and of new writers and works to be discovered were the numerous public lectures announced and often reviewed in *Le Figaro* and other newspapers.

In addition to lectures in October and November such as Gide's on Philippe, Ossip-Lourié's on the current state of French drama, and Fauchois's on Racine, an astounding array of topics and lecturers appeared from January through June. Among those which might have compelled his attendance were the following: "Wagner" on January 11, "Gautier" on January 27, "Modern Russian Theatre" on February 3, "Bradley and Royce" and "Venetian Music" (the latter by Gabriel Fauré) on February 12, "Logic" by Bertrand Russell on March 22, "From Hegel to Bergson" on March 27, "Buddhism: Past and Present" on April 28, "Beethoven's Music" on May 19, and "Dante's *Commedia*" on May 22. Most intriguing on this list is the lecture by Russell, who was to become an important figure in Eliot's life only a few years later.

The cultural scene in Paris during the period from January through June was as stimulating as the intellectual scene. Indeed, it was a season in which sensation followed sensation in the fields of dance, music, drama, and the visual arts, all the more so because of the extensive experimentation in and interpenetration of the various arts occurring at the time. A cultural feast of extraordinary richness was laid before the young Eliot.

In the winter months a fair number of intriguing opportunities presented themselves. From January 18–28, he could have seen the shockingly innovative and indeed scandalous American dancer Isadora Duncan, who gave four performances at the Théâtre du Châtelet. André Nède waxed poetic in predicting to readers of *Le Figaro* on January 18 that "Paris will applaud Mademoiselle Duncan because the lovable gods of antiquity sent her to awaken the city to the happy dream of the ancient past" (5).

In February, numerous cultural events took place, such as art exhibitions of the Orientalistes, Women Painters and Sculptors, and Rousseau. However, most compelling for the young man who already admired this work was the revival at the Opéra-Comique of Debussy's only opera, *Pelléas et Mélisande*, a highly sensuous and intensely emotional work whose passionate lovers may be reflected ironically in various modern couples in Eliot's early poetry, particularly *The Waste Land*.

In the sports arena, an extraordinary boxing match lasting for 25 rounds between Harry Lewis, the world middleweight champion, and Blink Mac Clowsky took place on February 22 at the Hippodrome, as reported in *Le Figaro*'s column *La Boxe* the next day. It was one of several such matches that may have inspired Eliot to take boxing lessons at a "toughish gymnasium in Boston's South End" (Aiken, "King" 20–1) upon his return to Harvard in the autumn of 1911.

In late February he wrote a charming letter to his niece Theodora Eliot Smith, one of only three letters from his Parisian year to have survived. He told her about French children and incidentally revealed some of his own activities. He noted, in language appropriate for a youngster, that he took frequent walks in the Jardin du Luxembourg, where he saw children sailing boats in the pond, rolling hoops, and spinning tops (Figure 12). After commenting that they seemed quite happy despite not having as many playthings as American children, he described the little donkey carts in which they rode on Sunday afternoons on the Champs-Élysées, which he identified as "a long wide street." Finally, he described the proper behavior and the black pinafores, black capes, and bare legs of Parisian school girls, the mild winter weather, and "the little steamboats [that] go up and down the river like black flies: 'fly-boats,' they call them." He ended with a remark on the time difference between France and the United States: "Just about now you are having supper in America, and here, it is my bed time. Isn't that funny?" He sent his love to "mother and father and all the dolls," signing himself "Your Uncle TOM" (*Letters* 16). This letter gives us one of only a few glimpses of his Parisian experience as it was occurring, as well as conveying his affection for his little niece and his effort to write on her level, thereby revealing a side of him not often seen.

March brought additional stimulating events. Throughout the month, the Concert Mayol, a highly-popular café-concert, presented a new production featuring Mayol himself singing the "lively, light-hearted songs" that had made him a celebrity as well as attractions such as a one-act comedy, a female impersonator, and "the tragedienne of song" Damia (Feshotte 41, 37). As for high culture, Maurice Maeterlinck's enchanting verse drama *L'Oiseau bleu* [The Blue Bird], which opened on March 2 at the Théâtre Réjane, played to capacity crowds for two months. Ultimately, however, Eliot rejected the approach of this famed playwright and poet, who received the Nobel Prize for Literature in that very year.

Also, in early March the Société Musicale Indépendante, an organization promoting contemporary music, presented several concerts. One of these featured piano pieces by Erik Satie and a work for clarinet and piano entitled "Rhapsodie" by Debussy with Maurice Ravel at the piano. "For some," wrote *Le Figaro*'s leading music critic Robert Brussel in his review of March 9, "it was a revelation" (5). It is a tantalizing coincidence that "Rhapsody on a Windy Night" is dated March 1911, perhaps inspired by this performance and reflecting the title of Debussy's composition in its own title. This poem clearly shows the influence of the Parisian figure the *flâneur* (an upper-class, sophisticated male who walks through an urban setting observing its details) as its speaker describes aspects of the Parisian cityscape during a nocturnal journey.

In addition to this poem, Eliot wrote or at least dated four others in February: "Entretien dans un parc," "Interlude: in a Bar," "Bacchus and Ariadne: 2nd Debate between the Body and Soul," "The smoke that gathers blue and sinks." Another entitled "He said: this universe is very clever" is dated March 1911 (Ricks xxxix). Some or all of these may have been partly written earlier, with Eliot revising portions to reflect his Parisian experiences and observations and demonstrating the French use of lowercase in three of the titles. "Entretien dans un parc," with its title in French replacing the earlier title "Situation," reveals the influence of Philippe's *Bubu de Montparnasse* as well as Eliot's own observations of Parisian streets in the speaker's description of "a blind alley, stopped with broken walls / Papered with posters, chalked with childish scrawls!" (26–7). "Interlude: in a Bar" and "The smoke that gathers blue and sinks" reflect actual Parisian bars, bistros, cabarets-artistiques, and/or cafés-concerts that Eliot may have seen as well as scenes in Philippe's novel in their descriptions of smoke-filled venues; the latter in particular conveys the novel's bleak view of life in its "shifting smoke" (1) that settles across "the floors that soak / The dregs from broken glass" (4–5) and anticipates "Preludes" in its grimness. "Bacchus and Ariadne" in its meditation on time reveals the influence of

Bergson's *la durée réelle*, while "He Said" encapsulates the current conflict over science and the humanities raging in the academic community (as seen especially in *La Nouvelle Sorbonne*). The "He" may refer obliquely to Bergson's opposition to the scientific views of the universe so dominant at the time in his lectures: "He said: this universe is very clever / The scientists have laid it out on paper / Each atom goes on working out its law . . ." (1–3). The comparison of "The Absolute" (7) to "a syphilitic spider" (6) waiting in the middle of the "geometric net" (5) of scientific theories is echoed in Eliot's description in his 1934 "A Commentary" of "the spider-like figure of Bergson" swinging over all the other intellectuals in 1910–1911 Paris (452).

The Spring of 1911

On the first day of April, a highly publicized and, as it turned out, controversial boxing match took place between two black boxers, Sam Mac Vea and Sam Langford. The writer of *La Boxe* reported the next day in *Le Figaro* that it ended in a deplorable manner when, even though Langford was "considerably superior to Vea" and had clearly won, the referee declared it *match nul* [a draw], thereby enraging the spectators (2). Again, such an exciting match may have contributed to Eliot's taking boxing lessons in Boston in the fall.

Although this match dominated the sporting news at the beginning of April, the remainder of the spring of 1911 saw a veritable explosion of cultural offerings, many of which were on the cutting edge and set the stage for impressive developments in all areas of the arts. On April 2, three pieces from Ravel's score for the ballet *Daphnis et Chloé*, which he was in the process of composing for Diaghilev's Ballets Russes for the 1912 season, were performed as a concert suite at the Théâtre du Châtelet. Brussel noted in his review the next day that the young composer was opening new horizons by composing music for ballet legitimate in its own right (4). On April 6 Copeau and Croué's stage adaptation of Dostoevsky's novel *The Brothers Karamazov* opened as the inaugural production of the Théâtre des Arts, which was dedicated to presenting innovative drama, and a note in the *Letters* tells us that Eliot attended a performance (25).[30] The play held enormous interest for Eliot, not only because of the publicity surrounding it but also because he had read the novel earlier in the year at the instigation of Alain-Fournier. His tutor, along with Rivière, had a "zealous concern" for the play's success (Howarth 366) and may even have invited Eliot to a performance since he received eight tickets from Copeau (Rivière and Alain-Fournier 379–85). How exciting it must have been for Eliot both to see a play based on a novel which he greatly admired and to read Rivière's review in the May issue of *La*

Nouvelle Revue Française. Moreover, the same month featured art exhibitions of Ingres and of Dutch masters.

Following Bergson's classes of April 7 and 8, the Easter holidays ensued until April 28, when the courses resumed (Bergson 846). Taking advantage of the vacation, Eliot went to London, where, as he revealed to his cousin Eleanor in a letter of April 26 written the day after his return, he saw the major museums, Hampton Court, the City ("Thoroughly"), St. Paul's Cathedral, the London Zoo (where he "gave the apteryx a bun"), and a host of lesser known sites such as Cricklewood and five obscure churches. He deliberately did not go to the popular tourist landmarks such as the Tower of London, Madame Tussaud's Wax Museum, or Westminster Abbey, the last of which "was closed due to the coronation preparations" for George V, scheduled for June 22 (*Letters* 19). Although he assured his cousin that he "was out doors most of the time" and did not waste the opportunity of being in London, he revealed that, because of the cold weather with no hint of spring, "one continued to hibernate amongst the bricks. And one looked through the windows, and the waiter brought in eggs and coffee, and the *Graphic* (which I conscientiously tried to read, to please them)" (18). These details appear in only slightly altered form in the opening lines of "Interlude in London," dated April 1911 and apparently written in London or soon afterward: "We hibernate among the bricks / And live across the window panes / With marmalade and tea at six" (1–3). The grim urban scene with its "mouldy flowerpots / And broken flutes at garret windows" reflects the influence of Philippe, but with a different metropolis as its location. This London experience, intersecting and commingling with his Parisian experience, would be evident in other early poems, particularly "The Love Song of J. Alfred Prufrock," which he would complete in the summer in yet another metropolis, that of Munich. And of course London and Paris in various combinations with all the great cities of his lived experience appear throughout the remainder of his work.

While London's climate had been "very wintry and sedate," he discovered upon his return to Paris on April 25 (three days prior to the resumption of Bergson's lectures) that, as he wrote to his cousin, the city "has burst out, during my absence, into full spring" (*Letters* 18). It had also burst out with numerous art exhibitions, which were both praised and criticized in reviews and cartoons.

The most scandalous and, as it turned out, the most significant of these exhibitions was the controversial Salon des Indépendants, where the Cubists first displayed their works as a group in Room 41 from April 20–June 13. While its founders Pablo Picasso and Georges Braque did not participate, Robert Delaunay, Fernand Léger, Albert Gleizes, Jean Metsinger, and Henri Le Fauconnier caused quite a sensation with their avant-garde paintings, which evoked rage, outrage, and derision from most viewers and led to a near riot. It is hard to imagine that Eliot would not have visited this exhibition, which was the talk of Paris. Not only was it reviewed (typically in a hostile fashion) in all the newspapers, but also Bergson was linked with modern art, as Eliot points out in his 1934 "A Commentary" (452). Since Alain-Fournier attended on April 20 the *Jour de Vernissage* (Rivière and Alain-Fournier 383–4), he doubtless encouraged Eliot and Verdenal to see the exhibit, as noted earlier. Cubism, Futurism, and other avant-garde art movements were subjects of interest to Verdenal and Eliot, as indicated in Verdenal's letter of April 22, 1912, and Eliot's knowledge of modern art seems to have begun during his Parisian year.

The cultural events of May and June were even more spectacular than those of April. May 2 saw the opening of the Beethoven Festival with a performance of the first, second, and third symphonies at the Théâtre du Châtelet. It continued for ten days with presentations of a large number of his works, reflecting the high esteem in which the composer was held at the time. Indeed, Beethoven was idolized by the French not only as a composer but also as an ideal of virtue and fortitude, an attitude which Eliot maintained throughout his life, and Eliot's lifelong devotion to his music is reflected in many of his works, particularly *Four Quartets*.

Just three days after the Beethoven Festival began, a literary event of significance opened at the Bibliothèque nationale de France, an exposition on Théophile Gautier. The next day in *Le Figaro*'s column *Informations*, the lead piece entitled "Exposition Gautier" described "cette petite exposition" as "charmante," reporting that it consisted of eight glass display cases containing all the principle editions of his work, portraits of Gautier by a variety of artists, including one self-portrait, and even an 1851 study in which he seems to predict the advent of cars and planes. The article noted that these displays are "veritable treasures" for book-lovers, artists, and those who are simply curious (6). Perhaps Eliot's interest in Gautier, a figure who would influence him greatly just a few years hence, was augmented by this exhibition.

In addition to these events, the premiere of Ravel's one-act opera *L'Heure espagnole* [The Spanish Hour] took place on May 19 at the Opéra-Comique. Described by Ravel in a letter published on May 17 in *Le Figaro* as an attempt to "rejuvenate the opera-bouffe of Italy, but not in its traditional form" (5), its inventive score combined unusual musical effects with everyday events, perhaps inspiring Eliot to see that similar experiments could be tried in poetry.

Since Eliot's courses with Bergson ended on May 20, he was more or less entirely free after that date to attend the cultural events that were occurring, although his lessons with Alain-Fournier may well have continued for another month. Certainly the most spectacular cultural event of the month of May was the production at the Théâtre du Châtelet of Gabriele d'Annunzio's mystery play in verse, *Le Martyre de Saint Sébastien*, starring the seductive Russian ballerina Ida Rubenstein as Saint Sébastien in a daring reversal of gender roles and featuring music by Debussy, choreography by Mikhail Fokine, lavish sets and costumes by Léon Bakst, and an enormous cast of fifty actors and 350 musicians. Beset by controversy of all kinds, it was constantly in the news from its opening on May 22 to its last performance on June 1. It is quite likely that Eliot saw the production and was intrigued by its subject, treating it himself in his 1914 poem "The Love Song of St. Sebastian." Although in a letter of July 25, 1914 to Aiken he says that he had "studied" paintings of the saint, thus implying that they were his source of inspiration, his query, "[B]ut no one ever painted a female Sebastian, did they?" (*Letters* 44), suggests that he also had in mind the Paris production. Its experimentation with and synthesis of the arts on an international scale seem also to have influenced *The Waste Land*, while its use of poetry may have been one source of inspiration for his determination to write verse drama and restore it to prominence.

Eliot had no time to catch his breath in June, as his good fortune continued with two more sensational opportunities dominating the Parisian cultural scene. From June 6–17, the third season of Diaghilev's Ballets Russes presented two programs. Two of the ballets were sensational. *Le Spectre de la Rose* featured Nijinsky's spectacular leap through the casement window costumed as the Rose, a feat so exciting that dance historian Buckle comments, "Nobody who saw Nijinsky as the Rose ever got over it" (192). *Petrouchka* was a work of "extraordinary novelty" (Ghéon, "Saison" 251) with music by Igor Stravinsky, choreography by Mikhail Fokine, and Nijinsky dancing the lead role. Both of these, as well as the rather dismal failure *Narcisse*, demonstrated new freedoms in dance and interpenetration of the arts and offered Eliot the opportunity to see more of the culture of Russia in conjunction with his reading of Dostoevsky. All three are reflected in his poetry in various ways.

Serving as a most fitting conclusion not only to this dazzling spring season but also to Eliot's *annus mirabilis* in Paris was the performance of the Wagnerian tetralogy *Der Ring des Nibelungen*, presented in its entirety at the Opéra for the first time ever in Paris, beginning on June 10 and concluding on June 29, with the complete cycle given twice. Eliot surely took advantage of this rare opportunity by going to all or part of the tetralogy in the company of one or both of his French friends.

As for literature, if Eliot did not buy Benda's latest book, *L'Ordination*, on the day it appeared in Parisian book shops, he might have done so upon reading in a June 9 review in *Le Figaro* that in this small volume "a world of thoughts swirls around—new, moving, and strong, expressed in prose so personal, so pure, and so incisive that every word is necessary and precise" (4). These were elements of style which he admired and would attempt to capture himself; indeed, several passages on writing in *Four Quartets* seem to echo this review.

In the arena of popular entertainment, in addition to the ongoing options in cafés-concerts, music halls, and the like, two events in particular were literally dazzling. Both took place outdoors at night and featured electric lamps, a novelty at this time and a testament to French technological progress. In mid-May the permanent fairground Luna Park held *une soirée de gala* [an evening gala], with the lights making it sparkle like a fairyland, according to an article in the May 12 issue of *Le Figaro* (4). In early June the opening of an immense park with an Oriental motif called Magic-City took place, with foreign dignitaries among the revelers marveling at its "magnificent proportions, its artistic palaces, . . . and its daring structures," as reported in the June 3 issue of *Le Figaro* (5).

In mid-June, *Le Figaro*'s column "At the Schools" announced student dances and parties in the Latin Quarter celebrating the approaching end of the academic year. Le Bal des Quat'z'Arts [The Ball of the Four Arts] with a Babylonian theme held by the students of the École des Beaux-Arts was one of the best-known, and its description along with five photos in the July 15 issue of *Comoedia Illustré* gives us a good idea of what such a celebration was like. According to the article, starting at 6 p.m., troops of warriors dressed in loud colors and sporting saucepans adorned with feathers on their heads paraded down the peaceful rue de Rennes and the deserted boulevard Raspail and invaded the restaurants in the vicinity of the École des Beaux-Arts, which, from 7 p.m. on, echoed with licentious songs offensive to the chaste ears of the inhabitants of the quartier Saint-Sulpice. Beginning at 9 p.m., they filled the Place Clichy and assaulted the Hippodrome, with every vehicle disgorging unusual quantities of extremely gay warriors. Fanfares from bizarre instruments burst out from all sides, while the warriors stopped an autobus and terrorized peaceful customers at outdoor cafés in the neighborhood. After trooping rapidly and in a disorderly manner down the rue de Clichy, they performed "La Fantasia" in the courtyard of the Académie de Musique and finally disbanded in the courtyard of the École des Beaux-Arts after a brilliant concert and extraordinary dances in the fountain and the porticos. Then everyone went home to sleep, dirtier than anyone could imagine, and to gather strength to recommence next year more madly and more gaily than ever the tradition of this ball which is quintessentially French. The marvelous photos capture the parade, the Assyrian costumes complete with swords, the dancing in the fountain, and an open car bearing twelve revelers in the seats, on the running boards, and on the hood posing rakishly for the photographer as they pass (Figure 13), with the cut-line proclaiming, "Pauvres pneus!!!" [Poor tires!!] (De Malmoe 661–2). Eliot perhaps attended this party or others with his friends as a spirited close to a most spectacular year.

Summer Trip to Germany and Italy

Eliot left Paris toward the end of June on his trip to southern Germany and northern Italy, for Verdenal's second letter, written soon after Bastille Day (July 14), implies that Eliot was not there to attend the second performance of *Götterdämmerung* conducted by Nikisch on June 29. It is rather odd that Verdenal refers to having seen it "the other day," although it was over two weeks earlier (*Letters* 24–5).[31] Eliot went first to Munich, staying at Pension Bürger at Luisenstrasse 50, no doubt visiting its great art museum the Alte Pinakothek and hearing "something by Wagner," as Verdenal urged him to do (*Letters* 24), at Munich's famed opera house, the Bayerische Staatsoper, which had seen the premieres of a number of Wagner's operas. He also saw its public park, the Hofgarten, whose colonnades and outdoor café he re-creates in *The Waste Land* as the setting in which he portrays Marie, a character based on the Countess Marie Larisch. The niece and confidante of Empress Elisabeth of Austria, she was later disgraced when her role as the go-between for Crown Prince Rudolf and his lover Baroness Mary Vetsera was revealed upon the discovery of their shocking deaths at Mayerling in 1889. While G. K. L. Morris suggested in 1954 that much of Marie's conversation in the poem came from Eliot's reading of the countess's ghostwritten memoir *My Past* (1913), Valerie Eliot in the "Editorial Notes" to *The Waste Land: A Facsimile and Transcript of the Original Drafts* says that "in fact he had met the author (when and where is not known), and his description of the sledding, for example, was taken verbatim from a conversation that he had with [her]" (126). Perhaps this meeting took place in Munich in July of 1911, but one wonders how a twenty-two-year-old American graduate student managed to meet such a notorious member of the Austrian nobility.[32] The reference to the Starnbergersee in this section of the poem suggests that, while in Munich, Eliot made an excursion to this fashionable resort just south of the city (which was also the childhood home of the empress).

The most significant element of his sojourn in Munich— certainly for his immediate poetic goals—was the work he did on "The Love Song of J. Alfred Prufrock," as he himself confirmed in a letter of February 21, 1936 to Eudo C. Mason: "Most of it was written in the summer of 1911 when I was in Munich" (qtd. in Ricks 176). It seems likely that, being apparently alone, he found in Munich solitude and the opportunity to reflect on his Parisian experiences and observations and to incorporate them into this groundbreaking poem, an amazing work for such a young man, and also his first masterpiece.

Eliot also finished Part III of "Preludes," dated July 1911, to go along with Parts I and II, which had been written in October 1910, but whether before or after his arrival in Paris is uncertain. Part III clearly reflects the influence of his Parisian year in its epigraph, "Son âme de petite putain" [Her soul of a little whore], a commingling of phrases from *Bubu de Montparnasse* (Ricks 336). That influence is also evident in its bleak description of such a woman during the night and at dawn and in its original title "(Morgendämmerung) Prelude in Roxbury," the German word a result no doubt of his having just seen *Götterdämmerung* in Paris. When he completed Part IV in November 1911 back at Harvard, he gave it the title "Abenddämmerung" (Gallup 1240).[33]

On this summer trip he also visited Bergamo in northern Italy, perhaps in order to see the *San Sebastiano* (c. 1476) by Antonello da Messina in the museum Accademia Carrara (a painting which is today in the Gemäldegalerie in Dresden). He refers to it in a letter of July 19, 1914 to Aiken as one of the "*three* great" paintings of the saint (*Letters* 41; Ricks 268). Commissioned during an outbreak of plague, it is among the finest of da Messina's works in its depiction of the saint tethered to a tree with a look of patient forbearance and a Venetian cityscape in the background ("Antonella" 2). He could also have seen in this museum—considered one of the richest in Italy with approximately 1700 paintings by artists from the fifteenth to the eighteenth centuries—other paintings of the saint by Raffaello Sanzio and Jacometto Veneziano as well as Tarot cards painted by Bonifacio Bembo for Filippo Maria Visconti (*Bergamo* 16, 38). He may have remembered these cards in composing the passage on the fortunetelling scene in *The Waste Land*.

In Venice he saw another of the "*three* great" paintings of Saint Sebastian, Mantegna's third depiction of the saint (1490s) in the Ca d'Oro. He described it as "[f]irst quality" (Ricks 268) and told Sydney Schiff in a letter of March 24, 1920 that "Mantegna is a painter for whom I have a particular admiration—there is none who appeals to me more strongly. Do you know the St. Sebastian in the Franchetti's house on the Grand Canal?" (*Letters* 376). His interest in Mantegna was probably instigated by his having seen in the fall the painter's second version (1480s) of the saint at the Louvre, a new acquisition of 1910 and thus a star attraction at the time of Eliot's sojourn in Paris.[34] In Venice's Church of S.Maria della Salute he could also have seen other depictions of the saint, such as Tiziano's *San Marco in Trono e Santi* [*Saint Mark Enthroned and Saints*, one of whom is Saint Sebastian] and Basaiti's *San Sebastiano*.

Return to Paris and Departure for the United States

Eliot returned to Paris in early September and hoped to see both of his friends before leaving for the United States later in the month, having written in July to inquire about whether they would be there. Alain-Fournier replied in his letter of July 25 that, "unfortunately, I shall not be in Paris at the beginning of September" as he would be on military maneuvers and wondered what to do about returning some books to Eliot (*Letters* 27). Sadly, the two friends never met again. However, Verdenal replied in his letter of mid-July, "My dear fellow [*Mon vieux*], I shall be here in September, and very pleased to see you again" (*Letters* 23–4). They must have savored Eliot's last days in Paris together, gone to concerts, operas, and art exhibits, reminisced about the events of the year, and continued their discussions of philosophical, political, and literary issues, as Verdenal had indicated that they would when together again in the same letter: "We'll talk about all this again some time, if you like" (*Letters* 24). They must have pondered the most exciting event of the moment in the arts world: the theft of the *Mona Lisa* from the Louvre on August 21 and the arrest of Apollinaire on September 7, with Picasso implicated. This shocking occurrence dominated the newspapers for days, even after Apollinaire's release on September 12 (Mailer 317–34). Eliot bought a copy of Philippe's *La Mère et l'enfant* [Mother and Child] (1900), on the recommendation no doubt of Verdenal, who had just read and liked it, inscribing it "T. S. Eliot / Paris / September 1911" (*Letters* 21) and taking it with him when he left for the United States.

However, he took with him far more than Philippe's book, for the impact of that year not only on his mind and imagination but also on his heart and soul was to last a lifetime; he had become and would remain a devoted Francophile. Throughout his career, as a result of his knowledge of the language, the literature, and the culture as well as his connections with leading French figures in the intellectual and cultural arenas, the influence of his year in Paris was manifested in a variety of forms, including poems, reviews, essays, and translations as well as friendships and collaborations. In an immediate attempt to preserve something of the atmosphere of Paris and, I suspect, to demonstrate both his love of France and his new cosmopolitanism, he wore "exotic Left Bank clothing," carried a cane, hung a reproduction of Gauguin's *The Yellow Christ* in his room (Aiken, "King" 20–1; *Ushant* 143), subscribed to *La Nouvelle Revue Française*, and corresponded with Verdenal and perhaps with Alain-Fournier. But these were only the most tangible signs of the enormous and far-reaching effects of the "présent parfait" that he experienced when, along with Marc Chagall, Giorgio de Chirico, and other talented young people who would later become famous, he had the exceptional good fortune to come to the City of Light in 1910–1911. His Parisian year gave him the foundation to become a major writer of the twentieth century and the inspiration to produce his first masterpiece at the age of twenty-two.

· 2 ·

DAILY LIFE IN PARIS IN 1910–1911

In order to convey a comprehensive sense of Eliot's experience of living in Paris in 1910–1911, in this chapter I reconstruct the practical aspects of the city, beginning with a brief history from 1848 to 1911 to set the stage and then describing a wide variety of topics including domestic and international politics, the economy, buildings and landmarks, transportation, communications, electricity, sanitation, entertainment and photography, science and medicine, the status of men and women, and sports.

History of Paris from 1848 to 1911

The Paris of 1910–1911 can best be understood by returning to the mid-nineteenth century and the advent of the Second Republic and then tracing the major historical developments of the ensuing sixty years. After the Revolution of 1848, Louis Napoleon Bonaparte, the nephew of Napoleon I, was elected President of the Second Republic and in 1852 was proclaimed Emperor with the title Napoleon III. As Barbara Stern Shapiro points out, "The Second Empire was his creation, with his political imprint as the first modern dictator and with his social stamp, whereby festivities and the active pursuit of pleasure were the order of the day" (11). During this period, France enjoyed tremendous power and prosperity, with the arts as an important feature, with elegance and gaiety as dominant traits, and with the bourgeoisie as an increasingly significant political, economic, and social force. One of the most important and far-reaching accomplishments was Georges-Eugène Haussmann's massive renovation and modernization of Paris that included boulevards, parks, squares, public buildings, transportation facilities, a central marketplace (Les Halles), and a sewer system.

However, the Second Empire came to a catastrophic and humiliating end with the Prussian defeat of Napoleon III's army of 80,000 men at Sedan in September 1870. Two days later, the Third Republic was created with Adolphe Thiers as its first president. It attempted unsuccessfully to hold off the invading Prussian army, which besieged Paris until surrender was declared in January 1871. The French lost Alsace and Lorraine to the German Empire and had to pay huge reparations, "grievous losses which . . . caused permanent repercussions" (Shapiro 11). Worse yet, Prussian troops occupied Paris, representing yet another powerful blow to national pride (Evenson 8). Close on the heels of these devastating events came the debacle of the Paris Commune, a revolutionary municipal government which in March 1871 set itself against the new Third Republic seated at Versailles. After two months of bitter fighting, the Communards were defeated by the army of the National Assembly, but not before they destroyed a number of Parisian monuments, most notably the column at Place Vendôme, and set fires which raged throughout the city. As retaliation, mass executions of Communards took place, so that the Seine ran red with their blood (Evenson 9).

Amazingly, Paris and the nation recovered quickly, rebuilding not only the portions of the city which had been destroyed but also—and more importantly—national strength, stability, and confidence. Despite an unstable internal political situation which saw sixty different governments between 1870 and 1914 (Jones 221), the French embarked on a period of enormous financial prosperity, technological progress, and intellectual and artistic prestige. Paris was the acknowledged world center of culture and pleasure, symbolized by the completion in 1875 of the Opéra, designed by Charles Garnier. Indeed, in 1876, Henry James wrote in his *Parisian Sketches*, published in the *New York Tribune*, of "the amazing elasticity of France. Beaten and humiliated on a scale without precedent, despoiled, dishonored, bled to death financially . . . [,] Paris is today in outward aspect as radiant and prosperous . . . as if her sky had never known a cloud" (40). This period, called La Belle Époque, The Miraculous Years, or The Banquet Years, has been variously dated as beginning in 1875 with the completion of the Opéra, in 1878 with the Exposition Universelle, in 1880 with the Bastille Day celebration (Shapiro 12), or in 1885 with the massive state funeral of Victor Hugo (Shattuck 4–5). On the other hand, there is complete agreement that it ended in 1914 with the outbreak of World War I. The Paris that Eliot encountered during his sojourn there in 1910–1911 was very much the product of the rapid developments that occurred during this period, however we choose to date its beginning. As Péguy remarked in 1913, "The world has changed less since Jesus Christ than it has in the last thirty years" (qtd. in Shattuck 1).

Domestic Politics

In the years from the mid-1880s through the first decade of the twentieth century, France saw frequent changes in its presidents and cabinets and endured several crises in the political arena, with international discord simmering ominously in the background. Despite these disruptions, there was a rather amazing sense of political stability, which Jones attributes to "a deeper continuity" in the French nation (221).

Among the major crises was the Affaire Boulanger in 1887, named for the Minister of War whose strong military stance against Germany fed the popular desire for revenge against that nation at any cost and propelled him into a potential position of power, which he abandoned to follow his mistress to Belgium. Another was the Panama Canal Scandal of 1892, as well as various anarchist bombings of public buildings, homes of public figures, and the Chamber of Deputies in the 1890s with a few continuing into the early 1900s. Indeed, two bombings were front-page news in the October 15 and 22, 1910 issues of *Le Petit Parisien*, about the time of Eliot's arrival in Paris.

However, the most famous (or infamous) crisis was the Affaire Dreyfus, which began in 1894 and rocked the nation until 1906, although its repercussions were felt for many more years. Anti-Semitism had been gathering strength in France as a result of the growing Jewish population, which increased from 80,000 in 1880 to nearly 200,000 by 1920. It was fanned by the publication in 1886 of Édouard Drumont's virulent attack on Jews in his book *Jewish France*, followed by his organization in 1889 of the Anti-Semitic League and his founding in 1892 of the journal *La Libre Parole*, through which he spread his ideas (Knapton 440). When Alfred Dreyfus, a Jewish army captain, was unjustly accused in 1894 of selling military secrets to Germany, convicted, and sentenced to life imprisonment on Devil's Island, the nation became a cauldron of seething conflicts over Anti-Semitism as well as over the form of government for France (Republicanism vs. Monarchism), the military, and the Roman Catholic Church. In 1898 Émile Zola's famous letter "J'Accuse," in which he denounced both the military and the government in his defense of Dreyfus, brought matters to a head, causing many celebrated French figures to take sides. When Dreyfus was pardoned in 1899 and reinstated in the army in 1906 with a promotion to the rank of major, the immediate problem was resolved, but only on the surface, for Anti-Semitism was to fester in France in the ensuing years.

During the time of the Affaire Dreyfus, another great figure arose who was to have a profound influence on the French political scene and specifically on Eliot: Charles Maurras. In 1898 Maurras was one of the founders of the political group L'Action Française, devoted to "integral nationalism," specifically Monarchism (as opposed to Republicanism), the Roman Catholic Church, the military, and traditional values. It was openly and unabashedly opposed to Jews as well as Protestants, Freemasons, and foreigners, as noted in Chapter 1. His attacks on Jews appeared frequently on the front page of *L'Action Française*, which became a daily newspaper in 1908 and was sold in the streets by the Camelots du Roi, who also led demonstrations against Jews and others perceived as enemies to their cause. Eliot describes such a demonstration in "A Commentary" in the April 1934 issue of *The Criterion* (453). Eliot may have attended meetings of the student wing of the organization. He was influenced not only by the political views of Maurras but also by his belief that literature should be classical, restrained, and clear, avoiding the emotional excesses and vagueness of Romanticism.

Religious dissent was rife in France throughout the first decade of the twentieth century. The governments of the early 1900s adopted a strong anticlerical stance and "lurched into a campaign targeting the church establishment," particularly on the question of schooling: in 1904 religious congregations were prohibited from teaching, and in 1905 the formal separation of church and state was instituted, followed by the shutting down of thousands of religious schools (Jones 235). However, a movement to restore the Roman Catholic Church to its former power and prestige was in progress, as evident, for example, in the agenda of Maurras, himself ironically a nonbeliever, who nevertheless thought that a resurgence of Roman Catholicism was in the best interest of the nation (and his own conservative and traditionalist goals). Anti-Semitism was still quite virulent, its flames fanned by newspaper articles like those of Maurras. Meanwhile, some cosmopolitan, urban, and educated segments of the population, particularly those in Paris, turned their backs on religion altogether. The two buildings that dominated the Paris skyline, the Tour Eiffel and the nearly completed Basilique du Sacré-Coeur, symbolized the tension between the new technology associated with modern secularism, industrialization, and urbanization, and traditional religious values represented by the Roman Catholic Church.

International Politics

While these internal issues were clearly in the forefront during the years from the 1880s to the time of Eliot's sojourn in Paris, developments on the international scene, while less obvious, were also of importance. On the positive side, up to 1910 France "increased her overseas holdings ten-fold," including those in Africa, Indochina, and the Pacific and Indian oceans, so that its empire expanded to 300 million square miles and 50 million inhabitants, with the result that it became the world's second imperial power behind only the United Kingdom (Jones 225). On the negative side, international tensions were constant, the main conflict being with Germany, for, as Jones points out, the "smart to the national psyche caused by the loss of Alsace-Lorraine was never totally erased" (233). A strong desire for revenge was prevalent, provoked by the fact that Germany, "more and more irritable and irritating, incited incident after incident," rendering nearly impossible any hope of reconciliation (Maurois 178). Indeed, in the years immediately preceding World War I, European affairs in general were like "a powder keg awaiting a match" (Jones 233). However, these problems remained largely in the background, as indicated by the reduction between 1909 and 1912 of required military service from three years to two years (Horne 302).

It is no wonder that in the years surrounding 1910–1911 these troubling international issues seemed remote, for, as we can see in retrospect, this period was the pinnacle of nearly forty years of undreamed of prosperity, prestige, optimism, and achievements in all arenas throughout France in general and in Paris in particular. As Walter Benjamin notes, "Paris was the center of the universe of commodities and assets," as well as the most modern city in the world and "the capital of luxury and vice" (qtd. in Shapiro 11). With a population nearing 3 million at the end of the first decade of the twentieth century, Paris was a glittering showplace of great accomplishments of the past, as well as an artistic and technological venue "full of new wonders" (Horne 287).

Economics

Paris was the center of banking and finance as well as of commerce and industry for a strong economy that saw the national income double and industrial output triple after 1896, with the greatest increase in the decade preceding World War I. The key industries were iron, chemicals, and automobiles. Indeed in the production of automobiles, France was second only to the United States (Jones 227). The 1907 edition of Baedeker's guidebook noted that all the branches of French industry were represented in Paris, from the production of jewelry, leather goods, cabinetry, and toys to construction (xxiii).

These years also witnessed the rise of mass consumption and consumer culture, reflected perhaps most dramatically in enormous department stores, which were "essentially a Parisian invention" (Evenson 141) and "one of the most vital institutions of the epoch from 1880 to 1914" (Mumford, qtd. in Evenson 142). Parisian newspapers such as *Le Figaro* and *Le Matin* carried advertisements for a variety of products: automobiles; men's, women's, and children's clothing; *Pillules Pink pour Personnes Pâles* [Pink Pills for Pale People] that cured any ailment whatsoever; techniques for developing the bust or strengthening the physique; methods for losing weight safely; books hot off the press; Otono fountain pens; and that new invention the typewriter, which was "at the door of everyone for use at the office or on a trip for 175 francs or 10 francs a month" (*Le Matin* 22

June 1911:3), an indication of advanced technology as well as the availability of consumer credit.

Buildings and Landmarks

Concerning its buildings and other aspects of its physical presence, Paris was a masterpiece of architecture and design, and intentionally so. Emphasis was placed on the beauty of its architecture, as seen in the 1909 statement by Guillaume Chastenet to the Chamber of Deputies: "A great city . . . is a work of art. It is a collective and complex art, it is true, but this makes it an even higher form of art" (qtd. in Horne 279). At the time of Eliot's sojourn there, numerous landmarks already contributed to the "collective and complex art" of the Parisian cityscape, as well as testifying to its technological achievements. Chief among them was the Tour Eiffel, which had been built in 1889 for the International Exhibition and served as a symbol of French technological ingenuity and as "striking proof of the progress realized . . . by the art of the engineers" (Evenson 133). With a height of 300 meters, it was the tallest metal structure in the world at the time, while its modernistic design, electric lights, and elevators were on the cutting edge (Jones 225). Scheduled to be demolished in 1909, it survived partly because it was the site of radio transmissions, beaming the first overseas broadcast to Casablanca in 1907, and partly because it had become an integral part of the city's personality in the twenty years since its construction (Evenson 135–6). The Paris Exposition of 1900 added several other notable landmarks: the ornate Pont Alexandre Bridge, depicting on its four columns the past glories of France; the Grand Palais and the Petit Palais, "marvels of glass and steel" in which were displayed the works of more than 1000 mainly French artists; and the Arch at the Place de la Concorde with the statue of La Parisienne adorning its summit. In addition to these marvels of art, architecture, and engineering was the *trottoir roulant*, the electric moving sidewalk which connected the venues of the Exposition located on both sides of the Seine (Horne 292–3).

A stunning building which dominated the Paris skyline along with the Tour Eiffel was the Basilique du Sacré-Coeur on the crest of Montmartre, representing spiritual as opposed to technological and material concerns. Begun in 1875 as a symbol of repentance for the disastrous events of the early 1870s and of hope for the future, it was nearing completion in 1910–1911. Its consecration was scheduled to occur in October 1914, but the outbreak of World War I forced its delay until 1919 (Burton 174–96; Harvey 311–40). Built of a curiously (miraculously?) self-cleaning white stone (Caine 162), its brilliant central dome flanked by four smaller domes rose dramatically from Montmartre. Indeed, Baedeker refers to it in his 1907 guidebook as "the most grandiose religious edifice of this period" (xxvi).

Other recent buildings indicated important modern developments in Paris. Luxury hotels such as the Astoria and the Claridge (Horne 289) were built to accommodate the many tourists—both foreign and domestic—who flocked to this city of art, progress, and pleasure (some would have said vice), although there was criticism in 1909 that two new hotels near the Arc de Triomphe were too tall and resembled American skyscrapers (Evenson 157), a violation of French taste. Two massive and highly ornate train stations, the Gare de Lyon and the Gare d'Orsay, were completed around 1900 and served as monuments to the technology and progress represented by this growing mode of rapid transportation. As noted earlier, huge, elaborately decorated *grands magasins* [department stores], such as Le Bon Marché, Au Printemps, Les Galéries Lafayette, and La Samaritaine, which were built, expanded, and/or remodeled in the mid to late 1800s and early 1900s,[1] testified to the increasing role of consumer centers as luxury destinations, "palaces of the people" that "provided an atmosphere conducive to enjoyment and spending" (Evenson 140–2; see also Jones 229). Balzac's description of Le Bon Marché as "a cathedral of commerce for a congregation of customers" (qtd. in "History of Le Bon Marché") shows the nearly religious level to which such stores were elevated at the time. Other types of new buildings reflecting the modernism of Paris were banks, factories, warehouses, markets, theatres, and apartment houses (Evenson 139).

Another significant aspect of the physical presence of Paris at the time was its parks, which served many functions. In addition to their natural beauty, they promoted good health by providing open spaces with sunlight (thought to prevent tuberculosis) and by encouraging recreation. As Evenson notes, they were considered to be "indispensable to public hygiene" and thus should be easily accessible to all Parisians (269–70). Baedeker's guidebook reveals that parks and gardens were also venues for modern art, observing that they "have been transformed into veritable museums of modern art in displaying sculptures bought each year by the city at various art expositions" (xxvi). In addition, concerts of military music were presented there in the summer months. Among the most popular parks were the Jardin des Tuileries, the Jardin des Plantes, the Bois de Boulogne, and the Jardin du Luxembourg. Eliot often walked in the last, which was near the Pension Casaubon and which, as noted in Chapter 1, he described in detail to his niece Theodora Eliot Smith in a letter of February 1911: "I often go out and walk in the Luxembourg Gardens, which is a sort of park like the Boston Public Gardens, or the park back down the hill from your home in Brookline, where you used to go. There is a pond there too, and the children play boats when it is not too cold. There are lots of boats and they sail right across the pond and right through the fountain and never upset. They spin tops and roll hoops" (*Letters* 16). This park was also the setting of his nostalgic memory of Verdenal in his 1934 "A Commentary," in which he describes "a sentimental sunset" when he saw his friend "coming across the Luxembourg Gardens in the late afternoon, waving a branch of lilac" (452). His memory ends on a sorrowful note with a reference to Verdenal's death in the Dardanelles in World War I.

Baedeker closes his introduction to the city with a delightful description of Parisian *quartiers* [neighborhoods], noting that their diversity may be a surprise to visitors who have heard that the modern-day city is very homogeneous:

> Certain neighborhoods recall vaguely old Italian cities because of the melancholy of their grand palaces which have been abandoned or transformed. Others are gay and noisy, with many activities outside, as in the south of France. Still others are picturesque or sinister, with old lanes from the Middle Ages. The Seine, with its flotilla of commercial boats and big barges, creates the illusion, especially in the evening, of a great port. At night, the grand boulevards, with their bright lights, evoke the feeling of a city of pleasure, always celebrating. Finally, the pleasant suburbs with the forests of Boulogne, Vincennes, Meudon, and Montmorency add to the diversity, which is one of the charms of the capital, the seductress that no one leaves without regret. (xxvi)

This charming description encouraged readers such as Eliot to experience for themselves the variety of Parisian neighborhoods.

Transportation

Technological advances were evident everywhere, but especially in the new modes of transportation which operated alongside older ones in 1910–1911. On the streets of Paris, traffic was heavy, as seen in photographs from the period, with a mixture of automobiles, horse-drawn carriages and omnibuses, trams, motorbuses, and bicycles. Indeed, Baedeker notes that Paris "has preceded all other cities in the creation of modern means of transport," particularly since 1900 with "new electric or mechanized trams in great number, and especially the Métropolitain" (24). He lists the various modes of public transport in Section VI, *Moyens de Transport* [Types of Transportation], under the larger heading *Renseignements pratiques* [Practical Information].

The car had been introduced at the end of the nineteenth century, with the first car race taking place in 1894 (Horne 287). By the time Eliot arrived in Paris, both open and closed cars filled the streets, some driven by "emancipated women in bee-hive veils to keep out the dust" (Horne 295), and France was a world leader in automobile production, as noted earlier. Automobile ads filled the newspapers: a company called Voiturette Lion featured an elegant open car, boasting that it was "the great success of the year—for physicians, travelers, tourists, and businessmen" (*Comoedia* 29 May 1911:7), while Eugène Boulogne et Fils appealed to women by using a photograph (Figure 14) of Mlle Madge Lanzy driving a closed car, with what appears to be a uniformed chauffeur (just in case?) in the passenger seat in the fashionable Bois de Boulogne (*Comoedia Illustré* 15 June 1911: 597). And a delight-ful postcard circa 1910 with the caption *La Route Libre?!!* . . . [The Open Road?!! . . .] depicts an open car at the entrance to a country village. It is blocked by a large group of people celebrating what appears to be a wedding, much to the consterna-tion of the car's frustrated and impatient occupants, who are standing and gestur-ing for them to move out of the way. Furthermore, the car had quickly become a means of public transportation in Paris, as *voitures de place* [taxis] equipped with *taximetres* were introduced in 1904 and in just a few years had become so numerous that they could be found at two or three locations, according to Baedeker's entry *Voitures de place et de remise. Automobiles* (25).

Horse-drawn omnibuses, the earliest type of public transportation, were still operating in 1910, with both two- and three-horse versions. Trams, however, had largely supplanted them; in 1910, twelve companies operated more than 100 lines, and fixed stops had just been established. The motor bus, introduced in 1905 with two decks and a speed of fourteen kilometers per hour, had by 1911 given way to a single-deck closed vehicle with an open rear platform for second-class passengers (Evenson 80–85). Baedeker lists the hours of operation (from 6 or 7:30 a.m. to 11 p.m. or 12:30 a.m.) in the entry *Omnibus et tramways; autobus*, informing his readers that the omnibus-automobile, called the autobus, has been operating since 1906, with prices the same as for the regular omnibus. He adds that the top decks are covered and that the principal stops are fixed and marked by blue plaques at lampposts (26–7).

Another form of transportation seen on the streets of Paris was the bicycle [the *vélocipède* or *vélo*]. Introduced at the end of the nineteenth century, it was inexpen-sive, easy to master, and speedy, giving individuals a great degree of independence. Thus it was extremely popular with diverse segments of the populace. Rioux and Sirinelli assert that "the parish priest and the civil servant, the craftsman and the sophisticated woman, the young person in the country and the impecunious stu-dent, the unskilled laborer and even the curious idler, all pedaled with joy" (76), and Horne points out that it was "all the rage among à la mode Parisians" as well as the working class (287). The bicycle offered a new measure of freedom and independence for women in particular, as seen in an advertisement circa 1900 for Papillon bicycles that featured a beautiful young bride on a bicycle leaving her groom at the altar (Jones 230). In October 1900, the first issue of a new magazine entitled *L'Auto-Vélo* asserted that, because of the car and the bicycle, "We live better and more quickly than in the past . . . ," assuring its readers that, despite the advent of the automobile, "the bicycle has not said its last word, far from it." These were prophetic words indeed, for the number of bicycles increased from 326,000 in 1896 to 3.5 million in 1914 (Rioux and Sirinelli 76). And, as we will see, bicycling became one of the hottest new sports of the early twentieth century.

In addition to these types of transport found on the streets of Paris, riverboats, numbering over 100 in 1900 (Caine 108), provided transportation on the Seine until the outbreak of World War I. Listed by Baedeker as *Bateaux à vapeur* [Steamboats], he reminds his readers that "another means of transportation, which is inexpensive and pleasant, is 'les bateaux-omnibus' [boat-buses] circulating on the Seine." He notes that one pays on the boat itself, that the hours of first and last departures vary from 6 to 7 a.m. and 6 to 9 p.m., depending on the season, and that service is suspended if the river becomes too high, if it is full of ice, or if the fog is too dense (28–9).

From 1900 to 1910, several other systems of transport continued to develop. The railroad experienced further expansion, transporting passengers at ever greater speeds from Paris to destinations within France and far beyond through the advent of *wagons-lits* [sleeping cars] and the exotic Orient Express (Horne 287). Its rapid growth was indicated by the construction of the massive and ornate new stations, the Gare de Lyon and the Gare d'Orsay, as noted earlier. Canal and road-building also increased enormously (Jones 228), the latter in response to the mounting number of automobiles.

Far below the streets of Paris, the most exciting and technologically advanced mode of public transportation was developing: the Métropolitain, or "Métro," as it quickly became known, described as "the most important work Paris has experienced since its foundation" (Guerrand, qtd. in Evenson 106) since it "embodied . . . the image of the French capital as the modern city reflecting the advanced standards of French science and technology" (Evenson 106). Begun in 1898 for the 1900 Paris Exposition, the first line of ten kilometers was opened in July 1900, and five additional lines were in operation by 1910. The ornately decorated stations and entrances in the Art Nouveau style reflected Garnier's assertion in 1886 that "'The Métro, in the view of most Parisians, should reject absolutely all industrial character to become completely a work of art. Paris must not transform itself into a factory: it must remain a museum'" (qtd. in Evenson 109–10). Quickly becoming a major mode of rapid public transport after its opening, it carried nearly 56 million passengers in 1901, 149 million in 1905, and 400 million in 1914 (Evenson 109). Baedeker includes information on locations of stations, prices, and schedules and comments on the Métro's importance. He even includes a note for those unfamiliar with this still new means of transport: "The speed of the trains and the crowded conditions of the cars will surprise foreigners. At first, and if one is in a hurry, one should take the express trains that by-pass secondary stations," adding encouragingly that "[t]he uneasiness sometimes felt by sensitive people is not due to a lack of air, but rather to the crowds and to the smell of disinfectants" (28). Although the terrible floods of January 1910, the worst in 150 years (Horne 300), closed the entire system until April (Caine 126), it was back in action during Eliot's residence, with additional lines under construction.

Transportation was advancing not only on and beneath the earth but also far above it, for the airplane was improving in spectacular fashion, with France at the forefront. After Louis Blériot successfully flew over the English Channel in 1909, aviation in France literally took off. The French took great pride in being world leaders in flight, as seen on a poster from the period depicting a red airplane leaving the coast of France with a large caption at the bottom reading, "The first flight over the English Channel: a Frenchman, Louis Blériot, 25 July, 1909," and a smaller caption at the top proclaiming, "The world owes its wings to France."

Aviation was first seen as a daring feat of technology and science, then as a sport, and finally as a commercial enterprise. The newspapers in 1910–1911 were full of reports of French achievements and disasters in flying competitions. For example, in late May, when the second stage of a flying competition from Paris to Madrid was won by the Frenchman Védrines, *Le Petit Parisien* celebrated his achievement with a front-page account on May 27, featuring a large photograph of the aviator as he was decorated by King Alphonse XIII of Spain. The accompanying article contained glowing comments on the significance of what was a sports event at the time, predicting accurately future developments and displaying French pride: "Védrines triumphs, and French aviation with him. He exemplifies French courage, while French industry demonstrates the skill and power of our airplane builders. We already excel and make money in the car industry, and we will now do the same in plane construction. This sports event will have unquestionable practical results, for it proves our superiority and thus contributes to national productivity. Who would have thought ten years ago that one could fly in several hours from Paris to Madrid? The most fantastic inventions of novelists have been surpassed by this thrilling reality." That success was not an isolated incident. A competition beginning on August 7, 1911 covered 790 kilometers in six stages. Ten days later, the French pilots Auburn and Leblanc returned to the point of departure, demonstrating that "the airplane was not a simple dangerous toy but a practical means of transport," and on September 9, 1911 George Chavez beat the altitude record by flying at 2600 meters (Chastenet 75).

However, the dangers faced by these early French pioneers of flight were great. A column entitled *The Conquest of the Skies* in the June 24, 1911 issue of *Le Figaro* reported that "the condition of the aviator Gaget, who crashed at Charleville and suffered two broken legs, is satisfactory, while that of lieutenant Gobert, who crashed at Épieds, is equally reassuring, although he lost his right eye" (4), while *Le Matin* on December 24, 1910 reported on the front page that the aviator Cecil Grace was lost in the North Sea. Perhaps most telling is *Le Matin's* front-page column entitled *Martyrs and Conquerors of the Skies* in its April 24, 1911 issue.

The commercial possibilities of aviation were realized by a Frenchman who began the world's first airmail service in 1911 (Jones 228). The Illustrated Literary Supplement of *Le Petit Parisien* for February 12, 1911 featured a full-page color illustration of six men on a plane just above a rural scene with the caption, "Roger Sommer, in a military biplane, establishes the first world record of airbuses," indicating the idea of a passenger plane (Figure 15).

The French mania over aviation was evident everywhere during the time of Eliot's residence in Paris. Two period postcards depict airplanes above the city, one in the setting of the Champs-Élysées and another in that of the rue des Écoles in the vicinity of Eliot's pension and the Collège de France (Figure 16). The airplane was celebrated in a poem entitled "The Winged Monster" on the front page of the November 7, 1910 issue of *Le Figaro*. Its head-note almost certainly would have been of interest to Eliot, since it promoted a young French poet named Maurice Levaillant as well as a very modern subject from the new technology: "We have the pleasure of offering our readers a very ingenious and eloquent poem on aviation, whose author is one of the most gifted writers of the young generation." Eliot would have been impressed by the French interest in poetry, in aspiring young poets, and in contemporary subjects indicated by the appearance of this poem on the front page of the leading Parisian newspaper. However, he may have been less enthusiastic about the praise heaped upon Levaillant for not abandoning "the traditional rules of French poetry: the beautiful fullness of his stanzas is the reward of his respectful faithfulness to established rhythms," to which was attributed his having won the previous summer the National Prize for Poetry. The head-note concluded by promising that readers would find a poem by Levaillant on the front page each month. The young American who came to France in search of a poetic voice inspired by Laforgue and his contemporaries would have been disheartened to find such devotion to established poetic style in the current generation of French poets, but perhaps it made him even more determined to continue in a daring direction stylistically.

Excitement about and knowledge of aviation are also evident in the correspondence of Alain-Fournier and Rivière. In a letter of August 11, 1910, for example, Alain-Fournier describes his emotional reaction upon seeing a monoplane, which he thought was flown by the American aviator Charles Torres Weymann, over Paris at 7:30 a.m. the previous Saturday: "I looked at *that*, flying above Paris, with an emotion that cannot be expressed. It is curious to record that there are not yet words for that emotion and there doubtless will never be, although everyone tries .... It's a simple emotion. Something which rises from the depths of the chest and which doesn't have a name. One cries out: 'A man who flies' and that's it" (353–4). In his reply of August 12, Rivière reveals both his own enthusiasm as well as a good knowledge of current planes and aviators in asserting that the pilot was not Weymann but the French aviator Hubert Latham: "I was delighted by all that you told me about airplanes. But if it was a monoplane that you saw, it was Latham and not Weymann" (357).

Communications

Similar advances occurred in the field of communications. Telephone service had been available in Paris since 1879, and public phone booths were introduced in the 1880s. The number of phones in use climbed from 12,000 in 1889 to over 300,000 in 1913. Postal, telegraph, and telephone services were combined in 1889 to form the PTT, an abbreviation for Poste, Télégraphes, et Téléphones [Mail, Telegraph, and Telephone Services] (Jones 228). Baedeker lists all pertinent information for these, including prices. For example, a phone call in the inner city cost 15 centimes for 3 minutes (30–4).

Additionally, the *pneumatique* transmitted letters in cylinders by subterranean pneumatic tubes across the city within an hour (Horne 287). Begun in 1866 with service for the stock exchange only, the system was opened to the public in 1879 and expanded to include the entire city by 1888 and suburban areas by 1907 (Hayhurst 1–2); it was quite widespread at the time of Eliot's residence. Baedeker informed his readers that forms could be bought in telegraph offices, which had special boxes for them, and gave the prices (32).

Electricity

Electricity was introduced at the end of the nineteenth century. At first it was limited to rather spectacular uses, such as the installation of electric lights for the 1886 Impressionist Exhibit (Shapiro 15) and the powering of electric elevators in the Tour Eiffel in 1889. However, at its inaugural ceremonies, the Tour Eiffel was illuminated by 20,000 gas lights (Jones 225). Electricity was a stellar feature of the Paris Exposition of 1900, which boasted an electrically powered moving sidewalk as well as a Palace of Electricity with "a galaxy of light bulbs" (Horne 292).

By 1900, electric power began to expand into everyday life, with electric street lamps replacing gas ones (Deedes-Vincke 44) and with electric lighting in many entertainment venues (Shapiro 15). In the first decade of the twentieth century, it slowly found its way into middle-class homes, which until then used candles and oil lamps (Shapiro 15), and in 1912 the first electrically lit advertisement appeared (Higonnet 145). The marvels of electricity were featured in an exciting exhibit which took place at the time of Eliot's arrival in Paris and to which he may have been drawn to see for himself the wonders described in *Le Petit Parisien* on October 20, 1910: "At the Maison Électrique larger and larger crowds come to see the House of Tomorrow, which is all-electric and has no servants. How can one not be interested in this marvelous invention born of French genius, always at the forefront of progress?" (5). However, as I suggest in Chapter 8, while Eliot may have been awed by such a futuristic exhibit, he also saw in modern technology a danger to the human soul and imagination.

Sanitation

Great improvements in sanitation had also occurred in Paris by the time of Eliot's sojourn. Called the "pride of Paris," a complex system of new sewers had been constructed from the 1840s to the 1890s from the designs of Eugène Belguard. By 1870 over 500 kilometers of new sewer lines were either in service or under construction (Schladweiler). Brown and Maxwell's *The Encyclopaedia of Municipal and Sanitary Engineering*, published in 1910, shows three different sewer designs for varied Parisian locations (429–30), and a postcard circa 1914 from the Museum of the Égouts de Paris depicts a view both above and below rue Saint-Antoine, the latter revealing just beneath the street the line for the Métro with a sewer on each side ("Photos"). Running water, tubs, and toilets in homes and other establishments were luxuries as late as 1906, but were soon seen as necessary for cleanliness and good health and thus became more widely available (Evenson 209–11). Furthermore, tours of the sewers began in the 1870s. Donald Reid's *Paris Sewers and Sewermen* contains an 1896 illustration of one such tour in which a boatload of well-dressed tourists floats through a sewer, while in the background others walk behind a guardrail (see Schladweiler).

As another important aid to sanitation and health, garbage collection had begun in the 1860s, with horse-drawn tipcarts picking up the household waste that had been dumped onto streets or sidewalks between 8 and 9 p.m. the previous evening. However, a regulation passed in 1870 required that it be put out in the morning instead and that none was to be thrown out of windows! In 1884 Eugène Poubelle, the Prefect of the Seine, added new rules for garbage collection and street cleaning, including stipulations about the size of garbage cans, their contents, and their regular cleaning to avoid strong odors. In retaliation, angry landlords gave his name to the garbage can, and it has held to the present day (Krupa 2). Thus, by 1910–1911, regular and regulated garbage collection had largely eliminated both the foul appearance and disgusting smell of garbage in Paris, so that the city was relatively clean, pleasant-smelling, and sanitary, deserving of its reputation as modern in every way.

Finally, Paris boasted numerous public baths and toilets. Baedeker's guidebook listed them in the entry *Bains. Coiffeurs. Cabinets inodores* [Baths. Hairdressers. Odorless Toilets]. He gave locations and prices for both hot and cold public baths (23–4), hairdressers (24)—a somewhat strange category to be included in this grouping—and public toilets, billed as being odorless. He noted that the toilets were "generally very convenient" as they were located on the streets and cost 5 centimes or 10 and 15 centimes with a sink, although some were free of charge. He then listed some that cost 15 centimes, including one in the vicinity of the Jardin du Luxembourg, between the main garden path and the boulevard Saint-Michel, and another to the right behind the museum, "with urinals" (24), both of which were near the university sector and Eliot's pension. Of course, public toilets were almost exclusively for men.

Entertainment and Photography

Technological advances were evident in the entertainment industry not only in the use of electric lighting in venues such as the music hall and café-concert but also in inventions such as the gramophone and the *théâtrophone* and developments in cinema and photography. The gramophone, which was a trademark for the early phonograph, was first available in 1894, and its use was prevalent at the time Eliot came to Paris. In *The Waste Land* the term appears in the passage on the typist, who "puts a record on the gramophone" (256) after the departure of her callous, unattractive lover. The *théâtrophone* was an electrical device by means of which one could hear live music, a play, or an opera without being at the venue itself. Proust famously commented after hearing a live performance of Debussy's opera *Pelléas et Mélisande* on a *théâtrophone* at his apartment that "the scent of roses in the score is so strong that I have asthma whenever I hear it" (qtd. in Horne 298).

Cinema, which had been invented in 1895 by the French brothers Louis and Auguste Lumière (whose last name appropriately means "light") with their

Cinématographe, had by 1910 expanded to become one of the attractions in Parisian cafés-concerts, music halls, circuses, and fairs (N. Perloff 41–2), as well as being a regular feature in at least three establishments: the Grands Magasins Dufayel, the Musée Grevin, and the American Biograph (see Chapter 8). According to Higonnet, there were two movie theaters in Paris in 1907 and 160 in 1913 (168),[2] and, in the years prior to World War I, France was the world's leader in the production and distribution of film (Rearick 297).

Photography made great strides as well, especially in new kinds of portable equipment and in the use of dry rather than wet plates. It came to be seen as an art form and a new type of career, producing famous photographers such as Jacques-Henri Lartigue, Eugène Atget, and Constant Puyo. Lartigue was the photographer of the privileged in the last years of La Belle Époque, capturing them in the latest fashions on motor car rides and afternoon promenades in the Bois de Boulogne, although he was also interested in airplanes (Deedes-Vincke 43–4). Atget photographed Paris from 1898 to 1918, including everything that he considered "'artistic or picturesque in and around [the city]'"; according to Deedes-Vincke, "he was to produce one of the most formidable catalogues of photographic history covering the transition of the city from the nineteenth into the twentieth century. His documenting of Paris was painstakingly extensive," including buildings and the small trades, the grand and the ordinary (see Beaumont-Maillet). Deedes-Vincke suggests that Atget became, "unwittingly," a modern artist in that he photographed the same views from different angles and in different lights (similar to Cubist experiments on canvas), both close up and at a distance, and in that his human subjects included butchers, cobblers, florists, and errand-boys (45). Puyo, who founded the Photo Club de Paris and was an exponent of Pictorialism, which argued that the photograph was a work of art, was a great chronicler of bourgeois life in Paris at the time. The city and its people attracted many fine photographers because, as Deedes-Vincke points out, at the end of the first decade of the twentieth century, Paris was "unrivaled for its charm and fashionable elegance despite its rapidly spreading suburbs and the industrialization taking place within the city walls" (50).

Science and Medicine

A number of French scientists living in Paris were worldwide leaders in medicine and science, chief among them Louis Pasteur, Pierre and Marie Curie,[3] and Henri Becquerel. Pasteur made numerous discoveries in the latter half of the nineteenth century in the field of microbiology that, in effect, formed the foundation of modern medicine. Among these were sterilization, which prevented the spread of diseases, particularly in hospitals, and pasteurization, the process by which high heat destroys harmful microbes in perishable substances such as beer, wine, and milk. He also discovered the bacteria staphylococcus, streptococcus, and pneumococcus and developed vaccines for the treatment of cholera, anthrax, and rabies. He established the Pasteur Institute in Paris in 1888 as a clinic for rabies treatment as well as a research and teaching center for infectious diseases. Other Pasteur Institutes were subsequently established throughout the world. He was elected to the Académie des Sciences in 1882 ("Louis Pasteur" 1–4).

In the field of physics, Pierre and Marie Curie (the first woman to receive a doctorate in France) furthered the experiments of Becquerel, who had discovered natural radioactivity. The three jointly received the Nobel Prize for Physics in 1903, making Marie the first woman to win the prestigious award. A front-page color illustration of the Curies in their laboratory in the June 11, 1904 issue of *Le Petit Parisien* (see Jones 218) indicates the extent of their popularity in France and the celebration of their achievements, which were a source of French pride. After her husband's death in 1906, Marie became the first female professor at the Sorbonne (and the first in any European university). In 1911 she was awarded the Nobel Prize in Chemistry for the discovery of radium and polonium (the first person to win it twice), was a founder of the Institut du Radium in Paris in 1914 and its first director, and later worked on the use of radium in medicine (L'Institut du Radium, Paris).

However, one honor which she clearly deserved—election to the Académie des Sciences—eluded her because she was a woman. Eliot was no doubt aware of the controversy surrounding her potential election in January 1911, for this story appeared on the front page of many a Parisian newspaper. In the January 4 issue of *Le Matin*, for example, the front-page headline read, "Will the Académie elect Mme Curie?" Accompanied by her picture, the article reported that the Académie would gather at a special meeting to decide if women should be allowed to become members and offered the opinions of several scholars, noting that this question "preoccupies public opinion." Some scholars said that anyone who deserved it should be elected, while others said that women could not be members because the rules forbade it and the founders "never even considered admitting a woman." The next day's issue revealed in another front-page article that the Académie voted to "stick to tradition and not admit a woman," passing a resolution stating, "There is an unalterable tradition, which it appears completely wise to respect." Thus, the article concluded, "the Académie is hostile to the eligibility of women." Interestingly, a front-page article on January 9 appeared to follow up this controversial issue with an exploration of the rights (or lack thereof) of women, beginning with the statement, "The question of the rights of women is more and more pressing today."

Another honor denied to her at the time of her death, burial in the Panthéon, was rectified in 1995 when her remains, along with those of her husband, were transferred there.

Other famous French figures made important contributions in a variety of fields: Claude Bernard in physiology; Marcellin Berthelot in organic chemistry; Alfred Binet and Pierre Janet in psychology; Jean-Martin Charcot in anatomy; Jules Henri Poincaré in mathematics; Émile Durkheim and Lucien Lévy-Bruhl in sociology; Alfred Loisy in Biblical Studies; and, most important to Eliot studies, Bergson in philosophy, Maurras in political ideology, and a host of literary figures such as Claudel, Philippe, Péguy, Gide, Perse, and Benda (see Knapton 454–5; Jones 217). In his 1934 "A Commentary" (451–2), Eliot famously acknowledged the intellectual excitement engendered by a number of these figures in the Paris of 1910–1911, as noted in Chapter 1. Eliot scholars have investigated or are currently investigating the contributions of some of them to Eliot's intellectual development and literary production. For example, Nancy Gish is exploring the influence of Janet's theories of *désagrégation* [disintegration of the personality] on "Gerontion" and *The Waste Land* ("Pierre"), while John Morgenstern is making the case that Eliot's encounter with Durkheim's new theories in Paris can be detected in his works, both immediately and later on ("Discerning").

The Status of Men and Women

Paris in 1910–1911 was very much a patriarchal society in which men held power and privilege in every sphere, both public and private. As Jones points out, the "cult of masculinity" existed throughout the Third Republic, as illustrated strikingly by the prominence of dueling until the 1920s (239). Men held all public offices, dominated the business world, and were the authority figures in the home, making most, if not all, decisions.

A particularly distinct Parisian male figure, a "phenomenon of his time and place" who clearly influenced Eliot, was the *flâneur*, a term coined by Baudelaire in the mid-nineteenth century to describe an upper-class, educated, cultured, and cosmopolitan Parisian man who strolled along the boulevards, observing and recording the contemporary urban scene as a "passionate spectator" (Shapiro 13). The *flâneur* was an outgrowth and further development of the dandy persona, which appeared in London and Paris in the late eighteenth and early nineteenth centuries. The dandy was highly concerned with dress, fashion, and manners, felt disdain for the bourgeois and working classes, was self-absorbed, and maintained an aloof, skeptical, and reserved attitude. Laforgue resuscitated and reinvented the dandy in the late nineteenth century, as described in Chapter 1. The *flâneur* differs from the dandy in that he wanders the streets in various areas of a great modern metropolis, specifically Paris, observing its sights and its people of all classes as an act associated with art (see Gill 8–11).

Eliot merges these two Parisian male figures to create the speaker and main character in a number of poems written at this time. In "Rhapsody on a Windy Night," composed in March 1911 and influenced by Baudelaire's *Tableaux parisiens* and Laforgue's *Dernier vers*, the first-person speaker strolls from midnight to 4 a.m. about the streets of a city which seems to be Paris. He observes the sights which he passes, including rows of street lamps, a prostitute in a lighted doorway, and a cat foraging in a gutter, each of which evokes memories or associations in him. In Section III of "Preludes" and in "The Love Song of J. Alfred Prufrock," both products of his Parisian year, he alters and experiments with the traditional *flâneur* and its predecessor: he creates a narrative voice which is far more complex, ambiguous, and subjective and is not limited to largely objective descriptions of the external urban environment but includes indoor settings, its own internal imaginings and thoughts, and those of the woman in Section III of "Preludes." Additional experiments with this figure include the creation of ambiguity in "Preludes" through the speaker's shifts from "you" to "One" to "I." In "Prufrock," while the speaker (or more accurately, the thinker) has an unchanging identity, Eliot expands both his locations and the range of his thoughts. Concerning the former, the speaker begins his musings while walking through the streets, observing and recording the details of the seedy urban area through which he passes on his way to an upper-class social gathering, adhering to the established role of the *flâneur*. However, the speaker's personal responses to the external urban scene add a new dimension. Eliot further breaks the mold by having the majority of Prufrock's thoughts occurring indoors in the elegant setting in which the *soirée* is held and by revealing the inner anguish of his protagonist as he ponders a wide variety of personal problems, so that the relative objectivity of the traditional *flâneur* entirely disappears.[4] At the age of twenty-two, Eliot takes two French character types, merges them, and rings many changes upon them, thus demonstrating early in his career an ability to experiment with and expand the possibilities not only of Baudelaire's *flâneur* and Laforgue's dandy but also of other established literary devices and forms.

As for men's fashions in Paris, they were quite conservative and formal with no bright colors or daring cuts. Advertisements for and articles about men's fashions, often with titles such as "La Mode Masculine" [Male Fashions], in the Parisian newspapers of the day featured suits with long jackets, either single or double-breasted; pants with narrow legs, some of which sported the recent trend of cuffs; hard, detachable collars reaching the chin; neckties; bowler or top hats; gloves; and canes (Figure 17). Concerning cuffs, François Boucher tells us that it was considered "elegant to turn up the trouser bottoms, but only in the morning, whether it be rain or shine," adding that Frenchmen who copied this British innovation said, "'You turn up your trousers in Paris because it is raining in London.'" Boucher also reveals that men "could take their canes into drawing rooms 'and the Opéra,'" but that they should be "'malacca canes with silver or enameled knobs'" (403–4). Prufrock's attire clearly reflects the current formality and dandyism then in vogue in Paris: "My morning coat, my collar mounting firmly to the chin, / My necktie rich and modest, but asserted by a simple pin" (42–3). His references to "white flannel trousers" (123) and to wearing "the bottoms of my trousers rolled [cuffed]" (121) indicate that Eliot was aware of the most current Parisian male fashion trends. Indeed, according to Aiken, Eliot caused "a sensation" upon his return to Harvard in the autumn of 1911 by wearing "exotic Left Bank clothing" (although exactly what Aiken means is not clear) and parting his hair behind in the style which Prufrock considers. He also "made a point, for a while, a conspicuously un-American point of carrying a cane—was it a Malacca?" (*Ushant* 143; "King" 21).

As for women, they had in general few rights at the time. They were unable to vote, and the idea of women's suffrage was typically denounced as ridiculous.[5] Women could not "hold public office, serve on juries, or take a job without their husband's consent." Wives convicted of adultery received more severe punishments than husbands. Their roles were restricted largely to the domestic sphere: overseeing the household, rearing the children, providing for the needs of their husbands, and doing charitable work; roles reflected in newspapers, advertisements, and literature (Jones 240–1).

However, some advances had been made. In 1907 married women were granted sole rights to their earnings, and in 1910 they were allowed eight weeks of unpaid maternity leave (Horne 294), contingent, of course, on their having obtained permission from their husbands to work in the first place. A small percentage attended universities; in 1913, for example, 4,254 women as compared to 37,783 men were university students, and sixty-nine women received the *licence* degree (Zeldin 344). The first woman joined the Paris bar in 1900, and 3 percent of physicians were women in 1914 (Jones 241). There were also outstanding individual women, such as scientist Marie Curie, artist Marie Laurencin, and writers Colette and Gertrude Stein. In the November 15 issue of *Comoedia Illustré*, a small notice offered congratulations to Judith Gautier, daughter of Théophile Gautier, on her election to the Académie Goncourt, describing her as "the delicate author of so many famous works" and referring to her beauty and modesty (89). However, successful women such as these were few and far between.

The battle over women's rights at the time can be seen in two articles appearing in *Le Matin* in January 1911, surely occasioned by the controversy over Marie Curie's possible election to the Académie. In a remarkably liberal front-page article in the January 9 issue, A. Gervais, Senator of La Seine, argued that men and women should have equal rights as regards work. He began by stating that the question of the rights of women was becoming more and more pressing since women participated alongside men in all areas of life, a situation which was only going to increase. After giving numerous statistics on how many women were already in the work force (7 percent in fishing, 32 percent in industry and transportation, 34 percent in agriculture and forestry, 34 percent in the professions and public service, 36 percent in commerce, and 80 percent in domestic jobs), he asserted that men and women must collaborate to produce a strong and yet gentle home and that women should have the same rights as men to defend and conserve "life, honor, and liberty." On the other hand, the January 23 issue contained a short but powerful front-page article by Jules Wogue, Professeur agrégé at the Lycée Buffon, on "the invasion of women in the university." He argued that "the introduction of women into a place reserved for men is scandalous" and confusing since schools at lower levels were separated into those for males and those for females. He ended by insisting, "I'm not anti-feminist, but women should not go to schools for men!" Interestingly, the next day's newspaper announced on the front page that M. Branly had been elected to the Académie, obviously as a result of Curie's rejection earlier in the month.

Since Paris was the fashion capital of the world and the center of *haute couture*, especially for women's fashions, current trends dominated Parisian society and were much in evidence in newspaper advertisements, cartoons, and articles on fashion. Sporting events, particularly horseracing, provided opportunities for both showing and showing off the latest fashions. So did theatre, where one went to display one's own clothing, to notice that of other (female) members of the audience, to admire or decry the costumes on stage, and only incidentally to attend to the performance. This emphasis on fashion at the theatre is strikingly illustrated in a cartoon entitled "Théâtre moderne" in the December 8, 1910 issue of *Le Figaro* (Figure 18), in which a gentleman in tails on a stage addresses the audience: "Ladies and gentlemen. The dresses in the play that we have had the honor of performing for you are by the fashion designer Ducoin. The hats are by Denface. I can't tell you the name of the playwright because the prompter has just left the prompt-box" (3). Clearly this cartoon suggests that the costume designers were far more important than the playwright, or the play, for that matter. Also attesting to the interest in fashion at the theatre were regular newspaper columns with titles such as *Le Figaro*'s standard feature *La Mode au Théâtre*.

The particular fashions in vogue for women at this time give us a keen insight into their positions, limitations, and aspirations. By 1910, women's fashions had changed dramatically from the S-shape that emphasized the female figure at the end of the nineteenth century and the very early years of the twentieth with curved bone corsets creating tiny "wasp" waists, bustles emphasizing "the movement of that body part to heroic proportions" ("Brief" 3), padded hips and breasts, full sleeves, long flowing dresses of heavy materials such as brocade or satin that swept the floor, and large hats adorned with feathers. All but the latter disappeared by the end of the first decade of the twentieth century. Thanks largely to the revolutionary designs of Paul Poiret, "le couturier explorateur" [the experimental fashion designer] from 1907 to 1914 (Musée de la Mode, Paris), dresses in 1910–1911 had straight lines, empire-style bodices, and hems that stopped at the tops of women's shoes, while suits were tailored with long jackets and straight skirts. These new styles can be seen, for example, in ads for La Samaritaine in the November 7, 1910 issue and for Pygmalion in the April 2 and May 1, 1911 issues of Le Figaro as well as in numerous drawings in articles not just on fashion but also on drama, dance, opera, and sporting events (Figure 19). They deemphasized the female figure and gave women more freedom. Indeed, Poiret said that his success was the result of his giving women exactly what they had always wanted—freedom ("Designer" 1). Toward that end, he also advocated the brassiere and other lighter foundation garments in place of boned corsets and padding.

In 1910–1911, his hobble skirt was all the rage, with "volume around the hips narrowing to an ankle-hugging bottom" ("Poiret"), so that women could only take small steps (see Borgé and Viasnoff 199 for a 1910 photo of young women in hobble skirts); later he added a slit in the front to make walking easier. However, the hobble skirt was deemed a "freak" in The New York Times in 1912 (qtd. in Steele 233). More daring and indeed scandalous were his divided skirt [la jupe culotte] and his pants for women. A cartoon entitled "Chez le Grand Culottier" [At the Shop of the Famous Designer of Culottes] in the February 24, 1911 issue of Le Figaro (Figure 20) depicts an older woman observing several young models in culottes and asking the designer, "Do you really think so? . . . a divided skirt for a married woman?," to which he responds, "But of course, madame! I dare even say 'especially' for a married woman . . . Today wearing culottes is more than elegant; it's the height of fashion" (3). Both Eliot and Verdenal were aware of this current fashion fad. On March 24, 1911 Eliot sent Eleanor Hinckley a postcard of a young woman wearing one at the Auteuil race track, with a caption noting that it "continues to amuse the race-goers, . . . intriguing them by the novelty of the mysterious undergarments." He expresses concern that the postcard may not "go through the American post" and adds, "I have not seen this costume on the street and I don't think it will be a success" (*Letters* 17). Verdenal, as noted in Chapter 1, described in a letter to Eliot of mid-July 1911 having glimpsed "a shapely leg through the slit of a 'fashionably slit skirt'" worn by a prostitute on a merry-go-round during Bastille Day festivities (*Letters* 24).

As for Poiret's pants for women, they were considered equally shocking as indicated in a cartoon by Abel Faivre entitled "La Rentrée d'Auteuil" [Opening Day at the Auteuil Race-track] in the February 23, 1911 issue of *Le Figaro* (Figure 21). It depicts two women wearing pants surrounded by a crowd which totally ignores the race itself to gawk at them in varying attitudes of curiosity, shock, and amusement as a photographer takes their picture; especially hilarious are the expressions of curiosity (or shock) on two race horses galloping by (3).

Influenced by Leon Bakst's designs for the exotic productions of the Ballets Russes, such as *Cléopâtre* in 1909 and *Schéhérazade* in 1910, Poiret introduced into women's fashion the vibrant colors of magenta, yellow, and green (Musée de la Mode, Paris), described by more conservative Paris designer Jean Worth as "hideous, barbaric!" (qtd. in Steele 234). He also launched an Oriental style with turbans, harem skirts and pants, fringed capes, and fur trim.[6] In June 1911 he gave his famous (or infamous) "Thousand and One Nights" party, at which women wore his split skirts, trousers, and Oriental gowns, while he himself sported a turban ("Designer" 2), celebrating *le style sultane* [the sultan's style] (Musée de la Mode, Paris).[7] With all these new and exciting fashions from which to choose, it is no wonder that, as Horne tells us, Parisian women changed their clothes as often as five times a day (294).

Sports

In the last decade of the nineteenth century and the first decade of the twentieth, sports took on a far greater role in daily Parisian life than previously. In part it was because of the beliefs of Pierre de Coubertin, who revived the Olympic Games in 1896 and advocated the idea that participation in sports both increased one's strength and agility and brought one a sense of calm amid the anxieties and agitations of modern life; in part it was because of additional leisure time for people in general (Rioux and Sirinelli 89, 76). Indeed, sports became yet another form of entertainment for the masses, and the rapid growth of a sports press stimulated interest in spectator sports (Rearick 297). Sports also had two other functions: to keep the French strong and fit in case a new conflict with Germany occurred—thus being to some extent a nationalistic enterprise built on anti-German sentiment (Rioux and Sirinelli 89–90; Jones 231)—and, more frivolously, to provide a venue for fashions. The importance of sports at the time that Eliot lived in Paris can be seen in Baedeker's entry *Sports. Clubs. Agences de Voyage*[8] as well as in a regular column in *Le Figaro* titled *La Vie Sportive*, which gave daily reports on a wide array of sports and sporting events in Paris and its environs, including older, more established sports such as horseracing, shooting, yachting, sailing, golf, tennis, rugby, soccer, boxing, and fencing, but also newer sports such as bicycling, automobiling, and aviation. In the spring of 1910, in fact, France had champions in tennis, riding, bicycling, automobiling, and aviation (Chastenet 74).

Horseracing was still the spectator sport of the upper classes and held a high place in the social sphere, as evident in its always appearing first in *La Vie Sportive* under the heading "Les Courses" [The Races] with a subheading indicating the particular racetrack, such as "Courses au Bois de Boulogne" or "Courses au Auteuil." Baedeker noted in Section X of his guide that the racing season lasted from February to December and listed the various locations and entry fees. The newspaper accounts typically began with a commentary (often in a romantic style) on the previous day's races, followed by a list of the winners, complete with financial details. For example, in the October 31, 1910 issue of *Le Figaro*, the column's writer, who identifies himself only as Ajax, gives a rather soulful eulogy for the last races of the season at Longchamp in the Bois de Boulogne: "The beautiful social gatherings at Longchamp are composed of brilliant days that are interesting, elegant, and sunny; one wishes that they could begin again, but not that they would continue because they would of necessity become somber and sad, ending in a sort of twilight in which all one's pretty memories would fade away so that one would abandon them with no regret, almost with pleasure. Image of youth that cannot be prolonged. Such was, I think, the general impression yesterday at the last race of the season at the Bois" (6). In the April 3, 1911 issue, Jean Septime celebrates the opening of the 1911 season with the following vibrant beginning of a six-paragraph commentary: "The first grand sporting event of the horse-racing season had all its usual glamour. I am even tempted to say that, despite a somewhat changeable sky, rarely has opening day been so brilliant" (5). The racetracks also functioned as the premier sporting event for Parisians to see and be seen in the latest fashions. While we do not know whether Eliot went to any races, since he sent Eleanor Hinckley a postcard of a model at the Auteuil races in a split skirt, he was aware of their serving as a fashion hotspot.

Boxing was extremely popular in France, with French boxing being different from English boxing in that it involved kicking, as Baedeker informed his readers (44). *La Boxe* was a standard feature in *Le Figaro*'s section *La Vie Sportive*, but especially outstanding bouts were reported in separate columns of their own. For example, as noted in Chapter 1, on February 23, 1911, a column entitled *La Boxe* with the subtitle "The Match between the Hammer and the Anvil" described "an extraordinary battle" of twenty-five rounds between Harry Lewis, the world middleweight champion, and Blink Mac Clowsky at the Hippodrome the previous evening (4). Another exciting match took place on April 1, 1911 between two black boxers named Sam Mac Vea and Sam Langford. On the day of the match, *Le Matin* devoted a full page to "les deux nègres pugilists" [the two black fighters] with photographs. Noting that "the heavy-weight champion of the world [Jack Johnson, another black boxer] could be challenged by either," it reported that Langford had never been knocked out and that Vea had been knocked out only twice, concluding that the match to take place that night at the Cirque de Paris would be "sensational" (6). And indeed it was, for it turned out to be the most controversial match of the season, ending in "a deplorable manner," according to *La Boxe* the next day: even though Langford was "considerably superior to Vea" and had clearly won, the referee enraged the spectators by declaring it a draw (2).

Eliot could also have seen films of boxing matches in Paris, a remarkable early combination of cinema and sports. Soon after his arrival, for example, the November 24 issue of *Le Figaro* contained an announcement that the first showing of the film of the famous match between Jim Jeffries and Jack Johnson would be shown that night at 10:30 p.m. at the American Biograph at 7 rue Taitbout. Boxing fans were urged to get their reservations immediately, a marvelous early tactic of "pressure" advertising: "This sensational film, which was acquired by the American Biograph for an enormous sum, presents all the preparations for and all phases of the match; large numbers of boxing fans will come to this premiere, so it would be prudent to reserve your seats right away" (6).

Boxing matches such as these—whether live or on film— probably inspired Eliot to take boxing lessons at what Aiken describes as a "toughish gymnasium in Boston's South End" following his return to Harvard in the fall of 1911. Aiken reveals that, "under the tutelage of an ex-pugilist with some such moniker as Steve O'Donnell, [Eliot] learned not only the rudiments of boxing, but also, as he put it, 'how to swarm with passion up a rope,'" adding that "his delight in this attainment was manifest." He reports that he and Eliot habitually met for dinner "after these gymnastic afternoons, usually at the Greek restaurant in Stuart Street," and that "on one unfortunate occasion" Eliot arrived with a "magnificent black eye," the result of having accidentally hit his instructor too hard ("King" 20–1). Eliot took his boxing lessons quite seriously, pursuing them with the same desire for excellence evident in his academic endeavors.

While the bicycle had first been utilized solely as a new mode of transportation, it soon brought about a new personal and spectator sport, providing not only a means of individual exercise and pleasure but also entertainment for the masses in the form of bicycle races. According to Rioux and Sirinelli, the earliest such race took place in May 1891 when twenty-two French and five British cyclists raced from Bordeaux to Paris. And what was to become the most celebrated bicycle race in the world, the Tour de France, was instituted on July 1, 1903 by Henri Desgranges, the owner of the publication *L'Auto*, in hopes of increasing its circulation (which it did—from 20,000 to 60,000 copies). This initial race took place between Villeneuve-Saint-George and Montgeron and was won by the Frenchman Garin, who in a photograph of the start of the race was already in the lead. The race definitively established the French as the champions of bicycle racing, allowed them to lay claim to this sport as their own, and served as a confirmation and celebration of the importance of recreation and leisure time (91–2).

At the time of Eliot's residence in Paris, bicycling as a sport was well established, with daily information about races as well as activities of bicycling clubs in the newspapers. For example, in *Le Figaro* under the heading *Vélocipédie* in *La Vie Sportive* for November 18, 1910 was a notice that the King of Belgium had accepted the title of Honorary Member of the French Union of Cyclists. The same column in the issue for February 12, 1911 reported that the Twenty-third Congress of the Union of International Cyclists met in Paris the previous morning and decided that the world championships for 1911 would take place in Italy in June while those for 1912 would take place in the United States. Whether Eliot rode a bicycle himself while in Paris, as a means of transportation or as a sport, or attended bicycle races, we do not know. If so, perhaps he heeded Baedeker's warning that, for a bicyclist, Paris traffic was dangerous, suggesting that one could take beautiful (and safer) rides in the outlying areas (44).

Bicycling also contributed to women's fashions in Paris, as it quickly became acceptable, even fashionable, for women to wear pants or bloomers in public as early as the 1890s, when women rode bicycles in the Bois de Boulogne. As noted by Arsène Alexandre in the August 1895 issue of *Scribner's Magazine*, "all Paris is a-wheel," and women "unblushingly don man's dress, or something alarmingly like it" (qtd. in Steele 173). The complete outfit typically included a bicycling cap of straw or felt and wool stockings of blue or black, other colors being "deplorable." Steele suggests that, because bicycling was a new sport and thus had no traditional feminine costume (as opposed to horseback riding, for instance), the outfit created for it was more liberal and daring (173–5). However, in 1895 it was not acceptable for women to wear bloomers in public *unless* they were on bicycles. In fact, "*pseudo-bicyclists* in trousers" caused a scandal by "promenad[ing] on the boulevards" without bicycles and were admonished by the Prefect of Police (Flobert, qtd. in Steele 176). In 1910–1911, thanks largely to the experimental designs of Poiret, trousers for women had become a fashion trend and no longer required a bicycle anywhere in the vicinity.

Automobiling was another new sport that had developed even more recently than bicycling, and Baedeker points out that it had grown more rapidly in France than anywhere else (43). The first car race took place in 1894 from Paris to Rouen, a distance of 123 kilometers (Horne 287), and by 1910–1911 car racing had become a sporting event of great interest and importance. Frantz-Reichel in a column entitled *Les Courses d'Automobiles* and subtitled "La Coupe des Voitures légères" in the June 24, 1911 issue of *Le Figaro* announced that the first ever race for the Cup of Light Automobiles, founded by *L'Auto*, would take place the next day at the racetrack at Boulogne-sur-Mer. Frantz-Reichel enthusiastically assured his readers that the next day's race represented "vigorous efforts to give the sport of French automobile-racing the vitality and brilliance which have won for the French automobile industry a dominant place in world-wide markets." And he closed with a grand flourish: "The race has created enormous interest in all sports circles. The track is very beautiful, very narrow and rapid, and we all know that such a race will be an impressive spectacle" (4). In *La Vie Sportive* under the heading *Automobilisme*, one could read descriptions of the latest models of 1910 and 1911 that bore suspicious resemblance to advertisements. For example, in the February 12, 1911 issue, the company Charron Exportation, which offered deluxe rental cars and whose address at 34 Champs-Élysées was conveniently given, announced a new model by Daimler without valves and assured its potential clients that its cars were driven by prudent and well-dressed chauffeurs (6). These pieces convey the excitement and pride engendered in France by this new sport.

Perhaps the most exciting new sport of all during Eliot's residence in Paris was aviation, in which the French were world leaders. Inspired by Blériot's daring flight over the English Channel in 1909, numerous flying competitions, which were reported with zeal in all the newspapers on a daily basis, took place in the next few years. Typically, a race was held in stages, with articles giving the names of the aviators, the number of kilometers of each stage, the number of hours taken to complete each stage, and finally the names of the winners along with the total number of kilometers and hours. *La Vie Sportive* included the subheading *Aviation*, with special separate columns reporting on the most noteworthy accomplishments. In the June 24, 1911 issue of *Le Figaro*, the column *La Conquête de l'Air* [The Conquest of the Air], subtitled *Le Circuit Européen* and signed F. R., reported that fourteen aviators landed at Utrecht, "a remarkable result," in the third stage of a flying competition that began in Paris, with the next day's stage to be from Utrecht to

Brussels. The article listed the aviators in order of their placement so far, the leader having covered the 630 kilometers in six hours, fifteen minutes (4). Eliot's interest in aviation might have been piqued by such reports as well as by Alain-Fournier's excitement about and knowledge of aviation. This glimpse into the thrilling and thought-provoking possibilities of the future in a setting which also preserved the great accomplishments of the past was yet another instance of that trait which Eliot so admired about the city as he experienced it on a daily basis.

1194 PARIS. — *Panorama sur la Seine pris de Notre-Dame.* — LL.

Figure 1. Panorama of Paris and the Seine from the top of Notre Dame. Panorama sur la Seine pris de Notre Dame. Paris (VIème arr.). Carte postale, vers 1900. © Roger-Viollet.

Figure 2. The Location of the Pension Casaubon, 151 bis rue Saint-Jacques. Rue Saint-Jacques, Hôtel Louis XIV, Porte et Balcon. Paris (Vème arr.). Impression photomécanique. Paris, Bibliothèque Historique de la Ville de Paris. © BHVP/Roger-Viollet.

Figure 3. Rue Soufflot and the Panthéon. Paris Vème arr. La rue Soufflot et le Panthéon. Vers 1900. ND-168 (13 × 18). © ND/Roger Viollet.

Figure 4. Alain-Fournier, 1913. Studio photograph by Dornac. Collection Alain Rivière, tous droits réservés. By permission of Alain Rivière.

Figure 5. Jean Verdenal. *2000M-9(f). By permission of the Houghton Library, Harvard University.

Figure 6. "—. . . . . Je peux bien vous dire, monsieur, que vous m'êtes infiniment sympathique" [I must tell you, sir, that I find you extremely attractive]. Abel Faivre, "Les Mauvaises fortunes" [Bad luck] *Le Figaro* (26 January 1911): 3. © 2010 Artists Rights Society (ARS), New York/ADAGP, Paris.

Figure 7. The Collège de France. By permission of the Bibliothèque nationale de France.

Figure 8. Henri Bergson. LC-DıG-ggbain-38388. Prints and Photographs Division, Library of Congress.

Figure 9. "Bergson 'Attrac'cheun." By permission of the Bibliothèque nationale de France.

Figure 10. Charles Maurras. By permission of the Bibliothèque nationale de France.

Par Albert GUILLAUME

UNE ENTRÉE EN SCÈNE

Figure 11. "—Allons, voyons, ma petite Dix-neuf-cent-onze, n'ayez pas le trac comme ça!
. . . Celle que vous remplacez était si exécrable que vous n'aurez pas de peine à être moins
mauvaise!. . ." [Go on, my little 1911; don't have stage fright like that! The year that you're
replacing was so abominable that you won't have any trouble being better!]. Albert Guillaume,
"Une Entrée en Scène" [A Stage Entrance] *Le Figaro* (30 December 1910): 3. © 2010 Artists
Rights Society (ARS), New York/ADAGP, Paris.

155 · PARIS · Jardin du Luxembourg

Figure 12. Children in the Jardin du Luxembourg. "155—Paris—Jardin du Luxembourg."
Carte postale anonyme. Paris, Musée Carnavalet. © Musée Carnavalet/Roger-Viollet.

Figure 13. Buffotot, "Pauvres pneus!!!" [Poor tires!!!] *Comoedia Illustré* (15 July 1911): 662. Jerome Robbins Dance Division, The New York Public Library for the Performing Arts, Astor, Lenox and Tilden Foundations.

Figure 14. Henri Manuel, "Mlle Madge Lanzy." Fabrique de Voitures & Automobiles De Luxe, Eugène Boulogne et Fils. *Comoedia Illustré* (15 June 1911): 597. Jerome Robbins Dance Division, The New York Public Library for the Performing Arts, Astor, Lenox and Tilden Foundations.

Figure 15. "Roger Sommer, sur biplane militaire, établit le premier record du monde des aérobus" [Roger Sommer, in a military biplane, establishes the first world record for airbuses]. *Le Petit Parisien: Supplément Littéraire Illustré* (12 February 1911): 51.

259 bis PARIS (V^e arr^t) — Rue des Ecoles près du Boulevard Saint-Michel · La Sorbonne

Figure 16. Rue des Écoles near boulevard Saint-Michel, La Sorbonne. Rue des Écoles près du boulevard Saint-Michel, La Sorbonne. Paris (Vème arr.). Impression photomécanique. Paris, Bibliothèque Historique de la Ville de Paris. © BHVP/Roger-Viollet.

LA MODE MASCULINE

Figure 17. Men's Fashions, 1911.
"La Mode Masculine" [Male Fashions].
Le Matin (2 April 1911): 4.

Figure 18. "—Mesdames, Messieurs. Les robes de la pièce que nous avons eu l'honneur de jouer devant vous sont de la maison Ducoin. Les chapeaux sont signés Denface. . . . . . Le nom de l'auteur . . . je ne saurais vous le dire. Le souffleur vient de quitter sa place" [Ladies and gentlemen. The dresses in the play that we have had the honor of performing for you are by the fashion designer Ducoin. The hats are by Denface. I can't tell you the name of the playwright because the prompter has just left the prompt-box]. Abel Faivre, "Théâtre moderne." *Le Figaro* (8 December 1910): 3. © 2010 Artists Rights Society (ARS) New York/ADAGP, Paris.

Figure 19. Women's Fashions, 1911. "Le Grand Prix de Paris: Quelques Toilettes." *Comoedia* (26 June 1911): 5.

par Albert GUILLAUME

CHEZ LE GRAND CULOTTIER

Figure 20. "—Vous croyez? . . . la jupe-culotte pour une mariée? . . .—Mais certainement, madame! J'ose même dire 'surtout' pour une mariée . . . Un jour comme celui-là, porter les culottes, c'est plus qu'une élégance, c'est tout un programme!" [—Do you really think so? . . . a divided skirt for a married woman? . . .—But of course, madame! I dare even say 'especially' for a married woman . . . Today wearing culottes is more than elegant; it's the height of fashion]. Albert Guillaume, "Chez le Grand Culottier" [At the Shop of the Famous Designer of Culottes] *Le Figaro* (24 February 1911): 3. © 2010 Artists Rights Society (ARS), New York/ADAGP, Paris.

LA RENTRÉE D'AUTEUIL, par Abel Faivre

Figure 21. Abel Faivre, "La Rentrée d'Auteuil" [The Opening of the Auteuil Racetrack] *Le Figaro* (23 February 1911): 3. © 2010 Artists Rights Society (ARS), New York/ADAGP, Paris.

· 3 ·

THE THEATRE

The richness and variety of the Parisian theatre scene provided Eliot with inspiration for both the aspiring poet and the latent dramatist within him. His description of Paris as a perfect present in its combination of past and future ("What France" 94) is brilliantly illustrated in that cultural arena. As Martin Esslin notes, "The Comédie-Française and other state-assisted theatres . . . continued on their centuries-old course of presenting the classics but were more and more influenced by innovations of pioneers like [André] Antoine and [Aurélien] Lugné-Poe" (374). The innovations were numerous and often conflicting. For example, the daring and sensational productions of the Ballets Russes, which first appeared in Paris in 1909, had numerous effects on stage design, such as bolder use of color. On the other hand, a reaction against such "spectacularly visual theatre" resulted in a desire for "simplicity, intellectual clarity, and the pure impact of the poetic word" (Esslin 375). Indeed, close on the heels of Eliot's arrival, the writer and theatre critic Jacques Rouché's article "L'Art théâtrale moderne" in the literary supplement of the November 12, 1910 issue of *Le Figaro* first made known to the French the ideas of various international pioneers in modern drama and proposed that set design should demonstrate the kind of experimentation occurring in modern art. He revived the Théâtre des Arts to put these ideas into practice in Paris, and Eliot went to see its inaugural production, the acclaimed adaptation of Dostoevsky's novel *Les Frères Karamazov*, in April 1911 (*Letters* 25).[1]

That his sojourn in Paris occurred in the midst of exciting developments in the field of drama is evident in a lecture on contemporary French drama given at the Sorbonne by the eminent scholar M. Ossip-Lourié on November 26, 1910. In his report of the lecture, which appeared in the column *Aux Écoles* [At the Schools] in *Le Figaro* directly beneath one on the beginning of courses at the Sorbonne, Jacques-Pierre revealed that it was "warmly welcomed" by the audience of students, playwrights, and critics. Ossip-Lourié explained that the theatrical movement of the last thirty years in France was highly influenced by the innovators Henry Becque and Antoine, that naturalistic, sociological, scientific, and psychological drama had recently come to the forefront, and that there had been a reciprocal influence between the theatre and the development of ideas. The lecturer concluded this part of his talk by exclaiming, "What a flowering, sirs, since Becque, and what a surprising diversity of subjects treated!" However, he also revealed that for several years the theatre in France had been experiencing a crisis, the causes of which were diverse, noting that, "with some exceptions, we look in vain in recent French drama for the France that works, thinks, and acts." He ended by asserting that the crisis would not last long (2).

Despite Ossip-Lourié's commentary on the crisis in French drama, the Parisian theatre scene at the time could only be described as flourishing, with numerous and varied offerings of both the established and the contemporary. Theatre was an integral part of the Parisian cultural, intellectual, and social scene. An amusing cartoon entitled "Théâtre moderne" in the December 8, 1910 issue of *Le Figaro* demonstrates how they were intertwined, as it spoofed the fact that the names of the costume-designers were of greater importance than the name of the playwright, as noted in Chapter 2. The influence of theatre on current fashions had been enormous since the advent of the Ballets Russes in Paris in 1909 and continued throughout Eliot's year there.

Eliot's interest in drama and his desire to immerse himself in every aspect of French culture suggest that he would have partaken of the wealth of theatre offerings. He could certainly have afforded to go because not only was his year abroad financed by his family, but tickets to most productions were extremely reasonable. For example, according to the article "Le Théâtre Shakespeare au Théâtre Femina" in the November 29 issue of *Le Figaro*, tickets to *A Midsummer Night's Dream* or *The Merry Wives of Windsor* were seven and ten francs for box seats and four and five francs for seats in the orchestra or balcony with a one franc booking fee (4), and at most theatres student tickets were available at even lower rates. And, despite the somewhat rudimentary nature of his French upon his arrival, his commitment to improving his ability to speak, read, and understand the language suggests that, in addition to reading contemporary French drama under Alain-Fournier's guidance, he attended as many plays as possible.

In this chapter, I will describe some of the major theatrical events during Eliot's year in Paris, indicating which ones he may have been most likely to have attended or at least known about, based on his own personal interests and on evidence of influences in his works. I will begin with an overview of the sheer number and variety of offerings throughout the year and will then focus on four events and an essay that were outstanding in one way or another and seem to have left their marks on the young man and his subsequent poetic and theatrical creations.

Overview of Parisian Theatre in 1910–1911

A summary of the plays presented during the 1910–1911 season at the Théâtre de l'Odéon appears in the column *Courrier des Théâtres* [Theatre News] in the June 16, 1911 issue of *Le Figaro* and captures in miniature the great variety of choices, as well as the inclusion of both contemporary and classical drama on the Parisian theatre scene. Eighteen new works and twenty-three classical French works had been performed. Of the new works, thirteen were in prose, while five were in verse, which may have been an inspiration to Eliot, since one of his major goals as a dramatist later was to compose verse drama. The classical plays made up an impressive list, with five by Racine (including *Andromaque*, *Iphigénie en Aulide*, and *Phèdre*), three by Corneille (*Le Cid*, *Horace*, and *Le Menteur*), and eight by Molière (including *Le Misanthrope*, *Le Médecin malgré lui*, and *L'École des femmes*). The article revealed that the "formidable number of 135 acts was performed at the Théâtre de l'Odéon during the season" and that "Molière made more money than Corneille and Corneille more than Racine" (6). Classic French drama was also performed at the Comédie-Française: for example, *Phèdre* in November, *Tartuffe* in January, and *Le Misanthrope* in April.

Classical Greek tragedies were also offered. The Comédie-Française presented *Oedipus Rex* in March, with the title role played by the acclaimed actor Jean Mounet-Sully, and *Électre* in April, while on June 29 at the Trocadéro the General Association of Students organized a performance of *Hécube*. The last, according to *Courrier des Théâtres* in the June 30 issue of *Le Figaro*, was a beautiful adaptation in French poetry by M. Paul Myrannes, "a true reconstitution of the ancient tragedy with its choruses and its music." An orchestra of two hundred musicians was conducted by M. Victor Charpentier, and the evening began with a lecture by M. Camille Le Senne (6). Eliot's interest in tragedy, particularly that based on Greek mythology (which he used as a framework in most of his own plays), suggests that he attended plays by Racine and Corneille as well as ancient Greek tragedies, while his penchant for comedy, so evident in his own drama, may have spurred him to see Molière's famous comedy of manners. The student-sponsored performance of *Hécube* at the end of the spring term was perhaps among the last cultural events he attended before departing for two months to Germany and Italy.

There were also numerous opportunities to see Shakespearean drama, ever popular in Paris. In April and May 1911, performances of *Hamlet* at the Comédie-Française may have attracted the young man who was in 1919 to write a famous essay on the tragedy. From December 1–8, 1910, the Shakespearean Theatre Company presented at the Théâtre Femina both *A Midsummer Night's Dream* and *The Merry Wives of Windsor*. The article "Le Théâtre Shakespeare au Théâtre

Femina" in the November 29 issue of *Le Figaro* commented that "the entire press, both French and foreign, enthusiastically welcomes the magnificent effort of M. Camille de Sainte-Croix and the Shakespearian Theatre Company in presenting these two triumphs from the previous season. Each play, to be preceded by a lecture given by M. de Sainte-Croix, will be a production of delicious fantasy and gaiety. Each will be the entire play, performed by agile artists and pretty actresses in original and noteworthy settings by the painter E. Simas. We only regret that the cycle is so brief" (4).

At the end of December, a new unexpurgated translation of *Romeo and Juliet* by Louis de Gramont with music by Berlioz appeared at the Théâtre de l'Odéon. In his review in the December 23 issue of *Le Figaro*, after noting that it had been the first of Shakespeare's works to be performed in France, Francis Chevassu waxed poetic: "Through the coarseness which seems the discharge of a bitter and violent soul and behind the tragic laugh and terrible irony of the playwright shines an ideal of dazzling beauty. There is certainly no other work in which love has spoken more loftily." If Eliot, a young man in the throes of romantic and sexual longings, happened to read this review suggesting that the play offered a highly positive vision of love, it may have encouraged his presence. The remainder of the review made this particular production sound even more attractive. According to Chevassu, the best thing about the translation was that it gave individuality to all the characters: Romeo was not a "sighing wimp, a sort of fop incapable of carrying a heavy sorrow, but an impassioned and even brutal man," while de Gramont "restored to Juliet, often poeticized to excess and made practically unreal, all the traits of a real woman." The style of cadenced prose and blank verse was true to Shakespeare, and "the beautiful music of Berlioz, played by the Orchestre Colonne, further intensified the sensation awakened by the genius of the poet" (5).

This poetic, highly positive review was countered by a wittily sarcastic review "La Soirée: *Roméo et Juliette* à l'Odéon" by Un Monsieur de l'Orchestre [A Gentlemen in the Orchestra], a regular feature of the newspaper's cultural section. The anonymous review punned wickedly on the French words *intègre*, *intégrale*, and *intégralité* to mock the vaunted "complete" or "unexpurgated" translation:

> You know that M. Louis de Gramont, the complete [*intègre*] translator, has offered us a complete [*intégrale*] translation in all its completeness [*intégralité*]. In the past, we've had numerous adaptations of the great Will; now we begin the cycle of complete translations; then we will tackle the cycle of juxta-linear translations, and finally that of textual performances in English. Thus there are some lovely evenings in store for lovers of Shakespeare. In confessing that the pleasure I get from a complete play like *Romeo and*

Juliet is a little arduous—prolix, confused, and convoluted [*diffus, confus, et touffu*]—I reveal that I am as little royalist as the king.

After stating that he found in such "complete reconstructions all the interest of a course in the archaeology of drama," the reviewer dutifully discussed each element of the production. Of the music, for example, he noted, "As is the fashion at the Odéon, the complete translation is accompanied by music. The complete Orchestre Colonne . . . plays not the music of Gounod but of Berlioz. I will not go so far as to say that the sauce surpasses the fish, but without doubt the music makes the complete chewing of it more enjoyable." And, after describing the ingenious décor which facilitated the numerous set changes required for the play, he expressed regret that such effort had not been expended on presenting "the ardent new work of a young unknown poet instead of consecrating the already consecrated glory, the unquestioned genius, of Shakespeare" (5). If Eliot read this review, in addition to enjoying its wit and sarcasm, which he himself not infrequently employed as a critic later in his career, he may have been encouraged by the reviewer's desire to see produced the poetic drama of a young writer. Such an open attitude toward new artists, evident in all of the arts in Paris at the time, may have been partly responsible for his ambition to live there and write in French (Hall 56).

Works by Ibsen and by the son of Leo Tolstoy were also presented during Eliot's Parisian year. The still shocking *Hedda Gabler* was performed in early January 1911. A review appearing on January 11 in *Le Matin* described the play as "a piteous study of a failed woman" and commented on the lead roles. Interestingly, Hedda was played by Mlle Greta Prozor, the daughter of the translator of Ibsen's works into French. She conveyed "with certainty all the nuances of the character," although in the reviewer's opinion she "insisted a little too much on each trait and analyzed rather than lived the role" (4). The male lead was played by the famous actor Lugné-Poe, who was also one of the leading French pioneers in experimental theatre. Among his most significant contributions was producing the works of contemporary playwrights such as Ibsen, Maeterlinck, Strindberg, and Claudel. Since Eliot was reading the works of Claudel under the tutelage of Alain-Fournier, he may have attended the play to see this important figure. Indeed, Lugné-Poe would premiere Claudel's *L'Annonce Faite à Marie* the next year, and although Eliot would not be there to see it, he no doubt read it as it was published serially beginning in the December 1, 1911 issue of *La Nouvelle Revue Française*, to which he subscribed on his return to the United States.[2] If he saw this production of *Hedda Gabler*, it was perhaps his first taste of the playwright whose work he found heavy-handed and prosaic, preferring verse drama (see, for example, "The Beating of a Drum" 12).

Because of his intense interest in Russian literature, the chance to see the literary début in France of Léon Tolstoy, the son of the great Russian novelist who had recently died in strange circumstances, may have drawn Eliot to the performance on January 7 of the two-act play *Marc*, sponsored by the Association Franco-Russe of the Université de Paris at the instigation of Mlle Genia Halpérise-Kaminsky, daughter of the translator of Tolstoy's works into French. After revealing that the play was first performed several years earlier at the Theatre of the Arts in St. Petersburg, Jacques-Pierre in his review in *Le Figaro* noted that it was too short for adequate character development (4).

Among all the varied theatrical events, four in particular stand out in the 1910–1911 season as the most likely to have captured Eliot's attention: two controversial Racine lectures in late October and early November 1910; Maeterlinck's *L'Oiseau bleu* [The Blue Bird], which opened in March 1911; Copeau and Croué's stage adaptation of *Les Frères Karamazov* in April 1911; and the collaborative and multidisciplinary production *Le Martyre de Saint Sébastien* in May 1911. Even after his return to the United States, the influence of Parisian theatre continued, for an essay by the eminent French drama critic Henri Ghéon in the November 1911 issue of *La Nouvelle Revue Française* seems to have inspired some of his most basic ideas about drama.

The Affaire Fauchois

Soon after Eliot's arrival in Paris, the literary/political controversy known as the Affaire Fauchois or the Affaire Racine erupted. On Thursday, October 27 at 2 p.m. at the Théâtre de l'Odéon (Figure 22), a performance of Racine's *Iphigénie en Aulide* was preceded by a lecture given by a young poet and playwright named René Fauchois, whose recent work *Beethoven* had been well-received. In the course of the lecture, he criticized Racine's play "rather intensely," according to a front-page article entitled "Une nouvelle Affaire à l'horizon: L'Affaire Racine" and accompanied by a picture of Fauchois on which was superimposed that of Racine in the October 28 issue of *Le Matin*. The article began by asking, "Who would have believed it? There is still in the year of grace 1910 a Racine question. And on this question, the Parisian public—that was said to be so blasé—is still completely ready to fight! This incredible fact was verified yesterday in the course of Fauchois's lecture."

What could possibly have caused such a reaction? His criticisms of a revered French classical playwright, summarized in detail in *Le Matin*, were shocking to traditionalists. He asserted that, despite its admirable fourth act and some beautiful passages of poetry "now and then," *Iphigénie en Aulide* is "one of the most tiresome works of the classical repertoire, revealing on even the briefest examination the superficiality of melodrama or operetta; the catastrophe is caused by artificial devices which even Scribe did not employ with such deviousness." The characters are either "abominable mannequins, rigid and without warmth, or, more abominable, have the grating manner of students at the École des Beaux Arts. Rarely do they appear to have souls." Further, "one can't imagine a more bombastic style of senile decay." Pointing out that "frequent errors of taste sicken even the most tolerant," he concluded that the play is "the tragedy of a janitor." He was often interrupted by cries of "It's shameful to speak of Racine this way! Long live Racine!" and "Get rid of the lecturer!" from members of two groups who objected to his criticisms: high school students following courses in classical literature and members of the Camelots du Roi, whose opposition was as much political as literary. Counteracting these members of the audience were friends and supporters of Fauchois, who applauded and cheered. Throughout the turmoil, Fauchois remained calm and continued with his lecture, ending with some praise of Racine. When he left the stage, he was recalled twice to bravos intermingled with boos and hisses. Then the performance of the play proceeded without further incident.

When asked by *Le Matin* why he had attacked Racine so violently, he replied that he "felt a duty to show young people of his generation that the classical playwrights have flaws, despite their admirable qualities, because, in the name of their supposed perfection, new dramatic works, with flaws but also with beauty, do not receive the praise they deserve. While in painting and in music a considerable effort has been made to break free of old formulas, dramatic literature seems always to be trapped in the same vicious circle." Citing recent plays such as *Hécube*, *Hélène*, and *Prométhée* by contemporary French playwrights, he concluded by asking, "Are we thus condemned eternally to use the same old Greek and Roman subject matter? Isn't there a history of France?" ("Une nouvelle Affaire" 1).[3]

The subsequent lecture on Thursday, November 3 was highly anticipated and indeed produced a greater furor than its predecessor. The title of a report of the incident in the November 4 issue of *Le Figaro* was "A Heated Clash over *Iphigénie*," and its writer Serge Basset began, "Fauchois again caused a violent uproar yesterday at the Odéon" (3), while an article by Robert Oudot with the clever title "M. René Fauchois ne mange pas encore des pissenlits par la Racine" [Fauchois isn't dead—or finished—yet][4] in the November 4 issue of *Comoedia* noted with more than a touch of sarcastic humor that the announcement of this second lecture on Racine must have increased the number of tickets sold for this boxing match "because from now on the 'swings,' 'uppercuts,' and 'punches' will be literary arguments as in the heroic days of romanticism" (4). This highly publicized controversy coincided with the first weeks of the university term, with Basset's article appearing just beneath one describing the return of students to the Sorbonne.

In giving the details of the near-riot, Basset revealed that the hall was packed, seething, boisterous, and noisy as the audience awaited the lecture. Precisely at 2 p.m., Fauchois, monocle in place and lecture notes in hand, appeared to the applause of friends and supporters and a volley of whistles from opponents, who also tossed copies of *L'Action Française* from the balcony. After calmly pouring himself a glass of water, he began the lecture. Suddenly, Jean Gravelines, a physician and a member of the executive committee of the Camelots du Roi, mounted the stage, brandished his fists at Fauchois, attempted to snatch his lecture notes, and cried out, "I forbid you to speak!" Others rushed to the stage amidst a turmoil of whistles and bravos, with friends and adversaries of the speaker attacking each other. As police, who had been summoned by the theatre's director, entered the theatre and began to arrest some of the brawlers, the famous innovator and pioneer in modern drama André Antoine arrived and attempted to calm the crowd: "What's happening is deplorable! This should not be a question of politics." He insisted that the lectures at the Odéon should provide a forum where all opinions, other than political ones, could be expressed and offered the protestors the opportunity to give their views. He also announced that, in order to restore peace, the performance of the play would take place immediately, to be followed by Fauchois's lecture, at which time those who did not wish to hear it could leave.

After the performance, Fauchois, who exhibited "a quiet assurance," according to Basset, began his lecture again, repeating many of the criticisms of the previous week. His partisans supported him with applause, while his detractors interrupted, insulted, and decried him. A young man shouting, "Out the door with Fauchois!" was himself arrested and removed, while an exasperated woman cried out in a tart voice, "What ineptitudes, you whipper-snapper! We didn't pay good money to hear you insult Racine!" Basset noted with some wit that the "torrent of heated applause, passionate and offensive interruptions, approval here, disapproval there, made this part of the lecture resemble a meeting of the Chamber of Deputies on a day of uproar and dissension," observing that Fauchois went on unemotionally with his remarks, although by the end so vituperative was his criticism of Racine that the number of bravos decreased significantly (3–4).

Following the lecture, there was agitation on the streets outside the theatre for some time, with additional arrests. And *L'Action Française* reported that a column of demonstrators ran through the Latin Quarter after leaving the theatre. As noted earlier, Eliot may be recalling this particular incident in his 1934 memoir: "in 1910 I remember the *camelots* cheering the *cuirassiers* who were sent to disperse them, because they represented the Army, all the time that they were trying to stampede their horses" ("A Commentary" 453). Such passion evoked by a literary event would have been impressive to an American. However, we can only wonder whether Eliot was inspired by Fauchois's call for freedom from the established conventions of writing drama or appalled by his daring attack on a respected figure in the French pantheon of great dramatists. Did this particular incident, which was discussed in great detail in *L'Action Française* in the days following, bring to life for him the philosophy of Charles Maurras, to whom he had been introduced at Harvard and whose ideas were to influence him for many years?

While the accounts in such newspapers as *Le Figaro* and *Le Matin* were relatively objective, those in Maurras's newspaper were heavily slanted, attacking Fauchois not only because of his criticisms of Racine but also because he was a Jew. For example, a front-page article entitled "The Scandal at the Odéon" in the November 4 issue, described Fauchois as frightened and extremely nervous: "At exactly 2 p.m., the curtain rose, and the detractor of Racine advanced, pale, having barely recovered from his fright of last week. He had scarcely opened his mouth before there were many whistles that unleashed a tumult, with some applause from his friends and from Jews . . . . Indignant at this provocation from a third-rate actor, our friend Gravelines leapt onto the stage and ordered the lecturer to leave. Everyone applauded his dynamic action as he spontaneously carried out the will of the audience." The report continued in this vein, referring to the young protestors, most of whom were Maurras's followers, as "courageous avengers of our literary glory," criticizing Antoine for allowing the lecture to proceed, and describing "poor" Fauchois as being "so pale that he was green," with shaking hands and nervous gestures. The article concluded by noting that, although it was raining when everyone left, it had been a glorious afternoon "which would be a happy memory to those young people who were at the Odéon on November 3, 1910."

In a front-page article on the following day, Maurras insisted that the opposition was not politically motivated, but seemingly undercut that assertion by noting that "the brilliant youth of 1910 seems made to return to all our pure fountains [of classicism, nationalism, and tradition]." As noted in Chapter 1, Gide in his "Journal sans Date" in the December 1910 issue of *La Nouvelle Revue Française* with some sarcasm questioned Maurras's statement, saying that he feared that the whistles of opposition were less literary than political and that a friend who had attended the "brawl" reported to him that one of the "nationalist whistlers," upon hearing Antoine's announcement that the play would be presented before the lecture, complained, "Oh, what a pain! I'm going to have to see *Iphigénie!*" With tongue in cheek, Gide wrote that despite such a remark he was reassured by Maurras's insistence in his article in the November 5 issue of *L'Action Française* that "our young friends have scrupulously avoided mixing political beliefs with their ardent Racinian demonstration at the Odéon." After pointing out that a number of the young "literary" men seemed to have principles more like those of the "Palais-

Bourbon" than of Mount Parnassus and that these "young extremists of tradition" appeared to have indeed mixed politics with literature, he ended by sarcastically noting, "Decidedly, Maurras has done well to reassure us that such is not the case" (780–4).

Only two weeks after the Odéon incident, on November 18, the Students of L'Action Française held a meeting to welcome old and new members at the beginning of the school year, as noted in Chapter 1. Presided over by Maurras himself, the major figures of the organization gave rousing speeches. A front-page account in *L'Action Française* the next day reported that the room was packed with attentive and passionate students who gave the speakers an impressive ovation when they entered, followed by "an almost religious silence" when Maurras rose to deliver a stirring speech. Eliot may have been one of those students, drawn by curiosity over the scandal, by interest in the ideas of Maurras, and/or by his new acquaintance Verdenal, who was attracted by those ideas himself (Schlemmer, qtd. in Watson 469).

Maeterlinck's *L'Oiseau bleu*

A second theatrical event that was the talk of Paris was the production of Maurice Maeterlinck's *L'Oiseau bleu* which opened on March 2, 1911 at the Théâtre Réjane and played to packed and enchanted houses for two months. A fairy tale about the journey of two children in search of a magical bird which brings happiness to human life, the poetical drama was praised by the majority of reviews for its beauty and charm as well as its positive philosophy. In the column *Les Théâtres* in the March 3 issue of *Le Figaro*, the reviewer commented that Maeterlinck had realized magnificently Gautier's wish that fairytales become the sovereign expression of the theatre (5). Gautier, of course, would soon become an important influence on Eliot.

Léon Blum presented an analysis of the play's philosophical content in the March 3 issue of *Comoedia* with an impressive article entitled "*L'Oiseau bleu*," featuring nine photographs of the production. After noting its acclaim by all of Paris, Blum praised Maeterlinck's originality in uniting into one system the mysticism of the neo-platonists with Emerson's and Carlyle's practical philosophy of the moral value of daily acts and duties. He noted that Maeterlinck emphasized, like the mystics, the essential oneness of past, present, and future, as well as the permanence of a secret life which is an eternal reality beneath physical and temporal appearances, while at the same time teaching, like Emerson and Carlyle, the importance of the actions of ordinary life (3). The mysticism of the play as described by Blum was similar to the Bergsonian philosophy that Eliot was currently imbibing from the philosopher himself. Since Eliot was doubtlessly struggling to reconcile those concepts with the practical moral values he had learned from his parents, *L'Oiseau bleu* may have suggested to him the possibility of doing so. However, a review in the March 3 issue of *L'Action Française* argued that it was "ridiculous to talk about its philosophy," which was "puerile and simple." The play was no more than a "lavish entertainment that's very delightful," which "we would like to enjoy without worrying about deep meanings" (3).

In addition to being the work of an acclaimed contemporary poet and playwright, the play was praised with exuberant superlatives in many reviews for the stylized décor of the Russian painter Egoroff, who had worked with the famed director Stanislavsky of the Moscow Art Theatre. It also received praise for the charming costumes designed by Mme Georgette LeBlanc, the wife of Maeterlinck, who played one of the lead roles, and for the skillful lighting. J. M. Garet's comment in his review "*L'Oiseau bleu*" in the March 2 issue of *Comoedia* after seeing the open rehearsal seems best to sum up the general critical response to the play: "Pure poetry triumphs in the theatre" (3).

Yet some later critics felt differently. According to Joseph Chiari, Maeterlinck attempted a compromise in his drama between "the realistic tendencies of his time and his poetic aspirations by treating poetic subjects and situations in prose," leading him to use the most outworn conventions of poetry in a way that caused his dramas to lack life and vitality (26). Based for the most part on legends or fairy tales, as in the case of *L'Oiseau bleu* (his most popular play), his dramas are a blend of symbolism, mysticism, and romanticism. Eliot, who probably first saw Maeterlinck's work on stage that spring in Paris,[5] noted the absence of the real world as a weakness in his 1934 essay "John Marston": "It is possible that what distinguishes poetic drama from prosaic drama is a kind of doubleness in the action, as if it took place on two planes at once. In this it is different from allegory, in which the abstraction is something conceived, not something differently felt, and from symbolism (as in the plays of Maeterlinck) in which the tangible world is deliberately diminished" (189). So, despite the fame of Maeterlinck in 1911—the year in which he received the Nobel Prize for Literature—his was an approach to poetic drama that Eliot would reject for himself.[6]

Les Frères Karamazov

A third sensation in the world of Parisian drama, and one that Eliot did attend (*Letters* 25), was the production that opened on April 6, 1911 as the inaugural work of the Théâtre des Arts: Copeau and Croué's stage adaptation in five acts of Dostoevsky's towering novel *Les Frères Karamazov* (Figure 23), which Eliot had read for the first time earlier that year—as he himself acknowledged: "During the period of my stay in Paris, Dostoevsky was very much a subject of interest amongst literary people and it was my friend and tutor, Alain Fournier [*sic*], who introduced me to this author. Under his instigation, I read *Crime and Punishment*, *The Idiot*, and *The Brothers Karamazov* in the French translation during the course of that winter. These three novels made a very profound impression on me . . ." (qtd. in Pope, "Prufrock and Raskolnikov Again" 319).

How exciting it must have been for Eliot to see a stage production of the novel at this new theatre dedicated to presenting innovative drama; perhaps he was a guest of Alain-Fournier,[7] who had received eight tickets from his friend Copeau (Rivière and Alain-Fournier 379). Copeau was a cofounder in 1909 of *La Nouvelle Revue Française* as well as a leading figure in the move for theatrical innovation who in 1913 would open the Théâtre du Vieux Colombier to put into practice new ideas. It is not far-fetched to imagine that Alain-Fournier, who often met Copeau for dinner or conversation (Rivière and Alain-Fournier 383–4), introduced Eliot to him. Both Alain-Fournier and Rivière, whose review of the play appeared in the May 1911 issue of *La Nouvelle Revue Française*, reveal an intense interest in and concern for the play's success in their letters of this period, as Howarth points out (366).

French readers anticipated this production with excitement, for, as Adolf Aderer writes in his review "Premières Réprésentations" in the April 7 issue of *Le Petit Parisien*, they were well acquainted with Dostoevsky's "biting and powerful talent, his tormented genius" (4). Despite its difficult intellectual level, reviews were extremely positive, typically praising the adaptation for its brilliant presentation of such a complex novel. In the April 15 issue of *Comoedia Illustré*, there were three different reviews of the play. In the most spectacular one, a four-page article featuring six photographs of various scenes, Francis Chevassu commented that, "thanks to the skillful adaptation of Copeau and Croué, the general public, rather than just the educated public, is able to experience the emotion of this drama, whose violence surpasses the most shocking inventions of our own [French] dramatists." Chevassu also noted that "their clear and logical development of the plot reveals an intelligent and scrupulous respect for the original" (422). A second review began and ended by praising the theatre itself as "a theatre of literary art . . . [which is] the most innovative today," with its inaugural production "the happiest manifestation" of its lofty goals. The writer went on to assert that one of the play's marvels was the way in which Copeau and Croué "adapted this powerful novel for the stage without losing any of its force and grandeur and preserved and sculpted its striking characters in unforgettable high reliefs" (Casalonga 412). In the third review Ernest La Jeunesse reflected both the great admiration for Russian works current in Paris and the intense response to this particular play in a breathless and packed style: "[The play] is beautiful, tremendously beautiful! It is overwhelming as it displays all the horror, all the mystery of the human condition, . . . the fatality, the bestiality, the very nothingness of moral nihilism, the basest carnal passion causing conflicts—and what conflicts!—between a son who still has ideals and a father who has only fleshly lusts . . ." (414). Finally, Rivière's review in the May 1911 issue of *La Nouvelle Revue Française* praised the authors for having produced "the dramatic equivalent of the complexity of Dostoevsky's novel" (758) with a plot which is "admirably clear" and with each character "a living person who is individualized and matchless" (759). He concluded, "The two authors have proven in this adaptation such a knowledge of drama that we expect not only another collaboration but also, because of their distinctive abilities, additional works of the highest value" (760).

Despite such reviews, the complexity and length of the play seem to have limited its commercial appeal, for Alain-Fournier wrote to Rivière on April 21 of the depressing experience of having recently seen the play again with only about forty people in the audience, a situation which he attributed to the paucity of publicity, arguing that with "a little publicity it would have been the greatest success of the year" (383). Yet the column *Courrier des Théâtres* in the April 27 issue of *Le Figaro* reported that the play, "which the media have unanimously described as a great success, attracts an elegant audience to the theatre every evening, and all the writers and artists express their esteem for this remarkable work" (4), and another in the May 4 issue commented that *Les Frères Karamazov* is "playing every evening to praise from its large audiences" (4). So well-known was the play that a cartoon entitled "Toujours Dindonnette" [Always stupid or, in current slang, Always an airhead] in the April 12 issue of *Comoedia* used it to ridicule the stupidity of women (Figure 24): a well-dressed society woman asks a male companion, who is smiling condescendingly at her ignorance, "Tell me, are the brothers Karamazov Russian dancers?," a reference to the Ballets Russes so popular in Paris at the time (5).[8]

Specific influences which the play may have had on Eliot are suggested by Gide's article published just prior to its opening on the front page of the April 4 issue of *Le Figaro*. After quoting Nietzsche's comment that "Dostoevsky is the only person to have taught me something about psychology," Gide emphasized that the realistic characters speak powerfully to people in 1911: "These 'colossal figures' address themselves to us [the modern-day French], and their voices are urgent. The three brothers, so similar and yet so different, . . . share the moral world that their old father has shamelessly deserted." He then noted the importance of "recognizing their disconcerting voices," as well as identifying with and learning from their situation, and ended with the hope that Copeau and Croué's adaptation would capture the original so effectively that "those spectators who have not already penetrated the depths of this novel will look at it with sufficient attention." Gide's assertion that

Dostoevsky's novel spoke directly to the French in 1911 and taught them crucial moral lessons, as well as his hope that the dramatic version would do the same, seems to have influenced Eliot's concept of the social and moral relevance of theatre and demonstrated for him the necessity of creating realistic characters in order to convey his themes. Eliot was perhaps thinking of this play when, to explain the quality of doubleness in poetic drama, he suggested in "John Marston," "We sometimes feel, in following the words and behaviour of some of the characters of Dostoevsky, that they are living at once on the plane that we know and on some other plane of reality from which we are shut out: their behaviour does not seem crazy, but rather in conformity with the laws of some world that we cannot perceive" (190).

Le Martyre de Saint Sébastien

The final dramatic offering of this sensational spring season was in many ways the most spectacular. *Le Martyre de Saint Sébastien*, a medieval mystery play in five acts which premiered at the Théâtre du Châtelet on May 22, 1911, was an international collaborative venture, with the poetic script by the notorious Italian poet Gabriele d'Annunzio, the music by the French composer Claude Debussy, the lavish sets and costumes by the Russian artist Léon Bakst, the choreography by the Russian Mikhail Fokine, and, in a daring reversal of gender roles, the part of Saint Sébastien performed by the Russian ballerina Ida Rubenstein. An extravaganza featuring fifty actors and 350 musicians, it was the talk of Paris, even though it had only nine performances (including the open rehearsal), closing on June 1 because, according to an article in the May 30 issue of *Le Petit Parisien* (4), the theatre was booked for rehearsals of the Ballets Russes after that date.[9]

How this production came to be is a fascinating story. In June of 1910, d'Annunzio, who had come to live in France earlier that year to escape his creditors in Italy, saw Ida Rubenstein dance the lead role in the Ballets Russes' sensuous production *Cléopâtre* and was inspired to write a play about Saint Sébastien that he had long had in mind: "'She has the legs of Saint Sébastien, which I have been looking for in vain for years'" (qtd. in Jullian 224). In a daring reversal of the tradition of men playing female roles in mystery plays, d'Annunzio created the starring role specifically for her: "I will take revenge for the feminine sex—Ida Rubenstein will play Saint Sébastien. Tall, slender, and flat-chested, she is absolute perfection for this role. Where could I find an actor whose body was so ethereal?" In truth, he was also motivated by his infatuation with her and was following a suggestion by his friend Comte Robert de Montesquiou that he should "write a work that would in an exceptional way bring to light the unique qualities of this artist and would raise her to the skies." He convinced her the next spring to accept the role and engaged Debussy, the leading contemporary French composer, to write the score (Seroff 290–1).

He spent several months in the summer and fall of 1910 doing research on French medieval mystery plays at the Bibliothèque nationale, reading the fifteenth- and sixteenth-century manuscripts on the death of Saint Sébastien, and study- ing Bach's *St. Matthew's Passion*.[10] Indeed, according to Seroff, he even had the blind organist of Notre Dame play the music of the great masters for him at night in the cathedral (291). Amassing material that filled the Villa Saint-Dominique near Arcachon where he was living, he then wrote the script in verse, finishing it in February 1911, just three months before the opening. Debussy was even more pressed for time, not even beginning to work on the score until mid-March be- cause of prior commitments. The last bars were completed during rehearsals, the complexity of the music overwhelming the performers and musicians as it came in page by page (Thompson 211).

Despite the feverish anticipation evoked by the advance publicity, the play was beset by various troubles before it even opened. As the reviewer identified as Un Monsieur de l'Orchestre in "La Soirée: *Le Martyre de Saint Sébastien* au Châtelet" in *Le Figaro's* May 23 issue pointed out, "The birth of *Le Martyre de Saint Sébastien* was accompanied by all sorts of problems" (5). Just two weeks before the premiere, the Vatican put d'Annunzio's works on the Index, and on May 16 the Archbishop of Paris condemned the play as "offensive to Christian consciences" (Thompson 213) and threatened Roman Catholics with excommunication if they attended a performance. The ostensible reason was its portrayal of a Christian saint in a heav- ily sensuous atmosphere, but in addition Rubenstein was a Jewish dancer famed for her physical beauty and both d'Annunzio and Debussy were proclaimed non- believers. It was considered a sacrilege that d'Annunzio in particular—a writer known for his eroticism—had written a religious play (Gullace 88). In a letter published in Parisian newspapers, d'Annunzio and Debussy defended the play as "profoundly religious, . . . a poetic glorification not only of the admirable Christian athlete but of all Christian heroism" (qtd. in Un Monsieur 5), and in an inter- view published in *Comoedia* Debussy asserted his right to compose religious music despite his lack of religious belief: "Even if I am not a practicing Catholic nor a believer, it did not cost me much effort to rise to the mystical heights which the poet's drama attains" (qtd. in Lockspeiser 98). Although the Church's ban created highly negative publicity and kept some Roman Catholics away, so powerful was the play's appeal that others defied it, as evidenced by a cartoon in the May 25 issue of *Le Figaro* (Figure 25) entitled "La Confession de la Parisienne" [The Confession of the Parisian Woman]. It depicts a well-dressed woman in a confessional booth who reveals that she has seen the play and is then asked by the priest, "How many times?" (3).

A second problem occurred on May 21, the day of the open dress rehearsal, which had been planned as a spectacular gala for a large group of invited guests that included "all the artistic and intellectual greats" (Un Monsieur 5). As Un Monsieur wittily put it, "Someone must have forgotten to invite the wicked old fairy Carabosse to the Christening of *Le Martyre de Saint Sébastien* because she came, after the earlier incident with the Archbishop, to complicate again and how tragically the birth of this beleaguered 'mystère.'" Unfortunately, the French Minister of War had been killed by a propeller at an airplane race at Issy-les-Moulineaux, so the organizers felt compelled to cancel the gala and close the rehearsal to all except the press. "Alas!," noted Un Monsieur, "M. Gabriel Astruc [the director of the theatre] proposes, but destiny disposes!" Although attempts were made to publicize the change in plans, a huge crowd gathered at the stage door, and all were ultimately allowed to view the rehearsal. Un Monsieur described with amusement how Astruc could not tell the critics from the curious ("He couldn't make the critics show their claws!") and thus had to let all enter. He also revealed that the audience was variously dressed and "sat down wherever they found seats with no regard for seat numbers in the dimly-lighted theatre" and that all experimented with a "do-it-yourself cloakroom" since no workers were there (5).

Despite these disconcerting problems, the much-anticipated opening of the play took place the next day (May 22) to both acclaim and criticism. The plot traces the life and death of Saint Sébastien in five acts, representing the five "mansions" of French medieval drama, with Debussy's music an integral part of the action. Act I takes place in the Court of the Lilies as Sébastien, an accomplished archer, receives the stigmata, is converted to Christianity, strips off his armor, and walks barefoot on burning coals, portrayed in an ecstatic dance choreographed by Fokine and performed by Rubenstein to the music of a magnificent polyphonic chorus. So powerful was this episode that the sophisticated Parisian audiences exclaimed, "Mais elle va mourir!" [But she's going to die!] (Birnbaum, qtd. in Spencer 142). In Act II, whose prelude is "a glittering piece of orchestral writing with an undercurrent of terror," he destroys the temples of the false gods and converts to Christianity the virgin Erigone, who sings an aria derived from a medieval Italian song (Lockspeiser 230). Act III, which "unfolds like a sumptuous fresco" (Roger-Marx 538), begins with a prelude of "cruel fanfares" which foreshadows the action as Sébastien refuses the Emperor Diocletian's command to renounce Christianity, and the women of Byblos in a chorus dominated by the cry "Pleurez! Pleurez!" [Weep! Weep!] pour out their grief over his impending death. The scene of his death is dramatically rendered in Act IV, following a plaintive prelude of eerie tremulos, as he is bound to a tree and shot with arrows by the Emperor's archers while the women mourn. In the final act, he ascends to heaven to a series of majestic polyphonic choruses with a soprano voice representing his soul soaring above the chorus and orchestra, after which an impressive hymn, "Louez le Seigneur" [Praise the Savior], the French version of Psalm 105, concludes the play (Lockspeiser 231).

The role of Saint Sébastien, which is the very core of the play, was a showpiece for Rubenstein. With the exception of the solo sung by a soprano as the saint ascends to heaven, the part was entirely spoken, with episodes such as the walking on coals interpreted in dance by the ballerina. D'Annunzio envisioned Saint Sébastien as a combination of a Christian saint and the handsome pagan figure Adonis: "I have long dreamed of the bleeding youth . . . transfigured in the Christian myth, like the beautiful wounded god mourned by the women of Byblos before the catafalque of ebony and purple in the vernal equinox" (qtd. in Thompson 210). Rubenstein's physical beauty with its erotic overtones was, in his view, an ideal representation of his hero. He was defying tradition and deliberately provoking scandal by casting a woman in the role, and, by choosing this particular woman with her reputation for sensuality, he created a sensation. Un Monsieur rhapsodized, "How exquisite she is in Act I, so pale and svelte in her golden armor! She resembles a knight escaped from an old altar piece, a delicate St. Michael of Raphael, or a St. George escaped from a watercolor of Gustave Moreau" (5).

The most sexually provocative scene, mixing spiritual and sexual ecstasy and pain so intensely as to cause a shiver of excitement in each member of the audience, is that of Saint Sébastien's death, when he is bound to a laurel tree and shot by the archers after the Emperor commands that he be killed gently under a shower of blossoms "because he is beautiful" (Gullace 89). D'Annunzio said that he was inspired by the words of Veronica Gambara, a woman poet of the Renaissance, "He that loves me most, wounds me," which are echoed by Saint Sébastien as he awaits the arrows that will pierce his flesh: "He that wounds me the more deeply, the more deeply loves me" (Thompson 210). Indeed, Bakst's sketch of Rubenstein for this scene (Figure 26), in which she is bound with a thick rope and pierced by numerous arrows, was published in the June 1 issue of *Comoedia Illustré*, with a handwritten inscription by d'Annunzio that reads, "The heart must kill its love so that it can return seven times more passionate" (536).

Most reviewers, all of them male, seem to have been seduced by Rubenstein in the role and were as infatuated as was d'Annunzio, given her sensuality and the combination of passion and pain in her portrayal of the role. Emery in a review entitled "*Le Martyre de Saint Sébastien*: Comment ils ont joué" [How it was performed]" in the May 23 issue of *Comoedia* noted that she conveyed marvelously the ardent fanaticism and mystic exaltation of a Christian martyr. . . . Saint Sébastien like all martyrs was animated by a frenzy of love and grief which flowed in his veins like a devouring fire and burned both the flesh and the spirit. All who have loved—whether a woman, a god, or a sacred idea—know the irresistible need to sacrifice oneself, to suffer, to pant, to die for their love . . . . The melodious murmur of a woman's voice in ecstasy makes us feel in our hearts the grievous joy of her agony. This bizarre incarnation of the archer Sébastien by a woman with a supple and voluptuous body of pale and gleaming flesh who portrays, in languid and sensual dances, the Stations of the Cross is a savage, insane, but very impressive work of art, which produces piercing sensations, divine or diabolical, in our minds.(3)

Perhaps, however, Jean Cocteau was the most straightforward, for he ended his review "Madame Ida Rubenstein dans 'Saint Sébastien'" in the June 1 issue of *Comoedia*, which was dedicated totally to Rubenstein, with the comment, "*She is delicious*" (2).

D'Annunzio's decision to write the play in verse, and in a language not his own, was both daring and ambitious. Even more remarkable, he researched the verse of French medieval mystery plays in depth in order to produce an authentic reproduction of it. Léon Blum opened his May 23 review on the front page of *Comoedia* by declaring, "Today French poetry includes in its ranks another great poet" and marveled that "a foreigner (an Italian) is capable of writing French poetry with such freedom, certitude, and grandeur, that he has such mastery and knows the secrets of vocabulary and rhythm, that he can bring to life a language which is not his native language"; he ended by proclaiming that d'Annunzio had "enriched the repertoire of French lyricism, demonstrating more delicacy in rhythm, more certitude in vocabulary, more richness and grace in the creation and placement of images than contemporary French poets." Similar praise appeared the same day in Brussel's review in the column *Les Théâtres* in *Le Figaro*. He devoted three entire paragraphs to the verse, noting that the play was in octosyllables, the traditional verse of French liturgical dramas of the Middle Ages, commented on the use of the rondel and the villanelle, and concluded that the poetry gave the work "the most singular and rare beauty" (5).

However, there were also problems with the poetry. In addition to errors in grammar and syntax,[11] there was a jarring mixture of vocabulary. Blum himself pointed out that the play contained language from "different historical periods, that of the medieval epic, of Montaigne or Amyot, of Gautier or Banville, while the rhythms recall by turns the verse of medieval chronicles of heroic deeds and of the mystery plays, the techniques of the Parnassians, and those of the recent Symbolist poets" (1), with the result being that the poetry had an inconsistent, artificial, and stilted quality. In a review in *La Nouvelle Revue Française* entitled sarcastically "M. d'Annunzio et l'Art," Ghéon argued that the poet had committed a "blasphemy against art" (12), commenting that d'Annunzio used the diction of "our oldest writers and also of our most recent ones" and claiming that his octosyllabic verse was mechanical and monotonous (7). To make matters worse, as Emery bluntly put it in his review in *Comoedia*, Rubenstein has "a deplorable voice for the stage; she pronounces badly, declaims too violently; her accent deforms the words so that one can barely distinguish the author's text in her sighs and howls" (2). In a review in the column *Au Théâtre* in the May 23 issue of *Le Matin*, Guy Launay simply said, "It is impossible to understand Rubenstein because of her [Russian] accent" (2).

While the poetry received mixed reviews, Debussy's music and Bakst's sets and costumes were uniformly praised. In composing the score, Debussy ventured into new territory, most notably in producing music of a religious nature and in creating vocal music for both chorus and solo voices in addition to the orchestral music which had been his forte previously, thus expanding his range of accomplishments considerably. The music required 350 musicians for the orchestra and chorus. The famed André Caplet conducted the orchestra for the first time in Paris, while the chorus had three directors. In a review of the music in the May 23 issue of *Comoedia*, L. Vuillemin asserted that Debussy had "shed his old skin" and "given free rein to his harmonic aspirations" (2). Alfred Bruneau, in a review in the column *Au Théâtre* in the May 23 issue of *Le Matin*, proclaimed that the music was "among the most beautiful compositions that Debussy has written, striking because of its clarity, serenity, and power despite being written in a short time." He described as "meriting unreserved admiration" the chorus expressing the women's grief at the death of Saint Sébastien and the "vast and glorious final 'Alleluia'" (2). The writer of a short review in the May 25 issue of *Le Petit Parisien* said simply that "the music of Debussy revels in purity" (4), perhaps a not so subtle comment on the charges that, as a nonbeliever, he could not write religious music. Indeed, Debussy wrote the score in a state of exaltation and was so moved by the music at one rehearsal that he wept openly (Seroff 292, 297).

The sets and the 500 costumes by Bakst were spectacular, extravagant, and bold and, like the poetry, were a mixture of different cultures and historical periods. The Byzantine settings, which "suited Bakst's sumptuous oriental taste" (Spencer 142), merged antiquity and the Middle Ages "with a deliberate anachronism" (Roger-Marx 534). In his review "*Le Martyre de Saint Sébastien*: La mise en scène et les décors" [the set and scenery] in the May 23 issue of *Comoedia*, Louis Schneider described the "magic of [Bakst's] reds, emerald greens, golds, the song of his blues from deep sea waters—and the sophisticated naïveté of the design. . . . [The set] is like a dream in which stained glass windows come to life" (2). While each of the five sets was impressive, Diocletian's Palace in the third act was singled out for praise by Un Monsieur as "remarkable with its black twisted columns and its ceiling lighted with a somber and mystical blue" (5). The costumes included "medieval cowls, Moorish turbans, Greek tunics, and Roman togas" (Spencer 143). Rubenstein's various costumes were the most memorable: a suit of golden armor and helmet with a large bow, a full-length cloak made of hexagonal designs, and the appearance of near nakedness in the scene of the martyrdom. The extravagance of the costumes and their influence on Parisian fashions were reflected in a cartoon sarcastically entitled "Élégance" appearing in the June 15 issue of *Comoedia* (Figure 27): a woman wearing an enormous hat and dress decorated with geometrical designs and carrying a matching parasol answers a male observer's apparent query about where she got the idea for such an outfit, saying, "It's obvious, isn't it? I was inspired by the costumes in d'Annunzio's *Le Martyre de Saint Sébastien*" (3).

Despite its sensational nature, the play suffered from a number of defects. In addition to the artificial quality of the poetry and Rubenstein's poor pronunciation, the excessive emphasis on physical beauty and sensuality in the depiction of a Christian saint detracted from the spiritual aspect of the play. The sheer complexity of themes and images was confusing, made the plot and meanings difficult to comprehend, and slowed the dramatic action. With a five-hour running time, the curtain fell, as the reviewer in the May 25 issue of *Le Petit Parisien* reported, "precisely at midnight" (4). The vastness of the stage, the magnitude of the setting, and the large number of participants added more confusion and limited the audience's ability to hear both words and music (Blum 2).

Eliot must have seen a performance of this spectacular and controversial production, for various indications of its influence can be detected in both his poetry and drama.[12] Three poems written during or before 1914–15, "The Burnt Dancer," "The Love Song of St. Sebastian," and "The Death of Saint Narcissus," all reflect the subject matter and erotic atmosphere of this production.

The first describes a black moth caught in a flame, an apparent symbol of the agony and ecstasy of martyrdom: "The patient acolyte of pain, / . . . The singèd reveller of the fire / . . . Desires completion of his loss" (32, 34, 37). The refrain in French, "O danse mon papillon noir" [O dance, my black moth] (14, 29, 41), in combination with the fire, evokes Rubenstein's ecstatic dance depicting Saint Sébastien's walking on burning coals.

"The Love Song of St. Sebastian," which Eliot wrote not long before sending it to Aiken on July 25, 1914,[13] is even more erotic and brutal, describing what seem to be two methods of dealing with one's feelings of lust for a beloved: in the first stanza the saint dies on his beloved's breast after flogging himself, while in the second he strangles—or imagines strangling—her.[14] He indicates to Aiken that his immediate sources of inspiration were *paintings* of the saint: "I have studied S. Sebastians" (*Letters* 44), referring to the "*three* great" works which he listed for Aiken in a letter of July 19, 1914—those of Mantegna in Venice, Antonello of Messina in Bergamo, and Memling in Brussels (*Letters* 41). He had seen the first two in the summer of 1911 and the third in early July 1914. However, Eliot's apparent allusion to Rubenstein as Saint Sébastien in the July 25 letter to Aiken, "[N]o one ever painted a female Sebastian, did they?" (*Letters* 44), implies that the Paris production was another major source of inspiration. Furthermore, the title as well as the actual or imagined murder may refer to the play's sensational concept of the interaction between love and pain, demonstrated most dramatically in Saint Sébastien's death at the hands of the Emperor's archers, with whom he pleads,

O archers,
archers, if ever you loved me,
let me know your love
again, in the arrows!
I tell you, I tell you,
the one who wounds me
the most deeply loves me
the most deeply!

As noted earlier, d'Annunzio echoes this idea in the inscription on Bakst's sketch of Rubenstein tied to the laurel tree with an arrow piercing her throat. As the arrows penetrate Saint Sébastien's flesh in the play, he cries out in ecstasy, "Again! Again! Again! Again! Eternal love!" This dramatic and highly erotic love song may also have inspired "The Love Song of J. Alfred Prufrock," begun in Paris but completed in Munich just two months after the production.

While Eliot's letter to Aiken lists as sources only those three paintings of St. Sebastian, he saw other depictions of the saint during his Paris year. Mantegna's 1480s version of *Saint Sébastian*[15] was a 1910 acquisition of the Louvre and thus a showpiece at the time. In grayish tones, it portrays the saint tied to fluted columns with nine arrows piercing his body, as he casts an anguished and sorrowful look heavenward. The Louvre also owned a *Saint Sebastian* by Perugino, with an inscription at the bottom which read, "Your arrows pierce me." In this version the saint, who leans against a column with his hands apparently bound behind him, is pierced by only two arrows and gazes upward with a sweet, serene expression. In addition, during Eliot's possible stop-over in London on his way to Paris in October 1910 and/or during his holiday there in April 1911, he probably viewed in the National Gallery Pollaiolo's *Saint Sebastian* (see Ricks 268), in which "the saint's physical beauty provides a certain sensual abandon that stands out more than his mystical ecstasy" and which d'Annunzio claimed as his inspiration (Gullace 88).

Finally, I suggest that *Le Martyre de Saint Sébastien* and the ballet *Narcisse*, performed by the Ballets Russes in Paris in June 1911,[16] coalesced in Eliot's imagination to produce "The Death of Saint Narcissus," an erotic poem presenting this figure from Greek mythology as a religious martyr who devotes himself to God to escape the lustful desires of the body. The speaker's description of his dancing on the burning sand while waiting for flaming arrows of lust and/or of physical chastisement to penetrate his flesh (34–6) reflects rather directly both Saint Sébastien's walking on burning coals in the first act and his agonizing but ecstatic death in the fourth act of the former.

In addition to Eliot's poetry, his concepts of and goals for drama, as well as specific details of some of his plays, indicate the influence of this unforgettable production. An article entitled "Les Auteurs du 'Martyre du Saint Sébastien'" in the June 1 issue of *Comoedia Illustré* contains the statement that d'Annunzio's "desire to address the multitudes directly led him to write works for the theatre" (527). Eliot's wish to reach large audiences and his belief that the "ideal medium for poetry, . . . and the most direct means of social 'usefulness' for poetry, is the theatre" ("Use of Poetry" 94) may directly reflect d'Annunzio's reason for writing drama.

In addition, d'Annunzio's attempt to revive verse drama may have served as an early inspiration for Eliot's similar goal, although the latter surely saw as well a number of pitfalls to avoid. While d'Annunzio's verse was praised for its re-creation of ancient meters and rhymes and for its lyric beauty, those very meters and rhymes along with its jarring mixture of archaic and modern language gave it a stilted, old-fashioned quality unappealing to modern audiences. Eliot realized early on, perhaps as a result of d'Annunzio's problems, that, for the poetry of his plays to speak to theatregoers in the twentieth century, he would have to use meters and language close to those of actual speech and avoid calling attention to the poetry as poetry: "If you write a play in verse, then the verse ought to be a medium to look THROUGH and not a pretty decoration to look AT" ("Five Points" 10). In order to make his plays meaningful to modern audiences with "telephones and motor cars and radio sets," he used a flexible meter and largely deleted rhyme to "give the effect of conversation" ("Poetry and Drama" 141, 139).

Last, d'Annunzio's choice of a religious subject demonstrated that it was viable for a modern play, and the production of this religious verse drama may have been an inspiration for the difficult dramatic goal which Eliot later set for himself: to write verse drama in an age conditioned to prose and to write of spiritual and moral concerns in an age largely devoid of and unsympathetic to them. His belief that poetry rather than prose was the ideal medium for expressing the intensity and universality of spiritual states is reflected by one of the speakers in his essay "A Dialogue on Dramatic Poetry": "The human soul, in intense emotion, strives to express itself in verse. . . . The tendency . . . of prose drama is to emphasize the ephemeral and superficial; if we want to get at the permanent and universal we tend to express ourselves in verse" (34).

Of his seven plays, *Murder in the Cathedral* bears the most obvious signs of the influence of *Le Martyre de Saint Sébastien* with its portrayal of the twelfth-century martyrdom of St. Thomas à Becket. Perhaps remembering the problems of d'Annunzio's verse, Eliot was aware of the difficult challenge of creating a diction and style appropriate to the historical period that also appealed to modern audiences; he noted in "Poetry and Drama" that the style could not be modern since the subject was historical, nor could it be archaic since he wanted to convey the contemporary relevance of Thomas's martyrdom (139). Eliot met the challenge in a number of ways: he did not rely excessively on iambic meter; he employed occasional unexpected rhymes; and he chose a neutral vocabulary "committed neither to the present nor to the past" ("Poetry and Drama" 139), consisting of both formal, elevated words and simple, commonplace ones. He also effectively blended Christian hymns and liturgy (the "Dies Irae" and the "Te Deum"), Anglo-Saxon alliterative verse, rhymed doggerel (the knights' verbal attacks on Thomas), and jazz rhythms ("Come down Daniel"). The result linked not only the past and present but also the extraordinary martyr and the ordinary human being. Furthermore, the anguish of the poor women of Canterbury at the impending death of Thomas is very similar to—and perhaps inspired by—that of the women of Byblos, who in anticipation of the death of Saint Sébastien cry out, "Pleurez! Pleurez!" with "intolerable insistence and intensity" (Lockspeiser 231). Eliot also treats the theme of martyrdom in *The Cocktail Party*, in which a modern-day saint, Celia Coplestone, is crucified near an anthill in an African country, though her death is described rather than portrayed.

As with d'Annunzio's versification, problems with his treatment of a religious subject may have been instructive to Eliot. Because of the excessive sensuality in general and of Saint Sébastien[17] in particular and also because of the production's spectacular complexity and length, the play lacked "real religious emotion and psychological interest," it "dissolved into pure spectacle and music," and its "mysticism was purely decorative" (Gullace 89). As Ghéon pointed out in his highly critical review "M. d'Annunzio et l'Art" in the July 1911 issue of *La Nouvelle Revue Française*, the poet's confused mixture of the pagan and the Christian produced a phony religious drama, devoid of sincere belief: "From this confusion, this incoherence, a monster was born at once mystical and depraved, a black sun from which shone a gloomy malaise felt by all the spectators, even the greatest nonbelievers.

True faith wasn't apparent; we were in the presence of a counterfeit work, fake in its character, its essence, and in the presence of an author who had no respect for his subject" (13). In Eliot's drama, however, spiritual issues are foremost in importance, with spectacle and sensuality at a minimum and his sincerity never in question.

Ghéon's "Sur le 'Théâtre Populaire'"

In addition to the foregoing theatrical events, Ghéon's article "Sur le 'Théâtre Populaire'" in the November 1911 issue of *La Nouvelle Revue Française* seems to have influenced the latent dramatist in Eliot, for a number of its ideas are echoed in his essays on drama and in his own plays. The prominent French drama critic argued for the return of popular drama, while in the process defining it, giving its characteristics, and criticizing realistic theatre. He began by stating that "dramatic art requires *a priori* the immediate collaboration of the spectator, a direct contact with him, his acceptance, his enthusiasm, and his joy" (503). This idea is reflected in Eliot's essays such as "Marie Lloyd," in which he states that the working man who went to see her "was engaged in that collaboration of the audience with the artist which is necessary in all art and most obviously in dramatic art" (174). Ghéon then made a distinction between the theatre of the people and popular theatre. He stated that the former, "which has never ceased to exist," includes "farce, vaudeville, and melodrama, yesterday the drama of cape and sword, today the detective play," but it excludes the élite. The latter, however, is for all, and he cited the Greek theatre as an ideal example (504). The problem in creating popular theatre today is that "our modern era conspicuously lacks the common ground of a shared faith." However, he believed that there is a "store of common aspirations, of natural heroism, of a popular ideal—national, human, in truth humanitarian—a ground on which we would all be able to meet," and he expressed the hope that someone will accomplish the task of writing a work based on this belief (504–5). These words echo in Eliot's essays in various comments on the lack of common ground in the modern world and the need for artists to create innovative ways of connecting with their audiences. For example, Eliot asserts that the "present situation is radically different from any in which poetry has been produced in the past: namely, . . . now there is nothing in which to believe" ("Use of Poetry" 88).[18] And indeed the young Eliot may have imagined himself as the "one among a hundred" (505) who would produce the great drama of which Ghéon dreamed.

The remainder of this intriguing essay described the characteristics of popular drama, particularly in contrast to those of realistic drama. First, popular drama must adopt "an attitude of greatness," the lack of which is the "capital error of realism, the reason for its weakness and its tediousness." Realistic drama has caused the hero to "descend to the level of the public, and inevitably to the most mediocre and ordinary, since it welcomes the crude banal details of daily life" (505). While comedy can accommodate this diminution of the hero, tragedy cannot, and Ghéon suggested that "it is the popular theatre of tragedy which is uniquely the question here," calling for it to rise above the "atmosphere of the everyday," to "tear audiences from the earth and raise them to a higher truth," and to create main characters who are heroic (506). His conviction that a popular tragedy must present a clear, unified plot and employ lyricism and the power of the word to reach and "weld together" the varied members of its audiences (507) must have struck a chord with Eliot, who was to dedicate himself to restoring verse drama for a general audience.

In his powerful and somewhat daring conclusion, Ghéon first listed the characteristics of his ideal tragedy of popular theatre: "Tragic occurrences, human truth, lyricism, grandeur in simplicity, these are the characteristics necessary for popular tragedy, if indeed a society as confused as ours can welcome it. A great action, clear in its progression and with an admirable design, crowned with poetry, constitutes again for the spectators the highest reality. Certainly this drama is far from the pseudo-psychological war-clubs, the arguments based on law-briefs, the so-called paintings of morals and manners which the Parisian public seems to cherish." Then he closes with the unexpected statement that, while the "most urgent and least foolhardy course might be to direct our efforts towards creating a very exclusive theatre, to write especially for readers of poetry, and, if I may say so, to risk the failure of a *Phèdre*, as did Racine," other routes to achieving a popular theatre should not be barred, with the one caveat that it must remain artistic: "New dramatic art is open to the most diverse paths, the only condition being that it must remain or become again an art" (508). This essay issued two calls that Eliot himself answers in his later work for the theatre: a call for playwrights to re-create for the modern world the grandeur and heroism of high tragedy written in verse, and a call for new strategies to address the attainment of this lofty dramatic goal. Indeed, although overlooked in Eliot scholarship, Ghéon's essay seems to have been an important source in the formulation of Eliot's own ideas about modern drama, as seen in both his plays and essays.

The Parisian theatre world of 1910–11 thus had much to offer this eager and intelligent young man who was to dedicate a portion of his literary career to the revival of verse drama. As a hotbed of innovation and experimentation as well as a preserver of the great classics, Parisian theatre provided Eliot with a variety of experiences that would influence his views on and practice of the dramatic arts.

· 4 ·

THE VISUAL ARTS

Eliot's description of Paris as a stunning combination of the past and the future was also accurate for the visual arts, for the city was a magnificent and extensive repository of great art works of the past—from the ancient Greeks to the nineteenth century—as well as the acknowledged hotbed for a host of rapidly developing and shockingly innovative new movements that were to change the art world forever. With an interest in art from his Harvard years, he profited from this opportunity to immerse himself in the fertile and exciting Parisian art scene. In addition, he visited museums and exhibitions in London, Venice, Bergamo, and, quite probably, Munich. In this chapter, I describe both the classic works of art and the contemporary art movements which Eliot encountered during that year and which influenced his work, both immediately and in the future.

Eliot arrived in Paris with at least a rudimentary knowledge of the visual arts. At Harvard, he had taken two art history courses as an undergraduate: History of Ancient Art in the fall of 1907 and Florentine Painting in the fall of 1909 (*Letters* xix-xx). His detailed lecture notes for the second course in King's College Library indicate that it focused on painters of the fourteenth and fifteenth centuries and included, among others, Uccello, Filippo Lippi, Fra Diamante, Fra Angelico, Ghiberti, Donatello, Brunelleschi, and Masaccio.[1] According to his essay on Gordon Craig in King's College Library, Eliot also attributed to his undergraduate days at Harvard his discovery of Japanese prints, Édouard Manet (1832–1883), the French painter and printmaker who was an important forerunner of the Impressionists, and of Claude Monet (1840–1926), the French founder and leader of the Impressionists. Furthermore, after seeing a reproduction of Manet's *Woman with a Parrot* in a book on French Impressionism, he wrote a sonnet about it entitled "On a Portrait" in 1909 (Dickey 1). Thus, when he came to the art-rich city of Paris, he was familiar with a wide spectrum of the visual arts from ancient times to the Renaissance to the contemporary period and from both the occident and the orient—quite a considerable scope for a young man whose main academic focus was literature, foreign languages, and philosophy.

Established Works of Art in Paris

Soon after arriving in Paris in October, he no doubt went to the Louvre to see some of the great works of art from the past that he had studied or discovered for himself at Harvard. Since he owned a copy of Baedeker's 1908 London guidebook and marked the pieces of art which he wanted to see, we can reasonably assume that he did the same with Baedeker's *Paris et ses environs*, even though it has not survived. However, the 1907 edition of that popular Paris guidebook can help us to determine what he could have seen. Perhaps after viewing the Louvre's most famous works, *Winged Victory*, *Venus de Milo*, and *Mona Lisa*, he explored its rich collection of Italian art, which, according to Baedeker, contained a large number of masterpieces of the first order. Those of the fourteenth and fifteenth centuries were recent acquisitions, while those of the grand artists of the *Cinquecento* were largely acquired by François I. Baedeker stated that the Louvre had the richest collection of the great Italian masters of the *Cinquecento* on this side of the Alps, naming first Leonardo da Vinci (who spent the last years of his life in France) and listing among his paintings in the Louvre not only *Mona Lisa*, the "most celebrated portrait of a woman in the world," but also the original version of *The Madonna [Virgin] of the Rocks* (115–16).

Eliot must have viewed this version of the famous painting in the Louvre as well as the second version in London's National Gallery during a possible stopover in that city in October 1910 and/or during his Easter holiday in London in April 1911. The two versions of the painting have an intriguing and somewhat mysterious history. Commissioned from da Vinci by the Milanese Confraternity of the Immaculate Conception as part of a polyptych for the Confraternity's chapel in Milan's Church of San Francesco Grande, the original painting was completed between 1483 and 1486. However, it apparently did not meet with the approval of the Confraternity because of its unorthodox aspects, and a long legal battle ensued (Marani 124–5). This version was perhaps brought to France by the sixty-five-year-old da Vinci himself when he accepted the invitation of the young king François I in 1516 to live under his patronage at a small castle in the Loire Valley, where he died in 1519. Indeed, he may have given it to the king in appreciation for his support, for the painting is a part of the collection of François I in the Louvre. At the time of Eliot's residence in Paris, it was displayed in the Grande Galerie (Baedeker 124). The second, more orthodox version was completed between 1506 and 1508 and was installed in the Church of San Francesco Grande. After the dissolution of the Confraternity in 1781, it was sold to an Englishman and, following several changes of ownership, was acquired by London's National Gallery in 1886.[2]

Both paintings depict the Virgin, an angel, and St. John the Baptist and Christ as toddlers in front of a dark grotto of jagged rocks, with a lake in the background and various plants in the foreground.[3] However, there are significant differences in the two versions. In the original (Figure 28), the figures have softer faces illuminated with a golden-hued light, while the grotto in the background is darker, more mysterious, and more sinister. The Virgin's robe is very dark blue, she tilts her head toward St. John, and her face bears a gentle look. The angel to her right wears a robe of soft red and green, she points at St. John, and her face has a mild expression. The fingers of both the Virgin's and the angel's hands are sharply angled, creating what some have seen as a menacing effect.[4] None of the holy figures has a halo. In the second version, da Vinci apparently conformed to the wishes of the Confraternity by creating a more conventional painting with idealized figures and a less forbidding background with blue and green water and light behind the farthest rocks. The figures are slightly larger and closer to the viewer. The colors are more subdued with the colorful gown of the angel replaced by a dull beige, brown, and grey-blue one and with Mary's robe of lighter blue. Mary has gentler, more rounded hands, and the angel's hand has been removed altogether. The faces are cooler and more abstract; their skin tones are whiter so that they have what Robert M. Wallace describes as "a corpse-like pallor" (147). Most obvious, however, is the addition of conventional religious elements denoting the holiness of the figures: halos for the Virgin, St. John, and Christ, a cruciform staff for St. John, and wings for the angel (for side-by-side versions, see Marani 126–7 or Wallace 50–51).

When Eliot composed *The Waste Land* in 1921, he included an ironic allusion to *The Madonna of the Rocks* in the fortune of the protagonist in Section I: "Here is Belladonna, the Lady of the Rocks, / The lady of situations" (48–49). The woman's name and the appositives bear a complexity of meanings, suggesting in a variety of ways that, although she is beautiful, she is a danger to the protagonist. Literally, Belladonna is Italian for "beautiful woman," but it also evokes ironically the similar word "Madonna," while "the Lady of the Rocks" is a secular version of the title of da Vinci's painting, evoking the jagged, dark rocks of both paintings and suggesting hardness and danger in this modern context. Belladonna is also the name of the deadly nightshade, a highly poisonous plant cultivated in France in particular, from which were derived medicinal alkaloids used in sedatives, stimulants, and antispasmodics until the mid-twentieth century, when, because of its potential for causing death, it was superseded by synthetic drugs ("Belladonna," *Encyclopaedia Britannica* 950). Indeed, since ancient times, it served as both a sedative and a poison, and, in medieval Europe, witchcraft and devil-worship cults used it for its hallucinogenic effects. Eliot clearly implies that this beautiful woman in the protagonist's future is dangerous—capable of sedating, disorienting, or killing him, whether physically or emotionally.

Interestingly, as recently as the early twentieth century, women used belladonna as a cosmetic, placing a dot of the red substance in the inner corners of the eyes because of its ability to dilate the pupils, an effect thought to increase sexual allure. This aspect of the allusion reinforces the idea that a sexually attractive woman poses an emotional danger to the protagonist. This modern sensual woman functions as the opposite of the traditional concept of the Virgin as a gentle mother figure who comforts suffering humanity.

Knowledge of the two versions of da Vinci's painting increases the complexity of the allusion. The eerie grotto with its jagged, dark rocks in both versions, but more strikingly in the original; the sharply-angled fingers of the Virgin and the angel in the original; and the ghostly pallor of the faces in the second version all contribute to the sinister aspects of Eliot's Belladonna. Thus these two paintings, which Eliot must have seen during his year abroad in 1910–1911, contributed to one of the most complex allusions in *The Waste Land*.

Located quite close to *The Madonna of the Rocks* in the Grande Galerie are two paintings of the school of da Vinci that may have influenced the allusion to John the Baptist in "The Love Song of J. Alfred Prufrock": "But though I have wept and fasted, wept and prayed, / Though I have seen my head (grown slightly bald) brought in upon a platter, / I am no prophet—and here's no great matter" (81–3). *Salomé Receives the Head of Saint John the Baptist* by Bernardino Luini (1485?-1532) depicts Salomé holding a platter, while above it an unseen person's hand suspends the head of the saint by the hair (Figure 29). This dramatic work is from the collection of Louis XIV. Nearby is Andrea Solario's 1507 painting *The Head of Saint John the Baptist*, portraying the head (thought to be an autoportrait of the painter) on a footed platter. These two classic works of art seem to have combined with a source from the low-brow world of popular entertainment to inspire Prufrock's striking allusion: the popular decapitation act at Parisian street fairs in which, according to Nancy Perloff, "the performer cut off his head and presented it on a plate to his baffled spectators. This act—which evokes the decapitated head of John the Baptist delivered to the Princess Salomé on a silver platter—underscores the enormous appeal of the Salomé legend for artists . . . and for the Parisian public during the early decades of the twentieth century" (30–1; see also Chapter 8). Eliot this early in his career was thus already a master at blending high art with ordinary, everyday material, a technique which he employed most brilliantly in many startling images and allusions in *The Waste Land*.

Also in the Louvre were three works by Michelangelo, which, along with those in London's National Gallery, Royal Academy, and British Museum, may have contributed to the famous couplet in "The Love Song of J. Alfred Prufrock": "In the room the women come and go / Talking of Michelangelo" (13–15, 35–6).[5] The famous unfinished marble statues *The Dying Slave* and *The Rebellious Slave* as well as an unfinished drawing entitled *The Sorrow over the Dead Christ* are the only works by Michelangelo in the Louvre.

Two paintings in the Louvre portraying the martyrdom of Saint Sebastian may well have contributed to Eliot's interest in this saint (*Letters* 41, 44, 376) and specifically to his poem "The Love Song of St. Sebastian," completed in July 1914. As noted in Chapter 3, the Louvre in 1910 acquired Mantegna's 1480s version of *Saint Sebastian*.[6] Because it was an important new acquisition and thus a showpiece at the time, displayed in the Salle des Nouvelles Acquisitions, it perhaps instituted the "particular admiration" (*Letters* 376) which Eliot held for this painter.[7] Its portrayal of the saint tied to fluted columns with nine arrows piercing his body and with an anguished look on his face, which is turned toward heaven, is striking in its melancholy atmosphere (Figure 30). In contrast, the *Saint Sebastian* by Perugino, with an inscription at the bottom reading, "Your arrows pierce me," bears a serene, even sweet expression on his face as he too gazes upward while bound to a column, his body pierced by two arrows.

"The Love Song of St. Sebastian" seems to have been inspired by these two paintings along with several other works: the Pollaiuolo *The Martyrdom of Saint Sebastian* (marked in his London Baedeker) and other depictions of the saint in London's National Gallery; the spectacular d'Annunzio production *Le Martyre de Saint Sébastien*; and the "*three* great" *Saint Sebastian* paintings that Eliot refers to in a letter of July 25, 1914 to Conrad Aiken containing a copy of the recently completed poem (*Letters* 41, 44). As discussed in Chapter 3, these paintings are Mantegna's in the Ca d' Oro in Venice, da Messina's in the Academia Carrara in Bergamo, and Memling's in Brussels. Eliot saw the first two in the summer of 1911 during his trip to northern Italy (Ricks 268) and the third in early July 1914 during a trip to Belgium.[8]

While these particular works of art by established masters seem to have exerted the most influence on Eliot, many others were exhibited in Paris throughout the period of his residence, both in museums and in numerous exhibitions. Among the latter were exhibitions of great artists of the late nineteenth century in December, of Orientalistes in February, and of Ingres and Dutch masters in April.

Established Works of Art in London

Eliot also saw great works of the past in London in October 1910 and/or April 1911. In his Baedeker's *London and Its Environs*, he marked a wide array of works of art in the margins with short vertical marks, dots, or check marks, indicating an ambitious program that would take quite a number of days to complete. In fact, he accomplished most of this plan, for he wrote to Eleanor Hinckley upon his return to Paris from London in late April that he had been to the National Gallery, the British Museum, the Wallace Collection (where he "made notes!!"), and the South Kensington Museum ("in large part") and thus had not "wasted [his] time" (*Letters* 19).

In the section on the National Gallery, he marked Italian Renaissance painters of the fifteenth century, including Botticelli, Pollaiuolo, Cosimo, Fra Angelico, Uccello, da Vinci (specifically *The Madonna of the Rocks*), Correggio, and Titian (specifically *Bacchus and Ariadne*). The entry for da Vinci's second version of *The Madonna of the Rocks* reads, "*Leonardo de Vinci* (1452–1519), Madonna and Child, with John the Baptist and an angel, a studio-copy, with alterations of 'La Vièrge aux Rochers' in the Louvre" (Baedeker 170 and Ricks 268): his marking this entry confirms that Eliot knew both versions when he incorporated the ironic allusion into section I of *The Waste Land*. In the same location were Verrocchio's *Virgin and Child with Two Angels*, Michelangelo's *Virgin and Child*, and Ghirlandaio's *Virgin and Child with Saint John* and *Portrait of a Young Man in Red*, the latter two having just been acquired in 1910. Nearby was Michelangelo's unfinished painting *The Entombment*, depicting the placing of Christ in the tomb, as well as Titian's *Bacchus and Ariadne*, the latter perhaps reflected in the allusions to the Ariadne story in the epigraph and in the first two stanzas of "Sweeney Erect."

The Martyrdom of Saint Sebastian by Antonio and Piero del Pollaiuolo, a few rooms away from *The Madonna of the Rocks*, depicts the saint at the top of a tree which has been stripped of its limbs; his hands are bound behind him, his feet are bound by ropes, and six arrows have penetrated his body as he looks up to the left with a sorrowful expression. In a circle at the base of the tree are six archers, some of whom are in the act of shooting more arrows at him while others are preparing to shoot. This painting, in which "the saint's physical beauty provides a certain sensual abandon that stands out more than his mystical ecstasy," has added significance in that d'Annunzio acknowledged it as his inspiration for *Le Martyre de Saint Sébastien* (Gullace 88). In the same location was Carlo Crivelli's 1491 painting *Virgin and Child with Saints Francis and Sebastian*, acquired by the National Gallery in 1870, in which the latter is pierced by twelve arrows.

Eliot also marked in his London Baedeker numerous additional works of art: paintings by Constable and Turner in the National Gallery; the French School of the eighteenth Century in the Wallace Collection; the illuminated manuscripts of the tenth-sixteenth centuries, the Elgin marbles (with the word "glance" written in the margin), the Egyptian Antiquities and Religious Collections, the Room of Gold Ornaments and Gems, and the Asiatic Salon in the British Museum; and the Chinese and Japanese Porcelain Collection, the Ivory, Gold, and Silver Collection, the European Tapestry, the Indian Section, and the Turkish, Persian, Chinese, and Saracenic Collection in the South Kensington Museum. In addition, he may have sought out Michelangelo's marble relief *Madonna and Child with the Infant Jesus* at the Royal Academy and a number of his drawings in the British Museum.

Avant-Garde Art in Paris

Even more important to Eliot's development as a poet than great art works of the past were the innovative recent and contemporary ones exhibited in Paris at that time, for the City of Light was the center of an artistic revolution of staggering proportions; as Gertrude Stein famously noted, "Paris was where the 20th Century was" (qtd. in Lieberman 11). Artistically speaking, it was "a period and place of great vitality, when artists began to see their world in profoundly different ways" and "shattered the boundaries of the status quo" by creating new forms of art (Huber 7). Thus, Eliot was living in Paris at the very zenith of artistic experimentation and must have both read about and seen some of the daring new developments. Indeed, I would argue that his exposure to Parisian avant-garde art was to a great extent responsible for his ability to write innovative poetry early in his career, beginning in that very year with "The Love Song of J. Alfred Prufrock." It evoked from Ezra Pound his now-famous comment in a letter of September 30, 1914 to Harriet Monroe that it was "the best poem I have yet had or seen from an American," expressing amazement that Eliot had "actually trained himself *and* modernized himself *on his own*" (*Letters of Ezra Pound* 40; see Parisi and Young for an account of how the poem came to be published in *Poetry* in June 1915, 169–72).

Eliot was in Paris at the very time when, according to Virginia Woolf's celebrated 1924 statement, human character changed dramatically—a statement which, it has been persistently and convincingly argued, was predicated upon the changes occurring in the world of art: "In or about December, 1910, human character changed. The change was not sudden and definite . . . . But a change there was, nevertheless; and, since one must be arbitrary, let us date it about the year 1910" (320). As Parsons and Gale point out, she is "bold enough to specify a month as well as a year" based on the notorious exhibition of Post-Impressionist paintings displayed at London's Grafton Gallery from November 1910 to January 1911. Her friend, the art critic Roger Fry, had procured the paintings from Parisian art dealers, made arrangements for the show, and given it its now famous title. Featuring works by such innovative recent and contemporary artists as Paul Gauguin, Paul Cézanne, Vincent van Gogh, Henri Matisse, Pablo Picasso, and André Derain, it was a *succès de scandale* with its "boldly distorted and willfully unnaturalistic paintings" that engendered for the most part outrage and shock among viewers and reviewers (Parsons and Gale 11–12). Most of the fifty or so reviews published in November and December 1910 were hostile, attacking the exhibition's works as subversive and revolutionary: a reviewer for the *Morning Post*, for example, asserted that it revealed "the existence of a widespread plot to destroy the whole fabric of European painting," while another writing for *Connoisseur* stated that the paintings were "garishly discordant in colour, formless, and destitute of tone," sarcastically regretting that "men of talent . . . should waste their lives in spoiling acres of good canvas when they might be better employed in stonebreaking for the roads" (qtd. in Parsons and Gale 12). News of the scandalous exhibit was so widespread in Europe that Eliot surely read or heard about it, perhaps seeing some of these harsh reviews.

In the years immediately preceding Eliot's sojourn in Paris, the acknowl-edged center of artistic experimentation to which flocked aspiring young artists from around the world,[9] an explosion of radical art movements took place there. Fauvism burst onto the art scene in October 1905 at the third Salon d'Automne when a group of artists including Matisse, Derain, Maurice Vlaminck, and others displayed their works together in Room VII of the Grand Palais. They were chris-tened "Les Fauves" [The Wild Beasts] by Louis Vauxcelles, an artist and art critic, because of their unconventional use of extremely bright colors, their incoherent form, and their heavy, violent brushstrokes of thick paint. The chief offender was Matisse's revolutionary *Woman in a Hat*, in which his bold use of color appeared most shockingly in the blue and green on her face. The term was sometimes also used to designate (and ridicule) avant-garde artists in general, as in A. Warnod's re-view of the Salon des Artistes Français on the front page of *Comoedia* on December 19, 1910, with comments on and photographs of works by Matisse, Picasso, Henri Le Fauconnier, and Kees van Dongen. In February 1909, the first manifesto of the Italian Futurist movement was published on the front page of *Le Figaro*; it an-nounced the movement's celebration of technology and the machine, the modern metropolis and industrialism, and speed and dynamism, as well as its commitment to destruction and nihilism. In a provocative illustration of the Futurist credo, it as-serted that a race car was "more beautiful than the *Winged Victory*" (qtd. in Parsons and Gale 183). The second manifesto followed in 1910, and in 1911 several Futurists visited Paris to view the daring developments of avant-garde French painting, as a result of which they added a Cubist idiom to their art. A painting such as Giacomo Balla's *Abstract Speed: The Car Has Passed* (1913) testifies to the value which they saw in the "metallic, not . . . verdant, Arcadia" of the modern industrial world (qtd. in Parsons and Gale 185).[10]

Overlapping with these movements in time, but surpassing them in importance and influence, was Cubism. While it has often been dated as beginning with Picasso's 1907 painting *Les Demoiselles d'Avignon*, in fact its first phase, Analytical Cubism, developed between early 1909—when Picasso and Georges Braque first began to work together—and 1912, when the introduction of collage ushered in the second phase, Synthetic Cubism, which lasted until the outbreak of World War I. During the first phase, which spans the time that Eliot was in Paris, Picasso and Braque collaborated in experimenting with a host of new techniques. Chief among them were the distortion or fragmentation of the figure, still-life, or landscape into geometric planes or cubes (hence the title "Cubism," first used derisively by the same Vauxcelles who had coined the term "Les Fauves" earlier); the use of multiple perspectives so that the subject is presented from several angles simultaneously; the limitation of colors to dull, monochromatic shades of tan and grey; and the reflection of primitive art and culture.

Picasso and Braque typically spurned the large exhibitions, showing and selling their paintings at the gallery of the art dealer Daniel-Henry Kahnweiler. There Eliot could have seen paintings created in 1910 such as Picasso's *Woman with a Mandolin* and the three portraits of art dealers, *Wilhelm Uhde, Ambroise Vollard,* and *Daniel-Henry Kahnweiler,* as well as Braque's *Violin and Pitcher* and *Sacré-Coeur de Montmartre,* the last a Cubist depiction of the new architectural wonder which dominated the Paris skyline along with the Tour Eiffel. Their innovative techniques were widely known in the artistic community. Indeed, Jean Metzinger wrote about the originality of Picasso's work as early as 1910, pointing out in particular his abandonment of Renaissance perspective in favor of multiple viewpoints (Arnason 193).

However, Cubism as a movement made its sensational public debut in Room 41 of the Salon des Indépendants, located at the corner of the Pont d'Alma and the Quay d'Orsay, from April 20–June 13, 1911, when Metzinger, Le Fauconnier, Albert Gleizes, Robert Delaunay, and Fernand Léger first exhibited their works as a group.[11] The new style of the paintings displayed there, which included Delaunay's *Eiffel Tower* (Figure 31), Le Fauconnier's *Abundance,* Léger's *Nudes in a Landscape,* and Gleizes's *Woman with Phlox* (Altschuler 27), evoked either rage or derision in most viewers, leading to a near riot in Room 41 (see Brooke 17–18) and becoming the talk of Paris. The Cubist section was reviewed in all the newspapers, for the most part in a hostile manner. For example, L. Dimier castigates it in the May 2 issue of *L'Action Française* in the snide tone typical of most of the negative reviews: "Let me say a few words about Cubism because its eccentricity has become public knowledge. After so many past follies have worn out our sense of outrage, it was not easy to find a new one; however, they have succeeded. They create objects composed of prisms with sharp edges; in order to find a synthesis of nature, one must look at the paintings from a distance. But that only results in a chaos without consolation. An entire room is consecrated to this absurdity . . ." (5). Kahnweiler later wrote that "in front of certain pictures there would be groups of people writhing with laughter or howling with rage," adding that he, Braque, and Picasso "had no desire to expose ourselves either to their laughter or to their rage" (qtd. in Gosling 191).

As pointed out in Chapter 1, it is likely that Eliot went to the exhibition, and particularly to the portion of it which caused the scandal, because of the widespread publicity and because Bergson was linked with modern art, as Eliot noted in his 1934 "A Commentary." Furthermore, Alain-Fournier, who attended the *Jour de Vernissage* the day before the official opening, doubtless reported to Eliot on the Cubist section, giving him a personal impetus to see it himself. That Eliot and Verdenal discussed Cubism and other contemporary art movements is clear from Verdenal's pessimistic statement about the survival of the former and his awareness of the proliferation of new trends in art in his April 22, 1912 letter: "Incidentally, Cubism has been destroyed by Futurism, which protests against museums, etc. and has a big exhibition at Bernheim's. Such are the manifestations of the new school, unless yet another springs up while my letter is crossing the sea" (Letters 34).[12] The daring technical experiments of the Cubists were, I suggest, a source for the disjunctive structure of "The Love Song of J. Alfred Prufrock," much of which Eliot composed in July 1911 with the scandalous exhibition fresh in his mind.

Eliot doubtless read Ghéon's puzzled review of the Cubist section at the 1911 Salon d'Automne in the November 1911 issue of *La Nouvelle Revue Française*, to which he subscribed on his return to the United States. An astute and demanding writer on cultural topics of all kinds, Ghéon clearly did not know what to make of Cubism, reflecting the widespread bewilderment engendered by the new art form. Yet he still gave a very accurate definition of it, which may have played a part in Eliot's realization of its significance for the world of art and for his own literary creations. Ghéon noted that at the Salon d'Automne of 1911 only the Cubists, the "intellectuels-géometres," attracted him, "as much by their singularity as by the clamor which surrounds them." Although many said that "they don't have all their brains," he proposed trying to "understand them before laughing at them." In the entire Salon d'Automne, he argued, no group appeared to him more representative of "ultra-modern painting" than the Cubists (627), who evoked the same object in several aspects at once—back, profile, three-quarters, and front— and presented both the outside and the inside. They constructed their paintings following not nature, but geometry, de-composing objects into a series of blocks and dividing them into "innumerable facets by cutting them up at sharp angles" (629). At the review's end, he suggested that it was probably premature to draw a conclusion about Cubism, but asserted that it was only one example of a general state of mind in which young poets, musicians, and painters placed a system of creation before the work itself and portrayed everything in fragments (630). Thus, in capturing the essential features of Analytical Cubism, Ghéon, while critical of it, confirmed for Eliot and others the Cubists' profoundly new ways of conveying human experience.

The Influence of Parisian Avant-Garde Art on *The Waste Land*

The influence of Cubism along with that of the other major avant-garde art movements that developed between 1905 and the early 1920s can be clearly seen in *The Waste Land*. A major result of Eliot's year in Paris was that, through his exposure to the daring experiments of Fauvism, Futurism, and Analytical Cubism, he was in the next ten years attuned to and aware of the subsequent, rapidly developing movements of Synthetic Cubism, Vorticism, Dada, and Surrealism. Traces of all of these movements are incorporated into his innovative poem. Synthetic Cubism introduced the revolutionary technique of collage (the use of fragments of materials from the everyday world such as ticket stubs, newspapers, tobacco wrappers, and wallpaper) as well as employing a wider spectrum of colors than Analytical Cubism and revealing an increased influence of the studio, café, music hall, and circus.[13] The English movement called Vorticism, influenced by both Cubism and Futurism, advocated techniques such as abstraction, multiple perspectives, geometrical forms, and modern urban civilization as subject matter. While adopting some characteristics from Cubism and Futurism, Dada focused on destroying the traditions and beliefs of Western art and literature and stressed political anarchy, the intuitive, and the irrational, thus anticipating Surrealism, which was in many ways a compendium and culmination of avant-garde art in the early twentieth century.[14] "Above all a movement of revolt" against traditional subjects and techniques of the past (Carrouges 1), Surrealism conveyed the sterility, chaos, and anguish of the modern world, the absence of love, the overemphasis on materialism, and the importance of the irrational and unconscious, and it used the techniques of collage, the double image, the fracturing of the human figure into various facets, and the mixture of cultures and religions.

All of these avant-garde art movements, along with early cinema, the 1917 Cubist ballet *Parade*, and popular entertainments such as the music hall and the circus, exerted a powerful influence on *The Waste Land*, which Eliot began conceiving eight years after his Parisian residence. Most obvious in the poem is the general principle of revolution to which many of these were dedicated. Surrealism was "particularly occupied . . . with revolution and with the demolishing of ideals and standards"

(Fowlie 15). One of its most well-known practitioners, the great Surrealist film-maker Luis Buñuel, said, "All of us were supporters of a certain concept of revolution, and although the Surrealists didn't consider themselves terrorists, they were constantly fighting a society they despised. Their principal weapon wasn't guns, of course; it was scandal . . ." (113), a statement which is especially applicable to Dada as well. Similarly, when *The Waste Land* first appeared, it was revolutionary in its technical innovations—its rejection of traditional stanza form, meter, rhyme, and linear structure—and its daring content with its descriptions of sexual issues (infidelity, prostitution, and abortion), its portrayal of the modern metropolis and recent technology, and its frank criticism of excessive materialism. As Harding reminds us, although time and familiarity have robbed the poem of much of its shock effect today, it was "a formidable piece of anti-establishment writing" in its time (15).

The most radical technique which Eliot adapted for the poem was collage, the invention of Picasso and Braque which ushered in Synthetic Cubism and which is an important component in subsequent movements as well. Indeed, Marjorie Perloff calls it the single most significant development in modern art (46). Collage is manifested in a variety of ways in Eliot's poem. Structurally, the poem is a literary collage of urban, desert, and ocean scenes which seem to be disconnected and without order or meaning, causing a 1922 review in the *Times Literary Supplement* to declare that the poem brings the reader to the limits of verbal coherence (Hunt 167). In a daringly radical move, Eliot introduces the technique in the opening section where, after an overview of the attitudes of the waste land's inhabitants, he shifts abruptly into the middle of a woman's conversation in Munich, followed by a description of a desert, a memory of a moment of potential love, an encounter with a fortuneteller, and a Dantesque scene of City workers crossing London Bridge. In 1922, this experiment was on the cutting edge, incorporating the fade-in, fade-out technique of early cinema, the Futurists' emphasis on the speed of modern life resulting from the new technology (the automobile, the airplane, and the typewriter, for example), and the rapid succession of acts or "turns" of the circus and music hall.

Collage is also evident in Eliot's combination of material from the real world of the late teens and early twenties, including low-brow popular entertainment, with allusions to works of literature, art, and music from the past, as well as in the surrealist device of the double or simultaneous image. He uses this technique variously. He plays on the differences between merged images (as in the contrast between a meaningful past and a degraded present implied in the melding of the goddess of chastity Diana from the minor Renaissance work *Parliament of Bees* with the prostitute Mrs. Porter from the bawdy Australian ballad popular with soldiers during World War I). Conversely, he emphasizes their similarities (as in the melding of real landmarks of London's financial district with the eerie landscape of Dante's *Inferno*). Bringing together seemingly unrelated images creates ambiguity since their meanings are elusive, causing perceivers to question their conventional views of what the Surrealists call "False Absolutes."

A technique which was introduced and developed by the Cubists and later adapted by subsequent movements was that of fracturing the human figure, still-life, or landscape into various planes or facets. This technique reflected the conviction that neither humanity nor the world it inhabits is a unified entity that can be fully experienced from a single perspective but is complex and literally many-faceted and thus must be viewed from multiple perspectives. Eliot makes use of this technique in a variety of ways. He fractures or splinters the conventional protagonist (who has a single identity which remains constant) by creating a composite figure whose various identities emerge and recede as it moves though the space and time of *The Waste Land*. He suggests thereby not only the complexity of the human being and the shifting nature of reality, but also the fragmentation of the individual in the modern industrialized world and the unclear or changing identities of people in dreams and nightmares. However, for decades, scholars, accustomed to a conventional protagonist, have tried to force a single identity on this elusive figure. As for the numerous characters that fill the poem, Eliot often describes them not as whole persons but as body parts (arms, hair, eyes, back, knees, feet, hands, fingernails) or as machines (the typist, for example, "waits / Like a taxi, throbbing, waiting," 216–17), reflecting another element of avant-garde art.

Multiple perspectives also appear in the poem's array of cultures and religions and in the quickly shifting kaleidoscope of scenes, which move from a public park in central Munich to a scorching desert; from the ornately decorated flat of an upper-class urban couple to a working-class pub; from crowds of City employees crossing London Bridge to a desolate scene on Margate Sands. Finally, he fractures or dislocates readers by challenging their traditional, non-involved, outside position in relation to the poem through the direct addresses at the ends of Sections I and IV which force them to become participants. To add to the disorientation of readers, Eliot borrows from Cubism and early cinema the use of steep or contorted angles; they observe both the crowds crossing London Bridge in Section I and the "hooded hordes swarming / Over endless plains" (369–70) in Section V as if looking down on them from a very high angle, while they see the tolling bell towers "upside down in air" (383) in Section V looking upward from a low angle.

The Waste Land clearly reflects as well the innovative subjects of the modern metropolis, technological inventions, and speed and dynamism employed in most of the contemporary art movements. Among numerous striking examples are

Delaunay's Cubist depiction of the Tour Eiffel, which Eliot could have seen in the Salon des Indépendants in the spring of 1911 in Paris, his gigantic 1912 *The City of Paris*, and his 1914 *Homage to Blériot*, celebrating the airplane; Léger's 1919 painting *The City*, a collage of billboards and metallic structures with a telephone pole in the foreground that conveys the commercial, technological, and mechanistic nature of the metropolis; and numerous works by the Italian Futurists, such as Umberto Boccioni's 1910–1911 *The City Rises* that captures both urban chaos and speed. Set in London, Eliot's poem features bleak views of the city's sterility, commercialism, noise, and speed in a variety of ways. Most striking is the description of crowds of business people on their way to dull, stifling jobs in the offices of the City, where Eliot himself was buried on a subterranean floor of Lloyd's Bank on a daily basis:

> A crowd flowed over London Bridge, so many,
> I had not thought death had undone so many . . . .
> Flowed up the hill and down King William Street,
> To where Saint Mary Woolnoth kept the hours
> With a dead sound on the final stroke of nine. (62–3, 66–8)

Speed, noise, and modern inventions such as the automobile and typewriter are implied in the references to the traffic ("The sound of horns and motors" 197), the wealthy couple's "closed car" (136), the idling taxi (216–17), and the typist who "Paces about her room again, alone" (254) after the departure of her callous lover, as well as in the staccato tempo of the wealthy woman's desperate attempts to elicit a response from her husband or lover ("'What are you thinking of? What thinking? What?'" 113) and her threat to "rush out as I am" (132). While the Futurists in particular celebrated these aspects of the modern industrial world, Eliot clearly deplores and condemns them as devastating to the human soul.

Seemingly in contrast to the depiction of the modern city, another important and defining element of these movements, particularly Cubism, is primitivism. Influenced by primitive Iberian and African sculpture and artifacts such as masks, Picasso and other Cubists experimented extensively with injecting a primitive quality into their figures to suggest that the menace of savagery resides in the civilized contemporary world. Eliot's incorporation of this insight into *The Waste Land* is evident in Section I in the ironic evocation of the ancient associations of fertility in the hyacinths carried by the sensual young woman in the garden scene. It also appears in the allusion to the ritual of burying pagan fertility gods in the protagonist's present-day conversation with Stetson, which implies that rejuvenation is not likely in the modern world.

Finally, *The Waste Land* reflects many of the themes of avant-garde art, particularly those of Cubism and Surrealism. Perhaps most striking is the portrayal of modern civilization as fragmented, chaotic, sterile, and nightmarish. Eliot's poem conveys this view in a variety of ways: from its symbolic title to its jarring structure; from its cries of despair at life's emptiness ("What shall we do tomorrow? / What shall we ever do?" 133–4) to its description of a desert landscape, "where the sun beats, / And the dead tree gives no shelter" (22–3). The world of nightmare, portrayed often in Surrealist works, appears at several points in the poem, most memorably in the last passage of Section I and throughout Section V, culminating in the protagonist's nightmare vision of the destruction of civilization: "What is the city over the mountains / Cracks and reforms and bursts in the violet air" (372–3). Another theme is the inability to establish or maintain significant human relationships, as seen in the series of vignettes featuring, among others, the hyacinth girl and her potential lover, Sweeney and the prostitute Mrs. Porter, and the typist and the young man carbuncular. Yet another is the indictment of the materialism of the modern industrial age, as seen in the crowds of anonymous workers trudging to dull jobs in the City.

Thus, while all the avant-garde art movements of the early twentieth century contributed to *The Waste Land*, Cubism was a particular and significant gift of Eliot's Parisian residence which introduced him to new modes of seeing, thinking, and creating.

Allusions to Art in Contemporary Reviews of the Early Poetry

As noted by Jewel Spears Brooker in the introduction to *T. S. Eliot: The Contemporary Reviews*, many contemporary reviewers of his early poems through *The Waste Land* used analogies with both great art of the past and modern art in searching for ways to explain their essential qualities (xvi, xviii). Ezra Pound in a review in the August 1917 issue of *Poetry* compares Eliot's use of contemporary detail in the poems of *Prufrock and Other Observations* (1917) to that of the seventeenth-century Spanish artist Diego Velázquez: "[H]e has used contemporary detail very much as Velázquez used contemporary detail in *Las Meninas*; the cold gray-green tones of the Spanish painter have, it seems to me, an emotional value not unlike the emotional value of Mr. Eliot's rhythms, and of his vocabulary" (8). May Sinclair in reviewing the same volume in the December 1917 issue of *Little Review* compares his portrayal of harsh realities to that of the eighteenth-century British artist William Hogarth. After noting that his observations are "ugly and unpleasant and obscure," Sinclair asserts, "Now there is no earthly reason why Mr. Eliot should not . . . do in words what Hogarth did in painting" (11–12). And Robert Nichols in reviewing *Ara Vos Prec* (1920) on April 18, 1920 in the *Observer* suggests that Eliot presents "the terrible realities" of human interiors with "something of the understanding and compassion of a Rembrandt" (30), the seventeenth-century Dutch artist.

Even more striking and numerous are the analogies to recent and contemporary art and artists. In reviewing *Prufrock*, Babette Deutsch in the February 16, 1918 *New Republic* points out analogies to late nineteenth-century Impressionism, describing Eliot's observations as having "the hall-marks of Impressionism" (14), and Louis Untermeyer in a June 30, 1920 review of *Poems* (1920) refers to "Portrait of a Lady" as "a half-sympathetic, half-scornful study in the Impressionist manner" (45). Nichols in his *Observer* review remarks that Eliot uses "the most quotidian, sordid, and apparently unpromising materials" to create an interior which is "as unqualified in statement as a [Walter] Sickert" (30), the most important of the British Impressionists. Interestingly, among Sickert's typical subjects was the London music hall, a venue much loved by Eliot, and his 1913 painting *Ennui* is similar in subject and tone to Eliot's 1919 poem "A Cooking Egg." Marianne Moore in the April 1918 issue of *Poetry* likens Eliot's "two London pieces" to the "post-Impressionistic English studies" of the late nineteenth-century American artist James Whistler, but suggests that the poet's harsh realities are more directly presented (15).

Most striking are the analogies to such contemporary movements as Cubism and Vorticism. Arthur Waugh in a highly critical review of Pound's *Catholic Anthology* in the October 1916 *Quarterly Review* notes the similarity of its poems to Cubism: "This strange little volume bears upon its cover a geometrical device, suggesting that the material within holds the same relation to the art of poetry as the work of the Cubist school holds to the art of painting and design." After quoting from several of its poems, including "The Love Song of J. Alfred Prufrock," he warns that the "unmetrical, incoherent banalities of these literary 'Cubists'" threaten poetry with anarchy (3–4). Conversely, Clive Bell in a wholly positive sense associates Eliot's work with that of Picasso, Matisse, Braque, and Derain as well as with that of Stravinsky and Joyce (35), and e. e. cummings's unconventional review of *Poems* in the June 1920 issue of the *Dial* is studded with references to avant-garde art. Allen Tate in the December 1922 issue of *Fugitive* notes that Duncan Grant and Picasso remake and remold the material world "in a subjective order" in their paintings and suggests that Eliot does something similar in *The Waste Land* (90–1). And in a brilliant essay in the *New York Evening Post Literary Review* for November 25, 1922, Edmund Wilson defines contemporary literature, using Eliot's *The Waste Land* and Joyce's *Ulysses* as his major examples, as a reflection of the fragmentation, chaos, and meaninglessness of the postwar world: "James Joyce and T.S. Eliot reflect our present condition of disruption. We are all tumultuous fragments . . . ." Wilson refers to Expressionism and Dada as other forms of art focusing on the modern mind's perception of the world and using similar radical techniques (78–9).

Other Art Exhibitions in Paris

While the exhibition of the Salon des Indépendants with its controversial first appearance of the Cubists was without a doubt the most striking, many other exhibitions of both established and contemporary art were held in Paris during Eliot's residence. The autumn and winter saw the Salon de l'Union Internationale in October, the Salon d'Hiver in January, and the exhibitions of Women Painters and Sculptors, of Henri Rousseau, and of the Société Moderne in February. However, the spring witnessed an explosion of exhibitions, most of which presented new works of art. As noted in Chapter 1, upon Eliot's return to Paris on April 25 after his Easter holiday in London, he commented in a letter to his cousin Eleanor that "Paris has burst out, during my absence, into full spring" (*Letters* 18). Indeed, Eliot could equally well have noted that it had burst out with art exhibitions so numerous that reviewers in *Le Figaro* made such comments as "ten new exhibitions open every day" (21 April: 3) and "Never have the art expositions been more numerous in Paris than this spring to the great joy of art lovers whose pleasures are multiplied" (11 May: 1).

Some reviewers, however, were critical of the number and size of the exhibitions, as seen in a cartoon entitled "Les Petits Salons" [The Little Salons] in the May 4 issue of *Le Figaro* (Figure 32), in which the driver of a group touring a museum in an open car, one of whom is asleep, asks a gentleman, "How many kilometers to the exit?," to which he replies, "I don't know. I'm not from around here" (3). In another in the April 28 issue, the chauffeur of an old woman who has fallen asleep in her wheelchair in a museum laments, "Poor dear; she would have been better off to have stayed in the country" (4). In an April 29 article entitled "The Salons of 1911," *Le Figaro*'s art critic Arsène Alexandre seems quite irritated not only by the number and variety of exhibitions—some of which he sarcastically lists in a long catalogue to emphasize how many there are—but even more by the uneven quality of the works displayed: "Will we be content with the fifteen to twenty thousand things—I call them 'things' for lack of a better word that would include what is beautiful and what is commonplace, what is worthy of attention and what is absurd—contained in the two Salons, the Salon des Indépendants, the expositions of humorists, Parisianists, deformists, designers, engravers, interior decorators, the works of Ingres, the works of the Dutch masters, and all those that I've forgotten?" (5).

Despite the humorous digs at their excessiveness and the widely varying quality of the works displayed, the fact remains that Paris in the spring of 1911 was a veritable feast of artistic offerings, among which were radical avant-garde creations that could only have astounded, impressed, and inspired a young visitor with literary ambitions from the less artistically inclined American scene.

Recent and Contemporary Sculpture

Recent and contemporary sculpture in Paris revealed experiments that rivaled those in painting, with the works of Auguste Rodin and Émile Bourdelle serving as prime examples.

Rodin, called the father of modern sculpture, has been credited with single-handedly restoring sculpture to the important position which it had held through the seventeenth century (Arnason 64). In the mid- to late nineteenth century in works such as *Man with the Broken Nose* (1864) and *The Age of Bronze* (1877), Rodin rebelled against the "sentimental idealism of the academicians" by demonstrating "scrupulous realism," power, intensity, and a concern with the movement of the human body (Arnason 65–6). Inspired by Donatello and Michelangelo, he reexamined both the human body and the art of the Middle Ages and the Renaissance, producing figures of great physical and emotional realism, often in distorted poses suggesting violence and brutality or in sensual poses considered scandalous. In 1880, as a result of a commission to create a portal for the proposed Musée des Arts Décoratifs, Rodin began work on his masterpiece *The Gates of Hell*, which was unfinished at his death in 1917. Depicting a variety of scenes and figures from Dante's *Inferno* and also reflecting the influence of Baudelaire's *Les Fleurs du Mal*, the massive work may have contributed to Eliot's interest in both these writers; he knew Baudelaire's poetry before arriving in France, and he read the *Commedia* for the first time during his Paris year. Individual sculptures from the work, such as *The Thinker*, a representation of Dante himself in the top center of the gate, and *The Kiss*, a depiction of the *Inferno*'s lovers Paolo and Francesca, gained fame on their own. Other great masterpieces include the 1886 *Burgers of Calais* and several versions of Balzac.

Numerous exhibitions of Rodin's works took place in Paris just prior to and during Eliot's year there, so that Eliot must have known of him and seen some of his works. Indeed, Rodin's reputation as a modern-day Michelangelo was known worldwide in the early years of the twentieth century. In 1900 the Exposition Universelle featured a Rodin Pavillion at the Place de l'Alma in which 150 of his sculptures and drawings were displayed ("Rodin" 15, 983). In 1906 *The Thinker* was installed in front of the Panthéon, right around the corner from Eliot's pension. In 1907 *The Walking Man* was exhibited at the Salon de la Société Nationale des Beaux-Arts; in 1908 major exhibitions of his drawings took place in Paris, Vienna, and Leipzig; and in 1909 and 1910 exhibitions of his drawings were held in Paris at La Galerie Dévambez and La Salle Gil Blas, respectively. In 1911, Paul Gsell's book on Rodin, *L'art, entretiens réunis* [Art, Collected Interviews], was published in Paris ("August" 3–4). Thus Eliot must certainly have been aware of the revolutionary, often scandalous innovations of this great sculptor, another of the many examples of experimental and radical developments taking place in the arts in Paris.

Bourdelle had been a student and then an assistant of Rodin, by whom he was heavily influenced. In the first decade of the twentieth century he set out in new, revolutionary directions while working within the framework of the classical tradition, especially archaic and fifth-century Greek sculpture (Arnason 73).[15] He was among the French pioneers of twentieth-century sculpture, along with Aristide Maillol and Charles Despiau. Many of the works that he created and exhibited just prior to and during the time of Eliot's residence were considered shocking in their power and in their techniques, which anticipated and in some instances paralleled early Cubist sculptures. *Heracles the Archer* took the 1910 Salon de la Société des Beaux-Arts by storm, its success marking his public acknowledgment as a leading sculptor in France along with Rodin. The extreme power of the figure is conveyed in its musculature, its tension-filled pose, and its broken planes. Interestingly, in 1910 he also did a sculpture of Rodin working on *The Gates of Hell*. Bourdelle's versatility is evident in *The Fruit*, a larger-than-life-size young female figure of "sinuous grace" (Cannon-Brookes 43), exhibited at the Salon de la Société des Beaux-Arts in 1911, where Eliot could have seen it; it may have served as a source of inspiration for the girl in "La Figlia che Piange," written the next year. It is highly likely that Eliot saw some of Bourdelle's works and even visited his studio because Alain-Fournier was quite interested in the sculptor and had recently published in *La Nouvelle Revue Française* a description of him in his studio (Gibson 198).

At this time Bourdelle had also returned to the subject of Beethoven, which fascinated him throughout his life; he saw a physical similarity between himself and the composer, as well as a "spiritual parallel with the qualities he was trying to achieve in his sculpture" (Cannon-Brookes 14). Between 1888 and 1891, Bourdelle had created a series of sculptures of Beethoven's head that were stylistically straightforward with carefully modeled surfaces (Cannon-Brookes 14, 33). Between 1901 and 1910, however, his Beethoven sculptures became more emotionally frenzied and stylistically distorted and faceted. According to Cannon-Brookes, this development was "to lead to Cubism and abstract art" (35), since his teaching position at the Grande-Chaumière, which began in 1909, allowed him to influence many young painters such as Alberto Giacometti. Famous personages in other fields, such as Bergson, also came to his studio to listen to and learn from him (Gautherin 23). Bourdelle's sculpture entitled *Beethoven in the Wind* (1904–1908) is inscribed,

"To the man and the god Beethoven," reflecting the worship of Beethoven both as a musician and as a model of moral strength and virtue so prevalent in Paris at this time; indeed, the Parisian adoration of the composer may have played a role in Bourdelle's return to Beethoven as a subject. This second series "reaches its climax in the strongly architectural forms of the *Draped Beethoven*" of 1910, whose "strongly faceted structure and the rhythmical imposition of planes . . . provide a fascinating parallel to the earliest Cubist sculptures of Picasso," such as the 1909 *Head of Fernande Olivier* (Cannon-Brookes 36, 39).[16] As I suggest in Chapter 7, Eliot was highly influenced by the devotion to Beethoven in Paris at the time and doubtlessly attended many of the Beethoven concerts given then, another reason that Bourdelle's sculptures of the composer may well have been of great interest to him.[17]

In addition to Picasso, other avant-garde (mostly Cubist) sculptors creating works in Paris at this time included Matisse (who studied for a time with Bourdelle), Constantin Brancusi, Alexander Archipenko, and Raymond Duchamp-Villon.[18] These sculptures by Rodin, Bourdelle, and others demonstrated the highly experimental directions in which the plastic arts were heading as well as in many cases a look back to the primitive or classical, perhaps providing inspiration for the kind of poetry that Eliot was currently writing and would write in the near future.

The Theft of the *Mona Lisa* from the Louvre

Involving both a great work of art from the past and two names prominent in the Parisian contemporary artistic and literary scene, one of the strangest and most shocking occurrences in the world of art during Eliot's year in Paris was not an exhibition, a painting, or a new art movement, but the theft of da Vinci's *Mona Lisa* from the Louvre on August 21, 1911 and the arrest of the critic and poet Apollinaire as the prime suspect, with Picasso implicated as well. Norman Mailer in *Portrait of Picasso as a Young Man* gives a very complete account of this complicated situation, citing information from Francis Steegmuller's book on Apollinaire, Fernande Olivier's memoirs and her biography of Picasso, and various newspaper stories (317–34). In 1907 a young Belgian named Géry Pieret, who worked for a time as Apollinaire's secretary, stole two Iberian statuettes from the Louvre and sold them to Picasso. In May 1911 he stole another and hid it in Apollinaire's apartment, where he was staying. So, when the *Mona Lisa* disappeared a few months later, Apollinaire and Picasso were terrified, assuming that Pieret was the thief and that they would be implicated. Pieret supposedly returned the recently stolen statuette while the two statuettes stolen in 1907 were taken, perhaps by Apollinaire himself, to the offices of the newspaper *Paris-Journal* to be returned to the Louvre, on condition of anonymity. However, his name was apparently revealed to police by the newspaper or one of its reporters, perhaps even André Salmon, leading to his arrest and incarceration on September 7.

Since the story was carried in all the newspapers, Apollinaire's reputation suffered enormously, with all of Paris in a state of shock that such a prominent figure in art and literature was implicated in the crime. This account from the September 9, 1911 issue of *Le Matin* is typical: "It was not without emotion and surprise that Paris learned last night of the arrest [of Apollinaire] made by the Sûreté in connection with the recent restitution of Phoenician statuettes stolen from the Louvre in 1907. The mere name of the person arrested is enough to account for this reaction. He is . . . Guillaume Apollinaire, . . . arrested the night before last . . . on the charge of 'harboring a criminal'" (qtd. in Mailer 327). When Picasso was brought in and questioned by the judge, he initially denied knowing him, shocking Apollinaire deeply. On September 12, Apollinaire was released from prison on probation, but, according to Steegmuller, was for some time depressed by and bitter about the entire episode, especially his treatment by some friends and fellow writers (222–3). It was more than two years later, in December 1913, that Apollinaire was finally fully exonerated when the painting was found in Florence; the thief was a mentally disturbed Italian who had been employed at the Louvre and had stolen it in order to return the painting to its homeland (Steegmuller 210).

Since Eliot returned to Paris in early September 1911 after his summer trip to Germany and Italy (*Letters* 27), he would certainly have known about this shocking episode, which thrust the avant-garde art movement and some of its leading practitioners and champions into the glare of the public view. What effect it may have had on Eliot we can only surmise, but he and Verdenal no doubt discussed its possible lessons: how frail one's reputation may be, how scandal can touch one who seems above the fray, how one's friends may abandon one, how difficult the life of the artist and writer may be.

Eliot's Lifelong Interest in Art

Eliot's year in Paris, I suggest, nurtured what would become an extensive interest in and knowledge about art, both established and contemporary, throughout the remainder of his life.[19] Indeed, as noted earlier, on his tour of southern Germany and northern Italy in the summer of 1911, he saw paintings of Saint Sebastian by Mantegna (which he described as "First quality") in the Ca d'Oro in Venice and by Antonello da Messina in Bergamo (Ricks 268). Furthermore, according to Aiken, when he returned to Harvard in the fall of 1911, Eliot brought with him from Paris and displayed in his room on Ash Street a copy of Gauguin's 1889 painting *The*

Yellow Christ ("King Bolo" 21), a work innovative in its use of bold yellows both in the landscape and in Christ's body, suggesting "a natural interchange between religion and rural life that confounds any separation between the real and the imaginary" (Parsons and Gale 103). A measure of Eliot's early appreciation for and understanding of its experimental qualities (as well as a glimpse of his arrogance) is evident in his reply to the suggestion that it demonstrated "a kind of sophisticated primitivism," for he commented, Aiken tells us, "with a waspishness that was characteristic" that there "was nothing primitive about it" (21). Furthermore, because of his interest in avant-garde European art, Eliot was likely to have been among the 12,000 people who viewed the sensational Armory Show, with 250 works by European modern artists such as Matisse, Picasso, Braque, Léger, Delaunay, and Marcel Duchamp, when it was exhibited in Boston's Copley Hall in April and May of 1913.[20]

Eliot's return to Europe in the summer of 1914, when he intended to improve his German for several weeks in Marburg, Germany, before spending the academic year studying philosophy at Merton College, Oxford, provided him with additional opportunities to increase his knowledge of art. Although there is no evidence that he went to Paris on his way to Marburg, he surely heard or read about the performance there on July 5 of Arthur Cravan's scandalous show that anticipated the antics of the Dadaists; a letter written to his cousin Eleanor while aboard ship is postmarked "London, July 7, 1914" (*Letters* 37), indicating that his arrival in Europe coincided with reports of this artistic event in the newspapers. Eliot visited Belgium during the second week of July, telling Aiken in a letter of July 19 that "the paintings [there] are *stunning*! only one (great) one in Ghent, but *treasures* in Bruges and Antwerp and Brussels! Memling, van Eyck, Matsys, David, Breughel, Rubens—really great stuff! . . . (And O a wonderful *Crucifixion* of Antonello of Messina)" (*Letters* 41).

The outbreak of World War I in early August 1914 caused Eliot to leave Germany immediately for England, where his involvement with art and artists increased significantly. Among his closest friends were Pound, as great a champion of contemporary art as of contemporary literature, and Wyndham Lewis, "the leading avant-garde painter in England" (Tomlinson 73). Indeed, less than a year after his arrival, in a letter of April 1915, Eliot wrote to Isabella Stewart Gardner, the Bostonian patron of the arts, that he had come to know "some of the modern artists whom the war has so far spared," mentioning Gaudier-Brzeska, Lewis, and several others and commenting on an exhibition of contemporary art at the Goupil Gallery (*Letters* 94). This letter reveals both that this twenty-six-year-old graduate student had an established (and astonishing) friendship with a leading figure in the Bostonian art world and that he was forming new friendships among the young avant-garde artists in London and attending exhibitions of modern art there. In addition, when "Preludes" and "Rhapsody of [*sic*] a Windy Night," both products of his year in Paris in whole or in part, were published in the July 1915 issue of the Vorticist magazine *Blast*, they appeared between Lewis's essay "A Review of Contemporary Art" and a series of six Vorticist designs by such artists as Frederick Etchels, Edward Wadsworth, and Lewis (*Blast* 38–63). Eliot's proximity to modern art was quite literal in this case and indicates that he was deeply involved with its development and leading figures.

By 1918 Eliot was regularly moving in circles composed largely of those devoted to modern art and literature, attending art exhibitions, and often mentioning them in print. Among his acquaintances were Clive and Vanessa Bell, Leonard and Virginia Woolf, the Sitwells, and Roger Fry, all of whom constantly discussed, wrote about, and/or experimented with new theories of both the visual and written arts. In particular, Fry's ideas stressing the overriding significance of design, the rejection of the representational, and the necessity of reproducing in literature the current experiments in the visual arts doubtlessly had an impact on Eliot, as they did on Virginia Woolf (see Broughton).

In addition to participating in discussions about art and literature with this group, Eliot was involved in the art scene in other ways. In May 1918 Aldous Huxley reported to Lady Ottoline Morrell that at London's Gaudier-Brzeska exhibit he saw "almost everybody—the glorious company of Sitwells, the noble army of poets, including Graves and Eliot" (Glendinning 59). Eliot probably attended the January 1919 exhibition of modern French painting arranged by his close friends, the Sitwell brothers, as well as Lewis's one-man show of watercolors and drawings depicting World War I entitled *Guns* in February 1919 at the Goupil Gallery (Wyndham Lewis Exhibition). In June 1919 the Woolfs' Hogarth Press printed seven of Eliot's recent poems in a small volume bound in one of Fry's designs (Gordon, *Imperfect* 145), and the next month he published a review in the *Egoist* of three volumes of poetry, one of which, as d'Ambrosio points out, was *Vingt-cinq poèmes* [Twenty-Five Poems] by Tristan Tzara, the leading spokesperson for Dada (103–16). In January 1921 he wrote to his mother that during his recent trip to Paris he was "mostly with old and new French friends and acquaintances, writers, painters" and had bought Vivien a drawing by "one of the best of the modern painters, Raoul Dufy" (*Letters* 433). In his first "London Letter" for the *Dial*, which appeared in April 1921, Eliot commented that the Picasso Exhibition at the Leicester Galleries was "the most interesting event of London at this moment" (453), and in the third, published in August 1921, he argued that Cubism "is not license but an attempt to establish order" (215). Certainly, a variety of modern art movements were much on his mind in 1921, when he began work in earnest on *The Waste Land*.

Throughout his adult life, Eliot collected and displayed in his lodgings a variety of art works, in addition to those already noted. When Babbitt visited him in his London flat in the summer of 1928, he saw above the mantelpiece in the living room a painting by Wyndham Lewis, which, according to Belgion, shocked Babbitt, who deplored modern art (52). Ironically, one of the most well-known of Lewis's portraits was that of Eliot himself, painted in 1938. And Igor Stravinsky describes the art works that adorned the Eliots' flat when he visited them in the spring of 1963: they included watercolors by John Ruskin and Henry Moore, a landscape by Edward Lear, drawings by Wyndham Lewis, and a bronze head of Eliot by Jacob Epstein (92), attesting to Eliot's eclectic tastes and his close connections with leading contemporary painters and sculptors.

Eliot's 1910–1911 year abroad provided him with the opportunity to see a wide array of great works of the past and present and inspired a lifelong interest in and knowledge of art. His residence in Paris nourished and enriched his early explorations of ancient Greek and Roman art and Florentine painting in two undergraduate art history courses at Harvard as well as his personal discoveries of Manet, Monet, and Japanese prints in the same period; in that great city as well as in London, Munich, and northern Italy, he had access to museums housing many of the world's most famous works. Even more important were the recent and contemporary avant-garde works that were exhibited in Paris either in private galleries such as Kahnweiler's or in sensational—indeed scandalous—public exhibitions such as the Salon des Indépendants in the spring of 1911. The new art movements of Fauvism, Futurism, and Analytical Cubism rocked the world of art by demonstrating what were at the time outrageous, cutting-edge experiments, and they laid the groundwork for the subsequent movements of Synthetic Cubism, Dada, Vorticism, and Surrealism. Eliot adapted to his poetic needs many of their principles, themes, and techniques. Thus, the influence of both the great art of the past and the great contemporary art in Paris is more extensive and profound than has been acknowledged in Eliot scholarship.[21]

Figure 22. Théâtre national de l'Odéon. Photographie d'Étienne Neurdein (1832–1918). Carte postale. © Musée Carnavalet/Roger-Viollet.

Figure 23. Bert, Scene from *Les Frères Karamazov*. *Comoedia Illustré* (15 April 1911): 422. Jerome Robbins Dance Division, The New York Public Library for the Performing Arts, Astor, Lenox and Tilden Foundations.

Figure 24. "—Dis donc, les frères Karamazov, c'est-y des danseurs russes? . . ." [—Tell me, are the brothers Karamazov Russian dancers? . . .]. Moriss, "Toujours Dindonnette" [Always a Stupid Woman]. *Comoedia* (12 April 1911): 3.

Figure 25. "—. . . . . d'avoir été entendre *le Martyre de saint Sébastien.*—Combien de fois?" [—. . . . . have been to *The Martyrdom of saint Sébastien.*—How many times?]. Abel Faivre. "La Confession de la Parisienne." *Le Figaro* (25 May 1911): 3. © 2010 Artists Rights Society (ARS), New York/ADAGP, Paris.

Figure 26. Léon Bakst, Drawing of Ida Rubenstein as Saint Sébastien. *Comoedia Illustré* (1 June 1911): 530. Jerome Robbins Dance Division, The New York Public Library for the Performing Arts, Astor, Lenox and Tilden Foundations.

ÉLÉGANCE

Figure 27. "—C'est simple, n'est-ce pas? . . . je me suis inspirée des costumes du *Martyre de Saint Sébastien*, de M. D'Annunzio" [—It's obvious, isn't it? . . . I was inspired by the costumes in D'Annunzio's *The Martyrdom of Saint Sébastien*]. Moriss, "Élégance." *Comoedia* (15 June 1911): 3.

Figure 28. Leonardo da Vinci (1452–1519). *The Virgin of the Rocks* (also called *Virgin and Child with Saint John the Baptist and an angel*). Photo: Gerard Blot. Louvre, Paris, France. Photo credit: Réunion des Musées Nationaux / Art Resource, NY.

Figure 29. Luini, Bernardino (c. 1475–1532). *Salomé receives the head of Saint John the Baptist.* Oil on canvas, 62.5 × 55 cm. Louvre, Paris, France. Photo Credit: Erich Lessing / Art Resource, NY.

Figure 30. Mantegna, Andrea (1431–1506). *Saint Sebastian*, painted for the Gonzaga family of Mantua. Canvas, 255 × 140 cm. R. F. 1766. Louvre, Paris, France. Photo credit: Erich Lessing / Art Resource, NY.

Figure 31. Robert Delaunay. *Eiffel Tower (Tour Eiffel)* 1911. Oil on canvas 79½ × 54½ inches (202 × 138.4 cm). Solomon R. Guggenheim Museum, New York. Solomon R. Guggenheim Founding Collection, by Gift 37.463. © L & M Services B. V. The Hague 20080819.

Figure 32. "—S'il vous plaît, combien de kilometers avant la sortie?—Je ne sais pas. . . je ne suis du pays" [—Please, how many kilometers to the exit?—I don't know. I'm not from around here]. Abel Faivre, "Les Petits Salons" [The Little Salons]. *Le Figaro* (4 May 1911): 3. © 2010 Artists Rights Society (ARS), New York/ADAGP, Paris.

Figure 33. Léon Bakst, *Les Ballets Russes au Châtelet*. *Comoedia Illustré* (1 June 1911). Cover. Jerome Robbins Dance Division, The New York Public Library for the Performing Arts, Astor, Lenox and Tilden Foundations.

Figure 34. L. Roosen, Vaslav Nijinsky with Tamara Karsavina in *Le Spectre de la Rose*. No. 2108 Photograph. Jerome Robbins Dance Division, The New York Public Library for the Performing Arts, Astor, Lenox and Tilden Foundations.

Figure 35. The Opéra Garnier. Paris (IXème arr.). L'Opéra Garnier, vers 1900. ND-82. © ND/Roger-Viollet.

Figure 36. Bert, M. Van Dick [Dyck] in Richard Wagner's *Der Ring des Nibelungen*, Paris, 1911. Henry Gauthier-Villars, "La Tetralogie." *Comoedia Illustré* (1 July 1911): 613. Jerome Robbins Dance Division, The New York Public Library for the Performing Arts, Astor, Lenox and Tilden Foundations.

THÉATRE DU CHATELET

" Arsène Lupin contre Herlock Sholmès"

M. HENRY
JULLIEN
(*Arsène Lupin*)

" ARSÈNE LUPIN
CONTRE HERLOCK
SHOLMÈS ", pièce
policière en quatre ac-
tes et vingt et un ta-
bleaux, tirée des
romans de M. Maurice
LEBLANC, par MM.
VICTOR DARLAY et
Henri DE GORSSE.

PREMIER ACTE

Figure 37. Bert, Arsène Lupin disguised as a rooster and a scene from Act I in a review by Paul Boyer, "Théâtre du Châtelet: 'Arsène Lupin contre Herlock Sholmès.'" *Comoedia Illustré* (15 November 1910): 100. Jerome Robbins Dance Division, The New York Public Library for the Performing Arts, Astor, Lenox and Tilden Foundations.

Figure 38. Brod, "Pendant la Revue.—On 'en met'" [During the Revue.—The musicians really go at it] in L. Vuillemin, "Dans la 'Fosse' d'un Music-Hall" [In the Orchestra Pit of a Music-Hall]. *Comoedia* (12 January 1911): 5.

161

Figure 39. The Music Hall Ba-ta-Clan. By permission of the Bibliothèque nationale de France.

Figure 40. Harry Fragson. By permission of the Bibliothèque nationale de France.

Mlle MONTJOIE (*Le Bohémien*)

Figure 41. Anonymous. Mlle Montjoie (*Le Bohémien*) in a review by Joe Bridge, "Ba-ta-Clan: 'Et Ça!'" *Comoedia Illustré* (15 November 1910): 108. Jerome Robbins Dance Division, The New York Public Library for the Performing Arts, Astor, Lenox and Tilden Foundations.

· 5 ·

THE DANCE

Geoffrey Whitworth, a British dance critic, begins his little book on Nijinsky, published in 1913, by quoting a passage from the 1910 edition of the *Encyclopaedia Britannica* bemoaning the current stagnant state of the dance: "It seems unlikely that we shall see any revival of the best period and style of dancing until a higher standard of grace and manners becomes fashionable in society." Whitworth then points out that this prophet has proved to be "most happily at fault" in his gloomy forecast, for dance was experiencing tremendous changes, advances, and innovations even as the passage was being written, so much so that "[d]uring the last few years a mighty revolution has had to be worked in our ideas concerning the whole art of the dance . . . ; [we have been] forced to develop a completely fresh set of aesthetic standards so as to keep pace with the development of a tradition which for us, previously, had been little more than a dead and obsolete form" (1–3). These comments communicate something of the excitement aroused by the new developments in the world of dance in the first thirty years of the twentieth century, an "incredibly lively time for the dance which had never before generated so many new ideas or attracted so many people" ("Dance" 466).

Most of the excitement emanated from two sources: Isadora Duncan and Diaghilev's Ballets Russes. Both performed in Paris during Eliot's year there, so he could have seen them and certainly heard about them. He could hardly have escaped an awareness of the daring experiments not only with dance movements themselves but also with music, sets, costumes, plots, and, perhaps most of all, with the integration of the arts and the collaboration of various types of artists in their productions. Eliot also had two opportunities to see Duncan during his early years in London, and he did attend performances of the Ballets Russes there, as revealed in numerous sources. He commented in various essays written in the 1920s both on dance productions and on books about dance, and his famous essay "Tradition and the Individual Talent" reveals the influence of Whitworth's book on Nijinsky in its two major ideas.

Eliot's interest in and knowledge about the dance seem to have begun in Paris in 1910–1911, and it influenced his poetry, drama, and critical ideas far more heavily than has been generally realized.[1]

Isadora Duncan in Paris

Isadora Duncan, the American dancer whose innovations sent shock waves through the dance world beginning in the early 1900s, gave six performances at the Théâtre du Châtelet from January 18–28, 1911. At this point in her career she had already achieved widespread acclaim for the daring and novel elements in her dance, as well as notoriety for the unconventional nature of her private life. The most distinguishing characteristic of her dancing was her use of natural movements, a radical departure from the regulated movements of the classical ballet. In a 1903 lecture, Duncan argued that the "expression of the modern school of ballet . . . is [one] of degeneration, of living death. [Its movements] are sterile . . . because they are unnatural" ("Dance" 263). The rhythms of her dance were inspired by the waves of the Pacific Ocean (Duncan 10) and its movements by Greek art. Her own description of the freedom and indeed the wild abandon of her dancing suggests how daringly new and thus both thrilling and moving her performances were for her audiences: "I am only able to give you a vague indication . . . of what most dancers will be later on—masses rushing like whirlwinds in rhythms caught up by mad waves of this music, flowing with fantastic sensuality and ecstasy" (Duncan 144). Gordon Craig, an actor, director, and theorist in drama, commented that she "moved as no one had ever seen anyone move before" (qtd. in Macdougall 95), clearly conveying the originality of her dance movements, whose freedom can be seen in sketches done by Abraham Walkowitz (see Sachs, Plate 32).

To reinforce her emphasis on the natural beauty of the unfettered human body, she rejected the stiff toe shoes and rigid tutus of conventional ballet and danced in bare feet or sandals, wore a tunic made of transparent, flowing material, and performed alone before a simple blue curtain on a bare stage. Because her body was clearly visible, her costume scandalized many; she notes in her biography that "my transparent tunic, showing every part of my dancing body, had created some stir . . . . Many times I declaimed myself hoarse on the subject of how beautiful and innocent the naked human body was when inspired by beautiful thoughts" (157–8).

A second important innovation, closely linked to the first, was, in her words, "the divine expression of the human spirit through the medium of the body's movement. . . . [This is the] first basic theory of my art" (Duncan 75–6). The set designer Robert Jones proclaimed that "the difference between Isadora Duncan and the other dancers of our time . . . is that she dances with her spirit. . . " (19). Rodin, who made numerous sketches of her, noted, "Suppleness, emotion, these high qualities which are the soul of the dance, are her complete and sovereign art" (qtd. in Sorell 179).

Her exaltation of the human body in its natural state, in combination with her ability to convey the human spirit with intense emotion, typically evoked powerful responses from her admirers, many of whom wept with joy and often described the experience as a significant moment in their lives. Edith Wharton, after seeing her dance in 1909, wrote, "The first sight of Isadora's dancing was a white milestone to me. . . . All through the immense, rapt audience one felt the rush of her inspiration" (qtd. in Macdougall 123). The art historian Élie Faure admitted in his preface to a 1910 book of drawings of Isadora, "Yes, we wept when we saw her. . . . [We] rediscovered that primitive purity which, every two or three thousand years, reappears from the depth of the abyss of our worn-out conscience to restore to us again a holy animality. . ." (qtd. in Macdougall 124–5). And in his article "Isadora Duncan et M. Pierre Lalo" in the March 1, 1911 issue of *La Nouvelle Revue Française*, Ghéon described his emotional response to her performance in Paris in January: "We admired this performance, never before offered to the French in the 20th century: a beautiful woman with noble lines, without any marks of deformity [as in a classical ballerina in toe shoes], at ease in a floating tunic, in the healthy use of her entire body. Music accompanies her movements: a double joy grips our hearts, a new joy which forces us to weep" (475).

Finally, she broke new ground by dancing to famous pieces of classical music which had not been written expressly for the dance and which required collaboration with an orchestra, conductor, chorus, and/or vocal soloists. Among her favorite composers were Wagner, Gluck, Bach, and Beethoven. Rimsky-Korsakov disapproved of this innovation, writing six months before his death in 1908, "What I dislike about her is that she connects her art with musical compositions dear to me. . . . How vexed I should be if I learned that Miss Duncan danced and mimed to my *Schéhérazade*" (qtd. in Buckle 163). However, others such as the great Russian choreographer Mikhail Fokine were inspired by her to do likewise. Fokine, "taking his cue from Isadora," arranged dances to the music of established composers, including Rimsky-Korsakov himself (Buckle 163), and subsequently went further than Isadora in choreographing ballets in collaboration with contemporary composers.

By 1911 when she performed in Paris, Duncan was well-known not only in Europe but also in the United States. Perhaps Eliot's ever-vigilant mother warned him about her, for Duncan had been denounced publicly by a St. Louis minister of a large and wealthy church when she danced there in the fall of 1909. He charged her with bringing shame to St. Louis and with degrading Beethoven's symphony to which she had danced, since she was a "middle-aged woman who had been for years associated with the Parisian stage," a pejorative term in America at this time, calling on "the multitudes of good women and clean men in this imperial city [to] stamp such an exhibition with utter and absolute condemnation" (qtd. in Macdougall 129). His outrage no doubt issued as well from her unconventional lifestyle, for she had already borne one child out of wedlock and the next year would bear another.

In Paris, far from parental disapproval, Eliot had a golden opportunity to see her dance. During the summer of 1910, she had choreographed dances to the music of Gluck's *Orpheus*, which would be the highlight of her performances in Paris. According to *Courrier des Théâtres* in the January 18 issue of *Le Figaro*, her program at the six matinées would consist of Bach's *Suite in D*, an interlude featuring the air and allegretto of Handel's *Suite in D Minor*, and her interpretation of Gluck's *Orpheus*, with the chorus and orchestra of the Concerts-Colonne, conducted by M. Gabriel Pierné (5).

André Nède, in an article entitled "Isadora Duncan au Châtelet" in *Le Figaro* on the same day, waxed poetic in describing to his readers the delights which awaited them. First recounting the "strange and beautiful story" of a young girl in a "remote corner of America" who had been inspired by the paintings on Greek vases to "recreate the gestures, movements, and the true feeling of the dances of ancient Greece," he then described in detail the major piece on the program and concluded with a veritable cascade of praise for Isadora's ability to fuse the ancient and the modern: "*Orpheus* is a delightful mixture of the spirit of ancient Greece and a more recent taste. . . . Miss Duncan's performance will be an exquisite feast. . . . And," he predicted, "Paris will applaud Miss Duncan, whom the lovable gods of antiquity have sent to reawaken it to the happy dreams of ancient days" (5). Eliot may have been attracted to a performance by the opportunity not only to experience the new freedoms in dance, the music of a great opera, and the choreographic interpretation of a Greek myth well-known to him, but also perhaps to see for himself this woman who had so scandalized St. Louis a year and a half earlier.

He may also have followed the controversy among reviewers after her performances. For example, Pierre Lalo's scathing indictment in *Le Temps* was answered by Ghéon in his article in the March 1911 issue of *La Nouvelle Revue Française*, in which he took Lalo to task for having "cruelly executed the American ballerina" on the grounds that she does not follow the practices of classical ballet: "[It's] absurd to reproach an innovative dancer for the absence of all tradition." In a bitingly sarcastic tone, he asked, "Does [Lalo] seriously believe that lightness is possible only on toe, at the price of artificial deformity? Is he persuaded that this lightness, which he calls 'a victory over weight,' is necessarily a condition of all dance?" Ghéon then argued that what was most valuable in Isadora's dancing was precisely her naturalness, her very weight, her very body, "the terrestrial weight of a healthy, strong, harmonious body which is presented to us in its natural plenitude and which runs, jumps, and puts its dynamism into action without artifice" (474). He concluded by reiterating the importance of her natural approach to dance, an indication of how truly innovative it was at the time: "[She performed before us as] a creature of God, just as God made her, so that a new beauty was revealed to us" (476). Saint-Alban, perhaps in an indirect response to Lalo, also praised her natural movements, in an article provocatively entitled "Le Nu au Théâtre" [The Nude in the Theatre] in the April 1 issue of *Mercure de France* (454–5).

We can gauge the extent of Duncan's influence on the arts in general as well as on dance in particular in two very different types of works produced in 1913. The Théâtre des Champs-Élysées in Paris, which opened in April of that year, was decorated with her dancing figure in the murals in the auditorium, in the frescoes in the halls, and most imposingly in the marble bas-reliefs of the façade designed by none other than Bourdelle (see Chapter 4), who had seen her dance in 1909: "To me it seemed that there, through her, was animated an ineffable frieze wherein divine frescoes slowly became human realities. Each leap, each attitude of the great artist remains in lightning flashes in my memory." He drew from that memory in sculpting the bas-reliefs for the façade: "All my muses in the theater are movements seized during Isadora's flight; she was my principal source. . ." (qtd. in Macdougall 124). The other work was Whitworth's slim volume on Nijinsky. After commenting that, during the first decade of the twentieth century, "[n]ew artistic impulses were coming to life all over Europe," he singled out for special tribute "the liberating force which sprang from the art of Isadora Duncan, whose heroic practice has done far more than any precept of philosophy to widen our ideas as to the intellectual and spiritual possibilities of the dance" (17–18). The young Eliot with his keen and indeed voracious appetite for new developments in the artistic and intellectual realms may have been inspired by her daring innovations to undertake his own.

Isadora Duncan in London

Ten years later Eliot had another opportunity to see Duncan dance, for she performed twice in 1921 in London. In April, she appeared at the Prince of Wales Theatre with the London Symphony, doing her powerful interpretation of Tchaikovsky's *Slavic March*, which she had choreographed in 1917 upon learning of the Russian Revolution (Macdougall 178). Three months later, on her way to Russia, she gave a series of farewell performances, again accompanied by the London Symphony, at the Queen's Hall. Among many rave reviews, one by Ernest Newman was typical: "Imagine, a dozen statues expressive, say, of the cardinal phases of despair—the poses and gestures and facial expressions of the moment in which each of these phases reaches its maximum of intensity. Then imagine some hundreds of statues that represent, in faultless beauty, every one of the moments of slow transition between these cardinal phases, and you get the art of Isadora Duncan . . . . Her secret, so far as we can penetrate to it, is apparently in the marvelous cooperation of every cell of her brain and every movement of her face and limbs" (qtd. in Macdougall 181). The qualities of Isadora singled out for praise may have attracted Eliot to a performance, especially if he had seen her dance in 1911, since he often attended the London productions of the Ballets Russes in the company of his wife Vivien and their artistic and literary friends.

As a revolutionary who swept away the artificiality and decadence of traditional ballet, who turned for inspiration to great musical pieces of the past, and who made daring and radical experiments in dance movements, staging, and costuming, Isadora Duncan may have inspired Eliot to experiment similarly in literature. Her prediction in 1903 that the "dancer of the future shall attain so great a height that all other arts shall be helped thereby" (qtd. in Macdougall 103) captures exactly the sort of influence that she herself would have on the Ballets Russes as well as on artists of every kind. As de Mille notes, "She touched off a creative conflagration. Not since the discovery of ancient statues during the Renaissance had such a re-evaluation of standards been witnessed in the arts. . . . Her effect on contemporaries and successors has been incalculable" (135–6).

The Ballets Russes in Paris

Eliot's connections with the Ballets Russes, which are clearly verifiable in the late 1910s and 1920s, seem to have begun in 1911 when this famous company returned to Paris for its third season, giving eight performances at the Théâtre du Châtelet from June 6–17, with Nijinsky and Karsavina as its lead dancers. Eliot would have been attracted to its performances for a number of reasons: its enormous popularity among the intellectual and artistic elite of Paris; its innovations in dance; its ideal of fusing various art forms into one artistic whole; the opportunity to see the most acclaimed male dancer of the day; and the chance to learn more about the culture of Russia in conjunction with his reading of Dostoevsky under the tutelage of Alain-Fournier.

The Ballets Russes was the brainchild of a small circle of artistic figures in St. Petersburg, headed by the great impresario Sergei Diaghilev, a man of enormous vision, imagination, and business sense, who possessed the uncanny ability to recognize and develop new talent and to bring extraordinarily gifted people together. Under his leadership, this group instituted some of the most innovative ideas of the times in the world of art. His main goal for the Ballets Russes was to achieve an interpenetration of the arts, so that dance, music, set design, costume, and literature would combine in a new artistic whole; in a letter of May 22, 1911, Diaghilev wrote that "my specialty is to make painters, musicians, poets and dancers work together" (qtd. in Buckle 196). As a group, they were dedicated to discovering and employing new techniques, approaches, and devices that would reflect the changing modern world rather than the static past, reflected in Diaghilev's 1903 remark, "I am deeply convinced we are living at a great historical moment. The time has come for a new culture, to be raised by ourselves . . ." (qtd. in Nijinsky 68). Indeed, Whitworth pointed out as early as 1913 that "from the start a definite note of modernity was sounded which proclaimed the Diaghilew [sic] ballet as an exponent of the new revolution in the art of the dance" (20). Finally, Diaghilev was committed to securing first-rate artists in all areas, from choreographers to dancers, from set and costume designers to seamstresses, from composers to conductors.

Diaghilev encouraged his choreographers to explore uncharted paths; his policy was that they should produce "something quite different: a movement of liberation in choreography; some fresh form of achievement" (Percival 89). His major choreographer from 1909–12 was the Russian Fokine, who made many innovations in the ballet. While Fokine had declared many of his revolutionary ideas in 1904 (Lawson 97–8), he was inspired to put them into practice largely under the influence of Isadora Duncan, whom he first saw dance in Russia in 1905; De Mille asserts that "the direct inspiration, the spark that fired [his] genius, was the barefoot, tunic-clad Isadora on a bald stage, dancing alone to Beethoven" (138), while Propert, in similar language, notes that Duncan inspired Fokine to "implant the elements of a soul into the Imperial Ballet" (71–2). Perhaps even more importantly, he was *enabled* to put them into practice by Diaghilev's commitment to the new and revolutionary. Fokine set about to make his choreography interpret the music, requiring his dancers to understand the phrasing of rhythmic patterns (de Mille 139). Furthermore, he liberated ballet from its rigid classical tradition by using asymmetrical groupings and placing dancers on different levels (Buckle 121). Finally, following Duncan's lead, he first used the works of famous composers of the past, choreographing *Les Sylphides* in 1909 to the music of Chopin, thus "breaking fresh ground," while in 1910 he was even more daring, creating a dance drama to Rimsky-Korsakov's *Schéhérazade*, an extremely radical move at that time, according to Buckle: "By imposing a passionate drama on an elaborate symphonic composition complete in itself [in choreographing *Schéhérazade*], Fokine and his collaborators were going much further [than they had in creating *Les Sylphides*]— committing a different kind of outrage. This bending of music to serve an action for which it was not intended would become a common practice in the next half century" (163).

Fokine then went far beyond Duncan's use of great music of the past by working directly with young contemporary composers whom Diaghilev commissioned to write works specifically for the ballet. Beginning with the 1910 season, he convinced Stravinsky, then only twenty-seven years old and as yet barely known, to compose *The Firebird* over the objections of his collaborators, who thought the composer's avant-garde rhythms too difficult for dancing. By the end of the next season, he was on his way to becoming "the most glittering star in the brilliant constellation of . . . Sergei Diaghilev's pre-1914 Ballets Russes" and one of the "foremost composers in Europe" (Stravinsky and Craft 26, 23). In the ensuing years, Diaghilev evoked memorable pieces of music specifically for ballet not only from Stravinsky—who produced eight scores for the Ballets Russes (Sorell 166)—but also from Debussy, Ravel, Richard Strauss, Erik Satie, and Francis Poulenc so that his various choreographers—Fokine, Nijinsky, Léonide Massine, Nijinska, and George Balanchine—collaborated closely with outstanding composers of the day.

Massine was the major choreographer and lead male dancer of the Ballets Russes from 1914 to 1921, contributing to the modernist revolution in dance by "harden[ing its] soft and 'beautiful' line" with movements that were angular and mechanical, using simultaneity and speed and focusing on the abstract and primitive (Garafola 86–8). Not only did Eliot attend performances choreographed and danced by Massine, but he also wrote often of his admiration for his skill, and he dined with him on at least one occasion, as described later in the chapter.

Diaghilev's set and costume designers were painters of great talent on the cutting edge of art; indeed, using the same artist to create both set and costumes was an innovation in itself. His major designers in the years 1909–12 were his close friends and collaborators Alexandre Benois and Léon Bakst. The former's particular talent was in synthesizing new artistic developments from Western Europe and Russian folk traditions, his most famous creation being that for *Petrouchka* in 1911, while Bakst's was in his daring and versatile use of colors. Bakst's design for *Schéhérazade* in 1910, for example, was bold and brilliant, "a perfect tornado of colour" (Propert 17); the stage was "furnished with huge carpets, draped with lavish curtains, hung with golden lamps, piled voluptuously with huge cushions. . . . Who else before Bakst had dared to mingle such oranges and crimsons, to offer such a luxurious swirl of ornament, to hint at such wickedness . . . ?" (Percival 98). In 1911 his great success was, by contrast, the delicate white and blue setting of a girl's bedroom and Nijinsky's costume as the Rose in various shades of red and purple for *Le Spectre de la Rose*. Subsequent artists who worked with the company included the Russians Natalia Goncharova and Mikhail Larionov, beginning in 1914; the

American Robert E. Jones, in 1916 only; the Spaniard Picasso, beginning in 1917; and in the 1920s a virtual "rollcall of the artists, major and minor, of the time," such as Matisse, Gris, Braque, Max Ernst, Joan Miro, and Giorgio de Chirico, many of whom designed special front curtains for their productions (Percival 109–112, 57).

Diaghilev also featured the leading Russian dancers of the day, including Ida Rubenstein, Anna Pavlova, and Tamara Karsavina. His most spectacular dancer (and later choreographer) in the years 1909–13 was Nijinsky, who electrified audiences with his technical skills, particularly his leaps, and with his acting ability. During rehearsals just prior to his first appearance in Paris in 1909, he was rumored to be "un prodige, un garçon formidable" [a prodigy, a formidable young man] (Buckle 138). Whitworth in his 1913 book calls him a genius: "[T]here is really no other word which at all expresses that peculiar element in Nijinsky's art" because of the many talents, "rarely found together," which are combined in him. Whitworth lists "that union of strength with lightness which is, perhaps, the most obvious feature of his style," "that fusion of utter freedom of movement with unfailing sense for decorative effect," and "the force of a powerful histrionic imagination," concluding that Nijinsky's dancing is "a thing as much of head and soul as of heart and body" (25, 27, 30–2). Most viewers of the time agreed. Of his acting ability, Sarah Bernhardt commented, on seeing him perform in *Petrouchka* in 1911, "I'm afraid, I'm afraid, because I see the greatest actor in the world," while Ellen Terry became a "fervent admirer" when she saw that ballet in England (qtd. in Nijinsky 128). Equally impressive was the judgment by Stravinsky himself: "To call him a dancer is not enough, for he was an even greater dramatic actor. . . . [As Petrouchka], he was the most exciting human being I have ever seen on a stage" (qtd. in de Mille 149). In conjunction with Fokine, Nijinsky rescued the male ballet dancer from his secondary position as carrier of the ballerina and elevated him to starring status; as de Mille notes, "Never before in the Western theater . . . had men dancers held such a dominant role" (143). From 1914 to 1921, Massine was the company's outstanding male dancer and choreographer, expanding the experimentations in dance still further.

Diaghilev first brought his Russian troupe to Paris in May 1909 to present performances both of ballet and opera, sending shock waves of excitement through the Parisian cultural scene. Buckle asserts that the "conquest of Europe by Russian dancing and the reign of Diaghilev as Director of the Ballets Russes can be said to begin at the moment Nijinsky [took] the stage with [Tamara Karsavina and Alexandra Baldina]" (141). The resounding success of the first performance was evident in Raoul Brevannes's review the next day in *Le Figaro* entitled "Le Gala russe," which opened with the ecstatic exclamation, "What an evening, what a hall, what an audience!" (5). So popular was the company that it presented a special gala performance at the Opéra on June 19, the day after the official end of the Paris season.

For the 1910 season, Diaghilev dropped opera from the program to focus entirely on dance and commissioned Stravinsky—then unknown—to write a piece specifically for the ballet, *The Firebird*, which featured choreography by Fokine with Nijinsky and Karsavina in the lead roles. Buckle asserts that with this work Diaghilev "invented a new art form, the ballets as *Gesamtkunstwerk* [total work of art] . . . in which all the elements, story (if any), music, décor and choreography, were commissioned by himself to form a complete whole" (182). It was one of the two great successes of the season, the other being the stunning production *Schéhérazade*. The costumes and décor of *The Firebird* were Bakst's "unquestionable masterpiece" (Nijinsky 109), with "juxtapositions of colour hardly guessed at before in the West" (Buckle 170). Fokine's choreography introduced a new type of mime, Rimsky-Korsakov's music was intensely exciting, and the sensual dancing of Rubenstein and Nijinsky received raves (Nijinsky 109–110; Buckle 170–2). Proust, after attending a performance, asserted, "I never saw anything so beautiful" (qtd. in Buckle 172).

This season was even more successful than the first, with numerous established artists, musicians, and writers, such as Proust, Debussy, Saint-Saëns, Bourdelle, Fauré, and Ravel, among its greatest supporters. Even more significant, the most avant-garde of the young aspiring artists, led by Rostand and Cocteau, were not only present at performances but followed Diaghilev and his party all over Paris, "like a court in attendance" (Nijinsky 114).

So when the third season of the Ballets Russes opened on June 6, 1911 at the Théâtre du Châtelet, anticipation was at fever pitch as all of Paris waited to see what new marvels, what daring experiments expanding still further the possibilities of art, would be presented. Bakst's costume design for a Bacchante appeared on the cover of the June 1 issue of *Comoedia Illustré* and also served as the cover for the *Programme Officiel des Ballets Russes* (Figure 33). Adding to the already high interest was the fact that Nijinsky had become a permanent member of the company as a result of a controversy in St. Petersburg in February when he had danced the lead male role in *Giselle* without the customary trunks over his tights, a costume considered shocking in Russia. When Nijinsky refused to apologize, he was dismissed. Most dance historians agree with Buckle that it "is almost impossible to believe that Diaghilev had not engineered this dismissal, which released Nijinsky [from the Imperial Ballet] to be the star of his new company" (187).

Two programs were performed four times each. The first, presented on June 6, 8, 9, and 10, included *Carnaval*, *Narcisse*, *Le Spectre de la Rose*, the surprise triumph of that year, and *Sadko*, while the second, presented on June 13, 15, 16, and 17, included *Schéhérazade*, *The Battle of Kerjenetz*, *Le Spectre de la Rose*, and *Petrouchka*, the most innovative of the new works.[2] Interested in all elements of the Parisian cultural scene, Eliot no doubt joined the ranks of their admirers. He has directly indicated that he knew and was influenced by both *Le Spectre de la Rose* and *Petrouchka*, and there is evidence that he was inspired by *Narcisse* as well.[3] Eliot's comment in his "London Letter" in the August 1921 issue of the *Dial* that "the earlier ballet [of the Ballets Russes], if it had greater dancers—Nijinsky or Pavlowa [*sic*]—had far less significance or substantiality" than the current productions (214) suggests that he had seen Nijinsky dance. He must have done so in 1911, since he could not have seen him during the remainder of the dancer's brief career.

The first Paris program for 1911 began with *Carnaval*, in which Nijinsky danced the role of Harlequin for the first time. It was followed by *Narcisse*, featuring a recently completed score by the Russian composer Alexandre Tcherepnine, choreography by Fokine, and a set and costumes in green and white by Bakst. Nijinsky danced the role of Narcissus, wearing a blond wig with long curls and a short white mantle, with Karsavina as Echo, repeating on a different level of the stage many of the movements of Narcissus. Critical opinion in general was negative; even Benois admitted that "it was not a great success" (qtd. in Buckle 194). Some elements were silly, if not laughable, including Nijinsky's costume, the opening scene in which the dance of "frogs, forest denizens, green goblins and toady sprites" resembled vaudeville (Nijinsky 137), and the closing scene in which Narcissus disappeared into the pool (Nijinsky went down a trap door) and a six-foot daffodil then rose from it. Further, the music was dull and the dancing somewhat static since Narcissus spent most of his time gazing into the pool, while, according to Propert, Echo "trailed about rather miserably in the background." Propert succinctly said of Nijinsky's appearance, "[His] tunic was too short and his hair too long." Calling the ballet as a whole "tiresome," he commented sarcastically, "So it dragged along till at last Narcissus disappeared into the brook, somewhat to our relief" (20–21). Ghéon in his review in the August 1, 1911 issue of *La Nouvelle Revue Française* attacked with intense sarcasm not only the ballet itself—which he called a blunder—but also the Parisian snobs who, lacking any critical sense, applauded Tcherepnine's "mediocre" music, admired Bakst's set "swarming with little green fauns," and adored their idol Nijinsky, even though he was "too blond," "too undressed," and "as little Greek as possible, with his tunic swirling around his body like a tutu." He ended by charging that the ballet was simply a pretext for featuring a "star," without unity or dramatic rationale, and accused the Russians of having lost sight of their original goal of transposing an action into a dance drama (250).

Despite the flaws of *Narcisse*, it may have been one source of inspiration for

Eliot's "The Death of Saint Narcissus," completed by August 1915, when Pound submitted it to *Poetry*.[4] An equally important influence seems to have been *Le Martyre de Saint Sébastien*, which caused a sensation in Paris in May 1911, as described in Chapter 3. The two performances, I suggest, coalesced in Eliot's imagination to produce this subtly erotic poem, which presents the figure from Greek mythology as a religious martyr who recounts his various metamorphoses and then, to escape the lure of the flesh, becomes a dancer before and/or for God; he dances on burning sand until his flesh is penetrated with flaming arrows (33–6). Bernstein suggests that the description of Narcissus's eyes as pointed refers to Nijinsky's "almond-shaped eyes," one of his most prominent features ("Vaslav" 85). As Smith points out, several of its lines reappear in "Gerontion," *The Waste Land*, and *Ash Wednesday* (34–5).

In addition to their influence on the poem, these two performances along with critical commentaries by Ghéon and others taught Eliot some valuable lessons when he began writing drama. *Narcisse* demonstrated pitfalls to avoid in using Greek myths in modern pieces. Thus, rather than directly presenting the myths which provide the frameworks for his contemporary plays, thereby removing the action from the present and interfering with the application of its meaning to present-day life, Eliot keeps them in the background, providing a sense of the universality of the experiences and problems portrayed. For instance, Aeschylus's *Oresteia* informs *The Family Reunion* (1939), deepening the significance of Harry's expiation of both his personal and his family's curse in modern-day England by linking it to the age-old struggle with sin and guilt. However, Eliot did not entirely escape the dangers of directly presenting myth in modern works, for, in early performances of the play, the actual appearance of the Eumenides on stage (called for in the text) failed miserably, no matter what form was tried, so that ultimately they were left to the imagination of the audience ("Poetry and Drama" 143). *Le Martyre de Saint Sébastien* alerted him to the difficulties of presenting a religious subject and of using poetry in contemporary drama.

Le Spectre de la Rose, the most popular work of the season, was based on Gautier's poem in which a young girl is visited in a dream by the apparition of a rose given to her at a ball. The music, Hector Berlioz's orchestration of Carl Maria von Weber's piano piece "L'Invitation à la Valse," was especially appropriate since Weber was a composer much admired by Gautier; the Bibliothèque nationale's May 1911 exhibition on Gautier in celebration of the 100th anniversary of his birth was a happy coincidence.

The ballet was a 12-minute *pas de deux* choreographed by Fokine and performed in Bakst's delicate setting of a girl's blue and white bedroom with French windows opening onto a garden. Exquisitely performed by Nijinsky and Karsavina (Figure

34), it was a breathtaking *tour de force*, with Nijinsky leaping in at the casement window, dancing continuously, some of the time with Karsavina in his arms, and ending with another spectacular leap that covered the entire stage. His costume, designed by Bakst and sewn onto him prior to each performance by the company's seamstress, consisted of a silk elastic leotard covered with rose leaves in various hues of red, rose, pink, and purple and a close-fitting cap of rose leaves. His makeup, which he applied himself, was meant to personify the rose; Romola Nijinsky described his face as resembling that of "a celestial insect . . . , and his mouth was like rose petals" (136–7). The aura of strangeness created by the unusual costume, in which Nijinsky appeared sexless, combined with his stunning leaps, his physical strength, and his delicacy of interpretation to make his performance unforgettable; as Buckle notes, "Nobody who saw Nijinsky as the Rose ever got over it" (192).

The reviews were ecstatic. Brussel's "Ballets Russes" in the June 8 issue of *Le Figaro* is typical:

> The performance is exquisite. In the muslin setting of a young girl's room on a spring evening, the Rose—its spirit, the memories it preserves in its petals, the perfume that it exhales—appears at the window opening onto the garden. It's Nijinsky, dressed in the faded colors of dying roses; he first murmurs his dance, then he leaps, then he glides toward the chair where the girl sleeps, with a rose, no doubt very precious, enclosed in her fingers. He gently embraces her and carries her to the whirlwind rhythms of the waltz. . . . The dance ends; with a light kiss on her forehead, the Rose evaporates into the dawn. . . . *Le Spectre de la Rose* is a masterpiece. (6)

Because of its rave reviews as well as its having been inspired by Gautier, whose poetry would influence him a few years later, Eliot probably attended one of its 1911 Paris performances; he himself indicated that he did see the ballet, although he did not specify when. His memories of it inspired the direct allusion in Section III of "Little Gidding": "It is not to ring the bell backward / Nor is it an incantation / To summon the spectre of a Rose" (183–5). In replying to John Hayward's assumption that he is alluding to Sir Thomas Browne's *The Garden of Cyrus*, Eliot asserted rather forcefully, "Damn Sir T. Browne, a writer I never got much kick from: I suppose it *is* a reminiscence, though I was thinking of the Ballet . . ." (qtd. in Gardner 202).[5]

Whenever he saw the ballet, Eliot's use of the rose as a symbol of human or divine love throughout his work owes something to his memories of it. In the early poetry through *The Waste Land*, the only reference to a rose is found in "Rhapsody on a Windy Night," written in Paris in March 1911 prior to the performance of *Le Spectre de la Rose*: "[The moon's] hand twists a paper rose, / That smells of dust and eau de Cologne" (57–8). Here the rose seems to symbolize a stale and faded human love and has a somewhat sentimental effect.

However, in the middle and late poems as well as in the plays, the rose often appears as a symbol of meaningful human love, of human love that leads to divine love, and/or of divine love itself. In "The Hollow Men," the "Multifoliate rose" (64), which the "empty men" (67) can hope for but can never attain, evokes Dante's vision of the Godhead in the *Paradiso*. In "Ash Wednesday," II, the "Lady of Silences" (66), who may be either the Virgin herself—often referred to in medieval hymns as a rose—or a human beloved such as Beatrice leading one to divine love, is addressed as "Rose of memory / Rose of forgetfulness" (69–70). The former is perhaps an evocation of the ballet's Rose, which lived in the girl's memory. The lines, "The single Rose / Is now the Garden / Where all loves end" (73–5) can also be read as describing either the Virgin, who, through giving birth to Christ, produced the Garden of Eden, the destination of all human love, or the human beloved, whose mortal love inspires one to seek the purity required for divine love.

In *Four Quartets*, Eliot endows the rose with a complexity of meanings central to the work, beginning in "Burnt Norton" with the crucial mystical experience in the rose garden, which symbolizes all timeless moments in human time, and closing in "Little Gidding" with the union of human and divine love: "And the fire and the rose are one" (260). Between these images, the rose has numerous meanings. It symbolizes human passion in old age ("Late roses filled with early snow," "East Coker" 57), the divine love that inspires purgatorial cleansing ("If to be warmed, then I must freeze / And quake in frigid purgatorial fires / Of which the flame is roses, and the smoke is briars," "East Coker" 164–6), the appealing physical beauty of the natural and time-bound world ("The salt is on the briar rose," "The Dry Salvages" 26), the futility of politics in human history ("the future is a faded song, a Royal Rose, or a lavender spray / Of wistful regret," "The Dry Salvages" 127–8), and the mortality both of love and life ("Ash on an old man's sleeve / Is all the ash the burnt roses leave," "Little Gidding" 55–6).

The second program contained the most original work of the Ballets Russes's 1911 Paris season, *Petrouchka*, a product of the collaboration of Diaghilev, Stravinsky, Benois, Fokine, Nijinsky, and Karsavina in the months and indeed weeks prior to its first performance. This work of "extraordinary novelty" (Ghéon, "Saison" 251; see also Buckle 201) was based on a Russian folk-legend about the disastrous triangular love affair of puppets (a ballerina, a Moor, and Petrouchka, the Russian Pierrot) at the pre-Lenten street fairs in 1830s St. Petersburg; as Buckle notes, it was "a glimpse of old Russia through modern spectacles" (195). The folk aspects of the plot and characters were skillfully merged with the contemporary music of Stravinsky and the experimental dance movements choreographed by

Fokine and executed by Nijinsky and the other dancers. This ballet, more than any other that Eliot might have witnessed in 1911, demonstrated how the old and the new, the established and the experimental could be successfully fused to produce an innovative work of art. Valerie Eliot's comment that Eliot had in mind the marionette in *Petrouchka* in creating the straw men in "The Hollow Men" (Southam 155) clearly indicates that he knew the ballet, and the likelihood is strong that he saw it at this time. Perhaps he was encouraged by Alain-Fournier to attend a performance, especially since Rivière admired it immensely and wrote a highly positive review published in the September 1, 1911 issue of *La Nouvelle Revue Française*.

It was one of Diaghilev's greatest creations; each of its components was hailed as among its creator's supreme achievements. *Petrouchka* was Benois's most important contribution to ballet; he not only wrote the libretto but also designed an ingenious stage-within-a-stage set as well as costumes reflecting the Russian folk tradition of the story's origins (Percival 92–3; Buckle 180). Stravinsky's score was praised by Whitworth for "its vivid intimacy of feeling, its freedom from formality, [and] its utter abandonment of the conventional means of climax"; his "most daring effects," such as the barrel organ, were introduced "informally and by the way" (84–5). In his review of the ballet in *Le Figaro* on June 17, Brussel commented that the "young composer, whom nature has generously endowed with rare gifts, began his career [with the score for the ballet] in a manner in which earlier musicians ended theirs. . . . As he becomes surer of himself, he is taking more risks, experimenting more" (6). According to Romola Nijinsky, Fokine's extremely complex choreography was "his greatest masterpiece," exhibiting the "greatest steps . . . taken in the development of ballet since Petipa" (127; see also Lawson 111).

Finally, Petrouchka was Nijinsky's favorite role, giving him an opportunity both to experiment with less graceful dance movements and to act (Nijinsky 144); Whitworth suggested that portraying the human being as machine gave him "a whole new range of attitude and movement" (60). Nijinsky's performance as Petrouchka may have partly inspired Eliot's description of human beings as machine-like, particularly in *The Waste Land*. Furthermore, this melancholy, would-be lover may have contributed to his conception of Prufrock, since he was composing the poem during his Parisian year and completed it in Munich in the month following the ballet's Paris performance. Lawson's comment that Petrouchka's "pathetic attempts to make his limbs express his love, joy, sorrow, and rage are those of a human being *frustrated by his inability to communicate his thoughts to others*" (111; italics mine) describes a central element in Eliot's characterization of Prufrock. And, as noted previously, Valerie Eliot revealed that Petrouchka did influence Eliot's creation of the straw men in "The Hollow Men."

The Ballets Russes in London

Eliot's involvement with and interest in dance in the later teens and twenties in London is clear. Most of his literary and artistic friends were fervent admirers of the Ballets Russes. Among the Bloomsbury group, Lady Ottoline Morrell was their greatest supporter. She first met Diaghilev, Nijinsky, and Bakst in Paris, befriended them in July 1912 when the company performed in London, and was from then on completely devoted to them (Buckle 232). In her memoirs she notes, "Lytton [Strachey] and most of my friends were such enthusiastic admirers of [Nijinsky], that I, from contrariness, had rather pooh-poohed him, but when I saw him dance I was completely converted, for I saw that anyone who so completely lost himself and embodied an idea was not just a good ballet dancer—he seemed no longer to be Nijinsky, but became the idea he was representing" (226–7). She often invited the three to her house at Bedford Square, and Buckle suggests that a tennis match observed there by Nijinsky and Bakst in July 1912 provided the inspiration for the ballet *Jeux* (234; see also Morrell 227–8). Eliot first met Morrell in 1915 (Ackroyd 73) and soon began to move in her circle of friends,[6] sharing their interest in the Russian company.

Although World War I forced a hiatus in performances of the Ballets Russes in London, the company returned in 1918. On Armistice Day, Osbert Sitwell, Diaghilev, and Massine attended a party at the Adelphi, at which most of the Bloomsbury group were celebrating (Buckle 350). While Eliot's name is not among those mentioned by Sitwell (17–22), he was likely to have been among the revelers as he was often included in their activities, and four days later he visited Leonard and Virginia Woolf at Hogarth House (*Letters* xxiv).[7] As Garafola points out, beginning in 1918 the entire Bloomsbury group passionately attended the newest productions of the Ballets Russes, admiring their modernist elements and seeing in them "the design, rhythm, and texture [that they] sought in literature no less than painting" (336). Indeed, many of them, including Clive Bell, Roger Fry, James Strachey, Richard Aldington, Pound, and Eliot, wrote major articles and reviews about them, particularly in 1919.

In addition, Vivien took ballet lessons with aspirations of becoming a professional dancer and was intensely devoted to the Ballets Russes. She knew both the leading dancers and specific ballets so well that she announced to Brigit Patmore and Eliot in 1917, after leaving a dance hall and stopping in a drugstore for aspirin, "I think I can do what Karsavina does at that moment" and demonstrated the dance movement on her toes (Patmore 85).[8] In the company of various friends, Eliot and Vivien attended performances of the Ballets Russes, whose ballets since the production of *Parade* in 1917 had been even more avant-garde in style and international in content than previously. On May 13, 1919, for example, along with Patmore and Jack and Mary Hutchinson, they saw at the Alhambra Theatre a program featuring *Carnaval*, *The Firebird*, and *The Good-Humored Ladies* with Massine and Lydia Lopokova dancing (*Letters* 292). On July 22, 1919 the Eliots accompanied the Sacheverell Sitwells to the same theater for the opening night of Diaghilev's newest production *The Three-Cornered Hat* with music by Manuel de Falla, choreography by Massine, and set design, curtains, and costumes by Picasso; the lead roles were danced by Massine and Karsavina. In her diary Vivien describes it as "very interesting and the music very good. Massine really wonderful" (*Letters* 320). The next evening Eliot went alone with the Hutchinsons to see *The Three-Cornered Hat* again as well as *Papillons* and *Prince Igor* (*Letters* 320). These performances no doubt influenced him as he was conceiving *The Waste Land*, not only through their innovative dance movements and rhythms but also through their contemporary music and art. Also, Eliot's remark in his essay "Dramatis Personae" in the April 1923 issue of *The Criterion* that Massine belongs to "the future stage" because he is "completely unhuman, impersonal, abstract" (305) indicates another source in addition to Nijinsky's performance as Petrouchka for Eliot's portrayal of modern city dwellers as mechanical and nonhuman.

During their 1919 autumn season (September 29–December 2) at the Empire Theatre, the Ballets Russes presented for the first time in England the innovative ballet *Parade*, a work which Eliot saw then, in 1920 when it was revived in Paris, and/or in 1921 when it was again included in their London repertoire: *The Waste Land* bears unmistakable marks of its influence, which is as important as that of *Le Sacre du Printemps* [The Rite of Spring]. This sensational ballet had aroused a furor at its premiere in Paris in May 1917 because of its experimental elements, and Apollinaire's coining the term "Surrealism" to describe it points to the new movement in contemporary art which it engendered. So its revival in London and Paris was a major cultural event, one not to be missed by avant-garde artists and writers.

Created by Cocteau, with music by Satie, choreography by Massine, and a Cubist set by Picasso, it depicted a *parade* [preview] of a show by street fair performers who try to entice passersby to enter their tent. In addition to drawing its subject matter from such popular forms of entertainment as the circus, the fair, and the music hall, *Parade* was daring and original in incorporating contemporary elements: ragtime music, an imitation of Charlie Chaplin,[9] cranking a motorcar, and taking a photograph. Satie's music served as a background for noises of industrialized civilization, such as typewriters, sirens, trains, and planes (suppressed in the 1917 production in Paris but restored in the 1919 revival in London) to suggest the "staccato pace of contemporary life" (Rothschild 88). Massine, dancing the role of the Chinese Conjuror, swallowed an egg, breathed out fire, and walked with a jerky motion. Other memorable characters included two ten-foot Cubist stage managers, one of whom (the American stage manager) resembled a robot with a stovepipe hat like a ship's funnel and with Manhattan skyscrapers on his shoulders (Buckle 331), and a pantomime horse that cavorted on the stage. The finale was "a rapid, ragtime dance in which the whole cast made a last desperate attempt to lure the audience in to see their show . . ." (Massine 105). According to Sorell, "*Parade* had the atmosphere of the street, the music hall, the circus . . . with a touch of the disintegration of society after World War I. It was new, different, a scandal" (170). Its mélange of contemporary art, dance, set design, costuming, and music suggested to Eliot as he created *The Waste Land* how he could incorporate various art forms as well as the modern world into his poem. Its allusions to a recent ragtime song, to automobiles, and to a typist, for example, along with techniques borrowed from cinema, Cubism, and jazz rhythms, can legitimately be traced in part to this ballet.[10]

From May through July of 1921, the Ballets Russes gave performances at the Prince's Theatre featuring a revival of Stravinsky's *Le Sacre du Printemps* and two new works, *Cuadro Flamenco* and *Chout*. In his "London Letter" for the *Dial* written in July, Eliot notes that he has not yet seen the company's current offerings: "M Diaghileff [*sic*], who has lately arrived with his Ballet and with Stravinsky, has crowded houses. . . . Not yet having had the opportunity of going, I can say nothing about either of the new ballets, *Chout* or *Cuadro Flamenco*" (214). However, Eliot's familiarity with and appreciation of its recent ballets are clear, as are his excitement over their originality and his hope that they will influence "a new drama":

> Two years ago M Diaghileff's ballet arrived, the first Russian dancers since the war: we greeted *The Good-humoured Ladies*, and *The Boutique Fantasque*, and *The Three-Cornered Hat*, as the dawn of an art of the theatre. And although there has been nothing since that could be called a further development, the ballet will probably be one of the influences forming a new drama, if a new drama ever comes. I mean of course the later ballet which has just been mentioned; for the earlier ballet, if it had greater dancers—Nijinsky or Pavlowa [*sic*]—had far less significance or substantiality. The later ballet is more sophisticated, but also more simplified, and simplifies more; and what is needed of art is a simplification of current life into something rich and strange. (214)

Eliot's comparison of the earlier and later ballets of the company suggests that he had seen both, further supporting my contention that he first saw productions of the Ballets Russes in Paris in 1911 (and indeed Eliot would have to have seen

Nijinsky then as he had ceased dancing by the late 1910s). Eliot's last sentence indicates how greatly the new works of the Ballets Russes influenced his own views of poetry as illustrated in *The Waste Land*, in which he clearly transforms contemporary life into "something rich and strange"—although many readers would argue that he does not simplify it.

Soon after writing that "London Letter," Eliot attended a performance of *Le Sacre du Printemps*, for his next "London Letter," written in September and published in October 1921, contains his commentary on it. Because Massine, who choreographed the revival of the controversial ballet, felt that Nijinsky had followed the rhythms of the score too closely, he based his own choreography on "the simple movements of the Russian peasants' round dances, strengthened . . . by the use of angular and broken lines which [he] had evolved from [his] study of Byzantine mosaics and perhaps unconsciously also from the captivating spirit of cubism" (Massine 152). The program note remarked on the new choreography's greater freedom from the music, as did Stravinsky in an interview appearing in *The Observer* on July 3, 1921: "The choreographic construction of Nijinsky, being of great plastic beauty, was, however, subjected to the tyranny of the bar: that of Massine is based on phrases each composed of several bars. This is the sense in which is conceived the free connection of the choreographic construction with the musical construction" (qtd. in Buckle 386).

Such comments, in effect authorizing the artist to break away from restraints—whether of bars of music in the case of choreography or of regular stanza forms and meters in the case of poetry—further confirmed Eliot's similar beliefs as he worked on *The Waste Land*. However, when he saw the revival in London, which was nearly as controversial as it had been in 1913 in Paris and was withdrawn after only three performances, it was the freedom and modernity of the music rather than of the choreography which most struck him. In the September "London Letter," while he found the choreography "admirable," being a great fan of Massine, he noted in a now-famous passage that only the music possessed the sense of the present which he considered a vital component of art:

The spirit of the music was modern, and the spirit of the ballet was primitive ceremony. The Vegetation Rite upon which the ballet is founded remained, in spite of the music, a pageant of primitive culture. . . . In art there should be interpenetration and metamorphosis. Even *The Golden Bough* can be read in two ways: as a collection of entertaining myths, or as a revelation of that vanished mind of which our mind is a continuation. In everything in the *Sacre du Printemps*, except in the music, one missed the sense of the present. [Stravinsky's music] did seem to transform the rhythm of the steppes into the scream of the motor horn, the rattle of machinery, the grind of wheels, the beating of iron and steel, the roar of the underground railway, and the other barbaric cries of modern life . . . . (452–3)

Thus the ballet's music, as Howarth points out, "brought home [to Eliot] the continuity of the human predicament," as well as the necessity of conveying this theme by capturing "the frightening barbaric sounds . . . [and] the frightening or poignant images of man's environment" in his poem. Eliot also realized, Howarth suggests, that, if he could achieve these effects in poetry, he would "create the contemporary literature which no writer in English had yet created" and thus would "bring a literature which had not yet had a Stravinsky, and lagged behind, level with European music" (235).

Howarth notes further that Eliot's comments on the music in the September "London Letter" echo those of Rivière in essays on Stravinsky's ballets published in *La Nouvelle Revue Française* and in *Nouvelles Études* [New Studies] in 1911 and 1913 and that they reveal his own stylistic methods in *The Waste Land*. Rivière remarked on Stravinsky's "audacity . . . marked by his simplification," his "acceptance of the banal by speaking in its voice and using all its advantages," and his omission of transitions between parts. Speaking specifically of *Le Sacre du Printemps*, he concluded, "The work is blunt and straightforward, its parts are completely primitive; it is presented to us without anything to help us swallow it; everything here is open, whole, clear, and coarse" (qtd. in Howarth 236). Howarth remarks accurately that his words "might describe the organization" of Eliot's poem (236). Furthermore, Rivière's description of the harshness and violence of the ballet's unconventional portrayal of spring seems to be echoed in *The Waste Land*'s opening passage: "This is a biological ballet. . . . Stravinsky tells us that he wanted to portray the surge of spring. But this is not the usual spring sung by poets, with its breezes, its bird-song, its pale skies and tender greens. Here is nothing but the harsh struggle of growth, the panic terror from the rising of the sap, the fearful regrouping of the cells. Spring seen from inside, with its violence, its spasms and its fissions. We seem to be watching a drama through a microscope . . ." (qtd. in Buckle 252).

Diaghilev's production of *Le Sacre du Printemps*, and particularly its music, influenced or confirmed many of Eliot's artistic precepts at the time and inspired various elements in *The Waste Land*: its interpenetration of pagan rites and legends from the past and the activities of contemporary life; its jagged, irregular meters and stanza forms; its lack of transitions; its imagery of the modern metropolis; its incorporation of other forms of art (such as painting and opera); and its portrayal of the present-day human being as a machine, the last partly inspired by Nijinsky and Massine. When Gordon suggests that Eliot found in the Ballets Russes and especially in *Le Sacre du Printemps* in the summer of 1921 an answer to his search for "a philosophic principle that would master [the] multiple, disparate perceptions" of contemporary life that he was struggling to portray in his poem, she uses the words "oddly enough" to indicate that the source of his solution is surprising (*Early* 107). However, his interest in and knowledge of this company—probably since 1911—make the connection far from odd, indeed even completely to be expected, especially since Diaghilev's productions presented incredible innovations in all the arts. Of course, those ballets were not Eliot's sole inspiration, since he knew well the current developments in all the contemporary fine arts and saw in them the opening up of new directions that gave him the insights he needed to create his poem.

Even after the passage of several years, Eliot's admiration for and willingness to defend the ballet were evident. As he wrote in "A Commentary" in the October 1924 issue of *The Criterion*, "The writer of these lines recalls his efforts, several years ago, to restrain (with the point of an umbrella) the mirth of his neighbours in a 'family house' which seemed united to deride Sokalova [*sic*] at her best in the *Sacre du Printemps*" (5), a reference to a performance that Eliot had seen in 1921 with Lydia Sokolova dancing the role of the Chosen Virgin. Moreover, a parody of "Prufrock," which Eliot added to an article by Vivien (under the pseudonym Fanny Marlow) also published in *The Criterion* that year, refers to the ballet: ". . . if one had said, yawning and settling a shawl, 'O no, I did not like the *Sacre* at all, not at all'" (V. Eliot 127).

In 1922, Eliot again saw Massine dance when he appeared with his own company on a mixed bill at the Coliseum. When Mary Hutchinson told him of a possible meeting with the dancer, he replied on April 27, "I hope your news of Massine at the Coliseum is true, as I have been to see him and thought him more brilliant and beautiful than ever—if what you said was sincere it is I consider a great compliment, as I (having never been so close before) quite fell in love with him. I want to meet him more than ever, and he is a genius" (*Letters* 523). Two months later, following the hoped-for meeting, Eliot wrote to tell her "how much I enjoyed the evening. I liked Massine very much indeed—with no disappointment—and hope that I shall see him again. He was much as I expected him to be. I enjoyed the whole evening and thought it perfect." He added two questions at the end: "Do you think Massine liked me? and would he come and see me, do you think?" (*Letters* 529–30). We do not know whether or not that visit materialized, but Eliot maintained his interest in Massine's performances; for example, he wrote in the October 1924 issue of *The Criterion* of the upcoming season of the Ballets Russes, urging Londoners, with obvious sarcasm, to appreciate the company's offerings, clearly fearing that they will not:

From November 27 the London public is to have the inestimable privilege of a season of the Diaghilev Ballet, and will be able to see again Leonid Massine and Lydia Lopokova, as well as several new acquisitions of the finest ballet in Europe. Let us hope that Sir Oswald Stoll will be able to provide, at the Coliseum, other turns of sufficient liveliness to induce our London audiences to sit through the performance of the greatest mimetic dancer in the world—Massine—to the music of one of the greatest musicians—Stravinski. . . . May we at least tolerate a part of what Paris has appreciated! (5)

Eliot's love for and knowledge of ballet provided him with one of several highly positive symbols for the spiritual and artistic experiences which he attempts to capture in *Four Quartets*; it was thus one means of achieving that which he said Dante had done, "realiz[ing] the inapprehensible in visual images" ("Dante" 229). The dance variously suggests the unity, perfection, harmony, order, and beauty to be attained in spiritual fulfillment or in artistic creation.[11] In section II of "Burnt Norton," he describes the quality of timelessness in terms of dance: "At the still point of the turning world . . . , / there the dance is" (62–3). In "East Coker," he first uses it to convey a meaningful and ordered existence within time, portraying his own ancestors dancing around a bonfire in a celebration of marriage: "Keeping time, / Keeping the rhythm in their dancing / As in their living in the living seasons" (39–41). He then reveals that this dance of earthly time is trapped in mortality: "Feet rising and falling. / Eating and drinking. Dung and death . . . . / The dancers are all gone under the hill" (45–6, 100). However, he ends by brilliantly reintroducing the more significant symbolism of the dance as defining a spiritual condition outside time: "So the darkness shall be the light, and the stillness the dancing" (128). In "Little Gidding," the image of a dancer in Section II suggests the order, grace, and beauty of a soul willingly undergoing purgation of sin, echoing but transforming Yeats's similar image in "Sailing to Byzantium" and "Byzantium": "From wrong to wrong the exasperated spirit / Proceeds, unless restored by that refining fire / Wherein you must move in measure, like a dancer" (145–7). In Section V, the last appearance of the dance is in terms of poetic creation, suggesting the perfection attained in those rare but inspired instances when all the words work flawlessly together: "The complete consort dancing together" (224). Clearly, Eliot uses the dance to express that which is most beautiful, most meaningful, most ecstatic both within and without the human experience, drawing upon his own admiration for this art form and reserving it for a major symbolic role only in his late poetry of intense spiritual and artistic exploration.

The Dance and Eliot's Verse Drama

Throughout the 1920s the dance continued to interest and influence Eliot, especially in terms of his experiments with verse drama. The ballet, as Howarth notes, "led him towards the discovery of entirely new rhythms for the English poetic drama" (306). In "The Beating of a Drum" in the October 1923 issue of *The Nation and the Athenaeum*, Eliot describes the importance of restoring the rhythms of poetry, music, and dance to contemporary drama, revealing a rather extensive knowledge of dance: "It is the rhythm, so utterly absent from modern drama, either verse or prose, and which interpreters of Shakespeare do their best to suppress, which makes Massine and Charlie Chaplin the great actors that they are, and which makes the juggling of Rastelli[12] more cathartic than a performance of 'A Doll's House.' . . . The drama was originally ritual; and ritual, consisting of a set of repeated movements, is essentially a dance" (12). In addition, he comments on a book published that same year by W. O. E. Oesterley entitled *The Sacred Dance: A Study in Comparative Folk-lore* as "an excellent study of primitive religious dances," regretting that the author does not "pursue the dance into drama" (12).

Oesterley's book was not the only one on dance which Eliot read at this time, for he wrote a review, entitled simply "The Ballet," of *The Dance: An Historical Survey of Dancing in Europe* (1924), by Cecil J. Sharpe and A. P. Oppé, and of *Mudras: The Ritual Hand Poses of the Buddha Priests and the Shiva Priests of Bali* (1924), by Tyra de Kleen, for *The Criterion*'s April 1925 issue. In evaluating the two, he reveals his own in-depth knowledge of the dance as well as his interest in how ballet may develop in the future. After indicating that a legitimate critic of ballet should have studied "dancing amongst primitive peoples," should possess "a first-hand knowledge of the ballet from bar practice to toe work," should "frequent the society of dancers, musicians, choreographers, and producers," should understand "the evolution of Christian and other liturgy," and should "track down the secrets of rhythm in the (still undeveloped) science of neurology," he faults Cecil Sharp not only for lacking all of these criteria but also for never having "really understood the modern ballet (such as that of Diaghilev)," indirectly revealing that he himself has some insight into them. He also criticizes Sharp for his suggestion that a new ballet should be founded on what Eliot considers "a dead ritual," concluding his review by promising to consider "the question of what the ballet of the future should be 'founded on'" in a subsequent article (441–3). Howarth suggests that this review, along with Eliot's 1926 preface to *Savonarola*, reveals that "in the dance Eliot discerned the divine pattern," which he attempted to capture in his drama through the rhythms and rituals of a poetic speech requiring "new metrics, a new language, a new tone," concluding that he succeeded in the "difficult feat of eliciting the dance from the dialect" (308–10). Whether or not we agree that Eliot was successful, Howarth accurately describes one of the ways in which Eliot's knowledge of the dance influenced the type of drama that he himself wrote beginning in the mid-20s with *Sweeney Agonistes*.

Dance and "Tradition and the Individual Talent"

Finally, Eliot echoes in "Tradition and the Individual Talent" (1919) the two major ideas in Whitworth's 1913 book *The Art of Nijinsky*. First, Whitworth argues that, as great art is impersonal, one of Nijinsky's virtues as a supremely talented dancer is his ability to subordinate his individual talent to the art of the ballet as a whole:

> Nijinsky has chosen to throw in his lot with that movement in the modern theatre which is antagonistic to anything like an undue emphasis on the *talent of the individual*. That the whole is greater than the part is a hard precept for mime or dancer who happens to be blessed with personality. The temptation to dominate is strong. But he who will accept and act upon this principle is sure of his reward; for so he will participate in a greatness that is greater even than his own—*the supreme greatness of an impersonal work of art*. Now, it is a chief glory of the Russian Ballet that it has not only afforded a perfect medium of expression to one of the most outstanding geniuses of the modern stage, but that it has also found in that genius *an aptitude for subordination which is among the rarest and finest virtues an artist of the theatre can possess*. (7–8; italics mine)

Eliot echoes these words in his essay when he says that "Poetry is not . . . the expression of personality, but an escape from personality" and that "[t]he emotion of art is impersonal. And the poet cannot reach this impersonality without surrendering himself wholly to the work to be done" (43–4), as Whitworth suggests that Nijinsky does.[13]

Moreover, Whitworth's comments on the importance of tradition in the development of new forms of art influenced Eliot's views on the subject. Whitworth asserts, "Only that tradition which carries the seed of young vitality can persist. For it is obvious that tradition needs for its complete process not only the faculty of *handing down*, but also the grace of *being received* . . . [by] the most important individuals of the new generation"; since those persons typically seem to owe little to "what has gone before," tradition has fallen into disrepute. However, he suggests, "if a novel work of art possesses any qualities of real virtue, tradition . . . is at the bottom of it. For tradition can act . . . so subtly that its influence may long remain undetected, and then at last be only generally perceived through the revealing perspective of time. This is the reason why the mere layman is always ready to be surprised at strangeness, whereas the professional, who can detect the ever-exquisite relation of effect and cause, is seldom astonished . . ." (75–6). Eliot, ever striving to be the consummate professional, would have agreed with these words and even seen himself called to take up the cause of defending the significant new art appearing at the time as an outgrowth of tradition. Whitworth's words seem to have provided the inspiration for his opening statements in "Tradition and the Individual Talent": "In English writing we seldom speak of tradition, though we occasionally apply its name in deploring its absence. . . . Yet if the only form of tradition, of handing down, consisted in following the ways of the immediate generation before us in a blind or timid adherence to its successes, 'tradition' should positively be discouraged. We have seen many such simple currents soon lost in the sand; and novelty is better than repetition. Tradition is a matter of much wider significance" (37–8).

The remainder of Whitworth's argument is also echoed, albeit in an expanded and more detailed form, in Eliot's essay. Taking as his example Post-Impressionist art, Whitworth argues that "there's no such thing as a complete novelty either in life or in the arts," but only organic growth, for which "tradition in some form or other is the first essential. For tradition, you see, is only another name for that principle of continuity without which the very idea of growth—let alone progress—is impossible" (79). Whitworth's "principle of continuity" is reflected in Eliot's comment that tradition "involves, in the first place, the historical sense, . . . and the historical sense involves a perception, not only of the pastness of the past, but of its presence . . . . This historical sense, which is a sense of the timeless as well as of the temporal and of the timeless and of the temporal together, is what makes a writer traditional. And it is at the same time what makes a writer most acutely conscious of his place in time, of his own contemporaneity" (38).

Whitworth concludes his discussion of tradition's feeding new works of art by citing the Ballets Russes as the supreme example to prove his case: "Now, the right functioning of tradition has never, perhaps, been more perfectly exemplified than in the case of the Russian Ballet which, greeted here on its first appearance as something absolutely new, soon transpired to be the culmination of a long development which linked together in one long process the most seemingly extravagant novelties with the beginnings of modern ballet in the eighteenth century" (79–80). Whitworth's theories, in conjunction with Eliot's own experience of seeing performances of this company, in all probability as early as June 1911, made a remarkable contribution to some of Eliot's best-known ideas on the arts and the artist.

Eliot's debt to the dance, which, I have argued, began in Paris in 1911, is thus of significant proportions. It influenced much of his work, especially *The Waste*

Land, Four Quartets, and "Tradition and the Individual Talent," for it showed him innovations which might be carried over into literature and criticism. The rejection of the graceful movements of traditional ballet for angular, less fluid ones; the abandonment of harmonious rhythms and melody lines in music for jarring, discordant, and often intensely exciting ones; and the experimentation with bold, unexpected colors and designs in the early sets of the Ballets Russes and with angular lines, multiple perspectives, and materials from the everyday world in later sets created by avant-garde artists—all encouraged him to try his own hand at creating something new and original in literature, most strikingly in *The Waste Land*. The dance demonstrated as well how the arts could interpenetrate and influence each other, a development reflected particularly in allusions to the visual arts and music in his poetry and drama. Furthermore, it suggested to him that the present gives new life to tradition and that tradition is an integral part of any valuable contemporary creation. Finally, it provided him with a symbol—significantly appearing almost exclusively in his late poetry—of unity, perfection, order, and beauty, those qualities which he felt at the time could be attained only in spiritual fulfillment or in artistic creation. In short, the dance exerted tremendous influence on the ideas and techniques which lie at the very heart of much of Eliot's *oeuvre*.

· 6 ·

THE OPERA

Eliot's appreciation and knowledge of opera have long been recognized. However, the important role played by the operatic scene in Paris during his year there has been overlooked. My reconstruction of the operatic offerings, which include a revival of Debussy's only opera, the premiere of Ravel's first opera, and productions of Wagner's *Tristan und Isolde* and *Der Ring des Nibelungen*, reveals the extensive possibilities for the influence of this celebrated field of the Parisian cultural world on the young American.

Eliot arrived in Paris having already been introduced to both operetta and opera. According to a note in *The Letters of T. S. Eliot*, he had been taken by his older brother Henry to see Franz Lehár's popular operetta *The Merry Widow* sometime between 1905, when it was first performed, and September 1910, when he alludes to it in the poem "Goldfish," and it "remained a favourite" throughout his life (54). Although the note erroneously calls it a Broadway musical, it was in fact "a new style of Viennese operetta, introducing waltz tunes and imitations of the Parisian cancan dances as well as a certain satirical element" ("Lehár" 125). The same poem also refers to Oskar Straus's operetta *The Chocolate Soldier*, based on Shaw's play *Arms and the Man*; as it was first performed in Vienna in 1908 (see Ricks 148–9), the reference suggests that Eliot kept up with current musical productions. In addition, at the Boston Opera House in 1909, he saw Wagner's *Tristan und Isolde*, which inspired the poem "Opera" (dated November 1909).

Operatic Venues and Performances

In addition to this previously established interest in the genre, Eliot's two French friends were fellow lovers of Wagner's music and thus further encouraged that interest. Indeed, Verdenal's comments on Wagnerian operas in letters written to Eliot both during the summer of 1911 and after his return to the United States provide evidence of their shared devotion and suggest that Eliot's Parisian experience nourished his love for and knowledge of opera.

Three important Parisian opera houses, described in some detail in the 1907 edition of Baedeker's *Paris et ses environs*, presented some of the greatest operas in the repertoire as well as a number of contemporary ones. The premier location was the Théâtre Nationale de l'Opéra, popularly known as the Opéra, designed by Charles Garnier in 1875 (Figure 35). According to Baedeker, it was universally renowned for its excellent productions of operatic masterpieces as well as for its grandiose ballets and sets. Performances took place on Mondays, Wednesdays, and Fridays, and, during the winter, on Saturdays as well, with prices from 2.50 to 17 francs, so that a student like Eliot could purchase tickets at a reasonable cost. Formal evening dress was required in the best seats, but women were admitted without hats to seats in the orchestra and balcony. The two other major venues for opera in 1910–1911 were the Opéra-Comique and the Théâtre Lyrique de la Gaité. Baedeker noted that the former originally presented "little operas with dialogue" but currently preferred "the pompous genre of the Opéra and lyric drama." The dress requirements were similar to those of the Opéra, and the prices ranged from 3 to 20 francs. The latter, he told his readers, had "already changed its purpose a thousand times and now presents a little of everything," with prices varying according to the productions (35–7).[1]

In researching operatic performances in Paris from October 1910 through June 1911, I was struck by three dominant traits. First, there was an astounding variety, with equal time given to young emerging musicians and to the long-established masters. This encouragement of new talent was a trait of the Parisian cultural scene that Eliot particularly admired, as he stated memorably in "What France Means to You" (94). As regards contemporary composers, the period was dominated by the French and Russians, which would also have been attractive to him, given his great interest in the literature and the culture of each at this time. Finally, the composer whose operas were most often performed during Eliot's sojourn in Paris was Wagner, whom he already admired. There were many opportunities to attend performances of Wagnerian operas, followed by lively exchanges on the subject with Alain-Fournier and Verdenal in particular, as confirmed by references to Wagner's music in Verdenal's letters to him. Soon after Eliot's departure from Paris for his summer trip, for example, Verdenal urged him, "Try, if possible, to hear something by Wagner in Munich" (*Letters* 24–5). In February 1911 Verdenal wrote that he had been listening to a great deal of music, mainly that of Wagner, and added, "I should be happy to know that you too are able to hear some Wagner in America" (*Letters* 31). Eliot's devotion to and knowledge of the works of the great German composer—who enjoyed enormous popularity in Paris at the time—are reflected not only in the well-known allusions in his poetry but also in poetic and dramatic experiments inspired in part by Wagner's daring innovations in form, subject matter, and techniques.

Two articles appearing in *Le Figaro* in October 1910, the month in which Eliot arrived in Paris, captured in miniature the great variety of choices for operatic performances as well as the openness to new talent typical in Paris during Eliot's sojourn there.[2] In the October 1 issue, an article on the up-coming season of the Théâtre Lyrique de la Gaité, identified as "a new musical theatre" which has become "an integral part of normal Parisian life," noted that its owners opened it because "everyone demanded it—young musicians eager to produce and anxious to know where their works could be performed as well as people of modest means who wanted to hear good music without ruining their budgets"—and because others had tried it earlier without success. According to the owners, "it *had* to be done in a city like Paris, so fertile in resources of all kinds. We had a theatre in a popular neighborhood, so we tried it. It opened its doors on January 7, 1908 as a 'municipal theatre' for ordinary people, so we mixed operas and comic operas, new works and old, such as *The Barber of Seville*, *The Marriage of Figaro*, and *A Midsummer Night's Dream*, performed by great artists and a good orchestra." Some of the productions to be presented during its fourth season were "new works by talented young composers, such as *Salomé* by Antoine Mariotte, *Elsen*, an opera in four acts by Adalbert Mercier, a prize-winner in the Paris music competition, and *Les Girondins* [members of a moderate republican political party in revolutionary France], an opera in five acts by Fernand Le Bourne, whom Paris does not yet know." The owners asserted that one of the duties of their theatre was to contribute to the "development of our young musicians," a statement conveying the supportive attitude toward young artists current in Paris. Finally, the owners announced that in the near future *Don Quichotte*, the new work of "one of the greatest of contemporary French musicians, the master Massenet," would have its Paris premiere at the theatre with some of the greatest French singers in the leading roles and that Isadora Duncan would perform her "Ancient Greek Dances," the latter a project which must have fallen through as she danced instead at the Théâtre du Châtelet in January 1911. The article concluded by crediting the Théâtre Lyrique de la Gaité with "keeping some of the greatest artists in Paris, rather than letting them go to foreign countries" (5).

In the October 20 issue, a front-page article entitled "The Season of the Opéra-Comique, 1910–1911" began by stating, "Faithful to its traditions, the Opéra-Comique has made a place on its program for established masters such as Saint-Saëns, Debussy, and Massenet as well as for an entire pléiade of new composers, some yet unknown, others already distinguished by works applauded in concerts." This was yet another demonstration of the mixture of old and new, the traditional and the experimental, which Eliot found so appealing about Paris. Among the established works to be presented in the coming season, two that would likely have appealed to Eliot were Wagner's *Fliegende Holländer* and Gluck's *Alceste*, to which his love of Greek mythology may have drawn him. Perhaps Eliot's interest in this myth, which provides the framework for *The Cocktail Party*, was first sparked by this particular production. Among the new works was Ravel's *L'Heure espagnole*, an opéra-bouffe described as "a little one-act sparkling with humor, the first work to be presented in this theatre by one of the youngest and most original of our young musicians." In addition to operas, the article announced concerts on November 5 and 12 on "The Primitives of Modern Melody in France and Italy," which may have nourished Eliot's interest in primitivism in modern art and literature. The article ended with a flourish that would have stirred a young man eager to absorb Parisian culture: "With such a program and such a gathering of artists, the 1910–11 season of the Opéra-Comique cannot fail to be exceptionally brilliant and rich in artistic results" (1).

An overview of operas presented during the period of Eliot's residence reveals the richness and variety for which the Parisian music world was so well-known, with performances of great works from the past and new ones from the present, with performers who were famous and those who hoped to be.

The wealth of choices during the week of October 20–27—about the time that Eliot arrived in Paris—is a good indication of what the entire year was like. The Opéra offered five works, including *Samson et Délila*, *Tannhäuser*, and *Tristan und Isolde*, while the Opéra-Comique presented seven works, among which were *Madame Butterfly*, *Die Zauberflöte*, and *Werther*. In addition, in his column *Courrier Musical* in the October 26 issue of *Le Figaro*, de Crémone announced a special November 1 performance of Hector Berlioz's *The Damnation of Faust* under the auspices of the Concerts Rouge at the Palais de Trocadéro, on the occasion of All-Saints Day. He assured his readers that this "superb gala matinée" was certain to be first-rate with well-known singers from the Opéra and the Opéra-Comique performing in the lead roles (6). In the following months, many of the great operas of all time were performed, such as *Aïda*, *Tosca*, *Carmen*, *Rigoletto*, *La Bohème*, *Le Mariage de Figaro*, and *Der Ring des Nibelungen*, while in the late spring during the Saison Russe at the Théâtre Sarah-Bernhardt Tchaikovsky's *Eugène Onegin* and Rimsky-Korsakov's *La Fiancée du Czar* were performed, the latter for the first time in France.

Recent and Contemporary Operas

In addition to established operas, the promotion of recent and contemporary works typical of the Parisian art scene at the time is evident in performances at the Opéra-Comique of Debussy's only opera *Pelléas et Mélisande* in February and of Ravel's first opera *L'Heure espagnole* in May.

Pelléas et Mélisande, based on Maeterlinck's 1892 poetic drama in prose,[3] was first performed in the spring of 1902 at the Opéra-Comique and was an immediate success. So great was its popularity that it was performed there again in the fall of 1902, in 1903, and in 1904. It gained international fame beginning in 1909 with a performance in London, followed by performances in 1910 in Vienna and Budapest, in 1911 in Turin and Paris, and in 1913 in Moscow and St. Petersburg (Lockspeiser 95–6).

The plot, conveying the pessimistic view that the lives of human beings are determined by forces over which they have no control and that the only certainty is death, follows the passionate but disastrous illicit love affair between Pelléas and Mélisande. Since Mélisande is married to Pelléas's half-brother Golaud, the two fight their growing attraction, but ultimately confess their love to each other. Overcome by jealousy, Golaud breaks in upon them and kills Pelléas. In the last scene, Mélisande is on her deathbed, having just given birth. Golaud implores her to reveal whether the baby is his or Pelléas's, but she dies without replying, leaving the answer unknown to both Golaud and the audience.

This highly sensuous and intensely emotional opera possesses a quietness and delicacy that set it apart from the more dramatic *Tristan und Isolde*, a major influence. Fleming and Macomber describe it as "a series of tableaux with dreamlike orchestral interludes linking one scene with the next" (324). Lockspeiser notes its simplicity, in contrast to the artificiality so much a convention of opera at the time; he quotes Verlaine's dictum, "Take hold of Eloquence and wring her neck" (224), and a passage from a review by Romain Rolland: "'*Rien de trop* [Nothing in excess]: that is [Debussy's] motto. . . . Like the Impressionist painters . . . , he paints with pure colours . . .'" (227).

Equally impressive and unique for the time is the way in which the music brilliantly corresponds to the language: "[It] is a masterwork in its wholly apt amalgamation of text and score, the inescapable rightness for its quiet dramatic purposes of Debussy's individual harmonies, the marvelous manner with which he made the sounds of Maeterlinck's French an integral element in a shimmering orchestral web" ("Debussy" 589). Lockspeiser comments that "No composer, unless it be Mozart, has ever made music accentuate speech more carefully, nor indeed more variedly" (219). Departing from convention, the opera has no arias, and the singers "simply intone the dialogue in delicate musical nuances that emerge as logical extensions of natural speech" (Fleming and Macomber 325), perhaps providing Eliot with a model of a musical attempt to create "natural speech" and inspiring him to make a similar poetic attempt. Finally, reflecting Maeterlinck's highly symbolic play, the opera is filled with water imagery, from Golaud's discovery of Mélisande beside a pool in the opening scene to her request to see the sea from her deathbed in the final scene (Fleming and Macomber 325). The water symbolism in the opera may have inspired Eliot to use similar symbolism—although in quite different ways—in *The Waste Land* and other poems.

Because Eliot already knew and admired this sensational opera, having discovered the plays of Maeterlinck, the music of Debussy, and especially the combination of the two in *Pelléas et Mélisande* during his Harvard undergraduate years (as he notes in an essay on Gordon Craig in King's College Library), it is hard to imagine that he would not have taken the opportunity to see this production in Paris, perhaps in the company of Verdenal and/or Alain-Fournier; increasing this likelihood is the fact that Rivière wrote a review of it for *La Nouvelle Revue Française*. Indeed, a measure of how it may have affected the young Eliot—admittedly full of passionate longings himself, as he revealed to Aiken—can be seen in Rivière's account of the intense way in which he and his friends had responded when first seeing it in 1902 and 1904 when they were only slightly younger than Eliot was in 1911. Rivière recalled the rapture evoked in "young people who welcomed the opera at its birth, those who were sixteen to twenty years of age when it first appeared." He described it as a "marvelous world, a beloved paradise where, entering a secret door, we escaped from the real world," a phrase perhaps echoed in Eliot's descriptions of the rose garden in both "Burnt Norton" and *The Family Reunion* many years later. Rivière defined the "power of its charm" and its beauty as lying in its innovative rejection of "linear music" for music that is "completely in each moment"; in the "extraordinary sweetness of its harmony"; and in the purity of its sentiment, which he described as "a lyric declamation of an admirable humanity." Throughout the review, he employed words such as "delicious," "exquisite," "soft," "ecstasy," "delicacy," and "fragility" to convey the qualities of the opera that were so appealing to the young. He concluded that, "while music, like the other arts, will soon cease to express only what is essential and re-establish the forms that it has suppressed, *Pelléas* is too perfect a realization of a certain ideal to fear future reactions against it and will stand as the true masterpiece of symbolism" (623–5).

I suggest that this opera, as well as the more well-known sources, informs a number of romantic moments in Eliot's poetry and drama involving lovers or potential lovers in gardens or parks, as two of the most intense scenes between Pelléas and Mélisande occur in those settings. At the end of Act I, soon after her marriage to Golaud, Mélisande meets Pelléas for the first time in the dark gardens of the castle of Golaud's grandfather Arkel, and they feel an instant attraction. At the beginning of Act II, when Mélisande and Pelléas are in a park, she accidentally drops her wedding ring into a well, an obvious symbol of her growing passion for Pelléas. Later in the act Arkel foreshadows her death when he tells her that she has the look of one awaiting an ominous fate as she stands in the garden in the sunlight, a passage perhaps reflected in the description of the young woman in "La Figlia Che Piange," written soon after Eliot's return to the United States from Paris: "Stand on the highest pavement of the stair—/ Lean on a garden urn—/ Weave, weave the sunlight in your hair—" (1–3).

Also, in Part I of *The Waste Land* the passionate love of Debussy's two lovers may hover behind that of Tristan and Isolde in the description of the failed relationship of the sensuous hyacinth girl and her potential lover, who is unable or unwilling to respond. The modern-day young people are an ironic contrast to the earlier two pairs of passionate lovers:

> "You gave me hyacinths first a year ago;
> "They called me the hyacinth girl."
> —Yet when we came back, late, from the Hyacinth garden,
> Your arms full, and your hair wet, I could not
> Speak, and my eyes failed . . . . (35–39)

Both the sensuality and the quiet delicacy of this scene seem to reflect Debussy's opera.

Other moments in Eliot's poetry and drama may have some connection—although more tenuous—with the opera. One example is found in "Burnt Norton," I, in the evocation of the two potential lovers in the rose garden ("Footfalls echo in the memory / Down the passage which we did not take / Towards the door we never opened / Into the rose-garden," 11–14), a motif which is then echoed throughout *Four Quartets*. Another is seen in *The Family Reunion* in Agatha's lines, "I only looked through the little door / When the sun was shining on the rose-garden," and Harry's response, "O my dear, and you walked through the little door / And I ran to meet you in the rose-garden" (276–7). Although this opera has never, as far as I can determine, been mentioned in Eliot scholarship as a possible source of ironic contrast to Eliot's failed lovers, it seems likely that he saw it in Paris in 1911 and that it lies quietly behind some of the characters he created in his poetry and drama.

A contemporary one-act opera which was impressive for its experimentation with a past form was Ravel's *L'Heure espagnole*, his first work in this genre. Premiering on May 19, 1911 at the Opéra-Comique on a double bill with Massenet's *Thérèse*, it was the thirty-five-year-old French composer's attempt, as he himself explained in a letter published on May 17 in *Le Figaro*, to "rejuvenate the opéra-bouffe of Italy, but not in its traditional form." Calling his opera a "comédie musicale," he asserted that the "humorous spirit of the work is purely musical. Laughter is evoked by unusual harmony, rhythm, melodic design, and orchestration" (5).

Based on Franc-Nohain's 1904 comedy of the same title, the opera is set in a clockmaker's shop in Spain and follows his wife's attempts to entertain two lovers during his one-hour absence. Ravel himself revealed that it appealed to him because of the "mixture of everyday conversation and deliberately ridiculous lyricism, the atmosphere of unusual and amusing sounds surrounding the characters in the clock shop, . . . [and] the opportunity to make good use of the picturesque rhythms of Spanish music" (qtd. in Larner 97). In the score he combines inventive musical effects with everyday prosaic events, anticipating in many ways the radical music of Satie in the scandalous 1917 ballet *Parade*. Among the wittiest effects, according to Larner, are the use of the lower instruments of the orchestra, such as the bassoon, trombone, and tuba, and the score for the orchestral overture, which incorporates the sounds of three metronomes at different speeds, bells ringing out of time, the crowing of a rooster produced by a sarrusophone, and the singing of a bird produced by a piccolo (101).

Ravel's experiments were widely praised in the reviews. René Lara in his column *Notre Page Musicale* [Our Music Page] in the May 27 issue of *Le Figaro* notes, "Ravel had the charming audacity to revive a type of musician that we rarely encounter among the pontiffs of the modernist school—the humorous musician. In returning to opéra-bouffe, he has victoriously proven that one can be a very subtle, advanced, and modernist musician and still possess the comic view, composing a score that is frankly amusing and clearly burlesque. It is full of ingenuity, demonstrating a rare mastery of sonority and tone in its comic effects and irresistible 'jokes'" (3). René Bizet in an interview with Ravel published in *L'Intransigeant* on May 17 reported the composer's comment that, "[a]bove all, I attempt to work on things which are very different. No principles, no principles which impose stereotyped formulas," and praised this "courageous statement, which is indeed that of a young man with bold ideas . . . who currently represents one of the finest hopes of the French school" (qtd. in Orenstein 412). And Ghéon in his review in the July 1, 1911 issue of *La Nouvelle Revue Française* described Ravel's playful, paradoxical music as very French, noting that his particular talent lay in "transforming into music the least musical subjects" and asserting that his music was "at the forefront [literally the frontier] of literary music and music in general" (136)—a great compliment from a tough critic.

The opera itself and these highly positive reviews confirmed yet again the openness of the Paris arts establishment to new ideas and techniques. Indeed, Ravel's rhythmic innovations and his use of ordinary materials—both in subject matter and orchestration—may have served as inspiration for Eliot to experiment with meter and to include elements of ordinary life, such as the music hall song "That Shakespearian Rag," in *The Waste Land* and other poems.

Wagnerian Opera

While the Parisian opera scene offered a wide array of both long-famous and new works by numerous composers, those of Richard Wagner were dominant. The Wagnerian vogue enjoyed both pervasiveness and power in Europe in the late nineteenth and early twentieth centuries, as described in Blissett's essay "Wagner in *The Waste Land*." It was at a peak of intensity in Paris during Eliot's residence, so that he was certainly swept up in it and for the rest of his life bore its indelible impress. Already enamored of this composer, he could have seen *Tristan und Isolde* in October or November, *Tannhäuser*, *Die Walküre*, and *Götterdämmerung* in November as well as several other times throughout the year, *Lohengrin* in February, *Die Meistersinger von Nürnburg* in March, and the entire cycle *Der Ring des Nibelungen* in June just before leaving Paris to travel to Germany and Italy.[4]

Wagner (1813–83) was a highly innovative composer who influenced Eliot in subject matter and technique and also provided him with several major allusions. A complex artist who explored entirely uncharted territory, Wagner was nevertheless influenced by a variety of sources. Among his musical influences were Mozart, Weber, and Gluck. However, most important was Beethoven, whom he worshipped. This is especially germane since devotion to Beethoven was a hallmark of the Parisian music scene during Eliot's year there (see Chapter 7). Wagner admired and was inspired in particular by Beethoven's quartets and symphonies and learned from him a mastery of construction; in 1870, he published an essay on Beethoven, arguing that music is the supreme art. Numerous other figures also exerted powerful influences upon Wagner: Aeschylus, Shakespeare, Schiller, Goethe, Schopenhauer, Nietzsche, and Freud. Christianity and Buddhism were influential as well. Interestingly, many of these also influenced Eliot.

Despite Wagner's reverence for composers of the past, he largely defied the musical conventions of the eighteenth and nineteenth centuries, rejecting traditional opera and inventing a revolutionary type of musical stage work for "the people," the *gesamtkunstwerk*, which united music, poetry, drama, dance, and painting. In this "music drama," as he called it, a poetic drama based on medieval Christian tales or Germanic and Norse mythology is sung against a complex orchestration. Even more astounding than his invention of this epical, interdisciplinary, and highly complex form was that Wagner himself single-handedly acted as composer, poet, dramatist, and set designer, a feat which no other composer before or since has even attempted, much less accomplished. Eliot no doubt found in this ambitious interweaving of various art forms inspiration for a similar type of innovation in his own poetry, most obviously in *The Waste Land*. Attending Wagnerian operas in conjunction with the similarly innovative interdisciplinary performances of the

Ballets Russes and the sensational production *Le Martyre de Saint Sébastien* during his Paris year—as I am convinced that he did—provided him with a powerful set of models for poetic possibilities.

Other elements of Wagner's operas also influenced Eliot. Wagner's creation of the *leitmotif*, a musical theme associated with a character, object, event, emotion, or idea, leading to great psychological complexity similar to free association, contributed to Eliot's creation of the "objective correlative," which he defined in his 1919 essay *"Hamlet"* as "a set of objects, a situation, a chain of events which shall be the formula of that *particular* emotion; such that when the external facts, which must terminate in sensory experience, are given, the emotion is immediately evoked" (48). Furthermore, Wagner's use of repeated themes, images, and phrases in part inspired Eliot to employ repetition as a structural technique in a number of works, in particular *The Waste Land* and *Four Quartets*. Inspired by Beethoven's experiments with repetition of themes, Wagner went a step further. Indeed, Howarth asserts that "no one understood better than Wagner how drama includes the ritual of ceremony (and how it requires a compelling repetitive pattern)" (383). Eliot's adaptations of these characteristics reflect debts to both of these great masters. In addition, Wagner's abandonment of discrete musical sections for a continuous musical flow (with which Beethoven also experimented) influenced the poet to use a stream of consciousness structure with little or no transition between parts, particularly in such poems as "The Love Song of J. Alfred Prufrock" and *The Waste Land*. Finally, Wagner's use of a multilayered symbolism on the three planes of drama, poetry, and music to convey his complex view of human beings and the world in which they live demonstrated a demanding and difficult, but highly effective method of communicating a similarly profound vision, which Eliot skillfully employs in such poems as *The Waste Land*, "Ash Wednesday," and *Four Quartets*.[5]

Having a preexisting interest in Wagner's work, Eliot must have been thrilled upon his arrival in October to discover that *Tristan und Isolde* was playing at the Opéra from October 22 to November 7. The reviews were ecstatic. In the November 1 issue of *Comoedia Illustré*, the reviewer asserted that "this immortal work of Wagner was presented with all the brilliance, all the tradition, and all the perfection worthy of the masterpiece. The two lead singers gave powerful expression to the major scenes, particularly the superb lyricism of the death of Isolde; their interaction and dramatic attitudes added to the intensity of the score" (64). Equally laudatory was the review in the October 30 issue of *Le Figaro*: "The last three performances of *Tristan und Isolde* . . . are among the outstanding events of the musical season. They have not only been perfect models of art, and of Wagnerian art in particular, but they have also shown how responsive the Parisian public has become, for we have rarely seen at the Opéra an audience more attentive, an atmosphere more rapt, and an enthusiasm more fervent. . . . Indeed, as a result of pressing requests, the Opéra may add one more performance if Mme Nordica, who is scheduled to leave for the United States for a series of concerts, can stay" (5).

Eliot may have been one of those rapt and enthusiastic members of the audience, perhaps attending the last performance on November 7 in the company of his new acquaintances Verdenal and Alain-Fournier. As mentioned earlier, two letters from Verdenal to Eliot refer to Wagner in a manner that conveys their intense interest in his works. In July 1911, soon after Eliot's departure from Paris, Verdenal urged him to see "something by Wagner" in Munich, while, in February 1912, he wrote that *Tristan und Isolde* "is terribly moving at the first hearing, and leaves you prostrate with ecstasy and thirsting to get back to it again" (*Letters* 31). Verdenal's intensely emotional response to that opera is quite similar to Eliot's description of his feelings about it in a conversation in 1956 with Stravinsky, who recalled that "Wagner was a principal [topic of their conversation]." He observed that "Eliot's Wagner nostalgia was apparent" and suggested that "*Tristan* must have been one of the most passionate experiences in his life" (92). Assuming that Eliot was referring to the 1909 performance in Boston in his poem "Opera," scholars have wondered at the absence of emotion. A possible explanation is that, in his conversation with Stravinsky, he was referring to a performance in Paris in 1910, when his passion for it may have been shared and reinforced by that of his friends.

Alain-Fournier and Rivière reveal their admiration for this Wagnerian opera in numerous letters of the time (Howarth 154). Also, Rivière wrote a highly personal and dramatic review of the 1910 Paris performance, which appeared in the January 1911 issue of *La Nouvelle Revue Française*. Some of its phrases seem to have influenced Eliot's use of the line "*Oed' und leer das Meer*" [Empty and blank the sea] from Act III of the opera to close the Hyacinth Girl passage in *The Waste Land*: "Monstrous masterpiece!," Rivière wrote. "I enter it like a black and blue night. There is no work more deprived of hope than *Tristan*; because desire is the opposite of hope. . . . The third act opens in solitude as empty as the sea. . . . The last measures of the opera express an immense outpouring of despair" (29, 32–3).[6]

The opera's portrayal of the intense and doomed love affair between the two famous lovers powerfully conveys Wagner's concept that love, destruction, and death are closely linked. Set in the legendary Celtic world at the beginning of the Middle Ages, the plot actually begins long before the curtain rises. The noble baron Tristan, in the service of his uncle King Mark of Cornwall, kills the Irish knight Morold and is himself severely wounded; he is cured by Isolde, Morold's fiancée, who, upon realizing Tristan's identity, intends to kill him for revenge until she looks into his eyes. Upon his return to England, he arranges a marriage between his uncle and Isolde, and the action of the opera begins as Tristan brings Isolde to Cornwall for the wedding. As his ship nears the coast, a young Irish sailor sings a plaintive 14-line song about the pain and anguish that he and his beloved feel as a result of their separation. In the last six lines, he imagines that her sighs of grief create the strong wind which fills the sails and pushes the ship farther away from Ireland:

> Westward
> turns my gaze;
> Eastward
> sails the ship.
> Fresh blows the wind
> Towards my homeland:
> My Irish child,
> Where are you dwelling?
> Do your drifting sighs
> Fill the sails?
> Alas, alas/Woe, woe/Blow, blow, you wind!
> Alas/Woe, ah alas/woe, my child,
> Irish maiden,
> You wild, adorable maiden! (*Tristan*, 1–14; translation mine)

The German is extremely complex and layered, as Wagner plays on the various overlapping meanings of *weht, wehen, wehe,* and *weh* ("alas/woe," "sighs," "blow/blowing," and "grief/sorrow"), so that each evokes the other closely linked definitions. The orchestral accompaniment, both melancholy and ominous, reinforces the emotional content of the words. Thus the opening passage of the opera sounds what Bernard Harris describes as "a tone of warning, even menace" (110) and functions as a sinister foreshadowing of the tumultuous love affair to come.

Eliot opens the Hyacinth Girl passage in *The Waste Land* with a quotation of four lines from the sailor's story. Blissett proposes that the poet knew the opera so intimately that his two small errors in the quotation in the original typescript indicate that he was quoting from memory (71–2). This intimate knowledge of the work suggests that Eliot intended the allusion to sound a similar note of anguish and/or warning for the modern-day couple on the verge of a love affair which holds the promise of sensuality and passion. Although their relationship, like that of Tristan and Isolde, is doomed, a crucial difference is that it never even gets underway: the young man is unable or unwilling to respond to the enticements of the young woman returning from a garden with wet hair and arms full of flowers. The ironic contrast to the intense love of Tristan and Isolde implies that passion such as theirs does not or cannot exist in the present.

However, because Eliot only uses lines 5–8 of the song—lines which out of context can appear to be positive—many Eliot scholars have erroneously described them as referring to happy love, quite the opposite of the song's significance in the opera. Cleanth Brooks in an otherwise brilliant analysis of *The Waste Land* published in 1948 describes the sailor as singing a song of "happy and naïve love" (11), an interpretation echoed by countless critics since then. Smith, for example, citing Brooks, notes that the "desolation in this second quotation [from the opera] . . . contrasts with the fresh breeze, a portent of happy love, in the first [quotation]" (76).

In the opera, Isolde responds to the sailor's song of love's anguish with anger, thinking that it alludes to her anguish over Tristan, and decides to kill both Tristan and herself with a poison drink. They both drink from the goblet, and, believing that they are dying and not knowing that her maid has substituted a love potion for the poison, they give in to their passion as the ship docks. In Act II, King Mark, led by the treacherous knight Melot, discovers the two lovers together, and Tristan, overcome with shame, allows Melot to wound him mortally. In Act III, Tristan lies dying at his ancestral castle overlooking the sea, hoping that Isolde will arrive by ship in time to cure him again. When his servant asks an old shepherd if her ship is approaching, the shepherd replies, "Oed' und leer das Meer"; this German usage of two words with the same meaning for emphasis ("oed" and "leer") conveys both literal and emotional desolation, reinforced musically "by the English horn and the empty thirds and fourths of the strings" (Zuckerman 188). Eliot chooses this bleak and despairing line to close the Hyacinth Girl episode, thereby indicating the failure of love and the lack of a cure for this sterile condition in contemporary civilization. The ironic contrast with the passion of Tristan and Isolde is deepened in that in the opera Isolde does appear, although too late to save Tristan, who dies in her arms. Grief-stricken, Isolde lovingly describes the features of his face, recalls their shared passion, and then dies on his body. In Eliot's poem, no such intensely passionate love seems possible in the present.

In composing the opera, Wagner deliberately reduced the stage action to a minimum to emphasize the psychological drama in the minds and hearts of Tristan and Isolde, noting that the essence of the opera is "endless yearning, longing, the bliss and wretchedness of love; world, power, fame, honor, chivalry, loyalty, and friendship all blown away like an insubstantial dream; one thing alone left living—longing, longing unquenchable, a yearning, a hunger, a languishing forever renewing itself; one sole redemption—death, surcease, a sleep without awakening" (qtd. in Fleming and Macomber 279). And he emphasizes that intense emotional content through the opera's symmetrical form: he opens with the sailor's song of love's anguish; he features in Act II the intimate, ecstatic love scene in which Tristan asserts that, should they die, they would nevertheless be joined forever; and he closes with Isolde's powerful "Liebestod," a "retrospective re-enactment of their sexual union, now transmuted from sensuality to spirituality" (Fleming and Macomber 281), followed by the orchestral playing of the motif of longing heard at the beginning. Influenced by Schopenhauer's *The World as Will and Idea* (1819), Wagner believed that the only way to overcome the insatiable will and find true fulfillment was to adopt Eastern mysticism's renunciation of selfhood (Fleming and Macomber 280–1). This belief, which is powerfully demonstrated in the opera's last act, made a long-lasting impression on Eliot, as is evident in his works throughout the entirety of his career.

One can imagine the way in which this passionate tale with its dramatic music affected the young Eliot, filled with romantic longings which he yearned to express. And it is easy to understand why he described the opera to Stravinsky as one of the most passionate experiences of his life, especially if he were referring to a performance in Paris in the fall of 1910 rather than to the one in Boston in 1909. Indeed, in an article in the April 17 issue of *Le Figaro*, Brussel referred to "the frenetic passion for *Tristan und Isolde*" so prevalent in Paris at the time (5), an indication that Eliot's response was widely shared by opera-going Parisians. Most important, at least for literary criticism, the two allusions to the opera in *The Waste Land* seem intended to resonate both as a parallel (both relationships are doomed) and as a contrast (one was passionate; the other was not) to romantic love in the modern world.

Finally, Eliot must again have marveled at his good fortune, for the entire cycle of the Wagnerian tetralogy *Der Ring des Nibelungen*, based on Norse and German mythology, was presented at the Opéra twice in June 1911, for the first time ever in Paris: *Das Rheingold* on June 10, *Die Walküre* on June 11, *Siegfried* on June 13, and *Götterdämmerung* on June 15 and again on June 24, 25, 27, and 29 (Figure 36). It is hard to imagine that he would not have taken advantage of this rare opportunity to see all or part of Wagner's masterwork at its inaugural Paris performance, perhaps in the company of one or both of his French friends. That he and Verdenal were intensely interested in the tetralogy is evident in Verdenal's letter of February 5, 1912: "I have been listening to [music] quite a lot recently (still mainly Wagner). I am beginning to get the hang of *The Ring*. Each time the plot becomes clearer and the obscure passages take on a meaning" (*Letters* 31). This comment reveals that the tetralogy was a topic of compelling interest to the two friends and that they struggled to gain a deeper understanding of the difficult and elusive work. Eliot must have attended the first set or the first operas of the second set, for Verdenal's letter of mid-July sent to Eliot in Munich indicates that the American had already left Paris by the time of the second performance of the final opera. Verdenal wrote that he went "the other day" to *Götterdämmerung*, conducted by Arthur Nikisch; as Felix Weingartner was the conductor for the first cycle and Nikisch for the second, Verdenal was referring to the performance on June 29. And Verdenal's comment that "the end must be one of the highest points ever reached by man" is a likely reflection of Eliot's own feelings about it (*Letters* 23, 25).

The first and last operas of the tetralogy are reflected in *The Waste Land*. *Das Rheingold* functions as the prologue to the entire work, setting up the action for the three succeeding operas. The complex plot begins at the bottom of the Rhine river where the Rhine-daughters, who are celebrating the beauty of the Rhine gold which they guard, rebuff the amorous advances of the hideous dwarf Alberich. The dwarf retaliates by stealing their treasure and thus invoking on himself the gold's curse: while the ring he makes from it will give him the power to rule the world, he is compelled to give up love and live in emotional desolation. Throughout Act I, the refrain of the Rhine-daughters appears again and again in a variety of forms. For example, in Voglinda's song which opens the act, it is "Wagalaweia! / Wallala weiala weia," while, near the end in one of several songs mocking Alberich, it is "Walala Walaleialala!" In despair over the loss of their gold, the Rhine-daughters pray to the king of the gods Wotan to restore it to them. He engineers the capture of Alberich and secures the ring, as a result of which he receives the curse of misery, death, and catastrophe, whose bitter working out is traced in the three following works. *Das Rheingold* ends on a bleak note, with the melancholy song of the Rhine-daughters rising from the dark waters of the river as they mourn the loss of their gold.

The second opera, *Die Walküre*, recounts how Brünnhilde, the daughter of Wotan, incurs her father's wrath by disobeying his orders to end the relationship of Siegmund and Sieglinde; he punishes her by turning her into a mortal and putting her into a deep sleep, but grants her request that she be surrounded by a circle of fire which can be traversed only by a mortal with great courage. In the third opera, *Siegfried*, the young Siegfried retrieves the ring after killing the dragon guarding it and then crosses the circle of fire to awaken Brünnehilde, whereupon the two fall in love. While Eliot no doubt saw these two works, he does not directly use them in his poetry.

The title, the dramatic finale, and the reappearance of the refrain of the Rhine-daughters in the final opera, however, provided Eliot with sources of inspiration. He could have seen *Götterdämmerung* on June 15 as the last work of the first cycle of the tetralogy, although it had been presented by itself both in November 1910 and March 1911. He seems to have attended one of these performances, since he chose as the original title for "Preludes," III, completed in July 1911, "Morgendämmerung. Prelude in Roxbury" [Morning Twilight] and as the original title for "Preludes," IV, completed in the fall of 1911, "Abenddämmerung" [Evening Twilight] (Gallup 1240).

Götterdämmerung depicts both the final destruction of evil and the redeeming qualities of love. Act 3, scene 1 opens with the Rhine-daughters mourning the loss of their gold and asking for a hero to return it to them, sounding in the middle of the passage another variation of their refrain: "Weialala leia." Although Siegfried appears almost instantaneously, he refuses to give them the ring, despite their warning that he will die that very day if he does not. He gives it instead to Brünnhilde, and the two pledge undying love to each other; however, he drinks a potion which causes him to fall in love with Gutrune and to retrieve the ring from Brünnehilde in order to give it to his new love. Distraught at this betrayal, Brünnhilde seeks revenge by revealing that he can be killed by a spear in the back. After Siegfried is mortally wounded, he remembers his love for Brünnhilde just before he dies. Overcome with grief, she orders a funeral pyre for him, returns the ring to the Rhine-daughters, thus removing from it the curse, and then dies on the pyre in order to be reunited with Siegfried in death. The redemptive power of love triumphs over evil, as Valhalla is engulfed by flames at the opera's dramatic conclusion.

The most obvious reflection of the tetralogy is Eliot's use in Section III of *The Waste Land* of the refrain of the Rhine-daughters from the opening song of Act 3, scene 1 of *Götterdämmerung*: "Weialala leia / Wallala leialala." Interestingly, its haunting power was noted by the composer Raoul Gunsburg in a front-page article entitled "La Musique" in the October 4, 1910 issue of *La Figaro*; he wrote that "it is the song of the Rhine-daughters that will remain in one's memory." Eliot first sounds the refrain after the bleak description of the present-day Thames river (277–8) and then repeats it after the idyllic description of the river in Elizabethan times (290–1), presaging in the manner of a Wagnerian leitmotif the songs of the three present-day Thames-daughters, who recount their emotionally sterile copulations and thus convey the absence of meaningful love in the contemporary world. Beginning at line 292, they end abruptly at line 306 with the two syllables of the refrain which close Act 3, scene 1 of the opera: "la la."[7]

A complex set of meanings emanates from the refrain in the poem. While the "gold" that has been stolen from these modern young women is their chastity, their responses differ so that, on the one hand, the refrain reflects the sense of loss and desolation of the third Thames-daughter who "can connect / Nothing with nothing" (301–2), but, on the other, it contrasts with the emotionless descriptions of the first two, echoing the emotional emptiness which was a major component of the curse. Perhaps Eliot also intends to suggest, at least implicitly, the destructive nature of absolute power and excessive materialism, which are important themes in the opera, in contemporary civilization. The "la la" in the single and separate closing line of their songs seems to be meant as a distant, faint trailing off of this mournful sound, suggesting the hopelessness and bleakness of their collective experience. Playing off against that melancholy musical sound as a perverse subtext is the flippant, casual slang expression "la la," indicative of the attitude toward sex in the modern world, especially as evidenced in the second Thames-daughter and earlier in the typist.

Finally, the dramatic conclusion of *Götterdämmerung* may have partly inspired several aspects of *The Waste Land*. In addition to Eliot's acknowledged sources in St. Augustine and Buddha, the negative connotations of the repeated "burning" at the end of Part III may also reflect the violent conflagration which destroys Valhalla as a result of commitment to power and materialism at the expense of love and compassion. Furthermore, it seems to be one of several sources for the nightmare vision of the destruction of modern civilization in Part V. On the other hand, the love of Brünnhilde may have suggested to Eliot the possibility of redemption in the contemporary world, although in altered and crucially different ways. Instead of human love, the means of redemption are to be found in the commands of the thunder to give, sympathize, and control and the protagonist's determination to set his own lands in order. Finally, the fast tempo of the breath-taking finale is perhaps reflected in the jarring final passage of the poem.

The reviews of the tetralogy were entirely laudatory. A review by L. Borgex entitled "Le premier cycle de la 'Tetralogy'" with photographs of the production by Bert, appeared in the June 16 issue of *Comoedia* with the subtitle, "The production was brilliant and bestowed great honor on M. Weingartner [the conductor]." After noting that "the Opéra has just presented [Wagner's *Ring*] for the first time in its entirety," Borgex enthusiastically described it as "above all a poetic work whose powerful drama includes in symbolic actions all the emotions that motivate the actions of human beings; and, instead of limiting itself to the single cadence of a harmoniously rhythmic verse . . . , it has underlined all the actions, accented its ideas, and expressed its emotions with the most formidable musical conception since Bach and Beethoven." Commenting that "the creative will of the great German master was able to incorporate all the arts in this work," he emphasized the importance of the presentation at the Paris Opéra of the entire cycle and praised the high quality of the performance. He described the skill of the conductor, especially in the finale of *Götterdämmerung*, which was "played at a dizzying pace that became more and more hurried and intense, producing a truly moving emotion and evoking cheers from the audience." He lauded the singers also, in particular M. Dumas in the role of Wotan and, concluded, "And now, let's rest for a week, while M. Nikisch [the next conductor] prepares for the second performance of the cycle," set to begin on June 24 (5).[8]

Reviews in *Le Figaro* were equally positive. Reporting on *Siegfried* in the June 14 issue, Brussel called it "splendid": "The admirable third part of this immense work was executed to perfection by an orchestra of the first order, directed by M. Weingartner with mighty mastery. The brilliant tenor M. Dalmorès, singing the role of Siegfried in his first performance on the stage of the Opéra, was acclaimed by the entire audience, while Mlle Grandjean, a marvelous Wagnerian singer, performed the role of Brünnhilde admirably." All in all, he declared, "it was a glorious evening" (6). His review of *Götterdämmerung* in the June 16 issue noted that it was an impressive musical experience and that the first cycle had a "unanimous and profound success that presaged the same for the second production" (5).

The glowing reviews of the second production of the tetralogy matched those of the first. Brussel in the June 26 issue of *Le Figaro* proclaimed the first performance of the second round, *Das Rheingold*, "an enormous success" and ended with a flourish: "Even greater joys are in store for us in seeing the entire tetralogy, that work which so closely resembles Wagner's guardian angel—music—which he himself described as this good angel 'which has come from the beginning of time burning with the sweat of human genius'" (5). After the final performance, he asserted in a review in the June 30 issue of *Le Figaro* that "the second cycle of the tetralogy ended in a magnificent manner," praising Nikisch for his thrilling direction of "this gigantic epic" and the singers for their artistry, mentioning that the trio of the Rhine-daughters demonstrated "exquisite freshness and perfect balance." He concluded, "These evenings, so long awaited in Paris, have been doubly happy since they presented the best music and proved that Parisian audiences, reputed to be more frivolous than attentive, have an artistic conscience" (6).

So the first-ever production of *Der Ring des Nibelungen* in Paris was a glorious success, perhaps best captured in Brussel's proclamation in the June 18 issue of *Le Figaro* that "these four evenings when we have successively heard all four parts have been a fantastic revelation for Wagnerians who have not been to Bayreuth, Vienna, or Munich" (5). If Eliot was one of those Wagnerians, he experienced the same rush of enthusiasm and excitement conveyed in these reviews. Blissett asserts, "No one can listen to a Wagner music drama without being changed by it; no one can go on a pilgrimage to Bayreuth without being marked for life" (76), a statement applicable to Eliot, who was "marked for life" by performances of Wagnerian opera in Paris and perhaps in Munich, Vienna, or even Bayreuth during his summer trip in 1911.

The Influence of Parisian Opera on Eliot

In Eliot's 1942 essay "The Music of Poetry," he notes that "a poet may gain much from the study of music," particularly as regards "the sense of rhythm and the sense of structure," indicating that he himself has done so, although he modestly denies having a "technical knowledge of music": "I know that a poem, or a passage of a poem, may tend to realize itself first as a particular rhythm before it reaches expression in words, and that this rhythm may bring to birth the idea and the image; and I do not believe that this is an experience peculiar to myself." He then specifies some of the ways in which musical elements may be transposed into poetry, again implying his own uses of music: "The use of recurrent themes is as natural to poetry as to music. There are possibilities for verse which bear some analogy to the development of a theme by different groups of instruments; there are possibilities of transitions in a poem comparable to the different movements of a symphony or a quartet; there are possibilities of contrapuntal arrangement of subject-matter. It is in the concert room, rather than in the opera house, that the germ of a poem may be quickened" (113–14). That study of music from which a poet may gain much seems for Eliot to have been nourished during his year in Paris, where, despite his claim that the music of the concert hall rather than that of the opera house inspires poetry, the operatic productions of the day fed his love for and knowledge of the genre and provided him with material for future poems.

Upon his return to Harvard, Eliot attended numerous operas, as well as other programs of classical music, perhaps inspired by his Parisian experiences of opera. For example, a set of programs dated from October 1913 to February 1914 in the Eliot Collection of Harvard's Houghton Library indicates that he attended no fewer than twelve operas and concerts in that brief period alone, including *Tristan und Isolde* on December 1, 1913, *Tosca* on December 22, 1913, and *Madame Butterfly* on January 2, 1914, all at the Boston Opera House. This interest in opera continued throughout the remainder of Eliot's life, providing him with sources of inspiration for his poetry, drama, and criticism and culminating in his discussion in the late 1950s with his close friend Stravinsky about collaborating on an opera, a project which never came to fruition (Boaz 218).

While Eliot must have seen the operas of Debussy, Ravel, and Wagner on many occasions, his probable viewing of them during his *annus mirabilis* in Paris made an indelible impression upon him, providing him with sources of inspiration as regards subject matter, structure, symbolism, and experimental techniques. The multifaceted operatic world offered him numerous opportunities to hear works that would significantly influence his literary production and enrich his personal life.

MUSIC OF THE CONCERT HALL

The classical music scene in Paris in 1910–1911 was spectacular, featuring (as did the other Parisian arts) the works of both established masters and young aspiring composers. In this chapter, I re-create that scene, describing performances, the venues in which they were presented, and the specific composers whose works were most noteworthy. In exploring this amazingly rich Parisian cultural arena which has been largely overlooked in Eliot studies, I suggest those which seem likely to have attracted and influenced him based on his own personal interests and on evidence in his works.

Arriving in Paris with some knowledge both of opera and music of the concert hall and finding two companions who were passionately devoted to music, attended performances on a regular basis, and discussed what they had heard, Eliot must have marveled at the wealth of opportunities to hear music of the concert hall. Verdenal's letters variously reporting on his own responses to certain pieces of music and urging Eliot to hear the works of particular composers confirm their enthusiasm (*Letters* 24–5, 31).

In the company of these friends or on his own, Eliot had the opportunity to attend numerous concerts in world-renowned halls during his stay. The most prestigious concert series and concert halls are described in some detail in Baedeker's 1907 guidebook. Under the heading *Théâtres. Concerts. Expositions artistiques* in the section *Renseignements pratiques*, listed first are "the celebrated concerts featuring masterpieces of classical music" given at the Conservatoire de Musique from November to April on Saturdays from 1:30 to 3 p.m. and on Sundays from 1 to 2 p.m. Seats not used by season ticket holders were sold to the general public at prices ranging from four to fifteen francs, so that a student such as Eliot could afford them. Two other concert series presented both classical and modern music on Sundays during the winter: the Concerts Lamoureux at the Théâtre Sarah-Bernhardt with prices from two to ten francs and the Concerts Colonne at the Théâtre du Châtelet with prices from one to eight francs. Also in the winter, three other halls offered concerts of chamber music, with details available on posters and in newspapers (39).

As with the other arts, there was an astounding variety, with equal time given to young emerging musicians and to the long-established masters, revealing the richness for which the Parisian music world was so well-known. While the music of French and Russian composers was regularly featured—especially as regards contemporary figures—the composer whose works were performed most often in the concert hall during Eliot's sojourn in Paris was Beethoven, for whom he developed a great admiration and whose works and experiments greatly influenced some of his poetry; indeed, his devotion to Beethoven may well have begun at this time.

An Overview of the Concert Scene

Soon after Eliot's arrival, several concerts featuring the music of Russian composers could have attracted him because of his interest in Russian culture, fostered by his reading of the novels of Dostoevsky at the instigation of Alain-Fournier. In the October 24 issue of *Le Figaro* in his column *Les Concerts*, Brussel reviewed two concerts given the previous day: the Concerts Lamoureux featured Borodin's *First Symphony in E Flat*, while the Concerts Colonne included in its program several "modern works that are little known" (such as "the prestigious 'Cappricio Espagnole' of Rimsky-Korsakov, performed with a verve and rhythm that were dazzling"), as well as Beethoven's *Heroic Symphony* and Bach's *Fifth Brandenburg Concerto* (4). The Concerts Colonne presented another concert of Russian music in late November, which concluded with Alexander Borodin's *Polovtsian Dances* from his opera *Prince Igor*. In a review in the January 1 issue of *La Nouvelle Revue Française*, Rivière commented that this music "touches what is most primitive in us and awakens in our depths the mysterious image of Asia" ("Les Scènes" 172). This review conveyed the emerging interest in the primitive and in the Orient in Paris at this time, an early probable influence on Eliot's own fascination with both.

On November 27 the first concert of a new music association presented Saint-Saëns's *Third Symphony*, Stravinsky's *Fireworks*, and "The Death of Isolde" from Wagner's *Tristan und Isolde*, all of which, according to Brussel in an article in the November 28 issue of *Le Figaro*, were very well done, despite the fact that they are "not easy works to perform." This concert was perhaps Eliot's introduction to the young Russian composer (just three years older than he) whom he was to admire throughout his life. Stravinsky's avant-garde music was to inspire him, especially in the composition of *The Waste Land*, and in the 1950s the composer was to become a close friend. Brussel had high praise for Stravinsky in the review: "We still remember the triumph of Stravinsky's *Firebird* [performed by the Ballets Russes] last spring, when he appeared with his dazzling orchestra, his mastery of composition, and his inventiveness as a type of prodigy. The personality of the young composer—he's only twenty-five—imposed itself in serious music circles as one of the most brilliant and gifted of the new Russian generation of composers." Brussel described his score as "a study of sonority and rhythm, whose prestige is equal to that of the ballet, with the same shades of color, vivacity, and instrumental seduction. Its genius attests to an artist of whom we can expect much. Although the work is complex and very difficult, the young orchestra and its conductor surpassed themselves" (4).

In his column for December 20 in *Le Figaro*, Brussel remarked that the music season had been full of first-rate concerts by such famous performers as the violinist Fritz Kreisler, the "captivating pianist Ernest Schelling," and "one of the most moving singers of lieder of our time, Mme Povla Frisch." He also described a concert that featured Mme Marie Olénine singing songs by the Russian composer Mussorgsky with moving sensitivity and four young girls playing quartets by Brahms, Beethoven, and Fauré (4). Rivière reviewed Olénine's performance in the February 1 issue of *La Nouvelle Revue Française*, calling Mussorgsky's music the true voice of Russia "with its church bells and prayers" and noting that its "account of humility" was highly moving (314, 317). With his interest in Russian music and in Beethoven—whose quartets in particular he admired and cited as a source of inspiration for his poetry—Eliot perhaps attended this program.

In late February or early March, the first of a series of three performances sponsored by the Société Musicale Indépendante, an organization promoting contemporary music, featured three piano pieces by Erik Satie, with none other than Ravel at the piano. Reviewing all three performances in the March 9 issue of *Le Figaro*, Brussel proclaimed this initial concert a revelation for some but for others a reminder of the amazement evoked by the bizarre art of this composer twenty years ago. Even more intriguing, the program also featured a work for clarinet and piano by Debussy entitled *Rhapsodie*. The March 3, 1911 composition date of "Rhapsody on a Windy Night" suggests the tantalizing possibility that Eliot attended this concert and that Debussy's piece inspired its title and form.

The poem reflects the definition of a rhapsody as an instrumental composition irregular in form, like an improvisation: the poem's open structure traces the speaker's observations of random sights, all of which are grim and depressing aspects of the modern urban scene, as he walks the streets between midnight and 4 a.m., in the tradition of the French *flâneur* who strolls along the city streets dispassionately observing its details. The influence of Eliot's Parisian sojourn is evident in several other elements of the poem: the line in French, "La lune ne garde aucune rancune" (51); the streetlamps, a Paris hallmark; the prostitute in a doorway and "female smells in shuttered rooms" (66), likely reflecting his reading of Philippe's *Bubu de Montparnasse* rather than personal experience; the "Smells of chestnuts in the streets" (65), evoking the ever-present odor of roasting chestnuts at Parisian vendors' street stands in autumn and winter; and the memory of a child stealing a toy on a quay, a probable reference to the paved bank along the Seine. The poem thus provides a tangible reflection of a specific musical performance in Paris and an array of details drawn from the Parisian cityscape.

According to Brussel, the second concert included "an impressive song by Stravinsky" and "the magnificent *Quartet in G Minor* by Fauré," while the third was made up entirely of unpublished works by contemporary and as yet unknown composers, with the exception of a Debussy quartet (4). At this series of concerts Eliot may have heard for the first time Stravinsky, Debussy, and Satie, all of whom also composed scores for dance productions that were probable influences. As suggested in Chapters 3 and 5, in May he no doubt attended the sensational multimedia extravaganza *Le Martyre de Saint Sébastien* with music by Debussy and in June the Ballets Russes's *Petrouchka* with music by Stravinsky. In London in 1919 he probably saw the revival of the 1917 experimental ballet *Parade* with music by Satie, and in 1921 he saw and wrote a now-famous review of the Ballets Russes's revival of *Le Sacre du Printemps*, with music by Stravinsky. As I have argued, each of these influenced Eliot's works, most notably *The Waste Land*.

One additional concert in early March is worth noting: on March 7 at the Salle Gaveau, the world-renowned cellist Pablo Casals played the works of several composers who were or would become Eliot's favorites on a program comprising Bach's *Suite for Cello*, Beethoven's *Sonata in A*, and songs by Schumann and Wagner (*Le Figaro*, 5 March, 1911: 4).

The month of April was filled with outstanding concerts, as the spring musical season was in full swing. One of the most striking was the performance of a portion of Ravel's score for the ballet *Daphnis et Chloé*, which he was in the process of composing for Diaghilev's Ballets Russes for the 1912 season. "Le Nocturne," "L'Interlude," and "La Danse guerrière" [The War Dance] were performed as a concert suite as part of a mixed program by the Concerts Colonne at the Théâtre du Châtelet on April 2 (Larner 122–3). Brussel in his review in *Le Figaro* the next day asserted that the linking of contemporary music and ballet, instigated by Diaghilev's commissioning young composers to create scores for his productions, was opening new horizons in music, suggesting that Ravel was one of the first to compose music for dancers which was legitimate on its own. Of the previous evening's performance, he praised the first two pieces for their "instrumentation [which was] extremely ingenious and rich in striking inventions," concluding that Ravel's work had significant virtues which assured it of a warm welcome in Parisian music circles (4).

M. D. Calvocoressi's review in the April 15 issue of *Comoedia Illustré* echoed

Brussel's enthusiasm for Ravel's experimentation. He stated that the performance of the three sections of *Daphnis et Chloé* was "the most important cultural event of the last two weeks" and praised Ravel's creation of a new and original musical genre characterized by powerful rhythmic innovation: "[The] flexibility of its rhythmic elements gave his pieces the movement of what, in language, is lyric declamation . . . , creating music that was rich in nuances and free of conventional stylizations and thus necessitating a corresponding freedom and richness in the choreography" (449). This definition of Ravel's music with its emphasis on freedom, experimentation with rhythm, rich nuances, rejection of conventional techniques, and interpenetration of various art forms corresponds to the kind of poetry that Eliot was already writing in Paris, and its comparison of music to poetry suggests that the two can experiment in the same ways.

These reviews may have encouraged Eliot to continue his poetic experiments and impressed him yet again with the support of young talent by the Parisian arts establishment, contributing to his ambition at the time to settle permanently in Paris, give up English, and write in French (Hall 56).

Finally, Brussel's column *Les Concerts* for June 4 contained an account of a young pianist named Victor Gille, whose entire program was devoted to works by his master, Frederic Chopin. Brussel asserted that the genius of Chopin could not have found a more sensitive interpreter than "this excellent pianist," who demonstrated a "profound understanding of the very soul of the composer's canon, its ethnic origins heard in the nocturnes, the polonaises, and the fantasies that were inspired by popular Polish songs," a comment that may have suggested to Eliot the possibility of incorporating popular material into his own poetry. Brussel described the "delicacy and certainty of Gille's touch, . . . his crystal-clear trills, and the serene and majestic force of his chords," as the pianist put "his whole soul into his soaring, poetic playing." He performed with "unequalled mastery" the *Fantasy in F Minor*, a series of *Études* including the tragic *Étude in C Minor*, several nocturnes, two polonaises, and finally the *Scherzo in B Flat Minor*, receiving enthusiastic applause as "the just reward for his marvelous talent" (6).

The references to a concert of Chopin's music in "Portrait of a Lady," which Eliot began in February 1910, worked on during his Parisian year, and completed in November 1911, may have been inspired by Gille's concert, for the poem's young male narrator, who callously describes his relationship with an older woman, notes (with what seems to be annoyance) the latter's comments about a concert they attended featuring a contemporary pianist playing Chopin's Preludes:

We have been, let us say, to hear the latest Pole
Transmit the Preludes through his hair and fingertips.

"So intimate, this Chopin, that I think his soul
Should be resurrected only among friends
Some two or three, who will not touch the bloom
That is rubbed and questioned in the concert room." (9–13)

Performances of Beethoven's Music

The composer whose works were most frequently performed at concerts during the period of Eliot's sojourn in Paris was Beethoven, to whom the French were passionately devoted at this time. As Leo Shrade establishes in *Beethoven in France*, the composer served as an ideal of moral virtue and fortitude in the face of extreme suffering in the early years of the twentieth century, a period which seemed "godless and without saints and heroes" (146). To combat the pessimism of the times, Péguy, as noted in Chapter 1, ran a series called "Lives of Illustrious Men" in his *Cahiers de la Quinzaine* in order to inspire in the modern-day French a regeneration of the virtues of the past and thus to "ward off barbarism" (146). Indeed, the fear of being overrun by barbarian values such as materialism as a result of the decline of traditional virtues was widespread in France at this time, as indicated in Péguy's purpose for instituting this series, and may have in part inspired the nightmare vision of the destruction of civilization in Part V of *The Waste Land*. The first biography to be featured was Romain Rolland's 1903 book *The Life of Beethoven*, which enjoyed an astounding popularity and influence that extended to World War I. Its basic premise was that the faith, courage, and energy of Beethoven allowed him to wring triumph out of suffering, indeed to gain greatness through suffering. In the preface, Rolland asserted that "at the head of this heroic legion [of great men of the past], we assign the first place to the strong and pure Beethoven. . . . May we re-animate after his example the faith of men in life and in men" (qtd. in Shrade 156). Rolland found "every suffering that can occur to a human being, every extreme grief, in Beethoven. The extreme courage to live, the valor to endure, all the energy a man can raise, these too he finds in Beethoven . . . , the 'heroic force of modern art'" (qtd. in Shrade 162). This "French apotheosis of the composer . . . kept an intellectual France breathless with excitement for a full decade," during which his works were played constantly in performances acknowledged as the best in Europe (Shrade 164–5, 142).

A further indication of the overwhelming influence of Beethoven in France in general and in Paris in particular is that he was the subject of numerous biographies in the next ten years[1] as well as works of sculpture, painting, and literature. For example, Bourdelle produced a series of bronze busts of the composer conveying a sense of massive strength and ferocious energy, and the young dramatist Fauchois received great acclaim for his play *Beethoven*, performed at the Théâtre de l'Odéon in 1909 under the direction of the famous Antoine. This powerful and pervasive concept of Beethoven exerted an influence on the youth of France no less than on their elders, for, according to Séverine in an article entitled "Notre Père Beethoven" [our father Beethoven] published in 1909, a "profound cult" grew up about him in which he served as their "supreme recourse against decadence," leading them on "a march toward sacred truth and pure beauty" (qtd. in Shrade 191). Eliot gained both an appreciation of Beethoven's music and an admiration of his virtues in this French atmosphere of near-worship of the composer, views which stayed with him throughout his life and inspired his creations in a number of ways.

This widespread devotion to and celebration of Beethoven's genius, this near-worship of him as the ideal of moral strength and goodness, are evident in the extraordinary number of concerts featuring his works in Paris in 1910–1911. Soon after Eliot's arrival, the Concerts Colonne presented Beethoven's *Heroic Symphony* with Gabriel Pierné conducting, while the Concerts Lamoureux performed airs and lieder by Beethoven, Handel, and Schubert, as reported by Brussel in the October 24 and 31 issues of *Le Figaro* (4). Furthermore, according to Brussel in the November 21 issue of *Le Figaro*, the Concerts Colonne devoted an entire program to works of Beethoven, in honor of its founder: the program included the Overture of *Léonore*, the *Concerto for Violin* (played admirably by the famous violinist Fritz Kriesler), three of the Gellert lieder, and the *Ninth Symphony*, with an excellent chorus and remarkable soloists (4). L. de Crémone in his column *Courrier Musical* in the November 22 issue of *Le Figaro* announced that the Concerts Colonne would present the next Sunday the season's last performance of the *Ninth Symphony*, "whose success last Sunday took on the proportions of a triumph with five hundred performers and with Mlle Rose Féart, eminent artist from the Opéra, singing the soprano solo." In addition, he revealed that "the great event of the musical season" would be the concerts on December 17, 24, and 31 at "Les Soirées d'Art" presented by the Concerts Barrau and featuring the "two great artists Risler and Enesco" performing Beethoven's sonatas for piano and violin (4).

The month of December saw several concerts of Beethoven's music. On December 13 at the Salle Gaveau, Siegfried Wagner, the son of Richard Wagner and the grandson of Franz Liszt, conducted a gala concert in honor of Beethoven. However, as noted in Chapter 1, Siegfried's performance was dismal, for it drew this harsh criticism in *Le Figaro's* review in the December 19 issue: "His heavy heredity weighs down the life of M. Siegfried Wagner, assuredly preventing him from being himself. The glory whose reflections surround him condemns him without doubt to a thousand virtues, of which silence is the least" (4). If Eliot happened to read this mordant commentary, it may have served as a model for the witty sarcasm in some of his own later reviews. In late December, Brussel favorably reviewed the first concert sponsored by the "brilliant Société Philharmonique," which included four young women playing Beethoven's *Quartet Opus 18*, along with quartets by Brahms and Fauré.

The fact that in the first two months of Eliot's sojourn in Paris there were at least eight performances of pieces by Beethoven is an obvious testament to the esteem in which the composer was held at the time. The winter and spring of 1911 saw more of this French adulation of their musical hero. In mid-January, according to Brussel in the January 14 issue of *Le Figaro*, the Concerts Barrau featured on the second program of "Les Soirées d'Art" Beethoven's *Second Quartet* and *Fourth Quartet* as well as his sonata *Clair de Lune* (7). In early March, the cellist Casals included Beethoven's *Sonata in A* in his concert, as noted above, while the Concerts Colonne presented his *Mass in D*, "a work rarely performed," according to Brussel in the March 8, 1911 issue of *Le Figaro* (4). And on April 30 and May 1, as announced by Brussel in the April 20 issue of *Le Figaro*, Fritz Kreisler, the "admirable violinist acclaimed throughout the world," presented in the Salle Gaveau concertos by Beethoven, Mendelssohn, Brahms, and Bach in the only two concerts that he would perform in Paris that season (5).

But the crown of the performances of Beethoven's music that year was the Beethoven Festival in early May. It opened "La Grand Saison de Paris" on May 2 at the Théâtre du Châtelet with a performance of the first, second, and third symphonies by the 100-member Orchestre Colonne under the direction of Felix Weingartner, renowned for his interpretations of Beethoven's works. In the next day's issue of *Le Figaro* in a review entitled "Châtelet: Le Festival Beethoven," Brussel reported that Weingartner, "one of the most brilliant conductors of our time," understood the genius of Beethoven as evident in his "faithful and straightforward interpretation, stripped of all artifice." His rendition of the first two symphonies was "stupendous," communicating their "grace and freshness and [giving] them an unforeseen seductive quality," while the "heroism of the third symphony under his baton attained the summits of the sublime" (4). Of the performance of Beethoven's quartets and lieder on May 5, Brussel in his column *Les Concerts* in the May 6 issue of *Le Figaro* observed that Weingartner demonstrated his skill in conducting the composer's more intimate works as well as the powerful ones, for which he was already well-known (5). *Le Matin*'s issue for May 9 reported in an article entitled "Le Festival Beethoven" that the concert of May 8, featuring the *Eighth Symphony* and *Ninth Symphony* performed by the orchestra and chorus of the Concerts Colonne with 1000 performers, was a triumph; the audience which packed the hall exhibited "the most extraordinary enthusiasm" with numerous standing ovations. So popular was this concert that the May 10 performance was already sold out, but an additional concert was scheduled for May 12, at which the *Fifth Symphony* and *Ninth Symphony* would be featured (4). Since this festival was so impressive, Eliot must have felt more than a tinge of chagrin that he would not be in Paris to attend the next Beethoven Festival, a "gigantic musical project" presenting the complete works for the first time ever, slated to take place from April 20 to June 15, 1912, as reported by L. de Crémone in his column *Courrier Musical* in the October 1, 1910 issue of *Le Figaro* (4).

The many opportunities to hear Beethoven's music during his Parisian year when the celebration—indeed the worship—of his music was so intense seem to have set in motion Eliot's lifelong devotion to the great composer, whose works, as he revealed later in his career, provided inspiration for his own poetry's content, structure, and techniques. Indeed, Beethoven's daring experimentation must have encouraged Eliot to try his own radical innovations; as Donald Grout, the noted music historian, makes clear, "Beethoven was the most powerful disruptive force in the history of music. His works opened the gateway to a new world" (491). The same claim can be made for Eliot in terms of twentieth century poetry.

While Beethoven's influence on Eliot is evident in poems written throughout his career,[2] the poet's late masterpiece *Four Quartets* reveals the most significant and pervasive influence. Its title and aspects of its content and form were in part inspired by Beethoven's string quartets, to which Eliot often listened. In March 1931, for example, he wrote Stephen Spender that he had been listening to the *Quartet in A Minor* (Opus 132), revealing a personal and deeply felt interpretation of and response to it as well as a desire to write something similar in poetry: "I have the A minor Quartet on the gramophone, and find it quite inexhaustible to study. There is a sort of heavenly or at least more than human gaiety about some of his later things which one imagines might come to oneself as *the fruit of reconciliation and relief after immense suffering*; I should like to get something of that into verse before I die" (54; italics mine). These words, particularly those in italics, echo the French view of Beethoven, so prevalent during Eliot's year in Paris, as a heroic figure whose faith, energy, and courage to endure allowed him to gain greatness through suffering. One of the dominant characteristics of this quartet and of all Beethoven's late works is their meditative quality, which Grout describes as "a feeling of assured tranquillity [and] . . . calm affirmation" (485), a trait which Eliot seems in particular to admire and to emulate in his late poetry. A further attraction may have been the "Heiliger Dankgesang" of the quartet, which music historian Glenn Stanley includes among "the best-known musical manifestations of Beethoven's religious sentiments in his later life" (31).

Reinforcing the influence of the worship of Beethoven as a musical genius and as a figure of moral strength which Eliot certainly absorbed during his Parisian year was the centennial of his death in 1927, celebrated throughout Europe with numerous concerts and with the publication of several new books on the composer. Chief among the latter was J. W. N. Sullivan's *Beethoven: His Spiritual Development*, published in 1927 and reviewed in the March 1928 issue of *The Criterion*. As Howarth notes, Eliot was acquainted with Sullivan, a fellow writer for the *Athenaeum* in 1919–1921, and knew the book (287), particularly the chapter on the last quartets, in which Sullivan argues that Beethoven is "presenting to us a vision of life, [which is that] the joy and energy of creation spring from a substratum of sorrow and suffering" (231, 234–5). The book was a powerful confirmation of the French views of the composer that Eliot witnessed in Paris, and Sullivan's descriptions of the three major last quartets, the *A Minor*, *B Flat Major*, and *C Sharp Minor*, captured the kind of poetry that he wished to write at that time. Sullivan's comments are not only echoed in *Four Quartets* but also serve as perceptive insights into many of the poet's intentions in that work. Of the *Quartet in C Sharp Minor*, "the greatest of [the] quartets," Sullivan writes that "the mystical vision is most perfectly sustained" (238), referring to the "exultant gaiety" of its "moments of illumination" (242). Of the *Quartet in A Minor*, which Eliot mentions in his letter to Spender, he writes that it is "the one most full of human pain"; relief from this anguish comes after the "heartfelt prayer," characterized as Beethoven's "pure and sincere communion with his God," which engenders "a rush of celestial joy." He suggests that "[r]elief from pain, in this most pessimistic of Beethoven's quartets, comes only from above" (245–6). And he concludes that, while the final Presto "rings out victoriously," listeners are left not with a "feeling of exultant triumph . . . , but rather with a feeling of slightly incredulous relief, of thankfulness still tinged with doubt" (247).[3]

In 1935, Eliot undertook to fulfill the goal expressed in his letter to Spender when he began the work that was to become *Four Quartets*. A number of passages that are moving direct commentaries on Eliot's personal suffering and subsequent reconciliation reflect his wish to "get something of that into verse." The most powerful of these are found, significantly, in "Little Gidding," his last major poem. In Section II, the speaker describes with a mixture of sarcasm, bitterness, and anguish "the gifts reserved for age / To set a crown upon your lifetime's effort" (131–2), the last of which is

> the rending pain of re-enactment
> Of all that you have done and been; the shame
> Of motives late revealed, and the awareness
> Of things ill done and done to others' harm . . . . (140–3)

Eliot caused emotional pain not only to Vivien but also to Emily Hale, Mary Trevelyan, and John Hayward (see Menan 126–31 and Seymour-Jones), who may be the biographical figures hovering behind the general reference to those whom an individual may have hurt—whether deliberately or not—during his or her lifetime and for which he or she feels remorse without being able to atone in any way. In Section III, however, after suggesting that "the use of memory" is "For liberation" (157–8), the speaker says, with what seems to be a sense of release and relief, "See, now they vanish, / The faces and places, with the self which, as it could, loved them, / To become renewed, transfigured, in another pattern" (164–6), a moving poetic rendering both of the speaker's admission that he was limited in his ability to love them and of "the fruit of reconciliation and relief after immense suffering." While the latter could not be described as "more than human gaiety," it does convey a simple human serenity that is confirmed in the closing passage with its notes of endurance, reconciliation, assurance, and even triumph:

> All manner of thing shall be well
> When the tongues of flame are in-folded
> Into the crowned knot of fire
> And the fire and the rose are one. (257–60)

Eliot's use of such highly personal material seems to reflect the highly personal nature of Beethoven's late quartets, which, according to David Barndollar, "are generally regarded as his most personal compositions, exploring far-reaching musical and emotional territories . . ." (182). Indeed, Barndollar concludes that perhaps "the best analogy between [Beethoven's late quartets and Eliot's *Four Quartets*] is their intimate, inward-looking personality" (192).

In addition to their meditative and emotionally charged qualities, other characteristics of Beethoven's late works from which Eliot drew inspiration for his last great work are the composer's "new conception of the possibilities of thematic *variation*[,] . . . repeating a given theme in new guises while recognizably preserving the essential structure of the entire theme in each repetition," and "a continuity . . . achieved by *intentionally blurring dividing lines*" (Grout 486–7; italics mine). Eliot adapted both of these, I would suggest, in composing *Four Quartets*. Music historian Nicholas Marston can help us see how Eliot did so. He points out that the slow movement of the *Quartet in A Minor* employs variation "as part of a broader scheme in which the theme and its variations are separated from one another by the intrusion of a sharply contrasting theme" (90) and notes Beethoven's "tendency to alter the conventional dynamic of multimovement works [by] his radical departure . . . from the conventional number and sequence of movements [and] his challenge to the autonomy of the individual movement itself." These techniques are especially evident in the last three piano sonatas and the five late string quartets (94), the latter being Eliot's particular favorites. Richard Kramer's description of Beethoven's experimental techniques in the late quartets seems as well to describe Eliot's techniques in *Four Quartets*, further indicating his debt to Beethoven: "[In] the music of the 1820s, and nowhere more eloquently than in Beethoven's last quartets, the fragile networking of 'fragmentary' pieces together into some work whose concept depends on the palpable ties between movements . . . can be said to renegotiate the terms by which the work claims to be a sum of its parts" (qtd. in Marston 94).

These experiments with form and variation were one source of inspiration for the numerous repetitions of themes, images, and phrases in *Four Quartets*, as in the opening passage on time in "Burnt Norton" and in the varied references to roses, a rose garden, a gate, children's voices, a waterfall, and music, as well as for the structure of contrasting movements and of passages within movements in the entire work. Grout's second characteristic is reflected in the shifts within sections of the individual poems from subject to subject with no breaks other than occasional spaces; this absence of breaks serves to reinforce the quiet meditative tone.

Also, the very concept of "four" linked quartets may have come from the most comprehensive of all Beethoven's innovations—the idea that individual quartets could be interrelated in an organic and complex manner. Music historian John Daverio's description of Beethoven's last four quartets could be said as well to describe Eliot's overall ultimate concept of his four interrelated poems and explains the somewhat confusing title (at least musically speaking, as Bebbington points out in his essay "Four *Quartets*?") of his final great poetic work: "Beethoven's conscious effort to forge palpable relationships among discrete works departs significantly from tradition. . . . In fact, certain aspects of the genesis of all the late quartets [specifically the four designated as op. 127, 132, 130, and 131] suggest that these works comprise a unified corpus. . . . Thus, significant elements of the finished works . . . indicate that Beethoven has replaced the traditional opus—a series of complementary but independent works—with a system of interrelated compositions, each of which was weighty enough to receive its own opus number" (149). This revolutionary development is reflected in Eliot's giving each individual poem its own title and making the four a "series of complementary but independent works." And Sullivan's comment that Beethoven's last quartets are unified by "a vision of life" (231), which he explains as the composer's realization that "one's creation necessitates one's suffering, that suffering is one of the greatest of God's gifts," a realization that "almost . . . reach[es] a mystical solution of the problem of evil" (233), is germane to understanding the vision of *Four Quartets*.

Helen Gardner in *The Art of T. S. Eliot* gives a brilliant and sensitive analysis of "the debt [Eliot] owes to the art of music in his solution of the problem of finding a form for the long poem," and, while she refers specifically to Beethoven only once, his compositions in particular seem to lie behind many of her references: "As the title shows, each poem is structurally a poetic equivalent of the classical symphony, or quartet, or sonata, as distinct from the suite. This structure is clear when all four poems are read, as they are intended to be, together, and is essentially the same as the structure of *The Waste Land*." She then reveals the musically based form in each section, noting that "each poem has five movements, each with its own inner necessary structure. The first movement suggests at once a musical analogy. In each poem it contains statement and counter-statement, or two contrasted but related themes, like the first and second subjects of a movement in strict sonata form" (37). However, this structure also resembles that of the innovative opening movement of Beethoven's *Quartet in A Minor*, which, according to Daverio, "deals with its apparently fragmentary materials quite differently," in that the first group "juxtaposes two ideas . . . [which] are open-ended, incomplete, and—at first blush—incompatible. Much of the remainder of the movement, however, is devoted to showing that these seemingly disparate gestures are or can be related" (158). After pointing out that the third movement is "the core of each poem, out of which reconcilement grows: it is an exploration with a twist of the ideas of the first two movements," Gardner directly refers to Beethoven in her description of the lyrical fourth section of each poem, citing as her example "East Coker": "The repetitive circling passage . . . where we seem to be standing still, waiting for something to happen, for a rhythm to break out, reminds one of the bridge passages and leading passages between two movements which Beethoven loved" (41). This description alludes to the composer's "blurring dividing lines" described by Grout above. Gardner's commentary makes clear how much Eliot owes to music in general and to Beethoven in particular in *Four Quartets* (36–42).

In *Four Quartets*, Eliot succeeds in achieving his poetic goal of producing poetry that is the equivalent of Beethoven's later works, described in an unpublished lecture: "I have long aimed [at writing] poetry so transparent that in reading it we are intent on what the poem *points at*, and not on the poetry, this seems to me to be the thing to try for. To get *beyond poetry*, as Beethoven, in his later works, strove to get *beyond music*" (qtd. in Matthiessen 90). Thus, the composer whose works he perhaps first heard in Paris in 1910–1911 was a source of multiple types of inspiration and encouragement to Eliot throughout his life, and his request that the second movement of Beethoven's *Seventh Symphony*, one of his favorite works, be played at his funeral was a fitting acknowledgment of the composer's importance to him.

Eliot's Lifelong Interest in Classical Music

Following his year in Paris, Eliot demonstrated a lifelong devotion to classical music, a direct influence of all that he experienced there musically. Back in Boston from 1911 to 1914, he attended numerous musical programs at Symphony Hall and at the Boston Opera House. As noted in Chapter 6, programs dated from October 1913 to February 1914 in the Eliot Collection of the Houghton Library reveal that he heard at least twelve concerts and operas in that period alone, including a concert featuring Beethoven's *Symphony in A Major* and Brahms's *Tragic Overture* on October 16, 1913 as well as a piano recital of Chopin's works on December 2, 1913. As noted in Chapter 5, in London in the late 1910s and early 1920s, he not only attended but also wrote about performances of the Ballets Russes with scores by a host of prominent avant-garde composers, most notably the revival in July 1921 of *Le Sacre du Printemps*. He famously commented in his "London Letter" in the October 1921 issue of the *Dial* that Stravinsky was the "greatest success since Picasso," describing the ballet's music as conveying a "sense of the present" by transforming "the rhythm of the steppes into the scream of the motor horn, the rattle of machinery, the grind of wheels, the beating of iron and steel, the roar of the underground railway, and the other barbaric cries of modern life" (452–3). These qualities of the score made it an important influence on *The Waste Land*, which he was writing at the time. Paul Chancellor in fact has argued that Eliot's musical sensibility in that poem is not that of Beethoven, as Gardner suggests, but "as distinctly a twentieth-century sensibility as Stravinsky's or Schoenberg's and, in 1922 at least, as new and startling" (122).[4]

Later in his life, in addition to attending live performances of classical music, he also listened to recordings of works by his favorite composers. In 1931, as noted earlier, he found inspiration in listening to Beethoven's *Quartet in A Minor* on the gramophone (Spender 54) for the poems that would become *Four Quartets*. In the 1950s, according to Mary Trevelyan's unpublished memoir, the two listened to records of compositions by Beethoven, Mozart, and Hayden (Gordon, *Imperfect* 470). When in the mid-1950s Eliot formed a close friendship with Stravinsky, the two discussed working together on an opera, a project which never came to fruition. However, in 1962 Stravinsky composed an anthem for an *a capella* chorus entitled "The Dove Descending Breaks the Air" from "Little Gidding" and dedicated it to Eliot, who remarked that Stravinsky could "get more out of me that way than any man living" (qtd. in Boaz 218). Even in death, Eliot's love of music was evident, for at his funeral two pieces important to him were played: the second movement of Beethoven's *Seventh Symphony*, in accordance with a wish he expressed to Trevelyan in 1949, as noted earlier, and Stravinsky's anthem (Gordon, *Imperfect*

526, 667). Less than a month after Eliot's death, Stravinsky composed a requiem which he described as "a Panikheda chorus in memory of the unforgettable Eliot" (Boaz 218).

The Influence of Classical Music in Eliot's Works

In the previous chapter, I quoted passages from Eliot's 1942 essay "The Music of Poetry" in which he describes the importance of music to him personally and poetically and asserts: "It is in the concert room, rather than in the opera house, that the germ of a poem may be quickened" (113–14). That study of music from which "a poet may gain much" seems to have been nourished in the concert halls of Paris, setting in motion his enduring love of classical music and providing him with a source of inspiration for his drama, his essays, but most especially his poems, as seen in their titles, structures, musical techniques—especially experimental ones—and allusions.

Eliot's Parisian musical experiences are reflected in his use of musical compositions in numerous titles of poems written at that time, more than in any other period. Such titles appear before his stay in Paris, confirming his early interest in music—as seen in two containing the word "Song" (1907, 1909), in "Ballade of the Fox Dinner," in "First Caprice in North Cambridge," in "Second Caprice in North Cambridge," and in "Opera" (all written in 1909). However, such titles are more numerous in 1910–1911. "Preludes," I and II, "Suite Clownesque," and "Fourth Caprice in Montparnasse" were written in October and November 1910, with his French residence reflected in the words "Clownesque" and "Montparnasse," while "Interlude: in a Bar," "Rhapsody on a Windy Night," "Interlude in London," "The Love Song of J. Alfred Prufrock," "Preludes," III and IV, and "Ballade pour la grosse Lulu" were written in 1911. Subsequently, musical titles appear from time to time, confirming his continued interest in music: "The Ballade of the Outlook" (1913), "The Love Song of St. Sebastian" (1914), "A Song for Simeon" (1928), "Triumphal March" (1931), "Five-Finger Exercises" (1933), "Choruses from 'The Rock'" (1934), and *Four Quartets* (1934–42). The sheer variety of musical compositions used in these titles reveals his extensive knowledge of numerous forms.[5]

Furthermore, a number of poems follow the structure of particular types of composition and/or contain allusions to musical instruments, musical performances, or specific pieces of music. *The Waste Land* and *Four Quartets* are the most obvious examples of the former, with the use of a structure similar to the five movements of a classical symphony, quartet, or sonata, as pointed out by Gardner. Chancellor, who argues that Eliot's sensibilities in *The Waste Land* are closer to those of Stravinsky and Schoenberg than to those of Beethoven, proposes that "its structure may be seen as that of a symphonic poem in sonata form using the chief symbols as its themes, and with a declaiming voice woven with it, partly to supply related but dissonant motifs" (123), an observation which also calls to mind Wagner's comprehensive influence on Eliot. Other poems, such as "Rhapsody on a Windy Night," reflect structural similarities to specific types of musical compositions. Examples of the latter appear in his poetry from beginning to end, along with allusions to musical instruments such as the piano, violin, cornet, and flute, to performances such as a Wagnerian opera and a Chopin concert, and to pieces of music, whether specifically named or alluded to through reference or quotation: *Tristan und Isolde*, *Götterdämmerung*, and *Invitation to the Dance*.

Finally, music itself serves in *Four Quartets* as both theme and symbol in a complex interplay of meanings; indeed it functions as a *leitmotif* of the poem. In "Burnt Norton," V, for example, it is a parallel to poetry and a symbol of the immortality of art:

Only by the form, the pattern,
Can words or music reach
The stillness, as a Chinese jar still
Moves perpetually in its stillness.
Not the stillness of the violin, while the note lasts,
Not that only, but the co-existence. (143–8)

And in "The Dry Salvages," V, it is one of several metaphors for the intersection of time and eternity, holding the climactic and most significant position in the list:

For most of us, there is only the unattended
Moment, the moment in and out of time,
The distraction fit, lost in a shaft of sunlight,
The wild thyme unseen, or the winter lightning
Or the waterfall, or music heard so deeply
That it is not heard at all, but you are the music
While the music lasts. (206–12)

The last lines testify to the significance of music as a moving experience in Eliot's life and to its power to convey what is clearly the supreme moment in his poetry—the intersection of time and the timeless.

The rich classical music scene in Paris presented numerous opportunities for Eliot to hear this type of music and appears to have instilled in him an enduring appreciation of and love for it. It not only nurtured his interest in established composers such as Beethoven—for whom he maintained an admiration akin to the near worship of him in Paris at the time—but also introduced him to contemporary composers such as Stravinsky, Ravel, Debussy, and Satie, whose daring experiments were inspiring examples of the new directions opening in all areas of the arts.

· 8 ·

POPULAR ENTERTAINMENT

While Eliot was without doubt drawn primarily to the offerings of high culture in Paris, he took advantage of being far away from his mother's certain disapproval[1] and in a more liberal environment than St. Louis and Boston to indulge his love of popular culture[2] by frequenting its famous (and infamous) lowbrow forms of light entertainment, whose motto was "Toujours du nouveau!" [Always something new!].[3] His sojourn in Paris coincided with an explosion of popular entertainment for the masses. While this type of entertainment had been a part of the Parisian scene for many years, beginning in about 1905 a significant increase in time for leisure and recreation for the lower classes took place as a result of a reduction in working hours and a revolution in access to and speed of transportation, as Rioux and Sirinelli point out. They cite the increased numbers of train travelers from 201 million in 1883 to 509 million in 1912 as well as the advent of the automobile and the ready availability of the bicycle, reflected in the statement in the first issue of *Auto-Vélo* in 1900, "We live better and we live more quickly than in the past" (75–6).[4] As a result of this new leisure time for the masses, the types of and venues for light entertainment expanded enormously from 1905 to the 1920s.

As Nancy Perloff notes in *Art and the Everyday: Popular Entertainment and the Circle of Eric Satie*, there were so many establishments presenting light entertainment in Paris in the early twentieth century that together they created "one vast entertainment world," whose hallmarks were diversity, speed, and interchange: "Their diversity reflected the startling simultaneity of modern urban technological life, with its intricate network of patterns, sights, and sounds" (20). Under what Rioux and Sirinelli call "the triple sign of music, light, and laughter" (79), these venues appealed to all social classes as well as to artists, writers, musicians, and intellectuals such as Cocteau, Picasso, Satie, and Francis Poulenc. In a letter of September 2, 1918, for example, Cocteau describes for Poulenc "the Spectacle Casino de Paris. Merry-go-rounds dizziness world upside-down velvet mirrors and enamel-painted Louis XIV horses which are rearing in a paradise of dentists and theatre loges," revealing his "love for the magical world of Parisian popular amusement . . . which crossed the bounds of individual milieux and dazzled the audience with its rapid succession of diverse images and its buoyant mood" (qtd. in N. Perloff 19). This "magical world" had its own section entitled *Cirques. Spectacles divers. Cafés-concerts. Bals publics* [Circuses. Various shows. Cafés with musical entertainment. Public dance halls] in the general information portion of Baedeker's guidebook (40) and its own daily column entitled *Spectacles et Concerts* [Shows and Musical Entertainment] in *Le Figaro*. I suggest that Eliot's love of popular entertainment can be traced to Paris as well as to the long-acknowledged American and British venues,[5] although this French influence has never been explored in Eliot scholarship.

In order to convey an idea of what Eliot could have seen, I will re-create the complexity of this colorful, dazzling world, describing the various types of light entertainment available at that time—melodramas, cabarets-artistiques, cafés-concerts, music halls, circuses, fairs and exhibitions, dance halls, and cinema—as well as noting specific shows, acts, and performers and suggesting the ways in which their influence seems to be reflected in Eliot's life and in his literary and critical works.

Melodramas

A prevalent form of Parisian light entertainment was *les pièces à grand spectacle* [plays with great spectacle], a type of melodrama which included music and dancing, roughly equivalent to Broadway musicals today; indeed the original meaning of the French word *mélodrame* was "musical drama." Among the most popular was the detective or police drama, filled with action and adventure. According to Baedeker, the premier theatre for such productions was the Théâtre du Châtelet, which had "a huge stage for 'les pièces à grand spectacle' and fantasies with ballets," with prices ranging from two to nine francs. A further attraction was that the luminous ceiling was removed in the summer to let in fresh air (38).

Soon after Eliot's arrival in Paris, an extremely popular detective play appeared there, which he may have attended since he loved detective works throughout his life, especially those about Sherlock Holmes. Humorously entitled "Arsène Lupin contre Herlock Sholmès," it was billed as a "pièce policière à grand spectacle" [a detective play with much spectacle] in four acts, with twenty-one sets, new musical pieces, ballet, and other types of entertainment (Figure 37). The play's preposterous plot, which included numerous complications, twists and turns, disguises, miraculous escapes, coincidences, a love interest, and a pet dog, followed the British detective's attempt to catch the French thief Arsène Lupin, who had stolen a diamond worth millions of francs. To elude capture, he adopted various disguises (including a giant rooster) that required twenty-two costume changes, according to a review in the October 29 issue of *Le Petit Parisien*. Additional comedy was provided by the blundering and stupid French policeman Ganimard. Furthermore, according to Paul Boyer's review in *Comoedia Illustré*, which was accompanied by photographs of the actors and sets, the authors had the great idea of including Sholmès's young son and his little fox terrier to aid him in his work, thus appealing to children in the audience.[6] Boyer described the play's lavish, sensational components, especially its "numerous, picturesque, and sumptuous" dances and its "superb sets," which included "entire streets, complete train stations," and a circus with comic cyclists, demonstrating the Théâtre du Châtelet's technological capabilities; in particular, he praised the street scene in which "the horses and carriages circulate with more ease than on the roads" (100–2).

Eliot's interest in detective literature is reflected in his works in various ways. His favorite type of light reading was the detective novel, with those of Wilkie Collins and Arthur Conan Doyle at the top of the list; however, as he wrote to his brother Henry in 1932, "I read any detective story with enjoyment" (qtd. in Jaidka 118).[7] Indeed, he produced both essays on and reviews of the genre as well, especially during the 1920s, revealing, as Jaidka has shown, an in-depth knowledge of his subject. He writes, for example, in a 1927 review entitled "Recent Detective Fiction" that "One likes in a detective story to have the pleasure of following the working of one keen mind" (362) and in an essay on Collins's *The Moonstone* criticizes modern detective characters, with specific reference to Sherlock Holmes. They are, he argues, "either efficient but featureless, forgotten the moment we lay the book down, or else they have too many features like Sherlock Holmes" (qtd. in Jaidka 145). As Chinitz has noted both in his essay in *PMLA* and in his book, Eliot in his essay "Wilkie Collins and Dickens" associates detective fiction with melodrama ("Cultural" 237; *Cultural* 108).

Elements from and specific references to detective literature are evident in Eliot's poetry and his plays: murders, dead bodies, unsavory characters, mystery, and suspense appear frequently. In "Sweeney Among the Nightingales" an air of mystery and danger hovers over the scene ("Death and the Raven drift above," 7), which is menaced by threatening characters such as "Rachel *née* Rabinovitch / [Who tears] at the grapes with murderous paws" (23–4), and it ends with the ambiguous and frightening allusion to nightingales singing in "the bloody wood" during the murder of Agamemnon (37). *The Waste Land* contains sinister references to "That corpse you planted last year in your garden" (71) and "White bodies naked on the low damp ground / And bones cast in a little low dry garret" (193–4). Criminal elements are presented much more directly in the plays, as in Sweeney's story in *Sweeney Agonistes* about the murderer who killed a girl, kept her in a bathtub filled with Lysol, and never got caught: "I knew a man once did a girl in / . . . Well he kept her there in a bath / . . . This one didn't get pinched in the end" ("Fragment of an Agon" 112, 116, 126). *Murder in the Cathedral*, whose title deliberately echoes those of detective novels,[8] actually presents on stage the murder of St. Thomas à Becket, while *The Family Reunion* is a mystery of sorts about a man who may have killed his wife by pushing her overboard on a transatlantic crossing: "You would never imagine that anyone could sink so quickly" (235).[9]

Finally, works featuring Sherlock Holmes in particular are reflected in two poems. As I note in *Landscape as Symbol in the Poetry of T. S. Eliot* (153), in Section II of "East Coker" Eliot alludes to Dr. Watson's remark in *The Hound of the Baskervilles* that "Life has become like that great Grimpen Mire, with little green patches everywhere into which one may sink and with no guide to point the track" (107), with the Grimpen Mire symbolizing the treacherous, trackless landscapes of life: "In the middle, not only in the middle of the way / But all the way, in a dark wood, in a bramble, / On the edge of a grimpen, where is no secure foothold . . . " (89–91). And, although the city in which "The Love Song of J. Alfred Prufrock" takes place is not specifically identified and seems a composite of Paris, London, St. Louis, Boston, and perhaps Munich, its fog may have been at least partly inspired by that found in many of Sherlock Holmes's adventures.[10]

Cabarets-Artistiques

The cabaret-artistique was a popular type of light entertainment focused on caustic wit and satire, featuring songs, short skits or shadow plays, and one-act revues, and mainly drawing intellectuals, artists, writers, and musicians, and thus a particularly apt venue for the young Eliot. The first of these to achieve fame was the Chat Noir in the latter years of the nineteenth century. There Satie, who was one of its pianists from 1888–91, received much of the inspiration for his innovative compositions incorporating popular and classical music. When it closed in 1897, others took its place. In the first two decades of the twentieth century, these establishments— some of which sponsored lavish parades—were considered fashionable night spots and attracted an elite clientele (N. Perloff 20–23). In Baedeker's guidebook they are described as "curious establishments . . . between cafés-brasseries [cafés serving food and alcohol] and cafés-concerts [cafés with musical entertainment]. They are for men who want to be entertained, in the evening and at night, and whose only concern is pleasure. They originated in the famous cabaret the Chat Noir, which was founded in 1882 by Rudolphe Salis and frequented by celebrated artists and writers, but which no longer exists" (42).

Of the six listed, five were located in Montmartre. At 58 rue Pigalle was the

Boîte à Fursy [Fursy's Nightclub], which presented political songs and charged expensive admission fees ranging from five to ten francs. As indicated in a notice in the April 13, 1911 issue of *Le Figaro*, Fursy himself and his new songs were to be featured in "La Revue de la Boîte" that evening at 9:30 p.m. (5). The Lune Rousse [The Harvest Moon] at 36 boulevard de Clichy typically offered a 9:30 p.m. program of songs by stars of the day, a humorous shadow play, and a one-act revue. The October 25, 1910 issue of *Le Figaro* contained an enthusiastic review of the current offerings by one E. G.: "I came out of The Lune Rousse totally charmed! It's a celebration of the French spirit, the Parisian spirit, and the Montmartrois spirit! . . . To tell the truth, every evening between 9:30 p.m. and midnight, one can spend superior minutes there, 150 minutes to be exact, because between the moment when the curtain rises—if there were a curtain—and the moment when one must regretfully leave, joy is continuously overflowing without the boredom of an entr'acte as a filler." E. G. praised the singers for their "ingenious rhythms," "biting satire," and "profound quips," especially Lucien Boyer, a well-known performer of comic opera who put his voice "at the service of lively inventions," and the "two masters of the house": Numa Blès, who sang songs and spoke verses that were amusing to hear, and Dominique Bonnaud, "the prince of song, whose eyes sparkled behind his lorgnon when he heard the tumult of laughter that he evoked without appearing to work at it." Clearly impressed with these performers, E. G. exclaimed, "What talent! What wit! What verve! And all so stripped of pretension! These song writers/performers, my word, don't seem to suspect that they have a hellish wit any more than Lucy Pezet seems to know that she has a delicious voice or the blond pianist Stanislas seems to have any idea that he is a musician of the first order!" They were followed by a humorous shadow play entitled "Ulysses in Montmartre," which "took us to the heroic time of La Butte, when at the Chat Noir—alas, now disappeared—the wit of [various performers] triumphed," and the evening's fare concluded with a one-act revue starring the aforementioned singer Lucy Pezet (4).

Other cabarets-artistiques were the Cabaret Aristide-Bruant, featuring "insulting remarks and farces that are more or less witty" (Baedeker 42); the Conservatoire de Montmartre, specializing in shadow plays; and the most popular at the time, especially for artists and writers, the Cabaret des Quat'z-Arts [Cabaret of the Four Arts], which had been the starting place for many popular singers such as Harry Fragson, Félix Mayol, and Paulus (Herbert 316–17) and which was famous for its midnight parades. Eliot was perhaps most likely to have gone to the cabaret the Noctambules (The Sleepwalkers) on the tiny rue Champollion near the Sorbonne, which, according to Baedeker, was a student hangout (42). Certainly the sharp, biting satire, the intellectual atmosphere, and the artistic/literary clientele at such establishments would have appealed to him and may have deepened his witty, satiric nature evident in such poems as "The Hippopotamus" and in many a critical piece.

Cafés-concerts

Cafés-concerts were born in the heart of Paris during the Second Empire (1852–75) and flourished until after World War I, when they were forced out of existence by the increasing popularity of music halls. Eliot's year in Paris occurred during a transition period in which cafés-concerts, while still very much in vogue, were in the process of converting to music halls, a form of entertainment which originated in England but became very Parisian (Rioux and Sirinelli 80). Thus at this time distinctions between the two were somewhat blurred, and it is in some cases difficult to determine which establishments were still cafés-concerts and which had become or were becoming music halls.

The major offerings of cafés-concerts were banal songs of a coarse, crude, and humorous nature, with a lengthy program progressing through *tours de chants* [turns or rounds of songs], with each series featuring a different singer, the most famous of whom typically appeared at the end. Some of the stars of cafés-concerts during 1910–1911 were Damia, Dranem, Fragson, Mayol, Mistinguett, Polaire, and Thibaud.[11] They sang sentimental or licentious love songs, patriotic songs, and idiotic songs, many of which had nonsensical refrains of *scies* [catch-phrases] heard in the streets (Caradec and Weill 30). One of the most popular of the idiotic songs was Dranem's "Ah, les p'tits pois" [Ah, green peas] with the refrain "Ça n'se mange pas avec les doigts" [Don't eat them with your fingers] following each of its ten verses. Over time, dances, short comic skits, musical comedies, operettas, and/or revues were added between the rounds of songs. Certain types of performers associated with cafés-concerts included *diseurs*, monologists who spoke rather than sang their songs; *comiques troupiers*, bumbling soldiers in clothes that were too small; and *gommeuses*, sensual singers of sexually explicit songs who were physically attractive but generally had poor voices (N. Perloff 25–6; Caradec and Weill 174).

Although originally called "theatres of the poor" (Rioux and Sirinelli 79) because they reduced or did away with admission fees and charged low prices for drinks, by 1910–11 cafés-concerts attracted a more diverse clientele. The customers smoked, drank beer, talked, moved around freely in the informal, noisy ambiance, and participated in the entertainment by interjecting comments and joining in the songs, especially the refrains and choruses. Indeed, many cafés-concerts sold sheets on which the refrains of the day were printed (Caradec and Weill 124).

Several accounts from the 1890s and the early 1900s quoted by Caradec and

Weill in their book *Le Café-concert* provide glimpses into what Eliot would have experienced in such an establishment. Jules Bertaut, for example, described "its coarse music played by an unrefined orchestra, . . . its unbreathable atmosphere of clouds of smoke and stale smells of beer, . . . [and] its lewd or obscene refrains repeated in chorus by the customers," concluding sarcastically that the café-concert provides "delectable memories, tipsy images for store clerks on a Sunday spree, maudlin working girls, and soldiers on leave" (7).

Victorin Joncières emphasized the same elements but added an account of the agitation evoked by the loud sounds and jarring rhythms of the music played by the low-class orchestra along with a pronouncement of the negative effects of these establishments:

> The songs of the café-concert produce their effect on the idiotic clientèle which enjoys this type of entertainment by the deformation of melodic design, the shock of violent rhythms, the brutality of the cry replacing the voice, and the excessively loud instruments that accompany them. Added to the attraction of obscenities and vulgarities is that of brazenness in these establishments where you can keep your hat on and smoke while drinking a glass of beer [*un bock*], where, intoxicated by the nauseating smells of tobacco and alcohol, you can take up in a chorus the idiotic refrain that the singer shouts, accompanied by the nervous excitation of the wind instruments and the drums.

He then commented that the "songs of the café-concert are certainly the main cause of the depravity of musical taste in France, and those who care about the moral state of the nation and its intellectual development are deeply saddened by the increasing success of these crass ineptitudes, which propagate themselves with the speed of an epidemic and end by instantly attaining the fame which real works of art often do not attain for years" (qtd. in Caradec and Weill 30).

Léo Claretie remarked in another contemporary account, apparently from a position of benign and generous superiority, on the songs and the audience participation in singing the refrains: "These little songs have their interest and aren't entirely negligible when one acknowledges that they represent the tastes and predilections of the masses. The literature of the café-concert is the expression of the masses and the resumé of the popular esthetic. There is direct contact between the song and the people; the penetration is intimate, for the audience takes up the refrain in a chorus, willingly accepting the invitation which often ends the last verse: 'Sing with me . . . . Repeat with me'" (qtd. in Caradec and Weill 30).

Eliot reflects many of these aspects of cafés-concerts in his poetry and in his theories on drama. The singular hallmark of these venues, mentioned by all three contemporary commentators, was audience participation, and Eliot's probable experience of joining in with the crowd as they sang refrains with performers at Parisian cafés-concerts contributed (along with similar experiences in English and American establishments) to his belief in the importance of the collaboration of audience and artist, best seen in his tribute to the famous British music hall star Marie Lloyd: "The working man who . . . joined in the chorus was himself performing part of the act; he was engaged in that collaboration of the audience with the artist which is necessary in all art and most obviously in dramatic art" (174). Further, the "stale smells of beer" from such an establishment may have inspired the lines in "Preludes," II, dated October 1910, "The morning comes to consciousness / Of faint stale smells of beer" (14–15). Also, parts I and III of "Portrait of a Lady," written in November 1910 and November 1911, respectively, seem to reflect cafés-concerts in the narrator's memories of the sound of "a dull tom-tom" (32) that echoes in his brain as he listens to a concert of classical music played by violins and cornets, introducing "one definite 'false note'" (35), as does his suggestion,

> Let us take the air, in a tobacco trance,
> Admire the monuments,
> Discuss the late events,
> Correct our watches by the public clocks.
> Then sit for half an hour and drink our bocks. (36–40)

While this scene seems to take place in the United States prior to the narrator's going abroad, Eliot's early experiences in Paris may well have informed the allusions to the "tobacco trance," to admiring monuments, and to drinking *bocks* [glasses of beer].

In addition, two poems written in February 1911, "The smoke that gathers blue and sinks" and "Interlude: in a Bar," seem to make use of them as well. The first opens with the speaker's description of the numbness induced in him by "after-dinner drinks" (3) imbibed in a smoke-filled entertainment venue. In the second stanza, the entertainment begins and rouses him somewhat from his torpor:

> What, you want action?
> Some attraction?
> Now begins
> The piano and the flute and two violins (11–14).

The last line describes the instrumental accompaniment typical in a café-concert. Then a woman matching the description of a *gommeuse*, "A lady of almost any age / But chiefly breasts and rings" (16–17), sings, "*Throw your arms around me—Aint you glad you found me*" (18), a slight variation of a somewhat maudlin love song published in 1907 (Ricks 245): Eliot may well have heard it in a Parisian café-concert, where American tunes were very popular. While this performance is "hardly strong enough" (19) to draw the speaker from his lethargy, the next "turn," a black dancer, succeeds in doing so:

Here's a negro (teeth and smile)
Has a dance that's quite worthwhile
That's the stuff!
(Here's your gin
Now begin!) (20–4)

Although the poem itself has perhaps negligible value, it does suggest that Eliot attempted to incorporate elements of Parisian café-concert entertainment into his artistic creations immediately.

So too does "Interlude: in a Bar," which seems to take place in such a venue, although its entertainment is not described. The haze of cigarette smoke and the fragments of broken glass cause the speaker to ponder the grim view of life here, in lines that echo Philippe's *Bubu de Montparnasse* and anticipate "Preludes," III, which he would complete in the summer of 1911:

Across the room the shifting smoke
Settles around the forms that pass
Pass through or clog the brain;
Across the floors that soak
The dregs from broken glass[.] (1–5)

The speaker ends with the observation that life is "Broken and scarred / Like dirty broken finger nails / Tapping the bar" (11–13), the latter a concrete detail that Eliot uses again in the song of the third Thames-daughter in *The Waste Land*, in her bleak memory of her seduction on Margate Sands: "The broken fingernails of dirty hands" (303).

Both contemporary newspapers and Baedeker's guidebook provide details of specific cafés-concerts that Eliot could have frequented and the performers and acts he could have seen. The latter contains this commentary under the heading *Cafés-concerts*: "These cafés, which offer drinks and songs of inferior quality and which also present little plays, are numerous and of greatly varying types. . . . The free admission, at certain cafés-concerts, is only a ruse to attract customers, because one is obligated to buy at least one drink, which costs, depending on the place, from 5 francs to 75 centimes and which is generally mediocre." The following list of sixteen of the "principal ones" is divided into the two categories of those operating in summer and those operating in winter. They include the Scala, the Eldorado, the Cigale, the Alhambra, and Ba-ta-Clan, the latter two already considered music halls. Indicative of the currently developing nature of music halls, this edition does not yet list them in a category of their own, but includes them with cafés-concerts, although the notation "today a Music hall" follows the listing of the Alhambra (41).

A typical program in a café-concert was presented at the Scala in October, the month of Eliot's arrival. According to the October 25 issue of *Le Figaro*, at 9:15 p.m. its current production entitled "Le Circuit du Leste" [The Agile Circuit] was an operetta-revue-fantasy-vaudeville in two acts and 17 "tableaux" or sets, beginning at 9:15 p.m. (4). The next day's issue carried this account: "Every evening Morton, the incomparable fantasist, and his witty partner Jane Marnac receive frenetic applause in the hall when they sing their famous duet 'My Heart is like a Sentry' in 'Le Circuit du Leste.' They evoke gales of inextinguishable laughter, and the audience calls them back to the stage with endless ovations. Furthermore, the production teems with ultra-joyous scenes that assure its long-lasting success" (4). And the November 24 issue of *Le Figaro* described a new production consisting of "Salominette," called a "profane tall-tale in one act," another one-act entitled "Gonzague," and "La Partie Concert" [The Part with Songs], featuring the singers Paul Morly, Pomponette, Sinoel, and Dufleuve (6).

Another café-concert was the popular Concert Mayol. Originally called the Grand-Concert Parisien, the famous café-concert singer and composer Mayol bought it in 1910 and renamed it for himself, playing on his fame to attract customers. From that year until 1914, it was among the most popular of the cafés-concerts in Paris. Well-known for his 1902 hit "Viens, poupole" about a working-class man who invites his wife to go to a café-concert on Saturday night as their "dessert," Mayol was a charming and elegant performer (Erismann 159) who spoke his songs. Feschotte notes that "his perfect diction, the artistry of his gestures (especially his hands), and the charm of his intonation assured Mayol a deserved celebrity. Elegant, always with a sprig of lily of the valley on his lapel, his hair raised in a tuft on top of his head, Mayol gained acclaim everywhere with a repertoire of lively, light-hearted songs" (41).

At the Concert Mayol, he featured great stars and elaborate revues. An article in the March 21, 1911 issue of *Le Figaro*, for example, describes the current successful program: "Since the return of Mayol, every evening people are turned away as Tout-Paris [Parisian high society] wants to applaud its favorite artist in his new productions. Damia [and other singers] triumph in their repertoires. Further, the one-act 'Service d'ami' [The Service of a Friend], which is beautifully acted by the exquisite comedienne Mlle Lyonel, . . . is a great success. And then there is M. Talera in his female impersonations, a magnificently-presented attraction" (6).

Damia, called "the tragedienne of song" because of her dramatic style, expressed "the very rhythm of the heart of the people" in realistic songs (Feschotte 37). She may have been among several early Parisian inspirations for Eliot's conviction that the link between the performer and the general public in theatre is of paramount importance.

The blurring of lines between café-concerts and music halls is especially evident in *Le Figaro*'s October 31 review of the revue "Mais z'oui!" [But, Of Course!] at the Cigale, a long-time café-concert specializing in the revue, which is, however, identified as "a pretty Montmartre music hall" (5).[12] Described as having long had "a pact with success," it has "assured itself of another one with 'Mais z'oui,' whose 15 acts, which evoked laughter, applause, and amazement, included ' The Triumphant Tenor,' 'Salomé and St. John the Baptist,' [and] . . . "The London Flower-Sellers," the latter featuring an increasingly popular import from England called simply "the girls." The "varied and lively" finale of the first act "took us to Brussels, Venice, Moscow, Seville, and London and ended with a dazzling general procession after having shown us dances from all the nations." The review concluded with a flourish of praise for the "extraordinary luxury of the costumes designed by Pascaud, the sets, and the scenes, whose ensembles and choruses were directed artistically by Bucourt of the Opéra. The cast deserved the bravos and accolades which they received, especially the incomparable Caruso and the beautiful Marthe Lenclud, whose voluptuous and savage dances created a sensation. It's above all, first and last, a great and enduring success" (5). The review demonstrates the major characteristics of what was to become Parisian music hall entertainment: diversity, speed, extravagance, performances by major figures from the world of high art, and international acts.

Music Halls

While Parisian café-concerts and music halls had many similarities, especially during Eliot's year there when they existed side by side with nearly equal popularity, there were several significant differences, as Nancy Perloff points out. First, although both presented quickly shifting acts or "turns" that included songs, circus acts, skits, dances, and revues, music halls expanded their offerings by presenting grander, more spectacular circus acts such as magicians, large animals, and acrobats as well as more sumptuous revues, called *revues à grand spectacle*, with numerous performers, an expanded orchestra, elaborate scenery, and electric lighting effects (Perloff 35). A cartoon by Brod in the article "In the Orchestra Pit of a Music hall" by L. Vuillemin in the January 12, 1911 issue of *Comoedia* (Figure 38) depicts the lively orchestra and the varied responses of the upper-class audience members to their music: entitled "During the Revue.—The Musicians 'really go at it,'" the cartoon cleverly presents the dynamic (and perhaps loud or discordant) quality of the music as a battle of large music notes (5). According to Caradec and Weill, "the revue was born in Paris" (181) and was not originally a part of the British music hall format. Second, in order to accommodate such features, which required greater technology and more space, and to attract a larger segment of the upper class, the buildings in which music hall entertainments were presented were both more spacious and more opulent. Rather than small cafés, the venues for music hall entertainment were often palatial. For example, the popular café-concert the Casino de Paris was transformed from a simple café into "'a veritable palace, a marvel of comfort and good taste,'" with gold leaf covering both walls and ceiling and new loges installed for the comfort of "a larger, wealthier clientèle" (qtd. in N. Perloff 34–5), while Ba-ta-Clan (Figure 39), a much-frequented establishment with 2000 seats, resembled a "gigantic pagoda" (Caradec and Weill 111). Other changes emphasized the shift from an informal café setting to "an elegant theatre," with the seats arranged in rows facing the stage rather than grouped around tables. Drinking and smoking were no longer allowed during the performance, and an admission fee was charged to take the place of the minimum drink requirement (N. Perloff 34–5). The result was a more formal setting and a more diverse clientele, the latter evidenced in a popular music hall song of 1903:

> Le music hall plaît à l'excès
> Au riche comme au prolétaire.
> Si son nom lui vient d'Angleterre,
> C'est un spectacle bien français . . . . (qtd. in Caradec and Weill 183)

> [The music hall is extremely pleasing
> To the rich as well as to the working class.
> Even though its name comes from England,
> It's a very French show . . . .]

Other traits of music halls which set them apart from cafés-concerts were their internationalism, with many acts imported from around the world, thus furnishing an appealing sense of the exotic and unusual, and their featuring famous figures from artistic fields such as opera, classical theatre, and cinema (N. Perloff 35). However, despite these expansions and refinements, Parisian music halls, like their sources the cafés-concerts and the British music halls, were still essentially rooted in their intimate connection with the audience. As W. Macqueen-Pope notes, music hall was a form of entertainment grounded in its audience, people who wanted something in which they could participate, something of which they would be an integral part, something which provided them gaiety, laughter, and music (3–6). Eliot seems to have found these qualities in particular most inviting.[13]

Although the number, sequence, and types of acts varied from music hall to music hall, so that they provided "a vast potpourri" (Feschotte 6), the program offered in December 1910 at the Nouveau Casino de Paris[14] is typical of what Eliot might have seen. Furthermore, the fact that the building had just been renovated indicates the growing popularity of music hall entertainment. An article in the December 14 issue of *Le Figaro* announced that the new owner's "dazzling success" on opening night placed this "splendid music hall," which had been entirely transformed, among the best in the capital. Predicting that the music hall would be packed because of the quality of this "family program" as well as its exceptionally reasonable prices and no-tipping policy, the writer described and incidentally defined this Parisian version of the British music hall: "This marvelous program presented for the select clientele which came to the remodeled Casino de Paris a procession of acts which were appealing, artistic, tasteful, and without triviality or excessive length. It's the true system of the English music hall with a rapid succession of attractions, a veritable kaleidoscope, charming and sparkling." He listed those acts which were most popular with the audience, revealing the move to greater technology, speed, and daring: a "dizzying motorcycle race" that took place high above the stage with speeds reaching 112 kilometers per hour, a juggler, five "ravishing English dancers" called the Ascot girls, a ventriloquist whose puppets sang a trio, and a troupe of mimes "who were unknown to Parisians yesterday but are famous today" (6).

Among the various music halls which Eliot may have attended, several in particular seem to be reflected in his literary goals and/or his works. When Eliot first arrived in Paris, the Variétés, described in Baedeker's guidebook as "excellent for vaudeville, farcical and bawdy plays, operettas, and revues" with prices ranging from twelve francs for the best seats to three francs for the cheapest ones (38), was presenting a satirical comedy entitled "Le Bois Sacré" [The Sacred Wood]. According to the October 30 issue of *Le Figaro*, its 100th performance had taken place the previous evening, with the box office taking in 9000 francs, and the first matinee of the season was scheduled for that very day (5).[15] While Eliot's title for his 1920 collection of essays has serious connotations, as discussed by Huismann (217–33), it may also reflect this piece of Parisian light entertainment, remembered from ten years earlier and perhaps functioning, at least for him, as a kind of inside joke undercutting or even mocking the seriousness of the essays in the collection.

Also in October the Alhambra, described in a review of its current offerings in the November 15 issue of *Comoedia Illustré* as "the prestigious Anglo-American Music hall" (92), offered a production featuring one of the great stars of the day,

Harry Fragson (Figure 40).[16] In a review in the November 5 issue of *Le Figaro*, he was hailed as "the national singer of wit and humor" who delighted the Parisian audience with his "inimitable cocoricos" (7). Eliot may first have heard this French onomatopoetic word for the crowing of a rooster, which was Fragson's comic hallmark, at one of his performances that autumn at the Alhambra and used it for quite a serious moment in Part V of *The Waste Land* when the protagonist, having reached the empty, ruined chapel, hears the cock on the rooftree cry, "Co co rico co co rico" (393).[17]

Eliot would have been impressed with Fragson's comic genius, praised in glowing terms in *Le Figaro's* review of November 5: "This time the genial artist, whose mirth-provoking irony and imperturbable calm are the ultimate symbol of the power of comedy, outdid himself. His famous repertoire, so varied and subtle, was enriched with new and surprising routines in which finesse and passion exploded in picturesque images. His triumph was indescribable!" (7). Eliot's appreciation of music hall humor and his realization that it could be effectively used in his own work—convincingly established by Schuchard in terms of the British music hall—may owe a great deal to his seeing Fragson and other comedians in Paris[18] in 1910–1911, in addition to those he had already observed in American vaudeville and minstrel shows.

Indeed, in the series of poems entitled "Suite Clownesque," written in the manner of Laforgue and completed in October 1910, Eliot makes several references to what appears to be a music hall comedian. While the series was apparently begun in the United States, so that the figure of the comedian may be drawn in part from American music hall and vaudeville,[19] it may also reflect his introduction to Parisian music hall during his first weeks in the French capital. The French word *Clownesque*, meaning "clownish," was added in pencil to the original title "Suite" (Ricks 162), a reflection no doubt of his French location. Sections I and IV describe a comedian with a scarlet "Nose that interrogates the stars" (I, 7, 16), with a "belly sparkling and immense" (I, 14), and with legs and toes spread apart; he leans across the orchestra, "[e]xplodes in laughter" (IV, 14), or "[i]nterrogates the audience" (I, 17). This figure may be a composite of several comedians appearing in Parisian music halls at the time. Also, in section II the women who "[p]erched on stools in the middle of the stage" (8) evoke female performers in Parisian cafés-concerts who sat on stools or chairs on the stage until their turn to perform.

In addition to comic songs, Fragson, who always dressed in evening clothes and was the first to accompany himself at the piano, sang sentimental and patriotic songs, with whose refrains audiences joined in (Caradec and Weill 148–9). In the show at the Alhambra, according to the article in the November 15 issue of *Comoedia Illustré*, he introduced a "deliciously attractive air [which] all the *tzigane* [gypsy] bands have made the vogue and which all of Paris hums, with exquisite words that everyone can sing." To facilitate its readers' ability to join in, the journal included the refrain of "this charming melody":

> O Manon, my lovely one,
> My heart says hello to you.
> For us the *tziganes* play their love song,
> Their love song, and this melody thrills me.
> Listen to it therefore.
> It's our first song. (92)

Here is yet another demonstration of the interaction of artist and audience in the music hall setting, which Eliot later described as an important component of drama.

Several acts in the Alhambra's production strikingly illustrated the attempt to draw audiences with ever more daring or unusual performers, many of whom were imported from other countries, thus contributing to the growing international flavor of music halls. Cited in the review in *Le Figaro* as noteworthy new acts were the "innovative dancers Moran and Tingley who were all the rage in New York for waltzing upside-down," an indication of the growing popularity of American dance partners in Paris, and the "screamingly funny Kelly," a comedian. The next day's matinee would see the debut of "Rudolf's famous elephants" (7). The article on the Alhambra in the November 15 issue of *Comoedia Illustré* announced that "several sensational acts" would appear in its next show, including Les MacBanns (jugglers with "electric devices") and an airplane performing such feats as taking off, climbing, and turning upside down (92). According to the May 3 issue of *Le Matin*, the Gaudschmidts' acrobatic dogs were hilarious, "provoking gales of laughter" in the current production (4). Perhaps viewing Les MacBanns instigated Eliot's admiration for jugglers, culminating in Enrico Rastelli, the great Italian performer who gained fame for juggling ten balls at once and whom Eliot could have seen at London's Hippodrome in 1922 when he appeared in Western Europe for the first time. His skill and artistry were so impressive that Eliot refers to him in "The Beating of a Drum," in a comment on the necessity of restoring rhythm to contemporary drama: "It is the rhythm, so utterly absent from modern drama, either verse or prose, and which interpreters of Shakespeare do their best to suppress, which makes Massine and Charlie Chaplin the great actors that they are, and which makes the juggling of Rastelli more cathartic than a performance of 'A Doll's House'" (12).[20]

Another performer whom Eliot could have seen at the Alhambra in Paris and/or at a music hall in London during his October 1910 or April 1911[21] visit there was the wildly popular Chinese magician Chung Ling Soo. Actually an American named William Ellsworth Robinson, the "Marvelous Chinese Conjuror" with over one hundred magic tricks was called "one of the two greatest illusionists in Europe" in a review of April 30 in London's *Sunday Times* (Dexter 17, 99). Performing annually at the Alhambra from 1910 until his accidental death in 1918, he was a "celebrity generally known by most people in Paris" (Rothschild 79) and was the inspiration for the Chinese Conjuror in the notorious 1917 ballet *Parade*, a likely influence on *The Waste Land*.

A leading female singer in a popular revue may have furnished the name which Eliot used over forty-five years later for a character in *The Elder Statesman* (1958). The enormous music hall Ba-ta-Clan, which began presenting showy *revues à grand spectacle* in 1910 (Feschotte 79), in the fall and spring of 1910–1911 mounted the lavish "Et Ça!" ("What About That!"). An enthusiastic reviewer in *Comoedia Illustré*'s June 15 issue proclaimed it "marvelous," noting that "in the loges of the hall that was filled to capacity were our most elegant society women and our most prominent Parisian men." He described the bold, chic costumes, the realism of the twenty-one sets, the excellence of the orchestra, and the cast of extremely beautiful singers. The first of the singers mentioned was Mlle Fina Montjoie, who played the role of "The Bohemian" and "whose burlesques were adorable." The accompanying photo (Figure 41) shows a rather buxom woman in a large hat, gypsy scarf, and cape (Bridge 108). Eliot's choice of the name Maisie Montjoy for the music hall star with whom Lord Claverton had a brief affair as a young man, and whose reappearance late in his life forces him to reevaluate his past actions, suggests that he attended a performance and remembered this particular Parisian singer.

Finally, the two most popular music halls of the time, the Moulin Rouge and the Folies-Bergère, presented spectacular productions during Eliot's year in Paris. The former, called the Théâtre-Concert du Moulin-Rouge in Baedeker's 1907 guidebook, presented "Revues, operettas, quadrilles realistes, etc." (41). At the time of Eliot's arrival in Paris, audiences thrilled to "La Danse Noire," described in the October 25 issue of *Le Figaro* as an "impassioned and brutal dance performed by Polaire and Gaston Sylvestre" in an "opérette à grand spectacle" there (4). Polaire, who began her career as a *gommeuse* in cafés-concerts, was called an *épileptique* because of her frenetic movements—shaking, jerking, and twirling her body in a manner considered scandalous at the time. Caradec and Weill describe her as "the agitating and agitated Polaire" and assert that she created "le genre épileptique" (177–8). She perhaps served as a model for the woman in "Sweeney Erect," who apparently suffers an actual epileptic seizure after having sex with the indifferent Sweeney. Caradec and Weill's description of Polaire's disheveled hair, immense black eyes that appeared bruised, and large voracious mouth (178) is strikingly similar to that of the woman in Eliot's poem: "This withered root of knots of hair / Slitted below and gashed with eyes, / This oval O cropped out with teeth" (13–15).

Also in late October 1910, the Folies-Bergère, described in the Baedeker guidebook as "a very popular place, half-theatre, half café-concert, where one can smoke and walk around in the promenade" for a fee of three to eight francs (40–1), offered a program filled with hilarious comic acts, according to various newspaper accounts. *Le Petit Parisien*, for example, reported in its October 20 issue, "Never has one heard such resounding laughter in a music hall as at the Folies-Bergère at the moment" (5). One cause of the laughter was a skit entitled "Bob et son chien" [Bob and His Dog] performed by Little Willem and Geo Ali, the "first dog impersonator," imported from London's Drury Lane Theatre. Other "attractions sensationelles," as noted in the October 25 issue of *Le Figaro*, were "Les Flying Girls" from Heidenreich (a trapeze act), Humpsti Bumpsti (comic acrobats billed as "The Kings of Mad Laughter"), The Moors of Abben-ben-Zair, and a ballet entitled "Les Niles" (5). The next month, according to an article in the November 27 issue of *Le Figaro*, a new show featured a pair of "extraordinary cyclists"; the 5 X-Rays in a "hilarious acrobatic skit"; the 3 Meers ("virtuosos of the high wire and laughter"); and at 10:15 p.m. precisely the famous cafe-concert singer Mayol with a new repertoire (5). A sumptuous revue with forty-six tableaux entitled "La Revue des Folies-Bergère" was presented in the spring of 1911, beginning with Les Jaxons in "Les Polichinelles" (a puppet show) and ending with a skit starring, among others, Maurice Chevalier, as reported in *Le Figaro* for March 25 (6). Programs such as these at the Moulin Rouge and the Folies-Bergère attest to the variety, the internationalism, and the sensationalism provided by music halls.

The influence of the music hall on Eliot is reflected in his essays, poems, and plays, as well as in his personal life.[22] Although it has typically been attributed to British and American venues only, Parisian music halls (along with cafés-concerts and cafés-artistiques) were also important early sources. In his critical essays, he often alludes to the music hall as a source of inspiration for a new form of verse drama. As early as 1920 in "The Possibility of a Poetic Drama," he makes the radical suggestion that, in creating contemporary poetic drama, the playwright should "take a form of entertainment, and subject it to the process which would leave it a form of art. Perhaps the music hall comedian is the best material" (70). Later, in the last essay of *The Use of Poetry and the Use of Criticism*, he suggests that every poet "would like to be something of a popular entertainer . . . [and have] a part to play in society as worthy as that of the music hall comedian" (154).

He puts these theories into action in various poems and plays, most obviously in the unfinished dramatic fragment *Sweeney Agonistes* (1926–7). There, as I note in my essay on Eliot in *Twentieth-Century American Dramatists*, he draws upon the traditions of the music hall to inject new vitality into poetic drama:

> The music hall format . . . provides him with a dramatic framework which fulfills his most pressing concerns. It is entertaining through its songs and its depictions of ordinary situations, and yet it also allows him to develop an underlying spiritual meaning and to write in verse; thus he can keep the audience's attention while at the same time conveying a significant theme in poetry. As he says in a humorous way in a letter to Ezra Pound [published in "Five Points on Dramatic Writing"], ". . . IF you can keep the bloody audience's attention engaged, then you can perform any monkey tricks you like when they ain't looking, and it's what you do behind the audience's back so to speak that makes your play IMMORTAL for a while. If the audience gets its strip tease it will swallow the poetry." (157)

Two radical aspects of the play are Eliot's injection into the text of popular tunes typical of music hall, such as "Under the Bamboo Tree" and "Ain't We Got Fun," and his combination of the rhythms of music hall patter, comic opera, and jazz in an attempt to create a new, contemporary meter for the dialogue. The pulsating, throbbing rhythms, the heavily accented syllables, and the hammering repetition, often in the format of an audience repeating the refrain first sung by the music hall or café-concert performer, echo what he may have heard in these Parisian venues:

> Sweeney: That's what life is. Just is
> Doris: What is?
>   What's that life is?
> Sweeney: Life is death. (98–101)[23]

While these examples from his essays and plays are obvious reflections of the influence of the music hall on his work, *The Waste Land* in far more subtle and largely unacknowledged ways makes extensive use of techniques and materials from Parisian music halls, cafés-concerts, and cafés-artistiques as well as from circuses, fairs, dance halls, and cinema.

Circuses

Circuses, a major form of popular entertainment much older than cafés-concerts and music halls, were creations of the late nineteenth and early twentieth centuries and offered a varied slate of acts, their main staple being the traditional fare of clowns, acrobats, trapeze artists, magicians, jugglers, and trained animals. At the time of Eliot's sojourn in Paris, these types of acts were still predominant in circus programs, but, in an attempt to compete with cafés-concerts and music halls, they were beginning to expand their offerings to include musical plays, dances, *pochades* [skits], pantomimes, operettas, and revues—although music, songs, and dancing girls were far less important in circuses than in the other two forms. As Feschotte points out, there was much interpenetration of the offerings of circus, café-concert, and music hall: "If the circus has lent many of its acts and performers to music hall, music hall has contributed a number of technical improvements to the circus, such as lighting effects. Both share dancers and troupes of girls. They have enriched each other" (118). Baedeker's guidebook listed five circuses: the Nouveau Cirque, the Cirque Médrano (also called Boum-Boum), the Cirque d'Hiver, the Cirque Métropole, and the Hippodrome, the first two of which were the most popular. During Eliot's year, the Cirque de Paris was operating as well. While most circuses attracted audiences that were predominantly of the lower and middle classes, the Nouveau Cirque in particular also drew members of the upper class and many foreign visitors (see N. Perloff 29, Adrian 53–4, and Bost 42–4). Artists, musicians, dancers, and writers, such as Cocteau, Picasso, Satie, and Massine, were especially interested in the circus and came often. Indeed, in the late nineteenth century Gautier—who would soon be an important influence on Eliot—wrote of the circus with the same respect that he gave theatre, opera, and ballet, noting that its appeal was that it had no speech and thus was "the opera of the eye" (qtd. in Speaight 161). As an aspiring poet, Eliot may have also been drawn there.

As with the offerings of cafés-concerts, music halls, and other types of popular entertainment, those of circuses were described in great detail in Parisian newspapers. Soon after Eliot's arrival, he might have read the description in the November 5 issue of *Le Figaro* of the program for that evening at the Cirque Médrano, which would present the debut of the "extraordinary cyclists" the Sisters Victoria, as well as the already successful acts of the juggling acrobats of the Balaquer troupe, the "musical eccentrics" the Haubons, the equestrian comedienne Mlle Léris Loyal, the "higher horsemanship" of Mlle de Bottoni, and the famous clowns from Chez Boum-Boum, including Carpi and Noppi, who were described as outstanding in the parody "The Waltz of the Open Boat" (7). This program and others presented at circuses during Eliot's year in Paris were still composed almost entirely of traditional circus acts, the adoption of "turns" from other forms of light entertainment being just underway. An article in the May 12, 1911 issue of *Le Figaro* announced that the director of the Cirque de Paris, "sparing no cost to add new acts to his show," had recently engaged "artists of the first rank," naming Al Schneider, who would debut with his twenty-two lions on May 13 in a program already loaded with such attractions as "the famous clown Chocolat, who continues to be the joy of the children" (4). Chocolat was one of several clowns, including the Fratellini Brothers, who often performed with a *cheval-jupon* [a horse with a skirt, beneath which two men performed movements such as dancing, kicking, and sitting down]. The daring appearance in the 1917 ballet *Parade* of a *cheval-jupon* was a major cause of the riotous response to that production.

Fairs and Exhibitions

Fairs and exhibitions were also integral elements of Parisian light entertainment during Eliot's year there. *Fêtes foraines* [itinerant fairs] provided circus acts and sideshows as well as games, rides, and the sale of foods (a particular favorite being spice bread), household articles, and decorative objects in an outdoor setting (see Borgé and Viasnoff 194 for a photo).[24] Rioux and Sirinelli assert that Paris launched the model of this type of entertainment with *La Fête à Neu-Neu* [The Fair of the Throne] and the country fair at Luna Park (located at Porte Maillot). The numerous street fairs of the boulevards featured merchants displaying their wares in booths on one boulevard, sideshows and entertainers on another, and games, lotteries, shooting galleries, and rides on yet another. The attractions abounded with new technical marvels, multicolored lights, and tempting sights (80), while a mélange of sounds filled the air: music from calliopes and small bands, cries of merchants selling their goods, shots from shooting galleries, and the turning of the merry-go-round (Fréjaville 246). This festive atmosphere attracted crowds from all social classes as well as artists, musicians, and writers such as Cocteau, Picasso, Satie, and Darius Milhaud, who drew inspiration from these lively venues. So too, it seems, did Eliot.

At the sideshows were fortune-tellers, dwarfs, bearded ladies, jugglers, wrestlers, boxers, trained animals, and magicians "who pulled rabbits out of a hat, made flowers appear in their buttonholes, and produced freshly laid eggs from thin air" (N. Perloff 30). One of the most spectacular and popular of the magic tricks was the decapitation act, in which, according to Nancy Perloff, "the performer cut off his head and presented it on a plate to his baffled spectators. This act—which evokes the decapitated head of John the Baptist delivered to the Princess Salomé on a silver platter—underscores the enormous appeal of the Salomé legend for artists (Aubrey Beardsley, Gustav Klimt, and Richard Strauss) and for the Parisian public during the early decades of the twentieth century." She mentions in particular Cocteau's use of the Salomé story in his scenario for Milhaud's ballet *Le Boeuf sur le Toit* (30–1).[25] As noted in Chapter 4, Eliot seems to have incorporated this act into "The Love Song of J. Alfred Prufrock" in the lines, "But though I have wept and fasted, wept and prayed, / Though I have seen my head [grown slightly bald] brought in upon a platter, / I am no prophet—and here's no great matter"

(81–3). Along with paintings of the saint which he saw in Paris, London, and other European cities, this unlikely source from the lowbrow world of popular entertainment appears directly to have influenced his literary creation, in this case almost immediately, and to have instigated his brilliant merging of popular and high art in his poetry.

Other elements of the fair appear to have influenced *The Waste Land* both directly and indirectly through artistic creations such as *Parade*. One of these was the *parade* itself, a preview of some of the acts to be performed inside the tent or stall set up on the street. Designed to entice onlookers to pay the price of admission to come in and see the entire show, the *parade* took place outside the tent, sometimes accompanied by a few musical instruments and presided over by a master of ceremonies or manager, who called out to potential audience members, describing the attractions, announcing the prices, and urging them to hurry in. A "pervasive feature" of street fairs (N. Perloff 31), this preview furnished the scenario for *Parade* and suggested to Eliot—either directly through his personal observations of *parades* at Parisian street fairs or indirectly through the ballet—the rapidly shifting series of scenes which form the structure of his poem.

The games, shooting galleries, and rides also provided inspiration to writers, musicians, and artists who sought to include the everyday world in their works. According to Nancy Perloff, a popular game called *Le jeu de massacre* [the game of massacre] challenged the player to knock down marionettes representing members of a wedding party with cloth balls, as the booth-keeper yelled, "Aim well at the groom! Knock down the mother-in-law!" Cocteau weaves this game into his 1921 work *Les Mariées de la Tour Eiffel* [The married couple of the Eiffel Tower], when the child of the bride and groom massacres the wedding party. Other games were the roulette wheel, betting booths, and shooting galleries such as *Le tir à surprise*, in which little dolls popped out of a door and danced to music from a music-box, perhaps the source of the title of Satie's composition *Jack in the Box* (N. Perloff 30). The rides included the merry-go-round, often accompanied by music, the Ferris wheel, and the train or roller-coaster, called *Montagnes russes* [Russian Mountains].

There were as well three permanent fairgrounds in Paris in 1910–11. One was the celebrated Grande Roue de Paris (the Great Ferris Wheel), which was open year-round and charged fifty centimes per ride (Baedeker 42). Another was Luna Park, which had been opened in 1909 by an American business and was "entirely mechanized" (Rioux and Sirinelli 80). It was appealingly described in the May 12, 1911 issue of *Le Figaro*: one could attend "La soirée de gala" [evening gala] currently underway and admire the "new luminous motifs which make the park sparkle with lights and give it the appearance of a fairyland, where, under the light of electric lamps, fashionable society men and women appear to walk in a golden powder, while in the restaurants they can enjoy gourmet dinners for 5 francs as famous Hungarian gypsy musicians play the most popular melodies" (4).

The electric lamps which allowed Parisians to enjoy outdoor nocturnal entertainment for the first time were a novelty and an exciting testament to the marvels of modern technological progress to be reveled in and appreciated, not only at Luna Park but also at Magic-City, an immense park in Oriental style which opened in early June 1911. An account in the June 3, 1911 issue of *Le Figaro* noted that "more than 20,000 people—truly the Tout-Paris of 1911—attended the opening along with ambassadors and great foreign figures. When this fairy-like city opened its doors at 8:30 p.m. last evening, all were amazed by its magnificent proportions, its numerous artistic palaces, . . . and its daring structures, created by the American engineer Biggs and the master French architect Fénard, aided by artists of great taste." The article described the "charming celebration amidst electric lights, fountains, and flowers in profusion. Among all the truly new and infinitely interesting attractions was heard the laughter of beautiful women drunk on the light and humming atmosphere of Paris enjoying itself, joyous and dizzy." Magic-City, the article predicted, would be the rendezvous for Parisian gentry for years to come (5).

The marvels of electricity, which had first been showcased in the Great Exposition of 1900 in Paris, heralded a great advance for the world of entertainment no less than for the world of technology and science. Indeed, electricity itself was featured in an exciting exhibit which took place at the time of Eliot's arrival in Paris and to which he may have been drawn to see for himself the wonders described in *Le Petit Parisien* on October 20: "At the Maison Électrique . . . larger and larger crowds come every day to see The House of Tomorrow, which is all-electric and has no servants. How can one not be interested in this marvelous invention born of French genius, always at the forefront of progress? Entry fee: 2 francs" (5). While Eliot may have been awed by such exhibits, he also saw beyond the surface glitter to the negative aspects of the modern world of technology and commerce, which he consistently attacked in his literary and critical works as dangers to the human soul and imagination.

Dance Halls

Another form of entertainment widely available in Paris was one in which the clientele themselves performed rather than watching others perform: the *bal* or dance hall. They fell into two categories: *le bal restaurant*, a restaurant with two or more stages for dancing and for song performances, and the *bal public* or *bal musette*, a dance hall where one drank and danced, in the latter to an accordion band.[26] As early as the 1880s, American dances and dance music had become popular in Paris. In the first decade of the twentieth century, performances by John Phillip Sousa increased the popularity of such types of American music and dance as ragtime and the cakewalk as well as marches and military music. In 1910–1911, many of the most popular dance tunes and dances in Paris were American; they were performed in music halls by both American and French professionals and in dance halls by Parisians eager to perfect the latest crazes.

In 1911, Vernon and Irene Castle, a well-known American husband-and-wife dance team, first came to Paris to perform in a revue at the Olympia music hall and popularized current American dances with daring names such as the Slow Rag, the Turkey Trot, the Monkey Glide, the Bunny Hug, the Grizzly Bear, and Shaking the Shimmy, which were performed to fast, syncopated music. These dances quickly spread to the dance halls (N. Perloff 45–59). Their popularity is evidenced in the 1912 ragtime tune "That Shakespearian Rag," whose refrain Eliot uses in a slightly altered form in Part II of *The Waste Land*, for it contains a reference to the Grizzly Bear dance in the lines, "I know if [Romeo and Juliet] were here today, / They'd Grizzly Bear in a diff'rent way" (Buck and Ruby). Sara M. Evans notes in her book *Born for Liberty* that in the first decade of the century young American working-class women flocked to dance halls, where they would have drinks and "join in the faddish 'tough dancing.' The raw sexuality of [these dances] . . . horrified the middle classes. By 1910 slightly more decorous versions . . . had become a new craze in middle-class cabarets. Such public eroticism shocked one magazine into announcing in 1913 that 'sex o'clock had struck'" (161).[27] The popularity of the Grizzly Bear in particular is further demonstrated by the title page of a 1911 calendar published in Sweden, featuring five photographs of the Swedish dance team Per Krohg and Lucy Vidil performing its various steps (Klüver 145).

Eliot probably went to Parisian dance halls (described in Baedeker's guidebook in its section entitled *Bals publics* as characteristic of Paris and open to all) and learned some of these popular dances, since both earlier and later in his life he enjoyed dancing and frequented dancing establishments (see Chinitz, "Jazz-Banjorine" 9–10). Indeed, he met Vivien at a dancing party in the spring of 1915 in Oxford, as mentioned in a letter of April 24, 1915 to Eleanor Hinckley: "I have . . . met a few ladies, and have even danced. The large hotels have dances on Saturday nights . . . . By being admitted to two dancing parties I have met several English girls, mostly about my own age, and especially two who are very good dancers" (*Letters* 97); one of these two was Vivien. He described them as "emancipated Londoners . . . [and] quite different from anything I have known at home or here . . . . They are charmingly sophisticated (even 'disillusioned') without being hardened; and I confess to taking great pleasure in seeing women smoke" (*Letters* 97).

The Bal Tabarin at the corner of rue Pigalle was listed in Baedeker as the principal dance hall on the right bank; offering "quadrilles réalistes, etc." (square dances of French origin composed of five figures and performed by four couples), it was open every night, the price of admission being two francs, except for Saturday when it cost five francs (42). In addition, special gala events took place on holidays (see Borgé and Viasnoff 200 and 203 for photos of Carnaval parades). For example, the November 24, 1910 issue of *Le Figaro* contained an announcement that, "as in every year, fashion designers and milliners will come to celebrate gaily the feast day of St. Catherine at the Bal Tabarin. Next Saturday, the Grande Fête des Muses, the triumph of St. Catherine, will feature a procession, in which one will witness the apotheosis of the Montmartre muses" (6). The February 4, 1911 issue of *Comoedia* announced that the "grand Egyptian celebration, The Triumph of Cleopatra" would take place that evening, featuring a saraband of pretty slaves, a farandole of sprightly courtesans,[28] a procession of priestesses of Isis, and the glorification of the divine Cleopatra (5), the last a reflection of the immensely popular production by the Ballets Russes the previous year. *Le Figaro*'s May 20, 1911 issue advertised "Le Bal des Petits Cochons" [The Dance of the Little Pigs] and "La Tentation de Saint Antoine" [The Temptation of Saint Anthony], a spin-off of the sensational production *Le Martyre de Saint Sébastien*, set to open at the Théâtre du Châtelet on May 22; a parade beginning at 12:30 a.m. would include one chariot of pretty she-devils and another depicting the temptation of the saint. An additional note promoted the "apéritif-concert" taking place daily at 5 p.m. with great success (4).

Soon after Eliot's arrival, an article in the November 1 issue of *Comoedia* announced the reopening on November 4 of the dance hall at the Moulin Rouge. Located next to the music hall, which "constantly attracted the Tout-Paris," it would feature a forty-piece orchestra, "cosmopolitan dances," and an innovation pleasing to its "elegant clientele": the installation of loges with access independent of the dance floor so that its occupants would not be bumped by dancers or the crowd (2).

While Eliot may have frequented this newly reopened dance hall or the Bal Tabarin and attended one or more of its special events, it is more likely that he would have gone to the Bal Bullier, located on the Left Bank and, according to Baedeker, "well-known as the dance-hall of students" (see Borgé and Viasnoff 193 for a photo of a *bal costumé* here) or to the Moulin de la Galette, which held masked balls during Carnaval; both were open on Tuesdays, Saturdays, and Sundays with entry fees of one to two francs. Baedeker further informed readers that, on Mardi Gras, young Parisians, both male and female, bombarded one another with confetti, a relatively new phenomenon since a definition of confetti as "small disks of colored paper" was included (42).

Cinema

The newest form of popular entertainment, the cinema, was also a part of the Parisian scene, although, because it was in its infancy, it was typically included as one type of entertainment in establishments that presented a variety of offerings; i.e., movie theaters showing films exclusively did not yet exist. Eliot's interest in cinema has been well-established, and it is highly likely that films showing in Paris in 1910–11 were among the earliest he saw. The development of French cinema began in 1895 when the brothers Louis and Auguste Lumière (whose last name appropriately means "light") invented a device called the Cinématographe, which could project films, and demonstrated it to the Parisian public in a rented room in the basement of the Grand Café, with the café chairs arranged in rows in front of a screen and with an admission charge of one franc for the twenty-minute show. From this modest beginning, cinema in Paris in the next fifteen years expanded to become one of the attractions in cafés-concerts, music halls, circuses, and fairs (N. Perloff 41–2).

By the time of Eliot's arrival in 1910, at least three establishments provided film showings as a regular feature of their evening programs—the Grands Magasins Dufayel, the Musée Grevin, and the American Biograph. While the earliest films were documentaries featuring everyday events, at this time they were often devoted to superhuman ventures such as scaling Mont Blanc, followed by a dance sequence such as "the curious cakewalk dance," and usually accompanied by orchestral music (N. Perloff 42). In the March 21 issue of *Le Figaro*, an ad for the five o'clock tea in the elegant winter garden of the Grands Magasins Dufayel commented on the "large audience, which, wishing to spend a pleasant afternoon, came every day to listen to the excellent symphony orchestra" and noted that from 2–6:30 p.m. the Cinématographe would present a new program suitable for families, "with humorous dialogue, musical adaptations, and marvelously colored scenes from the joyous Carnaval in Nice" (6).

As for the Musée Grevin, Baedeker's guidebook gives it its own heading under the rubric *Spectacles divers*, describing it in detail as follows: "The Musée Grevin, created by the celebrated artist of that name, . . . is a gallery of figures of famous persons and scenes of all sorts, both historical and contemporary . . . . There is also a theatre, which presents comedies, vaudevilles, operettas (entry fee: 2 francs, which includes entry to the museum). In the basement are the Roman Catacombs, as well as a room for luminous projections (cinématographe; entry fee: 50 centimes). Shows from 3–6 p.m. and from 8–10:45 p.m." (41). In the October 30 issue of *Le Figaro* is a commentary on the current productions showing in the theatre of the Musée Grevin: "'Coeur de Moineau' [Moineau's Heart], the charming play by M. Louis Artus, presents amorous and prettily sentimental scenes before packed houses both at matinée and evening performances, while at the 5 p.m. matinée the revue 'A-Musée-Vous' [Enjoy Yourself, a clever play on the French word for museum] is an enormous comic success, evoking much laughter, and Mlle Suzette Nelson, the pretty music hall star, triumphs" (5). An article in the April 1 issue of *Le Figaro* noted that the film showings at the cinema of the Musée Grevin "are all the rage in Paris. Its program, which is constantly changing and highly interesting, includes *The Foreign Legion*, *The Protests of the Vine-Growers of the Dawn*, *Viareggion Ravaged by a Tidal Wave*, and *At the Palace of Mirages*, the latter of which presents the luminous dances of the charming Mlle Christiane, which always create much enthusiasm" (5).

Sporting events were also the subjects of films. As noted in Chapters 1 and 2, a notice in the November 24 issue of *Le Figaro* announced, "Tonight at 10:30 p.m. the first showing of the film of the famous boxing match between Jim Jeffries and Jack Johnson will take place at the American Biograph at 7 rue Taitbout. This sensational film, which was acquired by the American Biograph for an enormous sum, presents all the preparations for and all the phases of the match. Because a large number of boxing enthusiasts will come to the première, it would be wise to reserve seats now" (6). Eliot's interest in boxing upon his return to America in the fall of 1911 suggests that he may have gone to see this film or others like it as well as actual boxing matches in Paris.

During and after World War I, American films, such as *The Perils of Pauline* (1914), and movie stars, such as Charlie Chaplin and Pearl White, were highly popular in Paris, influencing such artists as Cocteau, Picasso, Massine, and Satie in their creation of the ballet *Parade* in 1917, for example. Eliot too became a devoted fan of Chaplin, noting in the aforementioned passage from "The Beating of a Drum" that his rhythm makes him a great actor (12). By 1920 Paris had eleven theatres devoted exclusively to showing films (Caradec and Weill 186; see Borgé and Viasnoff 109 for a photo of an early movie theatre, date unknown). By the mid-1930s cinema had taken over as the major form of popular entertainment in Paris, replacing the music halls which had originally included cinema as just one of their multiple offerings and which later sometimes featured leading cinema stars (N. Perloff 44). Eliot's interest in cinema and his adaptation of cinematic techniques in *The Waste Land*, as described in the following section, may well have begun with the viewing of films such as those listed above during his student year in Paris.

Parisian Popular Entertainment and *The Waste Land*

The dazzling world of Parisian popular entertainment is reflected in the structure, technique, and content of *The Waste Land*, both through Eliot's own experience of its numerous forms during his 1910–1911 year in the French capital and through the intermediary of the scandalous avant-garde ballet *Parade*, which provided him with a model of how to incorporate this lowbrow entertainment into a legitimate work of high art.[29] In his 1920 essay "The Possibility of a Poetic Drama," he proposed the theory of creating a contemporary version of verse drama by taking "a form of entertainment [and subjecting] it to the process which would leave it a form of art," with the music hall comedian as "the best material" (70); the innovative, interdisciplinary *Parade* seems to have inspired him to apply this approach to poetry as well, specifically to the poem that he was struggling to create at that time.[30] Eliot's interest in the Ballets Russes and his love of popular entertainment, especially that in Paris on which the ballet is based, make it highly likely that he saw it. Since he attended several productions in May and July 1919 (*Letters* 292, 320), he no doubt went to the British première of the controversial ballet just four months later, especially since many of his literary and artistic friends, such as the Sitwell brothers, saw it. He could also have seen a revival in Paris during a weeklong visit in December 1920 and/or in London in 1921.

This extraordinary ballet was the result of the collaboration of some of the greatest artistic figures of the day: Cocteau, Picasso, Satie, Massine, and Diaghilev. Their goals were to create a work of art based on ordinary, contemporary life, specifically the lowbrow world of popular entertainment seen in the Parisian music hall, café-concert, street fair, circus, dance hall, and cinema; to incorporate new technology, such as the typewriter, the airplane, and the skyscraper; and to use techniques from the avant-garde developments in all the arts—in short, to create something entirely innovative and modern. As Massine notes, *Parade* was "an attempt to translate [popular art] into a totally new form . . . [and thus] we utilized certain elements of contemporary show-business—ragtime music, jazz, the cinema, billboard advertising, circus, and music hall techniques . . . . [We] were mainly concerned with creating something new and representative of our own age" (105). This commonplace material was considered unsuitable for the elite world of the ballet because it showed the "brash commercialism of modern life and the entertainments patronized not by the *beau monde* but by the general public"; according to Rothschild, that was the main source both of its originality and of its stormy reception (30, 71). Perhaps this ballet was a source for Eliot's assertion in his 1923 review-essay on Marianne Moore that "Fine art is the *refinement*, not the antithesis, of popular art" (595).

The scenario, created by Cocteau, is a *parade* of the acts of a troupe of performers at a Parisian street fair designed to entice spectators to come into the tent to see the entire show. Reflecting actual acts performed in 1917 and earlier in Parisian music halls, fairs, and circuses as well as American silent films and American music and dances popular in dance halls, they include the feats of a Chinese conjuror, a little American girl, and two acrobats, which are introduced by two managers and a *cheval-jupon*. The finale is "a rapid ragtime dance in which the whole cast [makes] a last desperate effort to lure the audience in to see their show" (Massine 105).

This format and subject matter, which recalled various types of Parisian light entertainment that Eliot himself probably saw during his year there, would have appealed to him and offered him inspiration for *The Waste Land*. Every aspect of the ballet from its guiding principles to its concrete details has striking correspondences in Eliot's poem. Since my essay "The Great Parade: Cocteau, Picasso, Satie, Massine, Diaghilev—and T.S. Eliot" discusses in detail these correspondences, I will highlight only the most significant, pointing out that much of what we see in the poem may be directly inspired by popular entertainments that Eliot saw in Paris.[31]

The most obvious reflection of popular entertainment both in the ballet and in the poem is the format of a series of turns or acts seen in street fairs, cabarets-artistiques, cafés-concerts, music halls, and circuses, reflecting as well the speed of modern life resulting from technological advances. The ballet presents three acts in quick succession, while *The Waste Land's* structure is a rapidly shifting series of scenes, many of which indicate the hurried tempo of the Machine Age with specific references to mechanization: "[The] human engine waits / Like a taxi, throbbing, waiting" (216–17). The cinema, too, may have contributed to the abruptly shifting structure, as well as to the techniques of the fade-in/fade-out, seen when the setting of the desert fades into Munich's Hofgarten, and of the close-up, seen when the panoramic view of the crowds crossing London Bridge zooms in to a close-up of Stetson.

The characters in the ballet, who were directly modeled on actual performers in Parisian venues in the early to mid-teens, have some ingenious counterparts in the poem. The Chinese Conjuror, danced by Massine, was based on the popular magician Chung Ling Soo, whom Eliot could have seen in Paris in 1910–11 and later in London and who may be reflected in Madame Sosostris; the warning she gives to the protagonist may allude to Diaghilev's lifelong fear of drowning, the result of having been told by a fortune-teller while a child that he would die by water.

The Little American Girl, a composite of Pearl White and Mary Pickford, two American stars of cinema well-known in France, as well as of young American women currently appearing in Parisian music halls, danced the ragtime, a staple of both music halls and dance halls, attesting to the popularity of American music and dances. Because the tapping of typewriter keys (reflecting this new technology and the resulting job opportunities for young working women) accompanies her dance, she may have partly inspired Eliot's creation of the typist.

Parade's ten-foot-tall Cubist managers, based on street-fair managers who attempted to convince spectators to come in to see the show and who then introduced the various turns, represented the crass commercial aspects, particularly advertising, that dominated the modern world of popular entertainment. Echoed in specific characters such as "the young man carbuncular" and Mr. Eugenides, they are perhaps most powerfully reflected in Eliot's general condemnation of the depressing and dehumanizing effects of commercialism in his description of anonymous, robotic office workers crossing London Bridge on their way into the City district: "A crowd flowed over London Bridge, so many, / . . . And each man fixed his eyes before his feet" (62, 65).

Finally, the *cheval-jupon*, taken directly from such popular Parisian clown acts as Chocolat and Footit or the Fratellini Brothers—both often featured at the Cirque Médrano—caused a furor as it cavorted on the stage in the ballet. As the most daring use of lowbrow entertainment, it may have encouraged Eliot to be equally innovative in his incorporation of popular culture in his poem. The horse exemplifies two other characteristics of contemporary art espoused by Eliot: the influence of the primitive and experimentation with duality. Not only was the *cheval-jupon* a part of primitive rituals, fairs, and folk festivals, but also Picasso's design for the head of *Parade's* horse reflects the African masks and double faces with which he was experimenting at the time; it conveys both humor and menace, the latter a trait that would never be seen in a circus or music hall horse. Eliot's infusion of these elements of the horse into *The Waste Land* can be seen in the allusion at the end of Section I to the ritual of burying pagan fertility gods in a present-day conversation about gardening, and in the implication that the traditionally friendly dog may destroy the possibility of resurrection.

The music and sounds of popular entertainment, reflected in Satie's innovative score for the ballet, are also evident in *The Waste Land*. Satie, who had been a pianist at the famous Montmartre cabaret-artistique the Chat Noir as well as at the Lune Rousse, was one of the earliest composers to insert popular music into his works; according to Ringo, "No musical style was too humble for him: that of the fair, the circus, the street corner" (qtd. in Rothschild 39). In his score, Satie combined classical music with American jazz and ragtime tunes popular in Parisian music halls, cafés-concerts, cabarets-artistiques, and dance halls, intentionally creating a discordant, jarring effect; as Cocteau pointed out in a review of the ballet in 1917, "two melodic planes are superimposed" so that the score "seems to marry the racket of a cheap music hall with the dreams of children, and the poetry and murmur of the ocean" (106). In the overture, which is a "fugue of a classical nature" (Cocteau 106), he "drops queer hints of squeaks and crashes [and] before the ballet is over he is rioting in rich and suggestive cacophony," as perceptively noted in a review of the revival of the ballet in London entitled "New Russian Ballet: 'Parade' at the Empire" in the November 15, 1919 issue of *The Times* (10).[32] For the ragtime dance of the Little American Girl, for example, he inserted into the score "The Steamboat Ragtime," actually Irving Berlin's "That Mysterious Rag," which was published in 1911 and appeared in a revue at the Moulin Rouge in 1913 (Rothschild 88), and the finale is a ragtime dance performed by the entire cast. These sudden, swift shifts from one type of music to another reflect the quickly changing acts of various forms of light entertainment, the flickering sequence of images in early cinema, and the chaotic, disjunctive quality of modern metropolitan life.

Eliot seems to have adapted elements of Satie's experimental score to reveal his vision of the chaotic, dissonant nature of contemporary civilization, a vision especially evident in *The Waste Land's* structure of quickly shifting scenes; in its discordant, jarring quality; and in its incorporation of common, popular material along with classical, canonical material. The last is seen in Eliot's combination of the lyrics of a bawdy ballad about prostitutes popular with soldiers in World War I and typical of the bawdy songs of cafés-concerts ("O the moon shines bright on Mrs. Porter / And on the daughter / Of Mrs. Porter / They wash their feet in soda water") with lines from two Renaissance poems, Marvell's "To His Coy Mistress" ("But at my back I always hear / Time's wingèd chariot hurrying near") and Day's "Parliament of Bees" ("When of the sudden, listening, you shall hear / A noise of horns and hunting, which shall bring / Actaeon to Diana in the spring"):

> But at my back from time to time I hear
> The sound of horns and motors, which shall bring
> Sweeney to Mrs. Porter in the spring.
> O the moon shone bright on Mrs. Porter
> And on her daughter
> They wash their feet in soda water. (196–201)

Eliot's inclusion of the lyrics of "That Shakespearian Rag," a 1912 tune popular in music halls, is no doubt indebted to the rags in Satie's score and to rags that he heard in Parisian venues of popular entertainment as well as in those in England and America (St. Louis in particular). The husband's thoughts in Section II contain a fragment of the refrain, reproduced almost exactly. The original version "That Shakespearian rag, Most intelligent, very elegant" (Buck and Ruby) is only slightly altered in the poem to "O O O O that Shakespeherian Rag—/ It's so elegant / So intelligent" (128–30); the odd spelling "Shakespeherian" is perhaps meant to indicate the way the word sounds when sung by music hall or café-concert singers or by the audience which repeats it. Finally, the closing passage with its dizzying, rapid shifts from fragment to fragment, some of which are in foreign languages, might be seen as the poetic equivalent of the ballet's exhausting finale.

Eliot may also have found inspiration in the ballet's sound effects from both the fairground, such as the klaxon, calliope, and lottery wheel, and the modern industrial world, such as airplanes, sirens, and the clicking of typewriter keys. These provide realism and convey the frenetic, staccato pace, the mechanization, and the discordant chaos of modern urban life. This transformation of commonplace sounds into art is echoed in the "dead sound on the final stroke of nine" (68) of St. Mary Woolnoth's bells (a sound which Eliot said in his notes to the poem that he had often noticed, obviously at the beginning of every working day as he entered Lloyd's Bank, just across a narrow street from the church). It is also reflected in the "sound of horns and motors" (197) of City traffic and the music of the typist's gramophone.

The dazzling, magical world of Parisian popular entertainment, which was loved by and provided inspiration to such early twentieth-century writers and artists as Cocteau, Picasso, Satie, Poulenc, and Massine, was also an influence—heretofore unacknowledged—on Eliot. The sheer scope and variety of its offerings were impressive, especially to a young American who arrived in Paris with a love of popular culture in his veins. The reflections of these Parisian lowbrow types of entertainment in his poetry, plays, and critical theories are numerous: the "inimitable cocoricos" of the popular comic singer Fragson; the star Fina Montjoie, in a *revue à grande spectacle* at the music hall Ba-ta-Clan; the boisterous repetition by the entire audience of the refrain of a song in a café-concert; the decapitation act at a street fair. Eliot's brilliant incorporation into his theoretical views and his works of materials drawn not only from the most intellectual and esoteric sources but also from the most frivolous and ordinary ones owes a great debt to the spectacular Parisian world of popular entertainment.

CONCLUSION

When Eliot left Paris in September 1911 to return to the United States, he took with him far more than the immediate indications of the influence of that magical, impressive, and life-altering year: wearing "exotic Left-Bank clothing," carrying a Malacca cane, hanging a reproduction of Gauguin's *The Yellow Christ* in his room (Aiken, "King" 20–21), subscribing to *La Nouvelle Revue Française*, and peppering his speech and letters with French expressions, attempts both to savor and to preserve its essence. It had a profound impact on his mind, his imagination, his heart, and his soul. Paris had gotten into his blood, and he would be forever marked by it; he had become and would remain a devoted Francophile. Its effect on his literary career was especially significant, for it gave him subject matter, techniques, and a willingness—indeed an eagerness—to experiment widely. The experience of that year was so far-reaching and extensive, as such experiences often are, that it is both a monumental and elusive undertaking to attempt to capture fully the complexity of its influence. However, because it is crucial to a deeper understanding of Eliot's life and his literary achievements, I will comment on what seem the most important of its contributions.

Perhaps most obvious are those tangible, if seemingly unremarkable, French elements that infiltrated Eliot's life both immediately and on a continuing basis. In addition to wearing French clothing and sporting a Malacca cane in the French style, he smoked French cigarettes, a habit acquired in Paris (Ackroyd, Illustration 17) and one which continued until his last years. He also maintained a fondness for Paris and other regions of France and made numerous visits to his favorite locations, establishing a recurrent pattern of finding there rejuvenation of his spirit, his intellect, his imagination, and his physical and mental health.

Eliot's Love of Paris, France, and the French People

For what must have been a multitude of reasons (the war; his grief over the deaths of Alain-Fournier, Verdenal, Péguy, and others; his and Vivien's health problems; a lack of money for holidays abroad), Eliot did not return to France for eight years after his departure in September 1911. In August 1919, he vacationed in Périgueux in the south of France (the site of his January 1911 trip), passing briefly through Paris en route. In letters written at that time to his mother, his brother, and his friend Sydney Schiff, he revealed his affection for France and the health benefit he derived from his sojourn in this much-loved country. His excitement at being again in France is evident in a letter of September 3, 1919 to his mother. After telling her that "I enjoyed my holiday thoroughly, and feel (and look) very well indeed," he recounted his trip from Le Havre to Trouville, describing "the boat crowded with people going to the races, and men with violins and singers passing their hats. It was all so French and so sudden that I was dazed by it." Going by train from Trouville to Paris, he then took a taxi to another train station to continue to Périgueux, giving the taxi driver a nice tip and telling him, "'That's because I have not been in Paris for eight years'; he roared with amusement, and waved to me as he drove off." Once on the train south, he "looked out of the window most of the way, being too excited to sleep" (*Letters* 328). To his brother Henry, he wrote on September 14, 1919, "I had a very delightful trip and feel in much better health for it. . . . France was certain to set me up," commenting that "being able to speak another language is a great stimulus and tonic" (*Letters* 330).

He returned to France on August 15, 1920 for a two-week holiday in the company of Wyndham Lewis, "a most excellent companion in travelling and a great comfort intellectually" (*Letters* 404). They first stayed in Paris at the Hôtel de l'Élysée and had dinner with James Joyce and Fritz Vanderpyl, art critic of the newspaper *Le Petit Parisien*; Eliot enclosed a sketch of the dinner in a letter to Sydney Schiff of August 22, noting that "Paris was a great relief after many months of London" (*Letters* 402–3), again revealing his great and lasting affection for the city. Following some days in Paris, he and Lewis took a walking and bicycling tour that included the Breton coast and the Loire (which Eliot had not previously visited and found "extremely beautiful," as he told Schiff in a letter of August 31) before returning to Paris, where they again saw Joyce. His love of France is clear in his comment to Schiff that "I was, as usual, very loth [*sic*] to leave France" (*Letters* 404).

Eliot was again in Paris just four months later for a holiday of six days before Christmas. In a letter of January 2, 1921, he confided to Max Bodenheim, an American poet, novelist, and playwright, "I of course escape to Paris whenever I can get a bit of a holiday, which is not very often," implying in following comments that it was an escape from the intellectual dullness of England. He referred to "the placid smile of imbecility which splits the face of contemporary London, or, more abstractly, the putrescence of English literature and journalism," and more or less included America in that indictment (*Letters* 431). Paris, in contrast, always represented for him lively intellectual and artistic energy and excitement. In a letter of January 22, 1921 to his mother, he confirmed that Paris was like an elixir to him: "My own health has been much better since my week in Paris before Christmas. It was such a complete change, and I enjoyed myself so thoroughly." He revealed that he stayed in "my old pension Casaubon," noting that he spent time with his brother-in-law Maurice and with "old and new French friends and acquaintances, writers, painters" and admitting that had he not met "such a number of new people there Paris would be desolate for me with pre-war memories of Jean Verdenal and the others." He also expressed a desire to return in the spring (*Letters* 433).

Years later he still felt an intense nostalgia and love for France, perhaps best seen in an obscure and little-known introduction which he wrote for *Inoubliable France* [Unforgettable France], a collection of forty-two photographs of France published by Alice Jahier in 1944 to preserve the memories of that country for those cut off from her during World War II. As she explains in the preface, dated June 1943, "For months, for years now, we have been in exile. And as we look at these pictures of France, the smooth, glossy photographs with all their shades of grey, from warm black to the pearly tones of light, stab us to the heart with glimpses of the land which lives within us" (n.p.). Eliot's introduction, entitled "To the Reader," which he surely agreed to write out of his own sense of being separated from this cherished country of his youth, echoes her anguish and strikingly reveals beneath the general terms he employs his own personal memories of and love for France: "Those who open this book, to study the photographs, of scenes so familiar and so strange, and to read the evocative text, are likely to be drawn to it first by its power of awakening memories from their own past lives. . . . To some, this book will bring . . . memories of studies pursued with the ardour and curiosity of youth; to some, memories of still more intense experience. . . . The picture of a place, however, as it evokes personal memories, may identify that place too closely with a life that is buried, or a chapter that is closed" (n.p.). Although he uses general terms ("Those" and "some") in describing how the photographs and text have the power to awaken "memories from [the readers'] own past lives," he clearly draws from his 1910-1911 year in Paris in the reference to "memories of studies pursued with the ardour and curiosity of youth." The ambiguous allusions to "still more intense experience" and to a photograph of a place identified "*too closely* with a life that is buried, or a chapter that is closed" (italics mine) suggest a still acute sense of pain and regret, perhaps associated with the deaths of Alain-Fournier and Verdenal in the war.

During his year in Paris, in addition to an affection for the city and the country as a whole, he developed a love for and admiration of the French people and their culture which was to last a lifetime and influence both his personal life and literary production. In particular he admired the analytical mindset of the French, their intellectual honesty, and their clarity of thought. For example, in a letter of

September 8, 1914 to his cousin Eleanor, written soon after his arrival in London from Marburg, Germany, he compared and contrasted the minds of the French and the English. Of a French woman whom he had recently met, he commented that "it is pleasant to be in contact with a French mind in a foreign city like this" and added, "it's ever so much easier to know what a Frenchman or an American is thinking about, than an Englishman. Perhaps partly that a Frenchman is so analytical and selfconscious that he dislikes to have anything going on inside him that he can't put into words, while an Englishman is content simply to live," the latter quality one that he wished to acquire, being himself more like the French. He concluded, "But on the other hand the French way has an intellectual honesty about it that the English seldom attain to. So there you are" (*Letters* 57). In a subsequent letter to her written on October 14, 1914, he continued his comparison and contrast of the two countries, telling her, "I don't think that I should ever feel at home in England, as I do for instance in France. Perhaps I admire the English more in some ways but find the French more congenial," adding by way of explanation that there is "a certain sense of confinement in England, and repression," with the implication that France provides freedom and openness (*Letters* 61).

He also considered France a highly civilized and cultured nation, being vastly superior in that regard to England, the United States, and Germany. For example, in a letter of April 1, 1915 to Isabella Stewart Gardner, the Bostonian patroness of the arts, he commented on the war and compared and contrasted the Germans and the French, clearly valuing the civilized nature of the latter: "The war is very real and very frightful to me . . . . [T]he Germans have that hospitality and cordiality which characterises the less civilised peoples. And not that I wish the Germans to be crushed—but France is so important, and defeat would do the French so much harm!" (*Letters* 93–4).[1]

French Friends and Colleagues

Eliot's year in France provided him not only with immediate French friendships—the most important of which were with Alain-Fournier and Verdenal—but also with French friends, acquaintances, and colleagues in the future, for the connections established by that year continued to be operative throughout his life. As noted in Chapter 1, his friendships with Alain-Fournier and Verdenal were quite extraordinary, providing him with two soul-mates who were intellectual, cultured, and sensitive and shared many of his interests. That both died in the early years of the war brought him much grief. Soon after the outbreak of war, he pondered in a letter of September 8, 1914 to Eleanor the painful situation of young men of his acquaintance in Germany and France fighting against each other: "I cannot but wonder whether it all seems as awful at your distance as it does here. I doubt it. No war ever seemed so real to me as this: of course I have been to some of the towns about which they have been fighting; and I know that men I have known, including one of my best friends, must be fighting each other" (*Letters* 58), a reference most likely to Verdenal. His death seemed to hit Eliot more forcefully than that of Alain-Fournier, since they were the closer of the two pairs of friends, as indicated by numerous references to him in letters as well as by the four dedications to him (see Ricks 3–4). In a letter of January 10, 1916 to Aiken, Eliot mentioned briefly in a list of (mostly negative) news items that "my friend Jean Verdenal has been killed" (*Letters* 125), while, in the letter of January 22, 1921 to his mother, noted above, he openly expressed his sense of loss, still keen over six years after Verdenal's death, when he stayed at the Pension Casaubon in Paris, where the two had been fellow boarders (*Letters* 433).

Throughout the remainder of his life, he made and maintained a variety of relationships with French friends and colleagues, such as Gide and Rivière. While Eliot first read the works of Gide during his Parisian year, he did not meet him then. However, as indicated in Chapter 1, ten years later, a long personal and literary acquaintance began when Gide wrote in December 1921 to invite him to become a regular contributor to *La Nouvelle Revue Française*, the journal which Eliot first came to know and admire while living in Paris. In his letter, Gide told Eliot that he was "an attentive reader of *The Sacred Wood*" and included some of his own work, hoping that Eliot could see the similarity of their thoughts (*Letters* 490–1), while Eliot in his reply indicated that he had been familiar with some of Gide's publications since his year in Paris (*Letters* 494–5). When Eliot went to Paris in January 1921 to finalize the arrangements for accepting the post, he did so not with Gide, as he had expected, but with Rivière, who had become the editor of the prestigious journal in 1919. He had met Rivière—Alain-Fournier's brother-in-law and then a contributor to the journal—once during his 1910–1911 residence in Paris, and this second encounter instigated a cordial relationship that lasted until Rivière's early death from typhoid fever in 1925, at which time Eliot wrote an obituary tribute to him. Other French figures with whom Eliot had friendships and/or professional relationships included Paul Valéry, whose photograph appeared in a gallery of photographs in his office at Faber and Faber (Hall 48), Valéry Larbaud, and Julien Benda.

Intellectual Influences

Another important aspect of the Parisian year was that Eliot encountered a powerful mix of ideas in a variety of forms which, as he acknowledged, contributed to his intellectual maturation and social, political, ideological, religious, and moral beliefs. The experience of observing such a number of differing views jostling for dominance demonstrated at the very least the wide number of compelling concepts among which one might choose for one's own and, I would suggest, gave him a broader range and more open mind than he has often been given credit for.

Easily overlooked as a source of Eliot's intellectual stimulation are the numerous public lectures listed and often reviewed in *Le Figaro* and other newspapers. The quality and variety of both the lecturers and their subjects are impressive, and many would certainly have been of interest to him, in particular those on Wagner, Gautier, modern Russian theatre, Bradley and Royce, Venetian music (by Fauré), Logic (by Russell), Philosophers from Hegel to Bergson, Buddhism, Beethoven's music, and Dante's *Commedia*.

Another major intellectual influence on the future critic, essayist, and journal editor can be found in the rigorous critical methods which he observed in French critics, reviewers, and essayists, such as Gide, Rivière, and Ghéon. In the November 1910 issue of *La Nouvelle Revue Française*, for example, he could have read and been impressed by Gide's powerful and daring critique of an essay attacking Baudelaire in an earlier issue by Faguet, a respected literary critic, professor of literature at the Sorbonne, and member of the Académie Française—a critique which no doubt caused Eliot to aspire to the same kind of no-holds-barred criticism himself. Rivière wrote astute reviews on a great range of cultural and literary subjects nearly every month for *La Nouvelle Revue Française*. The tough established critic, Ghéon, produced perceptive, provocative, and fearless commentaries on the newest cultural experiments, such as his review on the first exhibition of the Cubists in the spring of 1911. Ghéon was not one to back away from a confrontation, as when he took Lalo to task for his scathing indictment of Isadora Duncan in the March 1911 issue of *La Nouvelle Revue Française*. Eliot echoes in his essays on drama and in his plays a number of ideas in Ghéon's article "Sur le 'Théâtre Populaire,'" in which the French critic argues for a return to popular theatre in the November 1911 issue of the journal. This prestigious French journal was for Eliot a model of what an English literary journal should aspire to be.

Further contributing to his intellectual growth was a host of individuals who took strongly argued stances on a variety of topics. Gide, in addition to being a rigorous critic, was a novelist, poet, biographer, and essayist, as well as a social crusader who presented in several genres a penetrating examination of moral issues, such as a daring advocacy for homosexual rights and freedom from social and moral codes.

In Péguy, Eliot saw a proponent of French nationalism, of the Roman Catholic

Church (despite Péguy's non-practicing status), and of social and moral reform. Péguy was also an adversary of the excessive materialism and barbarism of the times, the latter reflected in Eliot's prose and poetry, most strikingly in *The Waste Land*. In his journal, *Les Cahiers de la Quinzaine*, Péguy published not only his own work but also that of leading thinkers of the day, as well as a series of biographies of individuals who exhibited strong moral values, since Péguy hoped to inspire a return to the virtues of the past. His journal was another model for Eliot to consider when *The Criterion* was launched later in his career. A "passionate Dreyfusard" (Kimball 8), Péguy offered in his book *Notre Jeunesse* a viewpoint in direct conflict with the anti-Semitism so rampant in France then, as demonstrated most powerfully by Maurras and L'Action Française. Finally, despite holding strong beliefs himself, Péguy was dedicated to the exchange of ideas and hosted a weekly discussion group in his bookshop, which Eliot may well have attended in the company of Alain-Fournier. Eliot's admiration for him is seen in his 1916 tribute to Péguy, in which he calls him "the incarnation of the rejuvenated French spirit" (qtd. in Kimball 2).

Other intellectual figures who were prominent in Paris that year, of whom Eliot knew, as he indicated in the 1934 "A Commentary," and whose ideas influenced him in various ways included de Gourmont, Barrès, Janet, Lévy-Bruhl, and Durkheim (451–2).

Durkheim was at the center of the controversy raging in the autumn of 1910 over the new emphasis at the Sorbonne on the scientific method of the social sciences, for which he was largely responsible, at the expense of the traditional study of language and literature. The flames of this controversy were fanned by a series of articles in defense of the latter entitled "L'Esprit de la Nouvelle Sorbonne" and signed with the pseudonym Agathon, later revealed to be Massis and de Tarde. Since Eliot read these, they no doubt led him to ponder the value and place of the two approaches in higher education. And Massis, who shared the beliefs of Maurras, later became a friend of Eliot, whose 1934 "A Commentary" originated as a review of Massis's memoir of those days.

However, without question the most significant of the intellectual influences were Bergson and Maurras. Eliot was swept up in "la ferveur bergsonienne" as he both attended the philosopher's courses and read the five major books of philosophy which had been published by the time of his residence in Paris. He embraced Bergson's key concepts of *la durée réelle*, *l'élan vital*, and *l'intuition*, valuing their spiritual, emotional, and humanistic nature, which was in opposition to the current emphasis on scientific and materialistic theories. Eliot was, as he himself acknowledged, "very much under his influence" during that year (Kumar, qtd. in Ricks 412), referring specifically to "the important influence that . . . *Matière et mémoire* had on my intellectual development" ("Lettre d'Angleterre," qtd. in Ricks 410). Bergson's ideas influenced Eliot's philosophic beliefs, aesthetic theories, and poetry, most obviously "The Love Song of J. Alfred Prufrock" and other poems written at the time, but also later works such as *Four Quartets*. While their powerful hold on him diminished somewhat in the years following his Parisian residence, that diminution was not as great as both he and many scholars would have us believe.

The ideas of Maurras and his political organization L'Action Française were equally powerful in Eliot's intellectual development. Maurras's advocacy of tradition, authority, and clarity, specifically expressed in his championing of nationalism, monarchy, the Roman Catholic Church, and the military, as well as his opposition to Romanticism in all its forms, was espoused to a large degree by Eliot during his Parisian year, when he read both Maurras's daily newspaper columns and his books. *L'Avenir de l'Intelligence*, in particular, influenced Eliot's views of the modern industrial world, as seen in poems such as *The Waste Land* as well as in essays. Eliot also observed the often violent activities of the Camelots du Roi and perhaps heard "Le Mâitre" speak at student meetings of L'Action Française. His devotion to Maurras, though tempered by his recognition of his flaws beginning in the late 1920s and early 1930s (Lockerd 10–11), seems to have lasted for most of his life. This devotion is evident in his preface to *For Lancelot Andrewes* and in his translation and publication of Maurras's "Prologue to an Essay on Criticism," both in 1928; in his dedication to Maurras in his 1929 essay on Dante; and in his homage to him published in 1948 in *Aspects de la France et du Monde*. In the homage Eliot not only described the great esteem in which Maurras was held in Paris in 1910–1911, but also asserted that in the present Maurras's "conceptions of monarchy and of hierarchy . . . [are] kin to my own, as they are to English conservatives, for whom these ideas remain intact despite the modern world" (qtd. in Asher 27). Finally, in the 1950s, Eliot wrote a defense of him, published in *Time and Tide*, and praised him in a speech entitled "The Literature of Politics" that subsequently was published by the Conservative Political Centre (Behr 71, 75).

These powerful and varied intellectual influences determined Eliot's own beliefs and appear in his criticism, drama, and poetry. How fully he absorbed and understood them and how immediately they became a part of his intellectual arsenal can be gauged by the fact that just five years later, in the autumn of 1916, he gave a series of six lectures in Yorkshire on the weighty subject of Social, Philosophical, and Religious Problems in Contemporary France and published a review of Durkheim's *The Elementary Forms of the Religious Life: A Study of Religious Sociology* (*Letters* 152).

Knowledge of French Language and Literature

The year in Paris also gave Eliot fluency in the French language which allowed him to read, write, and speak it with ease, along with an intimate knowledge of both established and contemporary French literature. Both played significant roles, often together, throughout his personal life and literary career. While he arrived in Paris with a good background in the language, his speaking ability was poor, as indicated by the remark of the *femme de chambre* at his pension (*Letters* 18). However, as a result of his conversation lessons with Alain-Fournier, his wide reading in French literature, and his extended immersion in a French-speaking culture, by the summer of 1911 his French was excellent, as confirmed by his tutor (*Letters* 26). His excellent command of French from then on is evidenced, for example, in a letter written by J. C. Squire, editor of *The New Statesman*, in support of Eliot's application for an Army commission in 1918; he asserts that Eliot's knowledge of the French language "is unusually great" (King's College Library). In an article entitled "Visite à T. S. Eliot," published in *La Gazette des Lettres* in 1946, Jean-Clarence Lambert comments that Eliot replied to his questions in very correct French (Eliot Collection, Houghton Library, Harvard University). And the fact that no translator is given for his essay "What France Means to You" in *La France Libre* suggests that he wrote it in French.

Eliot made both practical and literary use of this facility with the language. Concerning the former, he taught French (as well as Latin, mathematics, geography, history, drawing, baseball, and swimming) at Highgate Junior School in 1916. More significant, his ability helped him not only to get a job in the Colonial and Foreign Department at Lloyd's Bank in March 1917, but also to carry out his duties there successfully; as he wrote to his mother, "French and Italian I find useful [in my job], and shall have to pick up a little Spanish, Danish, Swedish, and Norwegian as well" (*Letters* 164). Eliot also interspersed French words and expressions, such as *tant mieux, au courant, métier, habile* (*Letters* 59, 67, 70, 90, 94), quite liberally in his letters, as well as, we can safely assume, in his conversations; he occasionally anglicized them, as in writing of a particularly good photograph that "Vivien is going to have it passe-partout'd [passed around to everyone]" (*Letters* 165).

His correspondence with certain French friends and colleagues was conducted entirely in French. Both Verdenal and Alain-Fournier wrote to him in French, and, since he wrote to the latter in French (*Letters* 26), it is reasonable to assume that he wrote to Verdenal in French as well, although none of those letters are extant. Other examples include his correspondence with Gide (*Letters* 490–1, 494, 502–3, 516), Hermann Hesse (*Letters* 509–10), and Paul Valéry (*Letters* 562).

Even more significant, Eliot made use of his knowledge both of the language and of the literature during his literary career in numerous ways. He often expressed his belief in the importance of French literature, as in his letter of April 1, 1918 to Eleanor Hinckley: he writes, "one must simply read French; let there be no nonsense about that; it is the most serious modern literature. Both for prose and poetry" (*Letters* 228). In a speech at a dinner in his honor given by the Alliance Française in Oxford in January 1949, he remarked that the study of French language and literature was a cause that he had always had at heart, and, in an interview in French with Radio-diffusion France in the same month, he expressed the hope that French readers of his poetry recognized him as "one of the inheritors of the legacy of Baudelaire, Laforgue, and Corbière" (King's College Library).

Cronin in a brilliant and somewhat overlooked essay describes some of the manifestations of this double influence of French language and literature on Eliot. First, he argues convincingly that the degree of intimacy with the language which Eliot gained in Paris, in combination with his previous knowledge of Laforgue, led to his writing poems during that Parisian year which are "nearer to translated French than to idiomatic English." He asserts that, "at the beginning of his career[,] translator and poet were so intimately linked as to be scarcely indistinguishable," citing in particular "Preludes" and "Rhapsody on a Windy Night" (131, 137). Cronin wonders how much of Eliot's first two books of poetry is "word-for-word translation and how much [is] totally original," an intriguing question. I suggest that, when Eliot composed "Prufrock," largely at the end of his year in Paris, he was able to inject his individual talent into the influence of Laforgue and a whole cast of French poets newly discovered to create his first masterpiece.

Second, Cronin points to the four French poems which Eliot wrote in the late teens as an aid to getting back to poetic composition. Eliot mentions in a letter of April 11, 1917 to his mother that "I have been doing some writing—mostly in French, curiously enough it has taken me that way—and some poems in French which will come out in the *Little Review* in Chicago" (*Letters* 175). He recalls the experience in 1959 in "The Art of Poetry": "At that period I thought I'd dried up completely. I hadn't written anything for some time and was rather desperate. I started writing a few things in French and found I *could*. . . . I did these things as a sort of *tour de force* to see what I could do. . . . I think it was just something that helped me get started again" (Hall 56). Cronin suggests that all four poems are "remarkable for their idiosyncratic wit and intimate knowledge of French—not the Academicians' language but 'as she is spoke'" (132). Eliot attained that level of idiomatic, vernacular French by living in Paris and immersing himself in the language over an extended period. Of "Le Directeur," Cronin notes that Eliot plays on sonorities that are "strictly speaking French," while "Mélange Adultère de Tout," which presents "the cosmopolitan *déraciné* with irony bordering on surrealism," breathes "the very spirit of the Left Bank, for which French is clearly the appropriate medium." Concerning the latter, I would add that Eliot combined the influences of Baudelaire, Laforgue, and Philippe with that of the emerging literary and artistic movement of Surrealism. Cronin goes on to describe "Lune de Miel" as owing its inspiration to a poem by Corbière, commenting on its "certain grossness [which is] permissible in French but not, perhaps, in English" and on its image of Saint Apollinaire, which is "one of the most striking . . . in all Eliot." He concludes this section with the "[s]ordid and scabrous" poem "Dans le Restaurant," which is "chiefly notable" for its last seven lines on Phlebas the Phoenician, lines that appear in Part IV of *The Waste Land*. Cronin makes the astute observation that this is a "curious instance of a poet translating one of his own translations back into English" (132).

Finally, Cronin takes up Eliot's role as a translator in the more common sense. As editor of *The Criterion*, he published in the late 1920s and early 1930s eight of his own translations of French works into English (seven prose pieces and a portion of one poem),[2] thus, according to Cronin, "transfer[ring] part of the civilization of one country to the civilization of another" (129). The translations of essays were "Poetry and Religion by Jacques Maritain, I and II" (January and May 1927), "Concerning 'Intuition' by Charles Mauron" (September 1927), "A Note on Intelligence and Intuition by Ramon Fernandez" (October 1927), "Prologue to an Essay on Criticism by Charles Maurras, I and II" (January and March 1928), "Fustel de Coulanges by Pierre Gaxotte" (December 1928), "A Humanist Theory of Value by Ramon Fernandez" (January 1930), which Cronin sees as the most important of the prose translations, and "On Reading Einstein by Charles Mauron" (October 1930). These pieces, as Cronin points out, all presented concepts or viewpoints with which Eliot himself sympathized and served to keep *The Criterion's* readership up to date on current French thought (133–4). The translation of Perse's poem *Anabase*, was, Cronin asserts, the most significant of all of Eliot's translations because it introduced this original and very difficult poet to English readers and because it greatly influenced Eliot's own poetry (134–7). Indeed, Eliot himself in a tribute to St.-John Perse in December 1949 commented that his translation "introduced a new and important poet" to British and American readers and "facilitated the understanding of his work," and also acknowledged that its influence appears in some of the poems he wrote soon after completing the translation "in imagery and perhaps also in rhythm" as well as in later work (King's College Library). Eliot must have read the poem soon after it appeared as a small book published by *La Nouvelle Revue Française* in 1925 and, recognizing its value, decided to translate and publish it, a portion appearing in the February 1928 issue of *The Criterion* with the full translation published as a book in 1930 by Faber and Faber.

While Cronin states that Eliot "repaid his debt to French literature by translating [*Anabase*]" (135–6), in fact he repaid it in a multiplicity of ways from the beginning of his career until his last days. Among these are reviews, essays, prefaces, introductions, and tributes to French literature in general, individual writers, and specific works. Most of his reviews were published early in his career in the *New Statesman*, such as those of Charles Sarolea's *The French Renascence* and Victor Boudon's *Avec Charles Péguy. De la Lorraine à la Marne* in 1916 and of Margaret Jourdain's *Diderot's Early Philosophical Works* and Paul Bourget's *Lazarine* in 1917. However, several important reviews appeared later, such as those of Arthur Symons's *Baudelaire: Prose and Poetry* in the *Dial* in 1928 (in which he was surely repaying his debt to the author whose book set him on the track of French poetry at Harvard), Peter Quennell's *Baudelaire and the Symbolists: Five Essays* in *The Criterion* in 1930, and Jacques and Raissa Maritain's *Situation de la poésie* in the *New English Weekly* in 1939. Essays include four "Lettres d'Angleterre" in *La Nouvelle Revue Française* in the 1920s, for which he was commissioned by Gide, and "The Classics in France—and in England" in *The Criterion* in 1923.

Prefaces, Forwards, and Introductions

Prefaces, forewords, and introductions are found largely from the middle of Eliot's career onwards, as his growing fame led to his being sought after to lend his approval to a variety of books. Among these are the prefaces to his translation of Perse's *Anabase* (1930) and to Philippe's *Bubu de Montparnasse* (1932); the foreword to Joseph Chiari's *Contemporary French Poetry* (1952); and introductions to Valéry's *Le Serpent* (1924) and *The Art of Poetry* (1958), to Baudelaire's *Journaux intimes* [Intimate Journals] (1930), and to Blaise Pascal's *Pensées* [Thoughts] (1931). Finally, he published a number of obituary tributes to outstanding French writers: to Péguy as a part of his review of Boudon's biography in the *New Statesman* (1916), to Rivière (1925) and Mallarmé (1926) in *La Nouvelle Revue Française*, to Perse in a speech (1949) located in King's College Library, to Maurras in *Time and Tide* (1953), and to Claudel in *Le Figaro Littéraire* (1955).

Speeches

Eliot also gave numerous speeches about France, the French language, and/or French literature, many of which are held in the Eliot Collection of King's College Library. One group of speeches was delivered in France (often in French) in the late

1940s and early 1950s. In them, he expressed his admiration of and debt to French literature and occasionally made personal comments. The most significant, entitled "Edgar Poe et la France," was given at Aix-en-Provence in December 1947 on the occasion of his receiving an Honorary Doctorate of Letters. He began by emphasizing the importance of the poets of Provence, which he called "the cradle of modern European poetry," and added, "here is a country and a language to which all poets of Europe, whether the language of their verse is a Latin language or not, must acknowledge their indebtedness." He then revealed, on a more personal note, that his understanding of the great French moralists, such as Ste. Beuve, had matured since he first read them "under the guidance of a wise, learned and enthusiastic teacher—the late Irving Babbitt, Professor of French Literature in Harvard University." He said that to Babbitt he owed "the beginning of my acquaintance with and admiration for French prose; I needed no master to arouse in me a passionate love of French poetry." Last, he considered the subject of the purity of language and "its current imperiled state," noting that "in France . . . the purity of language has been most consciously cultivated and most jealously guarded in the past." He paid tribute to Valéry because he "gave a lifetime to the study, the preservation and the renovation of the language" and asserted that poets have the "responsibility of maintaining the purity of language without which our civilization will surely decline." A note that Henri Fluchère translated it into French (although Eliot was quite capable of doing so himself) suggests that Eliot gave the speech in French. Among other speeches given in France were those at the opening of the Livre Anglais Exhibit at the Bibliothèque nationale de France in Paris in November 1951, at Nice in February 1952, and at the Université de Rennes in April 1952 (the last written in French on blue stationary).

Four speeches in the collection were delivered at gatherings in the U.K. of the Alliance Française, of which Eliot was a dedicated member. In January 1949, at a dinner in his honor held by the Alliance Française in Oxford, he conveyed his admiration of French culture in saying that "to be cut off from France [during World War II] was to live as if in an iron lung by artificial respiration," a striking simile since polio was prevalent at the time. In June 1951 he gave a speech as the Vice President of the Fédération Britannique des Comités de l'Alliance Française; in June 1952 he gave the presidential address with a French preamble in Edinburgh; and in May 1953 he spoke on Valéry at the annual banquet of the Alliance Française in Bristol.

Another speech in the collection, given in French in Brussels in December 1949, contained some personal biographical references; after remarking that his first and only other visit to Brussels was in July 1914, when he was a "young and quite unknown American," he revealed that his "design" for his life at that time was to become a professor of philosophy in the United States, a design which soon changed drastically for this "young pilgrim," as he called himself.

French Material in British Journals

When Eliot settled in London in the mid-teens, his knowledge of French language and literature enabled him to become a major player in the British literary scene, which, as Cyrena Pondrom shows in her fine "Introduction" in *The Road from Paris: French Influence on English Poetry, 1900–1920*, promoted recent and contemporary French thought, critical, artistic, and literary theories, and the literature itself in numerous publications at this time. Eliot published essays on these subjects in journals such as *The Egoist* and later *The Criterion*.

The Egoist, which was "predicated on the accurate assumption that a lively interest in literary France and at least some knowledge did exist among the *avant-garde*," presented its readers in the mid-teens with a variety of French works: recent poetry in French; translations of novels by such writers as Remy de Gourmont; reviews of new French books; substantial essays on leading French writers such as Péguy; and a literary causerie in each issue entitled "Passing Paris" (Pondrom 6–7). As the assistant editor of *The Egoist*, beginning in June 1917, Eliot continued the practice of featuring articles on French works and writers; as Pondrom notes, "French and English literary worlds were so contiguous that anyone seriously interested in poetry was presumed to be acquainted with recent French literature" (7).

In 1922 when he became the editor of the new journal, *The Criterion* (whose name was suggested by Vivien), his goals for it were modeled to a great extent on *La Nouvelle Revue Française*.[3] It would be truly European, indeed international, in content. It would offer reviews, originals and translations of contemporary works of literature and criticism, and editorials about contemporary intellectual trends, movements in the fine arts, and aesthetic theories. He defined its aims as "the examination of first principles in criticism, . . . the valuation of new, and the re-valuation of old works of literature according to principles, and the illustration of these principles in creative writing" (qtd. in Behr 26). He sought contributors from among the most highly regarded writers in various European countries—chief among them France. He called upon French literary figures who were already friends or acquaintances, and he also established new connections. Among the impressive French names from which he drew were Larbaud, Rivière, and Benda. In addition, he presented translations of French critical and literary works, eight of which were his own. The French pieces in the first four issues alone constituted an amazing collection, which included an essay on Joyce's

Ulysses by Larbaud (with an acknowledgement of *La Nouvelle Revue Française*); a translation of Mallarmé's poem "Hérodiade" by Fry; "A Preface" to *La Croix des Roses* [The Cross of Roses] by Benda; "Notes on a Possible Generalisation of the Theories of Freud" by Rivière; and reviews of French literary periodicals. Furthermore, *The Criterion* was the first English periodical to publish works of Cocteau, Valéry, and Proust (Ackroyd 248), an achievement in which Eliot took great pride. It is indicative of his devotion to and admiration for French literature that, in assessing the achievements of the journal in "A Commentary: Last Words" in its final issue in January 1939, he refers to publishing the best of European thought and introducing foreign authors to its readers, mentioning specifically those three French writers.[4]

French Literary Influences

The influence on Eliot of French writers, particularly Baudelaire and Laforgue, has been well-documented: his allusions to and actual quotations from their works, such as "'You! hypocrite lecteur!—mon semblable,—mon frère'" (76) and "*Le Prince d'Aquitaine à la tour abolie*" [The Prince of Aquitaine at the ruined tower] (430); his subject matter (urban industrial life, lower-class characters); his experimental techniques; and his aesthetic theories. In addition, he found in their works inspiration to break writer's block, most notably in 1917–18 when he wrote four poems in French and produced quatrains in the manner of Gautier's *Émaux et Camées* [Enamels and Cameos]. Concerning the latter, he said that he and Pound studied that work and then asked, "'Have I anything to say in which this form will be useful?' And we experimented" (Hall 54–5).

However, Eliot's year in Paris also had specific effects on the French literary influences that he had encountered previously. Although he found in Baudelaire and Laforgue models for the use of the sordid elements of the urban scene ("What Dante Means to Me" 126), actually living in Paris and observing the city himself in conjunction with reading Philippe's *Bubu de Montparnasse* and *Marie Donadieu* allowed him to discover ways to transform those models into something uniquely his own, as he did in "Rhapsody on a Windy Night," "Preludes," III, and "The Love Song of J. Alfred Prufrock." These poems show how, having walked the streets of Paris on his own and having observed its random details, he could appropriate the *flâneur* of Baudelaire into his own poetry with an intimacy and authenticity that he could not have possessed otherwise. Reading about it was not the same as actually experiencing it. Later in the passage on Baudelaire and Laforgue in "What Dante Means to Me," Eliot remarked,

It may be that I am indebted to Baudelaire chiefly for half a dozen lines out of the whole of *Fleurs du Mal*; and that his significance for me is summed up in the lines:

Fourmillante Cité, cité pleine de rêves,
Où le spectre en plein jour raccroche le passant . . .

I knew what *that* meant, because I had lived it before I knew that I wanted to turn it into verse on my own account. ("What Dante" 126–7)

While in the last sentence he is referring to his experience of the metropolis of St. Louis as an adolescent, he could have said the same thing of his experience of the metropolis of Paris as a twenty-two-year-old; the difference was that, in the latter case, he did know that he "wanted to turn it into verse on [his] own account."

Laforgue also provided Eliot with an ironic, detached, and cosmopolitan voice, the voice of a Parisian sophisticate, his updated version of the dandy, which he acknowledged in the essay quoted above: "Of Jules Laforgue, for instance, I can say that he was the first to teach me how to speak, to teach me the poetic possibilities of my own idiom of speech. Such early influences, the influences which, so to speak, first introduce one to oneself, are, I think, due to an impression which is in one aspect, the recognition of a temperament akin to one's own, and in another aspect the discovery of a form of expression which gives a clue to the discovery of one's own form" (126). Hearing French on a daily basis and absorbing its rhythms, inflections, slang, vulgarities, and idiomatic expressions gave Eliot the ability to echo them authentically in his own poetry, to write in a voice similar to what he so admired in Laforgue and yet to give it his own stamp.[5]

The works of recent and contemporary French literary figures, especially those to whom he was introduced by Alain-Fournier, also had a major impact on Eliot's aesthetic theories about and his creation of poetry and drama. These writers dealt with wide-ranging and innovative subjects and themes such as moral and philosophical issues and concepts of human love, served as models for writing in a variety of genres, and demonstrated experimental techniques.

Among the most important to Eliot's development as a writer, as I have shown, were Philippe, Claudel, Péguy, Gide, Perse, Rivière, and Alain-Fournier himself as well as Dostoevsky in French translation. Philippe's two novels showed him the Parisian underworld of prostitutes and pimps in grim areas of the city, an innovative subject, as evidenced in Alain-Fournier's and Rivière's letters, and inspired him to try his hand at creating similar portrayals of urban landscapes in poems such as "Preludes," "Rhapsody on a Windy Night," "The Love Song of J. Alfred Prufrock," *The Waste Land*, and *Four Quartets*. Eliot wrote in his 1932 Preface to *Bubu de*

Montparnasse that "the book has always been for me . . . a symbol of the Paris of [1910]" (qtd. in Ricks 405).

Claudel, Péguy, and Gide, who were very much a part of the contemporary Parisian literary scene, made important contributions as well. Claudel showed Eliot that a poet and dramatist could be intellectual, difficult, and religious, a rare combination that infuses Eliot's own works. Particularly influential was his religious verse drama *L'Annonce Faite à Marie* and his five-part religious poem "Cinq Grandes Odes." Péguy was a role model in undertaking a wide array of literary genres, including essays on a variety of subjects, religious poetry such as "Le Mystère de la Charité de Jeanne d'Arc," and political/philosophical works such as *Notre Jeunesse* on the Affaire Dreyfus. His devotion to moral and social reform and his founding of the journal *Les Cahiers de la Quinzaine* to promote it surely had a hand in Eliot's own efforts in that cause. Péguy's journal and *La Nouvelle Revue Française* served as models for Eliot later in shaping the content of *The Criterion*. Gide was another writer who took on subjects that were literary, political, and social in many different genres—from essays and newspaper articles to novels, poems, and memoirs. From him Eliot learned experimental techniques such as the use of an inner and outer narrator of his 1902 psychological novel *L'Immoraliste*; this type of narrator may have furnished the immediate inspiration for Eliot's similar technique in "Prufrock."

Finally, Perse, Rivière, and Alain-Fournier played significant roles in Eliot's literary education. The long, prose-like, but musical lines of Perse's 1911 poem "Éloges" are similar to Eliot's verse in "Marina" and "Choruses from 'The Rock,'" while its subject of an idyllic childhood was a likely inspiration for his evocations of youth in "New Hampshire" and in fleeting moments of *Four Quartets*. More importantly, Perse's 1924 long poem *Anabase*, with uncanny resemblances to *The Waste Land* in its journey though a desert landscape and its fragmented, difficult, heavily allusive style, struck Eliot as such an important innovative work that he translated and published it; its influence on Eliot is seen in "Journey of the Magi" and "Triumphal March." Rivière was a model of a critic whose astute reviews covered all aspects of the literary and fine arts scene, but who also produced creative work. Alain-Fournier inspired Eliot with his reviews and criticism. Furthermore, the subject of remorse in his memoir "Portrait" was to haunt Eliot throughout his life, appearing in subtle forms in early poems, such as "Portrait of a Lady," written in part during his Parisian year, and "La Figlia che Piange," as well as in late poems, such as "Little Gidding." Also influential was the novel that Alain-Fournier was writing at the time, particularly its motifs of a vanished idyllic youth, its regret for a former regime, and its anguished view of human love.

The Cultural Milieu and its Influence

Finally, the broad spectrum of the fine arts of high culture as well as the entertainments of popular culture in Paris during the astoundingly rich year of 1910–1911 presented Eliot with numerous opportunities for influence. The Parisian cultural milieu had a great impact on him, in myriad ways infiltrating and enriching his imagination, mind, and heart and contributing to his development as a poet, dramatist, and critic. In the process of researching exactly what was occurring then, I began to realize that this particular year was one of the most innovative, exciting, and sensational in the storied cultural history of Paris. Everywhere Eliot turned, there were stunning developments: interpenetration of the arts, collaboration among various types of artists, and experimentation with subject matter and style. At the same time, Paris offered a rich heritage of established and revered artistic achievements of the past.[6] He particularly admired this double richness, describing it most eloquently in his comment in his 1944 essay "What France Means to You," from which I quoted at the outset: "Tantôt Paris était tout le passé; tantôt tout l'avenir: et ces deux aspects se combinaient en un présent parfait." He was also well aware of his "exceptional good fortune" (94) in being in Paris at a time when the city was the intellectual and cultural center of the universe and thus embraced as much as possible of the city's high and popular culture.

Eliot's own words on the poet's special ability to store memories both from reading and the events of his or her life and then to use them in the creation of literary works are especially germane: "In some minds certain memories, both from reading and life, become charged with emotional significance" (qtd. in Matthiessen 56). In his essay "Wordsworth and Coleridge" in *The Use of Poetry and the Use of Criticism*, he elaborates on how the poet transforms each type of memory in the creative process. Concerning the matter of reading, he suggests that he or she "select[s] and store[s] up certain kinds of imagery from . . . books. And I should say that the mind of any poet would be magnetised in its own way, to select automatically, in his reading . . . the material—an image, a phrase, a word—which may be of use to him later" (78). Concerning the matter of life experiences, he remarks in the final essay of *The Use of Poetry and the Use of Criticism* that "of course only a part of an author's imagery comes from his reading. It comes from the whole of his sensitive life since early childhood. Why, for all of us, out of all that we have heard, seen, felt, in a lifetime, do certain images recur, charged with emotion, rather than others? The song of one bird, the leap of one fish, at a particular place and time, the scent of one flower, an old woman on a German mountain path, six ruffians seen through an open window playing cards at night at a small French railway junction where there was a water-mill: such memories may have symbolic value"

(148). These comments suggest that the works which Eliot read and the cultural experiences which he had during his Parisian year were stored in his amazingly retentive and synthesizing mind and imagination until he withdrew them for multiple, complex uses in the formation of his aesthetic theories and in the creation of his literary works. It is highly significant that a memory from France finds its way into his five examples of memories that may provide material for the writer; while the first three are vague and general, the last two are specific and have their origins in European rather than American locales.

A review of the highlights in the six areas of the cultural scene on which I have focused reveals that Eliot had many extraordinary opportunities. Four events in the theatre world were stunning in various ways. The two controversial Racine lectures demonstrated how passionately the French felt about drama and provided a memorable experience of Maurras's L'Action Française and the Camelots du Roi. Maeterlinck's highly popular L'Oiseau bleu demonstrated that poetic drama could be successful in the modern world, and its theme of the essential unity of past, present, and future reinforced the similar Bergsonian concept that Eliot was hearing and reading about; however, the play also revealed the pitfalls of using outworn poetic conventions and of distancing the action from the real world. The stage adaptation of Les Frères Karamazov at the newly-opened Théâtre des Arts, which Eliot did see, presented realistic characters who spoke urgently and meaningfully to modern theatregoers, a probable influence on Eliot's concept of the social and moral relevance of modern drama. The most spectacular event of all was the sensational multimedia production Le Martyre de Saint Sébastien, an international collaborative venture which demonstrated the interpenetration of the arts at the highest level; it portrayed the life and death of the saint, about whom Eliot would write the 1914 poem, "The Love Song of St. Sebastian," and illustrated that a religious poetic drama was viable in the present, but with certain cautions. In addition, a number of the ideas in Ghéon's brilliant essay on reviving popular drama in the November 1911 issue of La Nouvelle Revue Française are echoed in Eliot's concepts of drama as propounded in his essays and demonstrated in his plays. This is especially true of the French critic's call to re-create for the modern world the grandeur and nobility of high verse tragedy and his insistence that the playwright should be free to experiment. The Parisian theatre world thus offered inspiration and food for thought to this latent playwright and drama critic.

The great art museums of Paris—the Louvre chief among them—displayed famous traditional works which found their way into his poetry in sharply arresting images, as did those of museums in London, southern Germany, and northern Italy. Paintings of the decapitated head of John the Baptist, I suggest, combined in his imagination with the popular decapitation act in Parisian street fairs to produce

Prufrock's startling statement, "Though I have seen my head [grown slightly bald] brought in upon a platter, / I am no prophet" (82–3). I also propose that works of Michelangelo combined with memories of social gatherings in Boston to produce the now-famous couplet, "In the room the women come and go / Talking of Michelangelo" (13–14, 35–6), in this first masterpiece, completed in the summer following his Parisian year. Finally, I argue that paintings of the martyrdom of Saint Sebastian combined with the extravaganza *Le Martyre de Saint Sébastien* to inspire "The Love Song of Saint Sebastian" in 1914 and that da Vinci's two versions of *The Madonna of the Rocks* (the original in the Louvre and the second in London's National Gallery) evoked the complex reference in *The Waste Land* to "Belladonna, the Lady of the Rocks, / The lady of situations" (49–50).

Of even greater significance to Eliot's development as a poet in particular were the avant-garde art movements in Paris that were rocking the art world. They introduced him to a multitude of new ideas, subjects, and techniques which he quickly adapted to poetry. Cubism, the most influential, offered him the greatest and most immediate inspiration through the fragmentation into geometric planes of its subjects, the use of multiple perspectives, the incorporation of primitive art and culture, and the later development of collage, with Futurism supplying urban settings imbued with the speed and technology of a modern industrial civilization. Eliot must have visited Room 41 of the Salon des Indépendants, where the Cubists first displayed their works as a group in the late spring of 1911, perhaps in the company of Alain-Fournier and/or Verdenal, and read Ghéon's accurate, if puzzled, account of "les intellectuals-géometres" in the November 1911 issue of *La Nouvelle Revue Française*. The influence of the Cubists on Eliot showed up almost immediately in the techniques of "The Love Song of J. Alfred Prufrock" and explains, at least in part, how a twenty-two-year-old fledgling poet wrote such a remarkably daring and innovative poem. His remarks on Cubism in letters and later in reviews verify his knowledge of and interest in the movement. The concepts, themes, and techniques of a multiplicity of these avant-garde art movements, in combination with early cinema, the 1917 Cubist ballet *Parade*, and popular entertainments encountered in Paris (as well as in London, St. Louis, and Boston), all shaped his second masterpiece, *The Waste Land*. And the sculptures of Rodin, Bourdelle, and other avant-garde sculptors demonstrated that the commitment of Parisian artists to radical experimentation was widespread, perhaps further encouraging Eliot to pursue similar avenues in poetry and later in drama.

The dance scene, too, provided electrifying and sensational performances that were the talk of Paris. Isadora Duncan, the scandalous American dancer who introduced bold new dance movements in what was considered a bare minimum of clothing, presented six programs at the Théâtre du Châtelet from January 18–28,

1911. In these, she danced to classical music, such as Handel's *Suite in D Minor* and Gluck's *Orpheus*. Eliot may have taken this opportunity to see the dancer who had so scandalized St. Louis a year and a half earlier and been inspired by her daring innovations in a field that had been strictly governed by rigid rules in movements, costumes, and music. Indeed, Duncan has been credited with touching off "a creative conflagration. Not since the discovery of ancient statues during the Renaissance had such a re-evaluation of standards been witnessed in the arts" (de Mille 137). She herself fulfilled her 1903 prediction that the "dancer of the future shall attain so great a height that all other arts will be helped thereby" (qtd. in Macdougall 103).

The extensive innovation and the synergism of the arts demonstrated by Duncan were even more pronounced and flamboyantly displayed in the dance programs of the Ballets Russes, which returned to Paris in June of 1911 for a third highly popular season. This company demonstrated brilliantly the fruitful collaboration of dance, literature, music, and art. Eliot probably attended at least some of the performances of the ballets *Narcisse*, *Le Spectre de la Rose*, and *Petrouchka*. I suggest that he had the puppet Petrouchka in mind in creating the character of Prufrock, and Valerie Eliot has attested to its having been a source for the straw men in "The Hollow Men" (Southam 155).

As with drama and the visual arts, the dance performances in Paris instigated a lifelong interest in and devotion to dance. Eliot attended programs of the Ballets Russes in London in the summer of 1919 and the revival of *Le Sacre du Printemps* in the summer of 1921. He commented on them in his journal pieces and wrote reviews of books on dance. Furthermore, he incorporated their principles, themes, and techniques into his poetry (most obviously in *The Waste Land's* reflections of *Le Sacre du Printemps* and *Parade*) and into his theories about and creations of verse drama. Finally, Whitworth's slim 1913 volume *The Art of Nijinsky* provided Eliot with two major ideas in his 1919 essay "Tradition and the Individual Talent": the impersonality of the artist and the importance of tradition in the creation of new art.

Living in one of the premier cities in the world for opera, Eliot had the opportunity to attend performances of the greatest operas in the repertoire as well as exciting contemporary ones. Among the latter, the two that seem most likely to have impressed and influenced him were Debussy's only opera, *Pelléas et Mélisande*, and Ravel's first opera, *L'Heure espagnole*. Having discovered Debussy's sensuous and innovative work during his Harvard undergraduate years, he surely went to a performance; its powerful love story may have been an inspiration for the young woman in "La Figlia Che Piange" (written soon after Eliot's Parisian year), for the episode of the hyacinth girl and her potential lover in *The Waste Land*, for the scene of the potential lovers in the rose garden in "Burnt Norton," and for Harry and Agatha's meeting in a rose garden in *The Family Reunion*. Its departures from operatic conventions demonstrated yet again the widespread experimentation occurring in the arts in the early years of the twentieth century.

Ravel's one-act comic opera was an attempt to "rejuvenate the opéra-bouffe of Italy, but not in its traditional form," as he noted in a letter in the May 17, 1911 issue of *Le Figaro*. Its combination of inventive musical effects with everyday prosaic events perhaps inspired Eliot's experimentation with meter and his inclusion of elements of ordinary life in his poetry: for example, his use in *The Waste Land* of the music hall song "That Shakespearian Rag" and the bawdy World War I ballad about Mrs. Porter and her daughter. The praise heaped upon Ravel in the reviews for his bold experimentation could only have encouraged an aspiring writer to be daring as well.

However thrilling those operas were, the opportunities to see Wagnerian operas were doubtless the most exciting and influential events in the Parisian opera world that year. Soon after Eliot's arrival, the passionate *Tristan und Isolde*, which he had seen in Boston in 1909, was presented at the Opéra, confirming for him his exceptional good fortune in living in Paris when the Wagnerian vogue was at fever-pitch. Years later, Stravinsky deduced from a conversation with Eliot that "*Tristan* must have been one of the most passionate experiences of his life" (92). The quotations from the first and third acts which he uses to frame the episode of the failed relationship of the hyacinth girl and her unresponsive potential lover in *The Waste Land* evoke the intense though doomed love of Wagner's characters and serve as a powerful contrast to the modern relationship, which never even gets off the ground.

And his good fortune must have seemed unbelievable when the entire cycle of *Der Ring des Nibelungen* was performed for the first time ever in Paris in June 1911, a rare opportunity of which he took advantage, since letters from Verdenal indicate that the two discussed the brilliance and complexity of the tetralogy and since in *The Waste Land* Eliot models the songs of the Thames-daughters on the opera's Rhine-daughters. Furthermore, the final conflagration of Valhalla may be an unacknowledged source for the references to "burning" in Part III and for the nightmare vision of the destruction of civilization in Part V of the poem.

As operas in Paris laid the foundation for Eliot's lifelong devotion to that genre as well as supplying him with models for subject matter, structure, symbolism, and experimental techniques in his own works, so also did the numerous concerts of classical music; they were equally rich and varied, with both famous traditional works and daring and innovative new ones. Among the performances were concerts of music by Russian composers, such as Borodin, Rimsky-Korsakov, and

Stravinsky; a portion of Ravel's score for *Daphnis et Chloé* (which he was in the process of composing for the Ballets Russes); pieces by Satie and Debussy; and works by Chopin, played by an outstanding young pianist named Victor Gille. The last two seem to have made specific contributions to poems that Eliot was in the process of composing.

Debussy's work for clarinet and piano entitled *Rhapsodie*, performed at a concert in early March 1911, doubtlessly provided him with the title for "Rhapsody on a Windy Night," dated the same month. And it is likely that the Chopin concert was the source of a similar concert described by the young protagonist in "Portrait of a Lady."

As Wagner was the composer whose works dominated the Parisian operatic world, so Beethoven dominated the world of concert music, as well as serving as a model of the virtues of courage, fortitude, and integrity. Indeed, there was a Beethoven mania which matched the Wagner mania and seems to have sparked Eliot's love for Beethoven's music throughout the rest of his life, a love evident in his request that the second movement of his *Seventh Symphony* be played at his funeral. Dozens of performances of Beethoven's compositions took place during Eliot's residence in Paris, culminating in the Beethoven festival in early May 1911. His works, which Eliot knew well and in fact studied (Spender 54), influenced Eliot's poetry, particularly *Four Quartets*, in terms of content, structure, and technique; they also inspired Eliot to experiment widely and boldly, so that Grout's description of Beethoven as "the most powerful disruptive force in the history of music" (491) might justifiably be applied as well to Eliot in the history of literature. The most immediate influence of Beethoven on Eliot was the example of experimentation, which joined with similar examples in all the fine arts in Paris to impel him toward that kind of daring in his own work—to see that it was possible, that it was liberating, that it was admired and encouraged by the Parisian culture.

Finally, an unlikely source of inspiration for his future literary career as well as for much of the poetry that emerged that very year was the infamous Parisian lowbrow world of popular entertainment, a lively and dazzling concoction of melodramas, cabarets-artistiques, cafés-concerts, music halls, circuses, fairs and exhibitions, dance halls, and cinema. Eliot's daring use of these elements was encouraged and "authorized" by the fact that numerous artists and writers in Paris such as Cocteau, Picasso, Poulenc, and Satie openly attended, admired, and enjoyed such entertainments and incorporated them into their works in a forceful rejection of established convention. To give several of the most striking examples, the atmosphere of the café-concert suffuses Parts I and II of "Portrait of a Lady" (November 1910 and 1911, respectively), "The smoke that gathers blue and sinks," and "Interlude: in a Bar" (February 1911). Particular acts and performers of the music hall, such as Harry

Fragson (*The Waste Land*), Chung Ling Soo (*The Waste Land*), Fina Montjoie (*The Elder Statesman*), and Polaire ("Sweeney Erect"), furnished material in the form of allusions, characters, and techniques for his poetry, drama, and essays. The music hall format of a rapidly shifting series of acts is reflected in the structure of *The Waste Land*, its rhythms and characters in *Sweeney Agonistes*, and its songs in the inclusion of "That Shakespearian Rag" in *The Waste Land*. Early cinema demonstrated a variety of techniques such as the close-up and the fade-in/fade-out that Eliot adapted for *The Waste Land*. Both cafés-concerts and music halls contributed to his ideas about popular theatre, demonstrated in his plays and theories, as in his 1922 tribute to Marie Lloyd. But most striking is his merging of the decapitation act so popular in Parisian street fairs of the day with various paintings of the head of John the Baptist in the Louvre and London's National Gallery to create Prufrock's psychologically revealing comparison/contrast of himself to the prophet in "The Love Song of J. Alfred Prufrock." These examples amply demonstrate Eliot's ability to transform the most commonplace and frivolous aspects of the Parisian scene into material for his works of high intellect and culture.

Although largely unacknowledged, the effects of Eliot's Parisian year on his literature are thus profound and extensive, making significant contributions to his achievements in the literary sphere. *The Waste Land*, as I have shown in detail in several chapters, serves as the prime example of the year's later influence, but in closing I want to describe the multiplicity of ways in which Eliot's mind and imagination were immediately able to process, combine, and transform into art numerous facets of that experience to produce his first masterpiece, "The Love Song of J. Alfred Prufrock," begun in Paris but written largely in the summer of 1911 in Munich, when he had the time to mull over all that he had seen and done during the year.

The title itself is an ironic reflection of all the passionate love experiences that he had seen portrayed, from *Tristan und Isolde* and *Pelléas et Mélisande* to the erotic "love song" of Saint Sébastien, with the epigraph from Dante's *Inferno* coming from his reading that work in Italian for the first time that year. The character of Prufrock seems a combination of the melancholy would-be lover portrayed by Nijinsky in the Ballets Russes' production of *Petrouchka* (its most original work of the season), Baudelaire's *flâneur*, Laforgue's urbane and ironic speakers, and Eliot himself,[7] while his use of internal monologue to reveal Prufrock's hidden inner life in this highly psychological and innovative portrait seems inspired at least in part by a similar technique in Gide's 1902 psychological novel *L'Immoraliste*. The poem's fragmented and nonlinear structure which eschews transitions derives to some extent from the various avant-garde paintings, particularly those of Cubism, which he saw throughout the year but at their most spectacular in the Salon des

Indépendants in the spring of 1911; from experiments in the abandonment of discrete musical sections in the operas of Wagner and the compositions of Beethoven; and from abrupt shifts from scene to scene both in the music hall and in early cinema.

The opening setting of the seedy and depressing urban slum area through which Prufrock passes on his way to the élite social gathering combines Eliot's personal experience of walking in such Parisian streets with those of Philippe's *Bubu de Montparnasse*. Marjorie Perloff makes the astute observation that this depiction of such areas, which she terms "revolutionary urbanism," was most unusual in the poetry of the high modernist poets (*21st-Century* 26), and I suggest that the explanation for this striking singularity lies primarily in Eliot's actual and literary familiarity with the French capital.[8] Prufrock's self-demeaning and resigned comparison of his head cut off, psychologically speaking, to that of John the Baptist seems the product of several Parisian influences that coalesced in his imagination: the paintings of the saint's head in the Louvre (along with others in a variety of museums in London, Munich, Venice, and Bergamo); the popular decapitation act at street fairs; and the scene depicting Salomé and St. John the Baptist in the revue "Mais z'oui" at the café-concert the Cigale. His comparison of himself to Lazarus was inspired by Eliot's reading a French translation of Dostoevsky's *Crime and Punishment* during the year, as confirmed by Eliot in "Prufrock and Raskolnikov." Finally, Prufrock's elegant and formal clothing, his references to cuffed trousers and white flannel trousers, and his question, "Shall I part my hair behind?" reflect current Parisian fashion trends for men.

The crucial year in Paris, which enriched his knowledge and experience in a multitude of ways that helped to make Eliot into one of the major literary figures of the twentieth century, thus deserves to take its place in what we know of this extraordinary man and his works. As Howarth wrote many years ago, Eliot's debt to the Paris of this time is a debt of all of us who have an interest in exploring the development of this great creative and intellectual genius.

NOTES

Introduction

1. All translations from French are mine, with the exception of those from the letters of Verdenal and Alain-Fournier in *The Letters of T. S. Eliot* and newspaper accounts in Mailer's chapter on the theft of the *Mona Lisa*. Close translations appear in quotation marks. Newspaper articles are documented in the text.

2. Eliot himself also wrote in the 1934 "A Commentary" that "[t]he predominance of Paris [in 1910–1911] . . . was incontestable" (451).

3. Valerie Eliot reveals that, "On the deaths of his mother and brother, in 1929 and 1947, TSE recovered his correspondence with them and burnt a good part of it, together with their side, thus removing the family record of his final school year, his student days at Harvard and the period in Paris" (*Letters* xv). She does not explain why he did so.

4. I challenge Gordon's contention that "Paris did not change Eliot very much" and that he was disillusioned with the city by February 1911 (54–6). She offers little evidence for these statements and indeed interpolates the latter from several early poems; however, as we know, a writer's invented characters do not necessarily reflect his/her own feelings, attitudes, or beliefs.

5. For example, E. J. H. Greene's book (available only in French) *T. S. Eliot et la France* discusses the influence on his poetry of Laforgue, Rimbaud, Tailhade, Corbière, Gautier, Baudelaire, and Perse and on his prose of Gourmont, Benda, Maurras, Baudelaire, and Maritain. Grover Smith's wide-ranging *T. S. Eliot's Poetry and Plays: A Study in Sources and Meaning* identifies and explains various sources from French literature; John J. Soldo's *The Tempering of T. S. Eliot* contains chapters on Laforgue and Baudelaire; and Piers Gray's *T. S. Eliot's Intellectual and Poetic Development, 1909–1922* discusses Laforgue, Bergson, Benda, and Gautier. A number of essays explore the influence of a single French writer on Eliot, such as James Torrens's "Charles Maurras and Eliot's 'New Life,'" Philip Le Brun's "T. S. Eliot and Henri Bergson," Michael Hancher's "The Adventures of Tiresias: [Anatole] France, Gourmont, and Eliot," while Paul Douglass presents an in-depth study of the influence of Bergson on Eliot in his book *Bergson, Eliot, and American Literature*.

Chapter 1. "Un Présent Parfait"

1. He said in a speech given at Aix-en-Provence in 1947 that "I needed no master to arouse in me a passionate love of French poetry," suggesting that it grew on its own rather than having been inspired by a professor (King's College Library).

2. See Ricks's Appendix D for an excellent collection of Eliot's comments on a variety of subjects germane to this study, especially Section vi, "TSE on Arthur Symons, *The Symbolist Movement in Literature*, and on France and the French Symbolists" (399–409).

3. For example, in letters to Bertrand Russell of January 18 and May 23, 1916, one can see that she was indeed a force to be reckoned with; she attempts to enlist his aid in convincing Eliot to choose a career as a professor of philosophy—clearly her wish—rather than that of a poet. In the latter, she writes, "I am sure your influence in every way will confirm my son in his choice of philosophy as a life work. . . . I had hoped he would seek a University appointment next year. If he does not I shall feel regret. I have absolute faith in his Philosophy but not in the vers libre" (*Letters* 139; see also 131).

4. However, a note in *The Letters of T. S. Eliot* tells us that his first trip to London was in April 1911 (17), which may be erroneous, unless Eliot had ordered and received the London Baedeker prior to his departure.

5. Although the pension served dinner, Eliot may have eaten lunch at this little café or at the newly opened student restaurant nearby at 55 rue St-Jacques (as announced in the November 7 issue of *Le Petit Parisien*: 2).

6. According to the title page of the journal at the time of Eliot's residence, its offices were located at 78, rue d'Assas (for correspondence and manuscript submission) and 31, rue Bonaparte, where visitors were received on Mondays from 10 a.m. until noon. The board of directors was made up of Jacques Copeau, André Ruyters, and Jean Schlumberger, with Pierre de Lanux as secretary. A yearly subscription cost fifteen francs in France and nearby countries and eighteen francs in countries farther afield.

7. Alain-Fournier had read Philippe prior to the writer's death in 1909, while Rivière read *Bubu de Montparnasse* by the spring of 1911.

8. It is curious that, in the explanatory note on Alain-Fournier in *Letters*, Philippe and Claudel are omitted from the list of writers whom he and Eliot discussed (25).

9. Alain-Fournier wrote to Rivière on September 1, 1911 that he had read the second act of the play on the train. Since the play was not published until 1912, he must have been reading a draft; it is thus highly likely that he discussed it with Claudel, who had doubtless asked him for comments, and perhaps read other drafts as it was being composed (Rivière and Alain-Fournier 394).

10. A plaque in the Cathédrale de Chartres reads, "On June 15, 1912 Charles Péguy walked here from Paris to commit his children to the Virgin Mary; following his example and in his memory, students from France and other countries by the thousands make this pilgrimage each year."

11. In addition to Cronin's essay, I am indebted for some of the material in these two paragraphs on St.-John Perse to the three internet entries on this writer listed in Works Cited.

12. Eliot's identifying Rivière as the secretary of *La Nouvelle Revue Française* in 1910–1911 is in error, as that post was held by Pierre de Lanux at that time, according to the title page of the journal (see also Gibson 214).

13. Miller's arguments for a homosexual relationship, based largely on Verdenal's seven extant letters to Eliot, in his 2005 *T. S. Eliot: The Making of an American Poet, 1888–1922* are a continuation of his earlier efforts to establish such a case in his 1977 *T. S. Eliot's Personal Waste Land*. Many of them seem specious, none more so than his attempt to give homosexual overtones to an outing to St. Cloud by implying that the two friends went alone, when clearly four young men went together (Prichard and Child in addition to Eliot and Verdenal), for

Verdenal says that Eliot was "especially called to mind" by the landscape, which only "faintly recalled" the other two (*Letters* 34).

14. In a letter of December 31, 1914 to Aiken, Eliot reports that he has been "going through one of those nervous sexual attacks which I suffer from when alone in a city. . . . [T]his is the worst since Paris" (*Letters* 75).

15. Eliot's notebook of poems entitled *Inventions of the March Hare* bears the dedication "For Jean Verdenal 1889–1915, Mort aux Dardanelles," followed by the quotation from Dante's *Purgatorio*; *Prufrock and Other Observations* (1917) and *Poems* (1920) have only a shortened dedication, "To Jean Verdenal 1889–1915"; *Poems 1909–1925* (1925) is dedicated to Henry Ware Eliot, but on the half-title for the pages from *Prufrock and Other Observations* is the full dedication to Verdenal and the Dante quotation (Ricks 3–4).

16. Today it typically indicates the Université de Paris as a whole.

17. See Debaene, to whom I am indebted for much of the information in this paragraph, for a complete discussion of the controversy.

18. If there were a "Third Caprice in North Cambridge," which seems likely, it has disappeared.

19. Dufour's sonnet describes Dante as a "mysterious passerby / who, tragically alone, wandered far from Florence," coming eventually to Paris, a harsh, desolate, and terrifying city beneath which he felt the circles of hell yawning.

20. Eliot revealed in the preface to his 1929 essay "Dante" that "my Italian is chiefly self-taught, and learnt primarily in order to read Dante" (11), confirming in "What Dante Means to Me" that forty years earlier he had tried to figure out the *Commedia* by having a prose translation beside the original Italian version (125). Miller suggests that Dante would have been included in Santayana's Philosophy of History course at Harvard (91), while Gordon asserts, without citing a source, that Eliot had "some brilliant instruction in reading Dante in Italian" at Harvard (30). Eliot's list of courses does not include one in Italian or Dante. It is possible that he had some instruction in Dante prior to coming to Paris, but undertook to read the *Commedia* in Italian on his own while there, perhaps influenced by Alain-Fournier or Verdenal.

21. It has had a variety of names: Le Collège des Lecteurs Royaux or Le Collège Royal [The College of Royal Lecturers or The Royal College], reflecting its establishment and support by the king; Le Collège des Trois Langues [The College of Three Languages], reflecting its first three courses of instruction in Hebrew, Greek, and Latin; Le Collège National during the Revolution; Le Collège Impérial [The Imperial College] during Napoleon's reign; and Le Collège Royale again during the Restoration. It was given its current name in 1870 ("Collège," *Catholic* 1–2).

22. Gordon states that Eliot attended only seven of Bergson's lectures from early January to February 17, 1911, based on his notes in the Houghton Library (*Imperfect* 55, 568). However, it seems to me that he would have attended all the lectures from December 9, 1910 to May 20, 1911 since he was in Paris, at least for the record, for that specific reason. Furthermore, his comment in "What France Means to You" that "one had to have gone, regularly, every week" to the lectures to understand "la ferveur Bergsonienne" (94) implies that he himself did so for a substantial period of time, especially since he was a convert swept up in "la ferveur" (*Sermon* 5). A more plausible explanation for the limited notes in the Houghton Library is that those for the other lectures were lost.

23. T. E. Hulme, a British contemporary of Eliot, also attested to the power of Bergson's

lectures. Hulme noted that he "gave you the impression of a man describing with great difficulty the shape of something which he just saw. There was a curious pause and a gesture of the thumb and forefinger which looked as if he were pulling a fine thread out of a tangled mass. It carried over to one an extraordinary feeling of conviction. . . . [I]n a subtle way it gives one continually the feeling that one is helping the lecturer to discover something." To further explicate Bergson's method, he compares him to an artist "seeing for the first time a certain peculiar curve. . . . It is not that by his artistry he polishes up or decorates the previously existing curves, but simply that he has to create a new curve in order to say anything at all. It seems to me that this is the attitude of Bergson in everything that he has done" (206–7). And Evelyn Underhill, who wrote *Mysticism* and became a reviewer for *The Criterion*, wrote in a letter to a friend, "I'm still drunk with Bergson, who sharpened one's mind and swept one off one's feet both at once" (qtd. in Douglass 11).

24. Kristian Smidt, for example, demonstrates in *Poetry and Belief in the Work of T. S. Eliot* that Eliot continued to draw from Bergson's philosophy even after rejecting some of its facets, particularly in *Four Quartets*.

25. In a letter of 21 August, 1916 to Aiken, Eliot wrote that he was "preparing a set of six lectures on contemporary intellectual movements in France to deliver under the auspices of Oxford to the general public" (*Letters* 144). In a letter of 5 September 1916 to J. H. Woods he explains more fully: the lectures are on "Social, Philosophical and Religious Problems in Contemporary France," adding in a parenthesis that "the syllabus is given as 'Literature' and the course is advertised as 'Contemporary France,' but this is what it really is" (*Letters* 152). In fact, the material about the course published by the Oxford University Extension Lectures Program was entitled *Syllabus of a Course of Six Lectures on Modern French Literature by T. Stearns Eliot, M.A. (Harvard)*, and the reading list and outline which follow reflect the subject matter that he had indicated to Woods, along with modern French literature and politics (see Moody 41–9).

26. Eliot no doubt had in mind Gide's attack on Faguet in the November 1910 issue of *La Nouvelle Revue Française* in response to Faguet's criticism of Baudelaire as a poet of the second order who offered not a single new idea in the September issue of the journal (499, 503).

27. A similar incident took place in February 1911, when the Camelots disrupted performances at the Théâtre Français of a play by Henri Bernstein because he was Jewish and had deserted from the Army. While police ejected them from the opening performance, they continued their harassing tactics at subsequent performances, with large crowds gathering to observe the confrontations. Bernstein even fought duels with members of L'Action Française before being persuaded by the government to withdraw his play from the theater (Tannenbaum 100).

28. Eliot indicates in a letter about Maurras in the April 25, 1948 issue of *Aspects de la France et du monde* that he first discovered him through this book (see also Torrens 313).

29. The quotation reads, "La sensibilité, sauvée d'elle-même / et conduite dans l'order, est devenue / un principe de perfection" [Sensibility, preserved in itself and conducted in order, has become a principle of perfection].

30. The note erroneously states that he saw the play in 1910 (rather than 1911) at the Théâtre du Vieux Colombier (25), which did not even open until 1913. Eliot could have seen it either before or after his April holiday in London, since it continued to run well after his return.

31. Verdenal's first letter to Eliot is only dated "Sunday"; a 1911 calendar reveals that the first

two Sundays in July fell on the 3rd and the 10th, so I would speculate that it was likely to have been written on the 3rd, since the second letter was written soon after July 14 (*Letters* 20–4).

32. In the summer of 1911, she was living in Munich and was the wife of the musician Otto Brucks, whom she had married in 1897.

33. The titles "Morgendämmerung," meaning morning twilight or half-light, and "Abend-dämmerung," meaning evening twilight, echo *Götterdämmerung*, meaning The Twilight of the Gods.

34. I cannot help but wonder if Eliot went also to Vienna on his summer trip in 1911. There he could have seen Mantegna's first version (1459) of Saint Sebastian at the Kunsthistorisches museum. He could also have attended operas at the famous Staatsoper; operettas, such as *The Merry Widow*, to which his brother Henry had first taken him in the States prior to 1910 and which was a favorite of his (*Letters* 54), at the Volksoper; and concerts by the Vienna Philharmonic at the Musik Verein. Evidence of his having been in Vienna is his interest in and knowledge of Viennese nobility, specifically Countess Marie Larisch, and his inclusion of Vienna in the list of great centers of culture and learning partially destroyed by barbarians in Part V of *The Waste Land*.

Chapter 2. Daily Life in Paris in 1910–1911

1. Le Bon Marché was the earliest of the great department stores, established in 1852 by Aristide Boucicaut with an expansion built between 1869 and 1887 by L. A. Boileau and Gustave Eiffel ("History of Le Bon Marché"); it was the largest department store in the world until 1914 (Jones 229). Au Printemps opened in 1865 and was rebuilt after a fire in 1881; a new store with iron work in the Art Nouveau style was built in 1907 ("History of Au Printemps"). Les Galéries Lafayette was built in 1898 and La Samaritaine in 1905 (Evenson 142). Baedeker's 1907 guidebook listed in the section entitled *Les grands magasins de nouveauté* [the latest de-partment stores] Le Bon Marché, calling it "the most important, but a little far from the city center," as well as Au Printemps and La Samaritaine, but not Les Galéries Lafayette (51–2).

2. Marjorie Perloff, however, asserts that there were 200 cinemas in Paris in 1913 (14).

3. Marie Curie was a naturalized French citizen. She was born in Warsaw, Poland in 1867, came to Paris in 1891 to study physics and math at the Sorbonne, married Pierre Curie in 1895, and began a stunning career in science marked by many "firsts" for a woman.

4. "Prufrock's Pervigilium" opens with two stanzas utilizing a more straightforward *flâneur*, who observes the sights in the streets, with obvious influences from Philippe's *Bubu de Montparnasse* (see Ricks 39–47, 176–90). The similarities here with portions of "Rhapsody on a Windy Night" and "Preludes" suggest that Eliot was exploring various possibilities for the *flâneur* and his descriptions of the Parisian scene.

5. Women in France were not allowed to vote until 1944 (Zeldin 360).

6. Inspired by the combination of greens and blues in *Schéhérazade*, the jeweler Cartier first placed emeralds and sapphires together in the same setting. The Oriental themes and costumes of the early productions of the Ballets Russes also resulted in the popularity of heavy perfumes with names such as Shalimar by Guerlain, a fragrance still in existence today (Gray 4).

7. Poiret employed illustrators Paul Iribe and Georges Lepape, respectively, to illustrate his 1909 and 1911 brochures of designs. In 1911 he engaged the artist Raoul Dufy to design bold, avant-garde fabrics ("Designer" 2; "Poiret").

8. Baedeker gives information on many sports, including horseracing, automobiling, cycling, boating, soccer, cross-country, polo, shooting, ice-skating, fencing, and boxing (43–5).

Chapter 3. The Theatre

1. The information given in *Letters* that Eliot saw it in 1910 at the Théâtre du Vieux Colombier is erroneous.

2. Claudel's *L'Otage*, which was published serially in *La Nouvelle Revue Française*, beginning with the December 1, 1910 issue, was among this playwright's early plays which Eliot read with Alain-Fournier. As noted in Chapter 1, Eliot remarks in an obituary note on Claudel appearing in the March 5, 1954 issue of *Le Figaro Littéraire* that during his Paris year Alain-Fournier "put in my hands *L'Aigle* and *Connaissance de l'Est*. The impression that those two books, the prose essays and the five plays made upon my mind at that time is still very clear in my memory. The work of this period was his best. Claudel is not one of the writers from whom I myself have learned; his type of drama is very different from anything at which I myself have aimed." Nevertheless, Eliot calls him the greatest poetic dramatist of the century ("Le Salut" 1).

3. According to an article in the April 15, 1911 issue of *Comoedia Illustré*, Fauchois's play on Napoleon entitled *Rivoli* premiered on March 28, 1911 at the Odéon, demonstrating how French history could be used as subject matter in contemporary French drama.

4. This French expression, which means "he isn't eating the roots of dandelions yet," used wittily by Oudot with the play on Racine's name, is roughly equivalent to the expression in English that one who is dead and buried is "pushing up daisies."

5. Eliot indicates in an essay entitled "The Art of the Theatre: Gordon Craig's Socratic Dialogues," located in King's College Library, that he discovered the plays of Maeterlinck during his undergraduate period at Harvard. Thus he was familiar with the playwright's work when he came to Paris.

6. Eliot made other negative comments on Maeterlinck. In a review of Peter Quennell's *Baudelaire and the Symbolists* in *The Criterion* in 1930, he notes that Quennell "very rightly" omitted Maeterlinck (357), while in "Poetry and Drama," in discussing "plays which we call *poetic*, though they are written in prose," he refers to "the plays in prose (so much admired in my youth and now hardly even read) by Maeterlinck," pointing out their restricted subject matter, "dim" characterization, and limited scope (137).

7. As Eliot was in London for Easter holidays in April, returning to Paris on April 25, he could have either seen the play before his departure or after his return.

8. In French the word "dindon" means a male turkey, but also a fool or dupe, while the word "dinde" means a turkey-hen, but also a dull or stupid woman. "Dindonnette" is a slang term for a stupid woman, roughly equivalent to the contemporary term "airhead."

9. There is some confusion about the date of the final performance and hence the number of performances presented. While the program (a copy of which is located in the Bibliothèque Historique de la Ville de Paris) states that ten performances will take place from May 21–June 2, various newspaper accounts, including that in *Le Petit Parisien* cited in the text, give the date of the final performance as June 1 (with nine performances). So it appears that, after the program was printed, the last date had to be cancelled because of the conflict with rehearsals of the Ballets Russes.

10. Lockspeiser notes that Louis Laloy traces the origin of d'Annunzio's treatment of martyrdom to Anatole France's *Thaïs* and Gustave Flaubert's *La Tentation de Saint Antoine* (229).

11. These are pointed out, for example, in reviews such as Ghéon's "M. d'Annunzio et l'Art" in *La Nouvelle Revue Française* and Marnold's "Musique" in *Mercure de France*.

12. Harvey Gross in "The Figure of St. Sebastian" also argues the likelihood that Eliot saw the play in Paris in 1911 and that it was a source for "The Love Song of St. Sebastian," although he does not mention the other two poems or Eliot's drama (977–8). While studying at Harvard the next year, Eliot could have seen it again at the Boston Opera House in March 1912 with Teresa Cerutti in the lead role (Thompson 215). The play was also revived in the summer of 1922 at the Opéra in Paris with Ida Rubenstein as Saint Sébastien; it received bad reviews, which complained that it was long and boring ("It's painful to endure five hours of this atmosphere of an artificial paradise in the taste of Paris in 1911"), prompting Gullace to comment that it "seemed to be more the martyrdom of the spectators than of St. Sebastian." Other revivals occurred in 1926 at Milan's La Scala and in 1957 at the Opéra, the latter in a two-hour version (Gullace 90–1).

13. Eliot says in a letter to Aiken of July 19, "I have written some *stuff*—about 50 lines, but I find it shamefully laboured, and am belabouring it more. If I can improve it at all I will send it you" (*Letters* 42). In the July 25 letter, he encloses three poems, including "The Love Song of St. Sebastian," noting, "I enclose some *stuff*" (*Letters* 44).

14. Gross reads the second stanza as saying that he does strangle her (977), but the use of "should" and "would" renders the situation ambiguous. The speaker may be imagining what he would like to do or might do, not necessarily what he has actually done.

15. Mantegna painted three versions of Saint Sebastian—in 1459 (the Kunsthistorisches Museum, Vienna), in the 1480s (the Louvre), and between 1490–1500 (the Ca d'Oro, Venice, seen by Eliot in the summer of 1914).

16. For an account of the ballet *Narcisse*, see Chapter 5.

17. As Gullace notes, "The poet's attempt to revive the medieval mystery play and arouse feelings of a mystical nature were smothered by his inveterate sensualism. The primitive religious fervor of the main characters, cast against such a decadent background, appeared as a ridiculous anachronism" (89).

18. See Jewel Spears Brooker's informative essay "Common Ground and Collaboration in T.S. Eliot."

Chapter 4. The Visual Arts

1. These pages seem to me to be his notes on the first part of the course only (the forerunners and early painters of the period), for figures such as da Vinci, Raphael, and Michelangelo would typically be included, forming the major portion of the course. Perhaps the other notes were lost, or perhaps these pages constitute a partial summary or material for a paper.

2. Marani gives the date of acquisition as 1880 (133), but, according to the information on the painting in the National Gallery, it was 1886.

3. According to an explanation of the painting in the Louvre, it portrays "the Virgin come with Jesus to greet Saint John the Orphan, who has found refuge in a grotto, thanks to the protection of the archangel Uriel, who is kneeling on the right."

4. A curious example of a highly negative interpretation of the hands of Mary and the

angel is found in Dan Brown's popular novel *The Da Vinci Code* (2003): "More troubling still, Mary was holding one hand high above the head of infant John and making a decidedly threatening gesture—her fingers looking like eagle's talons, gripping an invisible head. Finally, the most obvious and frightening image: Just below Mary's curled fingers, Uriel was making a cutting gesture with his hand—as if slicing the neck of the invisible head gripped by Mary's claw-like hand" (138–9).

5. The lines were also no doubt influenced by discussions of art that Eliot had overheard or participated in at social gatherings in Boston. He may at that time already have met Isabella Stewart Gardner, the great patroness of the arts who had opened in 1903 the museum which bears her name and which she herself had designed in the style of a fifteenth-century Venetian palace to house her extraordinary collection of art (*Isabella Stewart Gardner Museum*); the museum contained a study by Michelangelo for *The Colonna Pièta*. Eliot certainly had made her acquaintance by the fall of 1912, for visits from him on September 16 and sometime between October 31 and November 3 of that year are noted in her guest book (*Letters* 93), and he corresponded with her a number of times after settling in England in 1914; letters written in April and July 1915 and in November 1918 are in *Letters* (93–5, 107–8, 250–2).

6. See note 13, Chapter 3.

7. Ricks notes that, when Eliot saw Mantegna's third version of *Saint Sebastian* in the Ca d'Oro in Venice in the summer of 1911, he described it as "First quality" and told Sydney Schiff in a letter of March 24, 1920 that "Mantegna is a painter for whom I have a particular admiration—there is none who appeals to me more strongly. Do you know the St. Sebastian in the Franchetti's house on the Grand Canal?" (268; *Letters* 376). As suggested in Chapter 1, in Venice, he may also have seen in the Church of S. Maria della Salute both Basaiti's *Saint Sebastian* and Titian's *Saint Mark on the Throne with Saints*, one of whom is Saint Sebastian.

8. See Chapter 3.

9. Some of the artists who came to Paris just prior to or during the period of Eliot's sojourn there were Brancusi (1904), Archipenko (1908) Léger (1909), de Chirico (1910), Chagall (1910), and Zadkine (1911).

10. The Futurists included Marinetti, Balla, Severini, Carra, and Boccioni.

11. The five painters had begun meeting at the Closerie des Lilas after the 1910 Salon d'Automne when they became aware that they had similar artistic goals; there they plotted, according to Brooke, "a virtual coup d'état against the hanging committee of the Salon des Indépendants" (16). It is possible that Eliot saw their works exhibited at the Salon d'Automne in October 1910 just after his arrival. Gris, who did not begin to paint seriously until 1911, first displayed his paintings with the group at the Section d'Or exhibition at the Galerie de la Boëtie in Paris in October 1912 (Parsons and Gale 180).

12. The Futurist Exhibition to which Verdenal refers was held in February 1912 at the Bernheim-Jeune gallery in Paris, their first in that city; it received much notice, including a favorable review by Apollinaire. The exhibition then appeared in London, Berlin, Brussels, and Munich, receiving an international reputation as a result (Arnason 221).

13. See Weiss, 1231–9, for an informative discussion of the café.

14. For a full discussion of the similarities between the principles, subjects, and techniques of Surrealism and those of *The Waste Land*, see the essay by Hargrove and Grootkerk, from which some material in this section comes. Other essays on the influence of modern art on

Eliot's work include those by Tomlinson and Brooker and Bentley on Cubism, by Tucker and d'Ambrosio on Dada, and by Hunt and Korg on modern art in general.

15. Given Eliot's interest in paintings of Saint Sebastian, it is noteworthy that Bourdelle in 1883 created in Toulouse a striking bronze sculpture of the saint, whose contorted body, outstretched arms, and anguished upward look convey extreme suffering. However, I have not been able to determine whether Eliot ever saw it.

16. In the last years of his life, from 1924 to 1929, Bourdelle returned once more to the subject of Beethoven, creating portrayals of the composer which range from grim to pathetic (Cannon-Brookes 117).

17. Bourdelle was also well-known for the bas-reliefs that adorn the façade of the Théâtre des Champs-Élysées, which opened in April 1913. Inspired by the dancer Isadora Duncan, whom he had seen dance in 1909, he noted that "All my muses in the theatre are movements seized during Isadora's flight; she was my principal source" (qtd. in Macdougall 124). Eliot may well have seen her perform in January 1911 at the Théâtre du Châtelet, as discussed in Chapter 5.

18. In 1911 Duchamp-Villon created a head of Baudelaire with the "repose and classic generalization of ancient sculpture" (Arnason 195). While Eliot probably did not see it during his Paris residence, it may have come to his attention later, given the acknowledged influence of the French poet on his poetry.

19. Scholars as astute and well-informed as Brooker and Bentley note cautiously before embarking on a discussion of the influence of Cubism on Eliot that "it is possible that he paid little attention to [modern art]" (28). However, the following summary (some of which first appeared in the essay by Hargrove and Grootkerk) makes clear his lifelong interest in and knowledge about it.

20. The official title was The International Exhibition of Modern Art, but, because it opened in the Armory of the 69th regiment in New York City, it came to be known simply as the Armory Show. While the Futurists refused to exhibit, the European section was otherwise "extraordinarily complete" (Arnason 427). The show was savagely attacked by most American critics and artists, in particular the Cubists, Matisse, and Duchamp's *Nude Descending a Staircase*, infamously described as "an explosion in a shingle factory" (qtd. in Arnason 426). It is also of interest to Eliot scholarship that John Quinn was among "a small but influential new class of [American] collectors" which came into being as a result of the Armory Show (Arnason 422).

21. Portions of this chapter first appeared in my essays "The Great Parade," "Parisian Theatre World," "Un Présent Parfait," and "*The Waste Land*," the last of which I co-authored with Grootkerk.

Chapter 5. The Dance

1. Howarth suggests that Eliot's debt to the ballet was greater than that to the music hall, seeing it as having mainly influenced the structure of *The Waste Land* and the rhythms of his verse drama (306). However, in reality, it influenced a great deal more of his work.

2. In the autumn of 2005 while I was teaching American Literature at the University of Vienna, I was fortunate to see at the Staatsoper *Le Spectre de la Rose*, *Petrouchka*, and *The Three-Cornered Hat*; the first and third were performed in their original versions, with the

same costume designs, so that I saw them exactly as Eliot would have and felt something of the excitement which they engendered in 1911 and 1919, respectively.

3. David Bernstein has also suggested that Eliot saw productions of the Ballets Russes in Paris in 1911 in two essays, "The Story of Vaslav Nijinsky as a Source for T. S. Eliot's 'The Death of Saint Narcissus'" and "Dance in the *Four Quartets*."

4. Both Valerie Eliot and Smith (who also speculates that the ballet influenced the poem) cite this date and note further that the poem was never published although the galley sheets were prepared (V. Eliot 129; Smith 34–5). However, Bernstein argues, unconvincingly, I think, that the composition date was between 1919 and 1922 ("Vaslav" 102–4).

5. In commenting on this exchange, Gardner implies that Eliot saw Nijinsky perform in this ballet in London in the mid- to late 1910s. However, that is highly unlikely as Nijinsky began having serious psychological problems by 1916 and stopped dancing altogether by 1919: "Eliot was much devoted to the Russian ballet in his early years in London and the words of Sir Thomas Browne blended in his memory with the ballet of *Le Spectre de la Rose*, in which Nijinsky made his famous leap" (202).

6. In December 1916, for example, he was invited to Garsington Manor along with Katherine Mansfield, Clive Bell, Aldous Huxley, and others.

7. However, as both he and Vivien were ill at the time of the Armistice Day party (Ackroyd 90), perhaps they were not well enough to attend.

8. Smith suggests that Vivien's interest in ballet was a possible influence on Eliot (307); see also Matthews (41, 54) and Sencourt (50).

9. According to Buckle, several of the characters invented by Massine reflect the influence of Chaplin, among them Niccolo the waiter in *The Good-Humored Ladies*, the Little American Girl in *Parade*, and the male Can-Can dancer in *La Boutique Fantasque* (565–6). Chaplin was a figure whom Eliot found very appealing in early cinema.

10. For a full discussion of the influence of the ballet on *The Waste Land*, see my essay "The Great Parade." See also Chapter 8.

11. Ted Hughes entitled his 1993 book on Eliot *Dancer to God: Tributes to T. S. Eliot*.

12. Enrico Rastelli was a famous juggler well-known throughout Europe for his extraordinary skills.

13. Lady Ottoline Morrell also found Nijinsky very impersonal, both as artist and man, a trait which she greatly admired; Nijinsky, she wrote, "completely lost himself and embodied an idea" when he danced and, even at social gatherings, was "a pure artist . . . and quite impersonal" (227, 239).

Chapter 6. The Opera

1. According to a short history of opera in France in Baedeker's guidebook, it originated there in the sixteenth century. In 1669 Pierre Perrin obtained the right to present operas in French, but in 1672 he gave the license to J.-B. Lully, whose operas charmed the French for a century. From 1683 to 1718, operas were performed at the Palais-Royal and at Porte St-Martin and from 1821 to 1874 at a theatre on rue Le Peletier. In 1875, Garnier's impressive Opéra opened its doors (35–7), maintaining its dominance as the preferred location for opera until the construction of the Opéra Bastille in the late twentieth century.

2. The promotion of new artists is also evident in an article in the November 24 issue of

Le Figaro announcing the inaugural Festival of the Literary and Musical Union, a society founded specifically "to perform and make known the works of the young," on November 29 at the Théâtre Femina, with the participation of artists from the Opéra, the Comédie-Française, the Odéon, and others, and featuring a one-act operetta and an "aéronautique" comedy in one act. Such works as the latter with its emphasis on modern technology may have influenced Eliot to include similar elements in his poetry, particularly *The Waste Land*.

3. As noted in Chapter 3, Eliot discovered the plays of Maeterlinck during his undergraduate days at Harvard and was thus familiar with the playwright when he came to Paris. While his poetical drama *L'Oiseau bleu* received accolades in the spring of 1911, Eliot later rejected him as a model to follow.

4. Wagner had decreed that *Parsifal* could be performed only at Bayreuth, an interdiction not lifted until 1914 when full productions took place in London's Covent Garden and in opera houses throughout Europe (Dana 268); thus, it was not performed in Paris in 1910–1911. However, a "Wagner festival" at the Théâtre du Châtelet in late March 1911 featured the scene of Brünnehilde's awakening from the fourth act of *Siegfried* and the "grand duo" from the second act of *Parsifal*. Eliot's use of the line "*Et O ces voix d'enfants, chantant dans la coupole*" [And O these children's voices, singing in the cupola] (202) in Section III of *The Waste Land*, a reference to Parsifal's hearing children singing in the choir loft of the chapel during the foot-washing ceremony that preceded the healing of Amfortas, may owe as much to Wagner's last opera as to Verlaine's poem "Parsifal," the source which he acknowledges in his notes. Interestingly, Howarth notes that the opera was performed in New York in 1904 and in London in 1913, with people flocking to see it on both occasions (383); an explanation for this seeming contradiction to Wagner's decree may be that only extracts were performed in New York and that the actual date for the London performance was 1914.

5. Some of the information in these three paragraphs comes from "Richard Wagner" in *Encyclopaedia Britannica* and from the websites *Richard Wagner: Master of the Music Drama* and *The Wagner Experience*. Adames indicates that both Baudelaire and Mallarmé wrote of the powerful influence on them of some elements of Wagner's music, thus providing Eliot with "significant precedents for considering how the suggestive range of theme and mood in a musical composition suggests analogies for creating a similar range of suggestiveness in a poem" (136).

6. As pointed out in Chapter 1, while Eliot was not a friend of Rivière at this time, meeting him only once that year, Rivière almost certainly influenced him indirectly through Alain-Fournier as well as through his reviews on all aspects of the arts published in nearly every issue of *La Nouvelle Revue Française* while Eliot was in Paris.

7. Eliot's note on this subject is confusing. He states that the "Song of the (three) Thames-daughters begins [at line 266, with the description of the modern-day Thames river]," but then he adds, "From line 292 to 306 inclusive they speak in turn." It is hard to see how their song begins at line 266 when the first of their three stanzas does not start until line 292, unless he means only that the refrain anticipates or announces the coming songs.

8. Weingartner, a very popular conductor in Paris who had been there the previous month conducting the symphonies of Beethoven, was engaged for the first performance of the tetralogy at the last moment as a result of the illness of the originally-scheduled conductor. Despite limited rehearsal time, he did an excellent job, according to reviews (see, for example, Borgex,

as well as Brussel's reviews in the June 14 and 18 issues of *Le Figaro*). Nikisch was the conductor for the second performance of the tetralogy.

Chapter 7. Music of the Concert Hall

1. Shrade describes books and essays on Beethoven by Bouyer, Canudo, Pioch, Prod'homme, Bellaigue, Tiersot, and D'Indy, among others.

2. For example, in 1930 he told G. Wilson Knight that he intended to write a poem inspired by Beethoven's *Coriolan Overture* and produced an outline the next year. He completed two parts, "Triumphal March" and "Difficulties of a Statesman," before abandoning the remainder of the project (Ackroyd 190).

3. I am indebted to Christopher McVey's paper "T. S Eliot, J. W. N. Sullivan, and Beethoven: Pointing Beyond Poetry in Eliot's Unpublished New Haven Lecture," presented in February 2008 at the Louisville Conference on Literature and Culture since 1900, for alerting me to Sullivan's book.

4. For further information on Stravinsky and Eliot, see Boaz and Bronzwaer.

5. A caprice is an instrumental composition in a more or less free form, often in a whimsical style. Chris Trombold notes that it also means "a head with hair standing on end, hence horror," thus conveying "a restrained sense of dismayed panic" in the poems bearing the word in their titles (92). An interlude is a short piece of instrumental music played between the parts of a song, the acts of a drama, etc.; a suite is an instrumental composition free as to the character and number of its movements; a ballade is a musical composition of poetic character, usually for piano or orchestra; a prelude is a section or movement introducing the theme or chief subject, as of a fugue or suite; a rhapsody is an instrumental composition irregular in form, like an improvisation; a march is a piece of strongly rhythmical music designed to accompany marching; a chorus is a musical composition sung by a number of voices in concert; a quartet is a composition in four parts, each for a single performer. All definitions are from *Webster's New Collegiate Dictionary*.

Chapter 8. Popular Entertainment

1. As noted in Chapter 1, Eliot's mother was not enthusiastic about his living in Paris, writing in her letter of 3 April, 1910, in response to his having apparently revealed his desire to study there in the fall, "I can not bear to think of your being alone in Paris, the very words give me a chill. . ." (*Letters* 13).

2. Chinitz notes Eliot's "lifelong attraction to various forms of low-brow culture," such as comic strips, boxing, street slang, melodrama, vaudeville, popular music, bawdy comedy, and sensational news stories ("Cultural" 237). It is worth noting that the term "vaudeville" came from a corruption of the French *voix de ville* [voice of the city or of the city's inhabitants], a reflection both of its appeal to common people and to audience participation.

3. A review of the program at the Olympia in the April 27, 1911 issue of *Le Figaro* suggests that this is the "self-imposed rule" of the owners (4).

4. As noted in Chapter 2, the article goes on to assert that "the bicycle has not said its last word, far from it," for it was an inexpensive mode of transportation that most could afford, with the numbers of bicycles increasing from 326,000 in 1896 to 3.5 million in 1914 (Rioux and Sirinelli 75–6).

5. Schuchard in his informative essay "In the Music Halls," after noting that Eliot was "already steeped in the songs of American vaudeville and minstrel shows" and had seen melodrama in Boston when he arrived in England in 1914 (104), discusses various British music hall performers whom Eliot saw from that year on.

6. The column entitled *La Soirée* [Evening Performance] in the October 29, 1910 issue of *Le Figaro* describes the "crowd of little boys in black evening clothes and little girls in long dresses" who enjoyed themselves at the opening performance, commenting that they had the same personalities as the adult members of the Tout-Paris who attended theatrical openings (5).

7. I owe a general debt to Jaidka's chapter on detective fiction and its influence on Eliot (118–53) in these two paragraphs.

8. The original title *Fear in the Way* was changed to the current one to make it more enticing (see Hargrove, "T.S. Eliot" 160).

9. See Jaidka for a detailed discussion of the elements of detective fiction in *The Family Reunion* (127–48). In addition to detective novels and plays, *Le Petit Parisien*, which was a sort of scandal sheet containing daily accounts of murders, suicides, bombings, and other violent occurrences, was another likely source of this type of material for Eliot.

10. Crawford asserts that the fog is that of London and seems to come directly from Doyle's detective novels (11), while Kenner suggests that the city is a composite of Boston, St. Louis, and Paris, with the fog being that of St. Louis: "If we tend to suppose that Prufrock treads the streets of Boston, still his surname and his yellow fogs are from St. Louis, and the Paris of Laforgue has left its impress" (27). My own view is that it was a combination of all four; since he had lived in or visited all of them when he wrote the poem, he could have drawn on both his own personal knowledge of each and his reading, a practice which he often followed. Furthermore, because he completed it in Munich during his summer trip, that German city may also have been a source. The three European cities may have been uppermost in his mind, while he could also draw on his memories of the two American cities.

11. For a description of numerous stars of the cafés-concerts and music halls of the time, see Feschotte 35–44.

12. A brief notice in the May 12 issue of *Le Figaro* announcing another appealing element of some café-concerts, the opening of an outdoor garden for the summer season, reveals yet again the overlapping of types of entertainment in referring to the Cigale as a "stylish théâtre-concert" (5).

13. Chinitz also suggests that the "vital element in the music hall format, for Eliot, is audience participation" ("Cultural" 239).

14. While today the word "casino" denotes a gambling establishment, in 1910–11 it meant a public hall with many kinds of entertainment, only one of which might be gambling.

15. The introductory section for the listing *Théâtres. Concerts. Expositions artistiques* in Baedeker's guidebook to Paris explained that matinées are given in the afternoon, despite the fact that the word means "morning" (34).

16. Fragson, born in England in 1869, spoke and sang with a slight British accent and introduced the *genre anglais* [the English genre]. In 1910, he had attained international acclaim and had completed a tour in Spain just prior to his stint at the Alhambra. He came to an untimely end, being shot by his 80-year-old father in a senile rage in 1913 (Caradec and Weill 148–9).

17. The Coq Gaulois [French Rooster] has been a national symbol of France since before the French Revolution, with the motto "Je veille sur la nation" [I keep watch over the nation], as illustrated in a display in the Musée des Arts and des Traditions Populaires in Paris. Thus there may be a connection between Fragson's use of the rooster's crowing as his trademark and his being called the "national singer of wit and humor." Eliot was no doubt aware of the French symbolism of the rooster, so that its cry in Section V of *The Waste Land* may suggest an element of protection as well as the more obvious meanings of a new day and hope for the future.

18. Schuchard describes Eliot's admiration of the powerful use of music hall humor as a moral tool and as a form of "comic purgation" for the English audience, and he suggests that Eliot experiments with it in the Sweeney poems and *Sweeney Agonistes* (105–7).

19. The references to Broadway in section III confirm an American setting at least for this part of the "Suite."

20. Rastelli was born in Russia to Italian parents in 1896 and lived and performed in his father's circus there until 1919, when his family fled to Western Europe. After appearing in England in 1922 and the United States in 1923, his fame was established, and he performed often in music halls, circuses, and fairs in Paris, London, and other European cities until his death in 1931.

21. Eliot may have also seen him at a London music hall during the years 1914–18.

22. Jaidka notes that Eliot's love of music hall songs was evident even in his old age when, seriously ill, he sang music hall ditties while his wife attempted to shave him (80).

23. See Jaidka for an extensive discussion of the play's reflections of music hall (82ff.).

24. My sources for this information include Nancy Perloff (29–32), Fréjaville (246), and Garnier (9–18, 274–86).

25. The popularity of this story is also evidenced in the scene "Salomé and St. John the Baptist" in the hit revue "Mais z'oui" presented in October 1910 at the café-concert the Cigale and in a contemporary opera entitled *Salomé* by Antoine Mariotte (see Chapter 6).

26. A musette was a small bagpipe with a soft, sweet tone, popular in France in the past, as well as a dance performed to the music of that instrument.

27. I am grateful to John Boaz for pointing out the information in this book to me.

28. A saraband is a stately court dance of the seventeenth and eighteenth centuries, done in slow triple time, while a farandole is a spirited Provençal circle dance.

29. See my essay "The Great Parade: Cocteau, Picasso, Satie, Massine, Diaghilev—and T. S. Eliot" in *Mosaic* for a fuller discussion of the subject.

30. As noted in Chapter 5, Gordon suggests that Eliot found in the Ballets Russes' production of *Le Sacre du Printemps* in the summer of 1921 an answer to his search for "a philosophic principle that would master [the] multiple, disparate perceptions" of contemporary life that he was attempting to portray in the poem (*Early* 107); while it was certainly a major influence, I would argue that it was only one of many sources of inspiration.

31. After writing the essay on *Parade*, published in *Mosaic* in 1998, I became convinced as a result of my subsequent research on Parisian popular entertainment for this chapter that the poem reflects both Eliot's own personal experience of it in 1910–1911 and its portrayal in the ballet.

32. Propert in his 1921 book on the Ballets Russes also comments on this aspect of the score, describing it as "noisy and discordant," but perceptively suggesting that the "blatancy and the dissonance were the deliberate choice of a clever musician" (56).

Conclusion

1. His affection for the French may partially be attributed to his French ancestry; his mother notes in a letter of May 23, 1916 to Bertrand Russell that "all our ancestors are English with a French ancestry far back on one line" (*Letters* 139).

2. Inexplicably, Cronin omits the first translation and also miscounts the total of those he does mention.

3. He looked to this French journal as a model to be followed in other ways as well, as when he diplomatically asked Scofield Thayer in a letter of January 1, 1921 in reference to the *Dial* if "the question of a more cheerful cover (. . . something as bright as the *Nouvelle Revue Française*) [had] ever been raised," adding that "for an English edition a cover which made more prominent some of the names familiar to this public might be well" (*Letters* 430). However, Marx argues (unconvincingly, to my mind) that by the mid-to late 1920s a rift between Eliot and the journal based on differing political views had developed, as indicated by Eliot's ceasing to publish pieces in it after 1927 and by the reduction of attention to French literature in *The Criterion* at roughly the same time ("Two Modernisms" 25–35).

4. In his Foreword to Chiari's *Contemporary French Poetry*, Eliot reiterates the importance of introducing readers to new writers: "If the poets to be discussed [in a critical introduction to contemporary poetry] are almost unknown, the critic's chief service is to bring their work to the notice of readers who are likely to appreciate them; and his critical acumen will be most appropriately exhibited by copious and well-chosen quotation. His main task is to persuade his readers that his poets deserve their attention, and to send them eagerly to the poetry itself" (vii).

5. Eliot's intimate knowledge of French vulgarities is particularly evident in "Vers Pour la Foulque" ("Verses for the Coot," with a play on the two meanings of the last word: a dark-gray aquatic bird or a foolish old man) in *Noctes Binanianae* (so named for Bina Gardens, the area in which Eliot was living at the time). He wrote this poem in French for fun in 1937 to rib John Hayward (Ricks 248) and as a kind of pastiche and parody of his own poems, especially "Prufrock," "Mr. Apollinax," "Whispers of Immortality," and *The Waste Land*. In stanza nine, for example, one line reads, in translation, "We're going to shit [*chier*] on the doorway [*la seuil*]," beside which is written in pencil, "perhaps best omitted." Part of it has a prose translation, but then he breaks off and types in a parenthesis, "The rest is untranslateable" (King's College Library).

6. An exception would be the dramatist Fauchois, who criticized one of the plays of Racine and thus incurred the wrath of Maurras's conservative and traditional organization L'Action Française, in particular the rowdy young Camelots du Roi, as noted in Chapter 3.

7. Marjorie Perloff asserts that "Prufrock cannot be separated from the poet who invented him" (*21st-Century* 24).

8. Other metropolitan areas such as St. Louis, Boston, London, and even Munich may well have merged with his experience of Paris to form a composite image of the low-class modern urban scene in general.

WORKS CITED

"About our Institution." *Le Collège de France*. http://www.college-de-france.fr/default/EN/all/college/english/index.htm (accessed March 29, 2007).

Ackroyd, Peter. *T. S. Eliot: A Life*. New York: Simon and Schuster, 1984.

Adames, John. "Eliot's *Ars Musica Poetica*: Sources in French Symbolism." *T. S. Eliot's Orchestra: Critical Essays on Poetry and Music*. New York: Garland Publishing, 2000. 129–46.

Adrian, Paul. *Histoire des cirques parisiens d'hier et d'aujourd'hui*. Paris: Paul Adrian, 1957.

Aiken, Conrad. "King Bolo and Others." *T. S. Eliot: A Symposium*. Ed. Tambimuttu and Richard March. New York: Tambimuttu & Mass, 1965.

———. *Ushant: An Essay*. New York: Duell, Sloan and Pearce, 1952.

"The Alain-Fournier Biography." *Biographie*. http://www.legrandmeaulnes.com/english/biographie.htm (accessed January 19, 2007).

Alain-Fournier. *Le Grand Meaulnes*. Paris: Éditions Émile-Paul, 1913.

———. *Lettres à sa famille et à quelques autres*. Paris: Éditions Fayard, 1991.

Alexandrian, Sarane. *Surrealist Art*. London: Thames and Hudson, 1970.

Altshuler, Bruce. *The Avant-Garde in Exhibition: New Art in the Twentieth Century*. Berkeley: University of California Press, 1998.

d'Ambrosio, Vinnie Marie. "Tzara in *The Waste Land*." *T. S. Eliot Annual*. Ed. Shyamal Bagchee. London: Macmillan, 1990. 103–16.

"André Gide." *Books and Writers*. http://ww.kirjasto.sci.fi/agide.htm (accessed January 29, 2007).

Antonella da Messina. http://www.mostraantonellademessina.it/eng/artist.html (accessed March 9, 2007).

Arnason, H. H. *History of Modern Art*. New York: Prentice-Hall, 1975.

"Art Poétique." *Paul Claudel: L'Homme et l'oeuvre: L'oeuvre en prose*. http://www.paul-claudel.net/oeuvre/art-poetique.html (accessed January 23, 2007).

Asher, Kenneth. "T. S. Eliot and Charles Maurras." *ANQ* 11.3 (Summer 1998): 20–29.

———. *T. S. Eliot and Ideology*. Cambridge: Cambridge University Press, 1998.

Atkielski, Anthony. *La Sorbonne*. http://www.atkielski.com/PhotoGallery/Paris/General/Sorbonne Small.html (accessed June 1, 2006).

"August Rodin: His Life, His Work." *Musée Rodin*. http://www.musee-rodin.fr/biotx-e.htm (accessed September 10, 2004).

"Les Auteurs du 'Martyre de Saint Sébastien.'" *Comoedia Illustré* (1 June 1911): 527–8.

Baedeker, Karl. *Paris et ses environs*. 16th ed. Paris: Paul Ollendorf, 1907.

Barndollar, David. "Movements in Time: *Four Quartets* and the Late String Quartets of

Beethoven." *T. S. Eliot's Orchestra: Critical Essays on Poetry and Music*. Ed. John Xiros Cooper. New York: Garland Publishing, 2000. 179–94.

Barr, Stuart. "À propos d'une letter retrouvée d'Alain-Fournier à T. S. Eliot." *Bulletin des Amis de Jacques Rivière et d'Alain-Fournier* 39 (1986): 7–18.

Beaumont-Maillet, Laure, ed. *Atget: Paris*. Paris: Hazan, 1992.

Bebbington, W. G. "Four *Quartets?*" *Essays in Criticism* (1989): 234–41.

Behr, Caroline. *T. S. Eliot: A Chronology of His Life and Works*. London: Macmillan Reference Books, 1983.

Belgion, Montgomery. "Irving Babbitt and the Continent." *T. S. Eliot: A Symposium*. Ed. Tambimuttu and Richard March. New York: Tambimuttu & Mass, 1965.

Bell, Clive. "Plus de Jazz." *New Republic* 28 (21 September 1921): 94. Rpt. in *T. S. Eliot: The Contemporary Reviews*. Ed. Jewel Spears Brooker. Cambridge: Cambridge University Press, 2004.

"Belladonna." *Encyclopaedia Britannica*. 15th ed. 1975.

———. *Yahoo Search Encyclopedia*. http://education.yahoo.com/reference/encyclopedia/ entry? id=4924 (accessed March 3, 2004).

Bergamo: Its Province. Provincia di Bergamo Culture and Tourism. Bergamo: Litostampa Istituto Grafico, 2005.

Bergson, Henri. *Mélanges*. Ed. André Robinet. Paris: Presses Universitaires de France, 1972.

"Bergson, Henri." *Encyclopaedia Britannica*. 15th ed. 1975.

Bernstein, David. "Dance in the *Four Quartets*." *Hebrew Studies in Literature and the Arts* 9 (1981): 230–61.

———. "The Story of Vaslav Nijinsky as a Source for T. S. Eliot's 'The Death of Saint Narcissus.'" *Hebrew Studies in Literature and the Arts* 4 (1976): 71–104.

Bizet, René. "*L'Heure espagnole*." *A Ravel Reader*. Ed. Arbie Orenstein. New York: Columbia University Press, 1990.

Blissett, William. "Wagner in *The Waste Land*." *The Practical Vision: Essays in English Literature in Honor of Flora Roy*. Ed. Jane Campbell and James Doyle. Waterloo, Ontario: Wilfred Laurier University Press, 1978. 71–85.

Boaz, Mildred Meyer. "Musical and Poetic Analogues in T. S. Eliot's *The Waste Land* and Igor Stravinsky's *The Rite of Spring*." *The Centennial Review* 24 (1980): 218–31.

Bonfante-Warren, Alexandra. *The Musée d'Orsay*. New York: Barnes and Noble Books, 2000.

Borgé, Jacques, and Nicolas Viasnoff. *Archives de Paris*. Paris: Éditions Michèle Trinckvel, 1996.

Bost, Pierre. *Le cirque et music-hall*. Paris: Hilsum, 1931.

Boucher, François. *20,000 Years of Fashion: The History of Costume and Personal Adornment*. New York: Harry N. Abrams, 1966.

Boyer, Paul. "Théâtre du Châtelet: 'Arsène Lupin contre Herlock Sholmès.'" *Comoedia Illustré* (15 November 1910): 100–2.

Bridge, Joe. "Ba-ta-clan: 'Et Ça!'" *Comoedia Illustré* (15 November 1910): 108.

"Brief Costume History, 1850–1919." *Fashions of the Ages*. http://www.fashionsoftheages.com/ history1850_1919.htm (accessed September 11, 2006).

Bronzwaer, W. "Igor Stravinsky and T. S. Eliot: A Comparison of Their Modernist Poetics." *Comparative Criticism* 4 (1982): 169–91.

Brooke, Peter. *Albert Gleizes: For and Against the Twentieth Century*. New Haven: Yale University Press, 2001.

Brooker, Jewel Spears. "Common Ground and Collaboration in T. S. Eliot." *Mastery and Escape: T. S. Eliot and the Dialectic of Modernism.* Amherst: University of Massachusetts Press, 1994. 65–78.

———. Introduction. *T. S. Eliot: The Contemporary Reviews.* Cambridge: Cambridge University Press, 2004.

———, and Joseph Bentley. *Reading* The Waste Land: *Modernism and the Limits of Interpretation.* Amherst: University of Massachusetts Press, 1990.

Brooks, Cleanth. "*The Waste Land*: Critique of the Myth." *T. S. Eliot: A Selected Critique.* Ed. Leonard Unger. New York: Oxford University Press, 1948.

Broughton, Panthea Reid. "The Blasphemy of Art: Fry's Aesthetics and Woolf's Non-'Literary' Stories." *Virginia Woolf's Multiple Muses.* Ed. Diane Gillespie. Columbia: University of Missouri Press, 1993. 36–57.

Brown, Dan. *The Da Vinci Code.* New York: Doubleday, 2003.

Brown, J. T., and W. H. Maxwell, eds. "Sewerage." *The Encyclopaedia of Municipal and Sanitary Engineering.* New York: Van Nostrand, 1910.

Buck, Gene, and Herman Ruby. *That Shakespearian Rag.* Music by David Stamper. London: Joseph W. Stern, 1912.

Buckle, Richard. *Diaghilev.* London: Weidenfeld and Nicolson, 1979.

Buñuel, Luis. "When Art was Revolution." *Vanity Fair* (September 1983): 108–25.

Burton, Richard D. E. *Blood in the City: Violence and Revelation in Paris, 1789–1945.* Ithaca: Cornell University Press, 2001.

Caine, Peter, and Oriel Caine. *Paris Then and Now.* San Diego: Thunder Bay Press, 2003.

Calvocoressi, M. D. "Aux Concerts." *Comoedia Illustré* (15 April 1911): 449.

Cannon-Brookes, Peter. *Émile Antoine Bourdelle: An Illustrated Commentary.* London: Trefoil Books, 1983.

Caradec, François, and Alain Weill. *Le Café-Concert.* Paris: Atelier Hachette/Massin, 1980.

Carrouges, Michel. *André Breton and the Basic Concepts of Surrealism.* Trans. Maura Prendergast. Tuscaloosa: University of Alabama Press, 1974.

Casalonga, Mte. "À propos des belles representations des *Frères Karamazov* qui vient d'inaugurer le 'Théâtre des Arts.'" *Comoedia Illustré* (15 April 1911): 412.

Chancellor, Paul. "The Music of *The Waste Land.*" *Comparative Literature Studies* (1971): 21–32.

"Charles Maurras: Action Man." *New Statesman* (9 April 2001). *The Crisis of the Modern World, the New World Order and Kali Yuga.* http://www.geocities.com/integral_tradition/maurras.html?200715 (accessed February 2, 2007).

"Charles Péguy (1873–1914)." *Books and Writers.* http://www.kirjasto.sci.fi/peguy.htm (accessed January 23, 2007).

Chastenet, Jacques. *Jours Inquiets et Jours Sanglants: 1906–1918.* Vol. 4 of *Histoire de la Troisième République.* Paris: Librairie Hachette, 1955. 7 vols.

Chevassu, Francis. "*Les Frères Karazamov.*" *Comoedia Illustré* (15 April 1911): 422–5.

Chiari, Joseph. *The Contemporary French Theatre: The Flight from Naturalism.* New York: Gordian Press, 1970.

Chinitz, David. "A Jazz-Banjorine, Not a Lute: Eliot and Popular Music before *The Waste Land.*" *T. S. Eliot's Orchestra: Critical Essays on Poetry and Music.* Ed. John Xiros Cooper. New York: Garland Publishing, 2000.

———. "T. S. Eliot and the Cultural Divide." *PMLA* 110 (1995): 236–47.

———. *T. S. Eliot and the Cultural Divide*. Chicago: University of Chicago Press, 2003.

Cocteau, Jean. "*Parade: Ballet Réaliste*: In Which Four Modernist Artists Had a Hand." *Vanity Fair* (5 September 1917): 37, 106.

"The Collège de France." *Catholic Encyclopedia*. http://www.newadvent.org/cathen/04113a. htm (accessed June 1, 2006).

Crawford, Robert. *The Savage and the City in the Work of T. S. Eliot*. Oxford: Clarendon Press, 1987.

Cronin, Vincent. "T. S. Eliot as a Translator." *T. S. Eliot: A Symposium for his Seventieth Birthday*. New York: Farrar, Straus & Cudahy, 1958. 129–37.

cummings, e. e. "T. S. Eliot." *Dial* 68.6 (June 1920): 781–84. Rpt. in *T. S. Eliot: The Contemporary Reviews*. Ed. Jewel Spears Brooker. Cambridge: Cambridge University Press, 2004.

Damase, Jacques. *Les Folies du Music-Hall: A History of the Paris Music-Hall from 1914 to the Present Day*. London: Anthony Blond, 1962.

Dana, Margaret E. "Orchestrating *The Waste Land*: Wagner, Leitmotiv, and the Play of Passion." *T. S. Eliot's Orchestra: Critical Essays on Poetry and Music*. Ed. John Xiros Cooper. New York: Garland Publishing, 2000.

"Dance, Western." *Encyclopaedia Britannica*. 15th ed. 1975.

Daverio, John. "Manner, Tone, and Tendency in Beethoven's Chamber Music for Strings." *The Cambridge Companion to Beethoven*. Ed. Glenn Stanley. New York: Cambridge University Press, 2000. 147–64.

Debaene, Vincent. "L'Inactualité d'Agathon." *Le Lettré de la Nouvelle Sorbonne. Fabula: la recherche en literature*. http://www.fabula.org/atelier.php?Le_lettre (accessed October 9, 2006).

"Debussy, Claude." *Encyclopaedia Britannica*. 15th ed. 1975.

Deedes-Vincke, Patrick. *Paris: The City and Its Photographers*. Boston: Little, Brown and Company, 1992.

De Malmoe. "Le Bal des Quat'z'Arts." *Comoedia Illustré* (15 June 1911): 621–2.

De Mille, Agnes. *The Book of the Dance*. New York: Golden Press, 1963.

"Designer Paul Poiret." *History of Fashion*. http://www.designerhistory.com/historyoffashion/poiret.html (accessed September 11, 2006).

Deutsch, Babette. "Another Impressionist." *New Republic* 14 (16 February 1918): 89. Rpt. in *T. S. Eliot: The Contemporary Reviews*. Ed. Jewel Spears Brooker. Cambridge: Cambridge University Press, 2004.

Dexter, Will. *The Riddle of Chung Ling Soo*. Bideford, UK: Supreme Magic, 1973.

Dickey, Frances. "Parrot's Eye: A Portrait by Manet and Two by T. S. Eliot." *Twentieth-Century Literature* 52.2 (Summer 2006): 1–34.

Douglass, Paul. *Bergson, Eliot, and American Literature*. Lexington: University Press of Kentucky, 1986.

Doyle, Arthur Conan. *The Hound of the Baskervilles*. New York: Grosset and Dunlap, 1902.

Duncan, Isadora. "The Dance of the Future." *What is Dance? Readings in Theory and Criticism*. Eds. Roger Copeland and Marshall Cohen. New York: Oxford University Press, 1983.

———. *My Life*. New York: Liveright, 1927.

Eliot, T. S. "The *Action Française*, M. Maurras and Mr. Ward." *The Criterion* 7.3 (March 1928): 195.

———. "The Ballet." *The Criterion* 3.11 (April 1925): 41–3.

———. "The Beating of a Drum." *The Nation and the Athenaeum* 34.1 (6 October 1923): 11–12.

———. "The Burnt Dancer," "Entretien dans un parc," "He said: this universe is very clever," "Interlude: in a Bar," "Interlude in London," "The Love Song of St. Sebastian," "The smoke that gathers blue and sinks," "Suite Clownesque." *Inventions of the March Hare: Poems 1909–1917.* Ed. Christopher Ricks. New York: Harcourt Brace & Company, 1996.

———. *The Collected Plays.* London: Faber and Faber, 1962.

———. *The Collected Poems, 1910–1962.* London: Faber and Faber, 1963; New York: Harcourt Brace & World, 1963.

———. "A Commentary." *The Criterion* 3.9 (October 1924): 1–5.

———. "A Commentary." *The Criterion* 13.52 (April 1934): 451–4.

———. "A Commentary: Last Words." *The Criterion* 18.71 (January 1939): 269.

———. *Dante.* London: Faber and Faber, 1929.

———. "The Death of Saint Narcissus." *Poems Written in Early Youth.* London: Faber and Faber, 1967; New York: Farrar, Straus and Giroux, 1967.

———. "A Dialogue on Dramatic Poetry." *Selected Essays, 1917–1932.* London: Faber and Faber, 1951. 31–45.

———. "Dramatis Personae." *The Criterion* 1.3 (April 1923): 303–6.

———. "Five Points on Dramatic Writing." *Townsman* 1 (July 1938): 10.

———. Foreword. *Contemporary French Poetry.* By Joseph Chiari. Manchester: Manchester University Press, 1952.

———. *Four Quartets.* New York: Harcourt Brace and Company, 1943.

———. "*Hamlet.*" *Selected Prose of T. S. Eliot.* Ed. Frank Kermode. New York: Harcourt Brace Jovanovich, 1975. 45–9.

———. "L'Hommage de l'étranger." *Aspects de la France et du monde* 2 (25 April 1948): 6.

———. "John Marston." *Elizabethan Essays.* London: Faber and Faber, 1934. 177–95.

———. *The Letters of T. S. Eliot: Volume I, 1898–1922.* Ed. Valerie Eliot. New York: Harcourt Brace Jovanovich, 1988.

———. "Lettre d'Angleterre." *La Nouvelle Revue Française* 21.122 (1 November 1923): 620.

———. "London Letter." *Dial* 70.4 (April 1921): 448–53.

———. "London Letter." *Dial* 71.2 (August 1921): 213–17.

———. "London Letter." *Dial* 71.4 (October 1921): 452–4.

———. "Marianne Moore." *Dial* 75.6 (December 1923): 594–7.

———. "Marie Lloyd." *Selected Prose of T. S. Eliot.* Ed. Frank Kermode. New York: Harcourt Brace Jovanovich, 1975. 172–4.

———. "The Music of Poetry." *Selected Prose of T. S. Eliot.* Ed. Frank Kermode. New York: Harcourt Brace Jovanovich, 1975. 107–14.

———. "The Perfect Critic." *The Sacred Wood.* 2nd ed. London: Methuen, 1928.

———. "Poetry and Drama." *Selected Prose of T. S. Eliot.* Ed. Frank Kermode. New York: Harcourt Brace Jovanovich, 1975. 132–47.

———. "The Possibility of a Poetic Drama." *The Sacred Wood.* London: Methuen, 1920.

———. Preface. *Anabasis: A Poem by St.-J. Perse.* Trans. T. S. Eliot. New York: Harcourt Brace, 1938.

———. Preface. *For Lancelot Andrewes: Essays on Style and Order.* London: Faber & Gwyer, 1928.

———. "Recent Detective Fiction." *The Criterion* 5.3 (June 1927): 359–62.

———. "Rencontre." *La Nouvelle Revue Française* 12.139 (1 April 1925): 657–8.

———. Rev. of *Baudelaire and the Symbolists*, by Peter Quennell. *The Criterion* 9.35 (January 1930): 357–9.

———. "Le Salut des trois grands poètes: Londres: T. S. Eliot." *Le Figaro Littéraire* 10.463 (5 March 1955): 1.

———. *A Sermon Preached in Magdalene College Chapel.* Cambridge: Cambridge University Press, 1948.

———. "To the Reader." *Inoubliable France.* By Alice Jahier. London: Sylvan Press, 1944.

———. "Tradition and the Individual Talent." *Selected Prose of T. S. Eliot.* Ed. Frank Kermode. New York: Harcourt Brace Jovanovich, 1975. 37–44.

———. "The Use of Poetry and the Use of Criticism." *Selected Prose of T. S. Eliot.* Ed. Frank Kermode. New York: Harcourt Brace Jovanovich, 1975. 79–96.

———. *The Use of Poetry and the Use of Criticism: Studies in the Relation of Criticism to Poetry in England.* London: Faber and Faber Limited, 1933.

———. "What Dante Means to Me." *To Criticize the Critic and Other Writings.* New York: Farrar Straus & Giroux, 1965; London: Faber and Faber, 1965. 125–35.

———. "What France Means to You." *La France Libre* 8.44 (15 June 1944): 94–95.

———. "Yeats." *Selected Prose of T. S. Eliot.* Ed. Frank Kermode. New York: Harcourt Brace Jovanovich, 1975. 248–57.

Eliot, Valerie, ed. "Editorial Notes." *The Waste Land: A Facsimile and Transcript of the Original Drafts.* New York: Harcourt Brace Jovanovich, 1971.

———, ed. "Introduction." *The Letters of T. S. Eliot: Volume I, 1898–1922.* New York: Harcourt Brace Jovanovich, 1988.

Erismann, Guy. *Histoire de la chanson.* Paris: Éditions Hermès, 1967.

Esslin, Martin. "Modern Theatre: 1890–1920." *The Oxford Illustrated History of Theatre.* Ed. John Russell Brown. New York: Oxford University Press, 1995. 341–79.

"Étonnant Collège." *Le Collège de France.* http://www.college-de-france.fr/default/EN/all/ins_pre/index.htm (accessed March 29, 2007).

Evans, Sarah. *Born for Liberty: A History of Women in America.* New York: Free Press, 1989.

Evenson, Norma. *Paris: A Century of Change, 1878–1978.* New Haven: Yale University Press, 1979.

Feshotte, Jacques. *Histoire du music-hall.* Paris: Presses Universitaires de France, 1965.

Fleming, William, and Frank Macomber. *Musical Arts and Styles.* Gainesville: University of Florida Press, 1990.

Fowlie, Wallace. *Age of Surrealism.* Bloomington: Indiana University Press, 1960.

Fréjaville, Gustave. *Au music-hall.* Paris: Éditions du Monde Nouveau, 1923.

Gaillard, Marc. *Paris de place en place.* Amiens: Martelle Éditions, 1997.

Gallup, Donald. "The 'Lost' Manuscripts of T. S. Eliot." *Times Literary Supplement* (7 November 1968): 1239–42.

Garafola, Lynn. *Diaghilev's Ballets Russes.* New York: Oxford University Press, 1989.

Gardner, Helen. *The Art of T. S. Eliot.* New York: E. P. Dutton & Company, 1959.

———. *The Composition of Four Quartets.* New York: Oxford University Press, 1978.

Garnier, Jacques. *Forains d'hier et d'aujourd'hui.* Orléans: Les Presses, 1968.

Gautherin, Véronique. "Bourdelle: Sa Vie, Son Oeuvre." *Dossier de l'Art: Bourdelle* (January-February 1993): 16–24.

Ghéon, Henri. "Les Cubistes contre le Salon d'Automne." *La Nouvelle Revue Française* 35 (1 November 1911): 626–30.

———. *"L'Heure espagnole,* par Maurice Ravel." *La Nouvelle Revue Française* 31 (1 July 1911): 136–7.

———. "Isadora Duncan et M. Pierre Lalo." *La Nouvelle Revue Française* 27 (1 March 1911): 473–6.

———. "M. d'Annunzio et l'Art." *La Nouvelle Revue Française* 31 (1 July 1911): 5–16.

———. "La Saison 'Russe' au Châtelet." *La Nouvelle Revue Française* 32 (1 August 1911): 250–1.

———. "Sur le 'Théâtre Populaire.'" *La Nouvelle Revue Française* 35 (1 November 1911): 503–8.

Gibson, Robert. *The End of Youth: The Life and Work of Alain-Fournier.* Exeter: Impress Books, 2005.

Gide, André. "Baudelaire et M. Faguet." *La Nouvelle Revue Française* 23 (1 November 1910): 499–518.

———. "Journal sans Date." *La Nouvelle Revue Française* 24 (1 December 1910): 780–4.

Gill, Patrick. "The Expatriate Experience, Self Construction, and the Flâneur in William Carlos Williams' *A Voyage to Pagany.*" Thesis. Bowling Green State University, 2007. http://www.ohiolink.edu/etd/send-pdf.cgi/Gill%20Patrick%20W.pdf?acc-num=bgsu118 (accessed July 10, 2008).

Gish, Nancy. "Pierre Janet's *Désagrégation* in 'Gerontion' and *The Waste Land.*" A paper presented at the T. S. Eliot Society Conference, St. Louis, Mo., 22 September, 2006.

Glendinning, Victoria. *Edith Sitwell: A Unicorn among Lions.* New York: Alfred A. Knopf, 1981.

Gordon, Lyndall. *Eliot's Early Years.* Oxford: Oxford University Press, 1977.

———. *T. S. Eliot: An Imperfect Life.* New York: W. W. Norton, 1998.

Gosling, Nigel. *The Adventurous World of Paris: 1900–1914.* New York: William Morrow, 1978.

Gray, Laurel Victoria. *Russian Orientalism and the Ballet Russe.* http://www.laurelvictoriagray.com/orientalism.htm (accessed October 18, 2006).

Gray, Piers. *T. S. Eliot's Intellectual and Poetic Development, 1909–1922.* Atlantic Highlands, N.J.: Humanities Press, 1982.

Greene, E. J. H. *T. S. Eliot et la France.* Paris: Éditions Contemporaines, 1951.

Gross, Harvey. "The Figure of St. Sebastian." *The Southern Review* 21.4 (October 1985): 974–84.

Grout, Donald Jay. *A History of Western Music.* New York: W. W. Norton, 1960.

Gullace, Giovanni. *Gabriele d'Annunzio in France: A Study of Cultural Relations.* Syracuse: Syracuse University Press, 1966.

Hall, Donald. "The Art of Poetry I: T. S. Eliot." Interview in *The Paris Review* 21 (Spring-Summer 1959): 47–70.

Hancher, Michael. "The Adventures of Tiresias: France, Gourmont, Eliot." *Modern Language Review* 73.1 (January 1978): 29–37.

Harding, D. W. "What the Thunder Said." *The Waste Land in Different Voices.* Ed. A. D. Moody. New York: St. Martin's Press, 1974.

Hargrove, Nancy D. "The Great Parade: Cocteau, Picasso, Satie, Massine, Diaghilev—and T. S. Eliot." *Mosaic* 31.1 (March 1998): 83–106.

———. *Landscape as Symbol in the Poetry of T. S. Eliot*. Jackson: University Press of Mississippi, 1978.

———. "Paris During Eliot's Residence in 1910–1911: A Practical Guide to the City." *Yeats Eliot Review* 24.1 (Spring 2007): 3–23.

———. "'Un Présent Parfait': Eliot and La Vie Parisienne." *T. S. Eliot at the Turn of the Century*. Ed. Marianne Thormählen. Lund: Lund University Press, 1994.

———. "T. S. Eliot." *Twentieth Century American Dramatists*. Vol. 7 of the *Dictionary of Literary Biography*. Detroit: Gale/Cengage Learning, 1981.

———. "T. S. Eliot and the Classical Music Scene in Paris, 1910–1911." *Publications of the Mississippi Philological Association* (2004): 10–26.

———. "T. S. Eliot and the Dance." *Journal of Modern Literature* 21.1 (Summer 1997): 61–88.

———. "T. S. Eliot and Opera in Paris, 1910–1911." *Yeats Eliot Review* 21.3 (Fall 2004): 2–20.

———. "T. S. Eliot and the Parisian Theatre World, 1910–1911." *South Atlantic Review* 66.4 (Fall 2001): 1–44.

———. "T. S. Eliot and Popular Entertainment in Paris, 1910–1911." *Journal of Popular Culture* 36.2 (Winter 2003): 77–115.

———. "T. S. Eliot's Year Abroad, 1910–1911: The Visual Arts." *South Atlantic Review* 71.1 (Winter 2006): 89–131.

———, and Paul Grootkerk. "*The Waste Land* as a Surrealist Poem." *The Comparatist* 19 (1995): 1–15.

Harris, Bernard. "'This music crept by me': Shakespeare and Wagner." The Waste Land *in Different Voices*. Ed. A. D. Moody. New York: St. Martin's Press, 1974.

Harvey, David. *Paris, Capital of Modernity*. New York: Routledge, 2003.

Hayhurst, J. D. *The Pneumatic Post of Paris*. http://www.cix.co.uk/~hayhurst/jdhayhurst/pneumatic/book1.html (accessed May 4, 2006).

"Henri Bergson (1859–1941)." *Books and Writers*. http://www.kirjasto.sci.fi/bergson.htm (accessed January 23, 2007).

Herbert, Michel. *La Chanson à Montmartre*. Paris: La Table Rond, 1967.

Higonnet, Patrice. *Paris: Capital of the World*. Trans. Arthur Goldhammer. Cambridge: Belknap Press, 2002.

"History." *Printemps: Department Store Paris*. http://www.departmentstoreparis.printemps.com/history/index.aspx?i=en (accessed October 15, 2006).

"History of Le Bon Marché." *Le Bon Marché*. http://www.lebonmarche.fr/anglais/index.htm (accessed October 15, 2006).

Horne, Alistair. *Seven Ages of Paris*. New York: Alfred A. Knopf, 2002.

Howarth, Herbert. *Notes on Some Figures Behind T. S. Eliot*. New York: Houghton Mifflin Company, 1964.

Huber, Richard L. "Sponsor's Statement." *Painters in Paris: 1895–1950*. New Haven: Yale University Press, 2000.

Hughes, Ted. *Dancer to God: Tributes to T. S. Eliot*. London: Faber and Faber, 1992.

Huisman, David. "Title and Subject in *The Sacred Wood*." *Essays in Criticism* (1989): 217–33.

Hulme, T. E. "A Personal Impression of Bergson." *The Life and Opinions of T. E. Hulme*. By Alun R. Jones. Boston: Beacon Press, 1960.

Hunt, John Dixon. "'Broken Images': T. S. Eliot and Modern Painting." The Waste Land *in Different Voices*. Ed. A. D. Moody. New York: St. Martin's Press, 1974.

Isabella Stewart Gardner Museum. http://www.gardnermuseum.org (accessed August 12, 2008).

Jaidka, Manju. *T. S. Eliot's Use of Popular Sources.* Lewiston, N.Y.: Mellen Press, 1997.

James, Henry. *Parisian Sketches: Letters to the New York Tribune, 1875–1876.* Ed. Leon Edel and Ilse Dusoir Lind. New York: New York University Press, 1957.

Jones, Colin. *The Cambridge Illustrated History of France.* Cambridge: Cambridge University Press, 1994.

Jones, Robert E. "The Gloves of Isadora." *Theatre Arts Magazine* 31 (1947): 17–22.

"*Le Journal.*" *Answers.com.* http://www.answers.com/topic/le-journal (accessed January 19, 2007).

Jullian, Philippe. *D'Annunzio.* Trans. Stephen Hardman. New York: Viking Press, 1973.

Kenner, Hugh. "The Urban Apocalypse." *Eliot in His Time.* Ed. A. Walton Litz. Princeton: Princeton University Press, 1973.

Kimball, Roger. "Charles Péguy." *The New Criterion* 20.3 (November 2001). http://www.new-criterion.com/archive/20/nov01/peguy.htm (accessed January 23, 2007).

Klüver, Billy, and Julie Martin. *Kiki's Paris: Artists and Lovers, 1900–1930.* New York: Harry N. Abrams, 1989.

Knapton, Ernest John. *France: An Interpretive History.* New York: Scribner, 1971.

Kolakowski, Leszek. *Bergson.* New York: Oxford University Press, 1985.

Korg, Jacob. "Modern Art Techniques in *The Waste Land.*" *The Journal of Aesthetics and Art Criticism* 18 (1960): 456–63.

———. "*The Waste Land* and Contemporary Art." *Approaches to Teaching T. S. Eliot's Poetry and Plays.* Ed. Jewel Spears Brooker. New York: The Modern Language Association of America, 1988.

Krupa, Fréderique. "Parisian Garbage from 1789–1900." *Paris: Urban Sanitation Before the 20th Century: A History of Invisible Infrastructure.* http://www.translucency.com/frede/parisproject/garbage17891900.html (accessed May 5, 2006).

La Jeunesse, Ernest. "La Bataille Théâtrale." *Comoedia Illustré* (15 April 1911): 414.

Larner, Gerald. *Maurice Ravel.* London: Phaidon Press, 1996.

Lawson, Joan. *A History of Ballet and Its Makers.* New York: Pitman Publishing Corporation, 1964.

Le Brun, Philip. "T. S. Eliot and Henri Bergson." *The Review of English Studies* 18.71 (August 1967): 274–86.

"Léhar, Franz." *Encyclopaedia Britannica.* 15th ed. 1975.

Lewis, Wyndham, ed. *Blast: Review of the Great English Vortex.* Numbers 1–2. Millwood, N.Y.: Kraus Reprint, 1974.

Lieberman, William S. *Painters in Paris: 1895–1950.* New Haven: Yale University Press, 2000.

Lockerd, Ben. "Maurras vs. Dawson: The Prime Influence on Eliot's Cultural Thought." *Time Present: The Newsletter of the T. S. Eliot Society* 63 (Fall 2007): 10–11.

Lockspeiser, Edward. *Debussy.* London: J. M. Dent & Sons, 1963.

"Louis Pasteur." *Embassy of France in Canada: Science and Technology Department.* http://www.ambafrance-ca.org/HYPERLAB/PEOPLE/pasteur.html (accessed May 15, 2006).

Macdougall, Allan Ross. *Isadora: A Revolutionary in Art and Love.* London: Thomas Nelson, 1960.

Macqueen-Pope, W. *The Melodies Linger On: The Story of Music Hall.* London: W. H. Allan, 1950.

Mailer, Norman. *Portrait of Picasso as a Young Man*. New York: Atlantic Monthly Press, 1995.

Marani, Pietro C. *Leonardo Da Vinci: The Complete Paintings*. New York: Abrams, 2000.

Marnold, Jean. "Musique." *Mercure de France* 92 (1 August 1911): 623–26.

Marston, Nicholas. "'The sense of an ending': Goal-directedness in Beethoven's Music." *The Cambridge Companion to Beethoven*. Ed. Glenn Stanley. New York: Cambridge University Press, 2000. 84–101.

Marx, William. *Naissance de la Critique Moderne: La Littérature selon Eliot et Valéry, 1889–1945*. Arras, France: Artois Presses Université, 2002.

———. "Two Modernisms: T. S. Eliot and *La Nouvelle Revue Française*." *The International Reception of T. S. Eliot*. Eds. Elisabeth Däumer and Shyamal Bagchee. London: Continuum, 2007.

Massine, Leonide. *My Life in Ballet*. New York: St. Martin's Press, 1968.

Massis, Henri. *Évocations: Souvenirs, 1905–1911*. Paris: Librairie Plon, 1931.

Matthews, T. S. *Great Tom: Notes Toward a Definition of T. S. Eliot*. New York: Harper and Row, 1963.

Matthiessen, F. O. *The Achievement of T. S. Eliot*. New York: Oxford University Press, 1959.

Maurois, André. *Histoire de la France*. Paris: Librairie Hachette, 1957.

McAlmon, Robert, and Kay Boyle. *Being Geniuses Together: 1910–1930*. London: Michael Joseph, 1968.

Menand, Louis. "The Women Come and Go: The Love Song of T. S. Eliot." *New Yorker* 30 September 2002: 126–31.

Miller, James E. *T. S. Eliot: The Making of an American Poet: 1888–1922*. University Park: Pennsylvania State University Press, 2005.

———. *T. S. Eliot's Personal Waste Land: Exorcism of the Demons*. University Park: Pennsylvania State University Press, 1977.

Moody, A. D. *Thomas Stearns Eliot: Poet*. Cambridge: Cambridge University Press, 1979.

Moore, Marianne. "A Note on T. S. Eliot's Book." *Poetry: A Magazine of Verse* (12 April 1918): 36–7. Rpt. in *T. S. Eliot: The Contemporary Reviews*. Ed. Jewel Spears Brooker. Cambridge: Cambridge University Press, 2004.

Morgenstern, John. "Discerning the 'Other' in *Other Observations*: T. S. Eliot as Cultural Anthropologist in 1910–1911 Paris." A paper presented at the T. S. Eliot Society Conference, St. Louis, Mo., 23 September 2006.

Morrell, Lady Ottoline. *Ottoline: The Early Memoirs of Lady Ottoline Morrell*. Ed. Robert Gathorne-Hardy. London: Faber and Faber, 1943.

Morris, G. K. L. "'Marie, Marie, Hold on Tight.'" *Partisan Review* 31.2 (March-April 1954): 231–3.

Nichols, Robert. "An Ironist." *Observer* (18 April 1920): 7. Rpt. in *T. S. Eliot: The Contemporary Reviews*. Ed. Jewel Spears Brooker. Cambridge: Cambridge University Press, 2004.

Nijinsky, Romola. *Nijinsky*. New York: Simon and Schuster, 1934.

Olivier, Fernande. *Picasso and His Friends*. Trans. Jane Miller. New York: Appleton Press, 1965.

"Paris." *Encyclopaedia Britannica*. 15th ed. 1975.

"Paris—Collège de France." *PlanetWare*. http://www.planetware.com/paris/college-de-france-f-p-cf.htm (accessed June 1, 2006).

Parisi, Joseph, and Stephen Young. *Dear Editor: A History of* Poetry *in Letters, The First Fifty Years 1912–1962*. New York: W. W. Norton and Company, 2002.

Parsons, Thomas, and Iain Gale. *Post-Impressionism: The Rise of Modern Art, 1880–1920.* Toronto: NDE Publishing, 1999.

Patmore, Brigit. *My Friends When Young: The Memoirs of Brigit Patmore.* London: William Heineman, 1968.

"Paul Claudel (1868–1955)." *Books and Writers.* http://www.kirjasto.sci.fi/pclaudel.htm (accessed January 23, 2007).

Percival, John. *The World of Diaghilev.* London: Studio Vista, 1971.

Perez, Claude-Pierre. "Connaissance de l'Est." *Paul Claudel: L'homme et l'oeuvre: L'oeuvre poétique.* http://www.paul-claudel.net/oeuvre/connaissance-est.html (accessed January 23, 2007).

"Périgueux." *JusttourFrance.* http://www.justtourfrance.com/aquitaine/town.asp?town=Perigu eux&area=Dordogne.htm (accessed September 16, 2007).

"Périgueux France." *Indigo Guide.* http://www.indigoguide.com/france/perigueux.htm (accessed September 17, 2007).

Perinot, Claudio. "Jean Verdenal: T. S. Eliot's French Friend." *Annali di ca' Foscari: Revista della Facoltà de lingue e letterature staniere dell università di venezia* 35.1–2 (1996): 265–75.

Perloff, Marjorie. *The Futurist Moment: Avant-Garde, Avant-Guerre, and the Language of Rupture.* Chicago: University of Chicago Press, 1986.

———. *21st-Century Modernism: The New "Poetics."* Oxford: Blackwell Publishers, 2002.

Perloff, Nancy. *Art and the Everyday: Popular Entertainment and the Circle of Erik Satie.* Oxford: Clarendon Press, 1991.

"Photos/Graphics: Paris 1." *Sewer History.* http://www.sewerhistory.org/grfx/wh_region/paris1. htm (accessed October 15, 2006).

"Poiret, Paul." *The Columbia Encyclopedia.* Sixth Edition. 2001–5. http://www.Bartleby. com/65/po/PoiretP.html (accessed September 13, 2006).

Pondrom, Cyrena N. *The Road from Paris: French Influence on English Poetry, 1900–1920.* Cambridge: Cambridge University Press, 1974.

Pope, John C. "Prufrock and Raskolnikov." *American Literature* 17.3 (November 1945): 213–30.

———. "Prufrock and Raskolnikov Again: A Letter from Eliot." *American Literature* 18.4 (January 1947): 319–21.

Pound, Ezra. *The Letters of Ezra Pound: 1907–1941.* Ed. D. D. Paige. New York: Harcourt Brace, 1950.

———. "T. S. Eliot." *Poetry: A Magazine of Verse* 10 (August 1917): 264–71. Rpt. in *T. S. Eliot: The Contemporary Reviews.* Ed. Jewel Spears Brooker. Cambridge: Cambridge University Press, 2004.

Propert, W. A. *The Russian Ballet in Western Europe, 1909–1917.* London: John Lane, 1921.

Rearick, Charles. "France's Cultural Clashes: Arts and Taste since the Impressionists." *French History Since Napoleon.* Ed. Martin S. Alexander. London: Arnold Publishers, 1999.

Reid, Donald. *Paris Sewers and Sewermen.* Cambridge, Mass.: Harvard University Press, 1991.

Richard Wagner: Libretti: Götterdämerung. http://www.rwagner.net/libretti/gotterd/e-t-gott. html (accessed September 20, 2007).

Richard Wagner: Libretti: Tristan und Isolde. http//www.rwagner.net/libretti/Tristan/e-tristan. alsl.html (accessed September 19, 2007).

Richard Wagner: Master of the Music Drama. 1997–2003. http://www.ffaire.com (accessed March 10, 2003).

Ricks, Christopher, ed. *T. S. Eliot: Inventions of the March Hare, Poems 1909–1917.* New York: Harcourt Brace & Company, 1996.

Rioux, J-P., and J-F Sirinelli. *Le Temps des masses: Le Vingtième siècle.* Vol. 4 of *Histoire culturelle de la France.* Paris: Éditions du Seuil, 1998.

Rivière, Jacques. "Moussorgski." *La Nouvelle Revue Française* 26 (1 February 1911): 314–17.

———. "Reprise de *Pelléas et Mélisande.*" *La Nouvelle Revue Française* 28 (1 April 1911): 623–5.

———. "Les Scènes Polovtsiennes du *Prince Igor.*" *La Nouvelle Revue Française* 25 (1 January 1911): 172–3.

———. "Sur le 'Tristan et Isolde' de Wagner." *La Nouvelle Revue Française* 25 (1 January 1911): 29–33.

———, and Alain-Fournier. *Correspondance: 1905–1914.* Vol. 2. Paris: Gallimard, 1926. 2 vols.

"Rodin, Auguste." *Encyclopaedia Britannica.* 15th ed. 1975.

Roger-Marx, Claude. "*Le Martyre de Saint Sébastien.*" *Comoedia Illustré* 17 (1 June 1911): 532–6.

Rothschild, Deborah Menaker. *Picasso's Parade: From Street to Stage.* London: Sotheby's Publishing, 1991.

Sachs, Curt. *World History of the Dance.* Trans. Bessie Schönberg. New York: Seven Arts, 1952.

Saint-Alban. "Le Nu au Théâtre." *Mercure de France* 90 (1 April 1911): 449–66.

"Saint-John Perse." *Poetry Portal.* http://www.poetry-portal.com/poets33.html (accessed February 1, 2007).

"Saint-John Perse (1887–1975)." *Books and Writers.* http://www.kirjasto.sci.fi/perse.htm (accessed February 1, 2007).

Schladweiler, Jon C. "Time Lines: Tracking down the Roots of our Sewer System, Paris." *Sewer History.* http://www.sewerhistory.org/grfx/wh_region/paris1.htm (accessed October 15, 2006).

Schuchard, Ronald. "In the Music Halls." *Eliot's Dark Angel: Intersections of Art and Life.* New York: Oxford University Press, 1999. 102–18.

Schwartz, Sanford. *The Matrix of Modernism.* Princeton: Princeton University Press, 1985.

Sencourt, Robert. *T. S. Eliot: A Memoir.* Ed. Donald Adamson. New York: Dodd, Mead & Company, 1971.

Seroff, Victor I. *Debussy: Musician of France.* Freeport, N.Y.: Books for Libraries, 1956.

Seymour-Jones, Carole. *Painted Shadow: The Life of Vivienne Eliot.* New York: Doubleday, 2001.

Shapiro, Barbara Stern. "Paris, The Capital of the Nineteenth Century." *Pleasures of Paris: Daumier to Picasso.* Ed. Barbara Stern Shapiro. Boston: Museum of Fine Arts, 1991.

Shattuck, Roger. *The Banquet Years: The Origins of the Avant Garde in France, 1885 to World War I.* Revised Ed. New York: Vintage Books, 1968.

Shrade, Leo. *Beethoven in France: The Growth of an Idea.* New York: Da Capo Press, 1978.

Sinclair, May. "*Prufrock and Other Observations:* A Criticism." *Little Review* 4.8 (December 1917): 8–14. Rpt. in *T. S. Eliot: The Contemporary Reviews.* Ed. Jewel Spears Brooker. Cambridge: Cambridge University Press, 2004.

Sitwell, Osbert. *Laughter in the Next Room*. Toronto: Macmillan, 1948.

Smidt, Kristian. *Poetry and Belief in the Work of T. S. Eliot*. Oslo: I kommisjon hos J. Dybwad, 1949.

Smith, Grover. *T. S. Eliot's Poetry and Plays: A Study in Sources and Meaning*. Chicago: University of Chicago Press, 1956.

Soldo, John J. *The Tempering of T. S. Eliot*. Ann Arbor: University of Michigan Press, 1983.

Sorell, Walter. *The Dance Through the Ages*. New York: Grosset and Dunlap, 1967.

Southam, B. C. *A Guide to the Selected Poems of T. S. Eliot*. London: Faber and Faber, 1994.

Speaight, George. *A History of the Circus*. New York: A. S. Barnes and Company, 1980.

Spencer, Charles. *Leon Bakst*. New York: St. Martin's Press, 1973.

Spender, Stephen. "Remembering Eliot." *T. S. Eliot: The Man and his Work*. Ed. Allen Tate. New York: Delacorte Press, 1966. 38–64.

Stanley, Glenn. "Beethoven at Work: Musical Activist and Thinker." *The Cambridge Companion to Beethoven*. Ed. Glenn Stanley. New York: Cambridge University Press, 2000.

Steegmuller, Francis. *Apollinaire: Poet among the Painters*. New York: Farrar Straus, 1963.

Steele, Valerie. *Paris Fashions: A Cultural History*. New York: Oxford University Press, 1988.

Stravinsky, Igor. "Memories of T. S. Eliot." *Esquire* (August 1965): 91–3.

Stravinsky, Vera, and Robert Craft. *Stravinsky in Pictures and Documents*. New York: Simon and Schuster, 1978.

Sullivan, J. W. N. *Beethoven: His Spiritual Development*. New York: Alfred A. Knopf, 1964.

Svarny, Erik. *"The Men of 1914": T. S. Eliot and Early Modernism*. Philadelphia: Open University Press, 1988.

Tannenbaum, Edward R. *The Action Française: Die-Hard Reactionaries in Twentieth-Century France*. New York: John Wiley and Sons, 1962.

Tate, Allen. "Whose Ox." *Fugitive* 1 (December 1922): 99–100. Rpt. in *T. S. Eliot: The Contemporary Reviews*. Ed. Jewel Spears Brooker. Cambridge: Cambridge University Press, 2004.

Thompson, Oscar. *Debussy: Man and Artist*. New York: Dodd, Mead, 1937.

Tint, Herbert. *The Decline of French Patriotism: 1870–1940*. London: Weidenfeld and Nicolson, 1964.

Tomlinson, David. "T. S. Eliot and the Cubists." *Twentieth-Century Literature* 26 (1980): 64–81.

Torrens, James, S. J. "Charles Maurras and Eliot's 'New Life.'" *PMLA* 89.2 (March 1974): 312–22.

Tristan und Isolde. Program from the Opéra National de Paris, 1998.

Trombold, Chris Buttram. "Earlier Versions of Eliot's Early Verse: The Newly-Published Drafts in the Berg Collection." *Journal of Modern Literature* 12 (1997): 89–108.

Tucker, Shawn R. *"The Waste Land*, Liminoid Phenomena, and the Confluence of Dada." *Mosaic* 34.3 (September 2001): 91–109.

Untermeyer, Louis. "Irony de Luxe." *Freeman* 1 (30 June 1920): 381–2. Rpt. in *T. S. Eliot: The Contemporary Reviews*. Ed. Jewel Spears Brooker. Cambridge: Cambridge University Press, 2004.

The Wagner Experience. http://www.utexas.edu/courses/wagner/htm (accessed March 10, 2003).

"Wagner, Richard." *Encyclopaedia Britannica*. 15th ed. 1975.

Wagner, Richard. *The Ring of the Nibelungen*. Trans. Stewart Robb. New York: E. P. Dutton, 1960.

Wallace, Robert M., and the Editors of *Time-Life* Books. *The World of Leonardo: 1452–1519*. New York: Time-Life Books, 1966.

Watson, George. "Quest for a Frenchman." *The Sewanee Review* 84.3 (July-September 1976): 465–75.

Waugh, Arthur. "The New Poetry." *Quarterly Review* 226 (October 1916): 386. Rpt. in *T. S. Eliot: The Contemporary Reviews*. Ed. Jewel Spears Brooker. Cambridge: Cambridge University Press, 2004.

Weber, Eugen. *Action Française: Royalism and Reaction in Twentieth-Century France*. Stanford: Stanford University Press, 1962.

Webster's New Collegiate Dictionary. Springfield, Mass.: G. & C. Merriam, 1958.

Weiss, Jeffrey. "Modernism and Memory: 1889–1914." *The Art and Spirit of Paris*. Ed. Michel Laclotte. Vol. 2. New York: Abbeville Press Publishers, 2003. 2 vols.

Whitworth, Geoffrey. *The Art of Nijinsky*. London: Chatto and Windus, 1913.

Wilson, Edmund. "The Rag-Bag of the Soul." *The New York Evening Post Literary Review* (22 November 1922): 237–8. Rpt. in *T. S. Eliot: The Contemporary Reviews*. Ed. Jewel Spears Brooker. Cambridge: Cambridge University Press, 2004.

Woolf, Virginia. "Mr. Bennett and Mrs. Brown." *Virginia Woolf: Collected Essays*. Ed. Leonard Woolf. Vol. 1. London: Chatto and Windus, 1966–7. 4 vols.

Wyndham Lewis: Art and War Exhibition. The Imperial War Museum. London. 25 June-11 October 1992.

Zeldin, Theodore. *France: 1848–1945: Anxiety and Hypocrisy*. New York: Oxford University Press, 1981.

Zuckerman, Elliott. *The First Hundred Years of Wagner's Tristan*. New York: Columbia University Press, 1964.

INDEX

Note: Illustrations are indicated by the notation *f* after the page number.

Ballets Russes: avant-garde tendencies, 179–80; *Daphnis et Chloé*, 51, 212; Eliot reviews, 222; *The Firebird*, 210–11; impact on fashion, 102, 287n6; impact on stage design, 101; impact summarized, 164; influence on Eliot, 174, 182, 183–84, 277; in London, 179–85; London productions, 169; opportunities to see, 277; Oriental themes, 287n6; *Parade*, 180–81; in Paris, 169–78; popularity of, 172–73; programs in June 1911, 54; Ida Rubenstein, 114; set and costume designers, 171; at Théâtre du Châtelet, 158f, 169; Whitworth on, 188

Bal Tabarin, 249

Barbarism, fears of, 19, 214

Basilique du Sacré-Coeur, 1, 62, 64–65; Cubism depiction, 134

Basset, Serge, 107–8

Ba-ta-Clan Music Hall, 162f, 235, 237, 241

Baudelaire, Charles Pierre: critics of, 20–21, 286n26; influence on Eliot, 266, 267, 271, 272; influence on Rodin, 143; influence of, on urban scene, 7, 77; sculptured head, 291n18; on Wagner, 293n5

"Beating of a Drum, The," 240

Becque, Henry, 101–2

Beethoven, Ludwig von: centennial of his death, 218; cult of, 215; Eliot's devotion to, 217; experimental techniques, 219–20, 279; frequency on concert scene, 210; influence on Eliot, 53, 211, 217, 279, 294n2; influence on Wagner, 198; late quartets, 219, 220, 221; Parisian devotion to, 145, 214–15, 217, 218; performances, 214–21; sculptures of, 144–45; significance to French, 53; Siegfried Wagner concert, 37

Beethoven Festival, 53, 216–17

Bell, Clive, 148

Belladonna, the Lady of the Rocks, 128–29

Belle Époque, 60

Belphégor (Benda), influence of, 46

Benda, Julian, 46, 54–55, 261, 270–71

Benois, Alexandre, 171, 178

Bergson, Henri, 1, 2, 37–43; appearance, 93f; Bourdelle's influence on, 144; Eliot on, 39; Eliot's attendance at lectures, 285n22; famous lectures, 39–41, 47, 52, 94f, 285–86n23; idea of attending his lectures, 8; influence on Eliot, 41–43, 50–51, 110–11, 263–64; influence on Péguy, 18; key concepts, 40; modern art link, 53, 135; oblique references, 51; as rationale for stay in Paris, 2; significance of, 38–39; Verdenal's interest in, 29

Berlioz, Hector, 104, 105, 193

Bernhardt, Sarah, 172

Bernstein, Henri, 286n27

Bicycles, 67–68, 83–85, 226, 294n4

Bicycling clubs, 84

Blast (Vorticist magazine), 148

Blériot, Louis, 69, 85

Bloomsbury group, 179

Blum, Léon, 110, 118

"Bois Sacré, Le," 238

Books consulted, overview, 3

Borodin, Alexander, 210

Boston, return to, 257

Bourdelle, Émile, 143, 144–45; busts of Beethoven, 214; on Isadora Duncan, 168, 291n17; Saint Sebastian sculpture, 291n15

Boxing: appeal to Eliot, 12, 251; described, 82–83; Eliot's lessons, 83; on film, 251; matches, 49, 51, 82–83

Braque, Georges, 134, 135

British journals, 270–71

Brothers Karamazov, The, 111–14, 150f; Eliot at play, 101; stage adaptation, 23, 51; success of, 113, 151f, 288n8

Brown, Dan, 290n4

Bubu de Montparnasse (Philippe): influence of, 14–16, 37, 50, 211–12, 234, 268, 271, 273, 274, 281, 284

Buddha, 206

Buildings, 64–65

"Burnt Dancer, The," 120

"Burnt Norton": influence of Alain-Fournier, 27; influence of ballet, 185; influence of Beethoven, 220; influence of Bergson, 43; influence of *Pelléas et Mélisande*, 195, 196; musical allusions, 224

Buses, 67

Cabarets-artistiques, 229–31, 254; influence on Eliot, 50

Cafés-concerts, 231–36; Concert Mayol, 50, 235–36; described, 231, 234–35; influence on Eliot, 50, 232–34, 255; music halls compared, 236–37; with outdoor gardens, 295n12

Cahiers de la Quinzaine, Les: contributors, 19; Péguy as editor, 19, 263

Camelots du Roi, 21, 44–45, 62, 107, 108–9, 286n27; Gide's characterization of, 109–10

"Cape Ann": lost innocence theme, 26

Caplet, André, 119

Carnaval, 174

Cars, 66–67, 96f; automobiling as sport, 85

Casals, Pablo, 212, 216

Catholic Church: on *Le Martyre de Saint Sébastien* play, 115–16, 151f

Chaplin, Charlie, 180, 251, 292n9

Chat Noir cabaret, 229, 230, 254

Chevalier, Maurice, 242

Children in Paris, 49

Chocolat (clown), 244–45, 254

Chopin, Frederic, 213

Chung Ling Soo, 241, 253

Cinema, 73–74, 287n2; boxing matches, 83; Eliot's interest in, 251; influence on ballet, 180, 292n8; influence of on Eliot's techniques, 253, 280; as popular entertainment, 250–51

Circus acts, 243–45; in music halls, 24, 236, 240, 242

Cirque de Paris, 244

Cirque Médrano, 244, 254

City, The (Léger), 139

City of Paris, The (Delaunay), 139

City Rises, The (Boccioni), 139

Civilization, destruction of, 140

Claridge Hotel, 65

Classical music: Eliot's funeral, 221, 222–23; Eliot's lifelong interest in, 222–23; influence on Eliot, 223–25, 278–79; influence on poems listed, 223; overview, of composers, 210; overview of Parisian scene, 209–10, 210–14; recordings, 222; structure of poems related, 223–24. *See also* Beethoven, Ludwig von

Classical tradition: merits of, 21

Claudel, Paul: Eliot's obituary of, 17–18; influence of, 16–18, 288n2; influence on Eliot's plays, 18; Lugné-Poe role, 105

Cleopatra theme, 249

Clothing. *See* Fashion

Clowns, 244–45, 254

Cocktail Party, The: martyrdom theme, 123

Cocteau, Jean, 245, 246, 253, 271

Collage as technique, 136, 137–38

Collège de France, 2, 37–38, 92f; history, 38; location, 10; names for, 285n21

Collins, Wilkie, 228

Comedy, 238–40

Commissaires de L'Action Française, 44

Common ground, lack of, 124

Communications, advances in, 71

Composers, overview, 210

Concert hall. *See* Classical music

Concert Mayol, 50, 235–36

Concerts Barrau, 215, 216

Concerts Colonne, 210; Beethoven concerts, 215, 216–17; prices, 209

Concerts Lamoureux, 209, 210, 215

Concerts of military music, 65

Connaissance de l'Est (Claudel), 17

Conservatoire de Musique, 209

Continuity, principle of, 188

Copeau, Jacques, 13, 23, 112

Corneille, Pierre, 222

Costume design, theatre, 79, 99f

Criterion, The, models for, 263, 270–71

Critic, Eliot on role of, 297n4

Croué, Jean, 13, 23, 112

Cubism: adopted by Futurists, 133; Armory Show (Boston), 147, 291n20; Eliot on, 148; fracturing human figure, 138; influence of, 133–34, 138, 141, 276, 291n19; influence on *Waste Land*, 136, 139–40; influencing sculpture, 144; primitivism in, 139

Cubist exhibit at Salon des Indépendants, 52–53, 276; sensational debut, 134–35, 290n11; Verdenal and, 31

Culottes, 80, 100f; Eliot on, 80–81; Verdenal on, 80, 81

Cult of masculinity, 76

Cultural events: influence summarized, 274–80; January through June, 48–54; overview, 1; range of, 11; re-creating the milieu, 3–4

Cultures and religions, array of, 138

cummings, e. e., 141

Cup of Light Automobiles, 85

Curie, Marie, 1, 75–76, 79, 287n3

Cycling, 67–68

Dada, 136, 148

Damia, 235–36

Dance: American popular, 248, 253–54; "divine pattern" of, 186; Eliot at dancing parties, 248–49; Eliot's verse drama, 186–87; influence on Eliot, 186, 188–89, 276–77; leading Russian dancers, 172; natural movements in, 165–67; rhythm analyzed, 186; saraband and farandole, 296n28; as symbol, 189; "Tradition and the Individual Talent," 187–89. *See also* Ballet; Ballets Russes; Duncan, Isadora; *Parade*; Rubenstein, Ida

Dance halls, 247–50

Dandy persona: appeal of, 7, 9; *flâneur* as outgrowth, 76; influence of Laforgue, 272. *See also* *Flâneur*

Daniel-Henry Kahnweiler (Picasso), 134

221; lost innocence theme, 26; multilayered symbolism, 199; music as theme and symbol, 224; repetition technique, 199; structures of music related, 223; suffering and reconciliation in, 218–19; thematic variation in, 219–20

"Fourth Caprice in Montparnasse," 37

Fragson, Harry, 162f, 239–40, 295n16, 296n17

France, 21; compared to other nations, 260; Eliot lectures on, 264; predominance of Paris, 283n2; representing poetry, 8

Francophile, Eliot as, 58, 257–60

Franco-Prussian War (1870), 59–60

French ancestry, Eliot's, 297n1

French friends and colleagues summarized, 260–61

French language skills. *See* Language issues

French people: analytical mindset admired, 259; love and admiration for, 259–60

French rooster symbol, 239, 296n17

Frères Karamazov, Les. See *Brothers Karamazov, The*

Fry, Roger, 132, 148, 271

Futurist artists/Futurism, 133, 135, 136, 290n12; on industrial world, 139

Gallipoli: battle of, 29, 33

Game of the massacre, 246

Games, 246

Garbage collection, 72–73

Gardner, Isabella Stewart, 147–48, 290n5

Garnier, Charles, 160f, 191, 292n1

Gautier, Théophile: on circuses, 244; exposition on, 53; on fairytales, 110; influence on Eliot, 110, 271; *Spectre de la Rose* (ballet), 175, 176

Gender, status of men and women, 76–81

Germany: Eliot on Germans, 260; Munich, 56; summer trip to, 56–57; tensions, 60, 62–63

"Gerontion," influence of, 76

Gervais, A., 79

Gesamtkunstwerk, 198

Ghéon, Henri: Affaire Fauchois, 45; on Cubism, 135–36; on Isadora Duncan, 166, 167–68; influence on Eliot, 124–25, 262; on *Le Martyre de Saint Sébastien*, 123–24; on *Narcisse*, 174; on *Petrouchka*, 177; on Ravel, 197; "Sur le 'Théâtre Populaire,'" 124–25

Gide, André, 1, 265; on Affaire Fauchois, 109–10; *Brothers Karamazov* play reviewed, 113–14; on Claudel, 16; Eliot's introduction to, 20; Eliot's personal and literary acquaintance, 21–22, 261; on *Éloges*, 22; influence on Eliot, 262; major works discussed, 20; on Maurras, 45; on Philippe, 35

Gille, Victor, 213

"Goldfish," 190

Gommeuse, 231, 233–34, 241

Gramont, Louis de, 104–5

Gramophones, 73

Grand Meaulnes, Le (Alain-Fournier), 26–27

Gravelines, Jean, 108, 109

Greek myths: in opera, 193; pitfalls in using, 175

Greek tragedies, theatre season, 103

Grizzly Bear dance, 248

Guilt, burden of, 24

"*Hamlet*," 103, 199

Health issues, 257, 258, 259

Hécube, 103

Hedda Gabler, 105

Hedonism theme, 20

L'Heure espagnole (Ravel), 193, 196–97, 277, 278

Hinckley, Eleanor, 3, 80, 82, 131, 248, 266

"Hippopotamus, The," 231

History of Paris (1848–1911), 59–60

Hogarth, William, 140

Hogarth Press, 148

Holidays in France, after 1911, 257–59

"Hollow Men, The": influence of ballet, 178, 277; rose reference, 177

Holmes, Sherlock, 29, 227, 228

Homage to Blériot (Delaunay), 139

Homosexuality: Gide's rights advocacy, 20, 262; Verdenal relationship, 28, 284–85n13

Horseracing, 82

"Humanism of Irving Babbitt, The," 46

Humanities versus social sciences debated, 35, 36

Ibsen, Henrik, 105

"Ideal, the" (*l'Idéal*), Verdenal on, 29–30

Imperial expansion, 62

Impressionist analogies, 141

Industrial production, 69

Inoubliable France (Eliot introduction), 259

Inspiration of Paris: cultural events, 11; leading French figures, overview, 76; overview, 2

Intellectual figures, overview, 1, 261–64

"Interlude: in a Bar," 50, 233, 234

"Interlude in London": writing of, 52

Introductions by Eliot, overview, 268

Intuition, Bergson on, 40

Iphigénie en Aulide (play), 106–10

Italian Futurist movement, 133, 139

Italy, 127

200–201; psychological drama, 202–3; Verdenal on, 31

"Triumphal March," 45–46

Typist, as creation, 254

Underhill, Evelyn, 286n23

Universe as a work of art, 17

Université de Paris, 35. *See also* Collège de France

Universities, women students, 78, 79

Urban renovation and modernization, 59–60

Urban scene as subject matter: Baudelaire as influence, 7; composite of cities, 297n8; *flâneur* as spectator, 76–77, 211, 287n2; fog, source of references, 295n10; "Fourth Caprice," 37; French literary influences, 271; as frightening, 173; influences summarized, 272–73, 281; London, 52; musical dissonance and, 255; in *Parade* (ballet), 252, 253; Philippe letters as influence, 15; portraying underside, 16; prostitutes, 15–16, 211; revolutionary urbanism approach, 281; Stravinsky scores, 222; in *Waste Land*, 137, 138–39, 253

Use of Poetry and the Use of Criticism, The, 242, 274

Valéry, Paul, 261, 265, 269, 271

Vandeputte, Henri, 15, 28

Vanderpyl, Fritz, 258

Velázquez, Diego: Pound's references to, 140

Verdenal, Jean, 28–34; correspondence with, 58; on Cubism, 135, 290n12; on culottes, 80, 81; death in battle, 261; dedication to, 33; described, 28, 91*f*; Eliot dedication to, 285n15; Eliot's nostalgia for, 33, 259; exchanges on opera, 191; final meeting, 58; friendship with, 28–29, 32–34, 260; as ideal friend, 12; interest in art, 31, 53; interest in literature, 30; interest in philosophy, 29; legacy for Eliot, 33; at Pension Casaubon, 31–32; personality, 29; political tendencies, 30, 110; response to music, 209; terms of address in letters, 28, 32–33; on Wagnerian opera, 31, 200, 203–4

Verse drama: d'Annunzio's, 118–19; Eliot on modern style, 122, 123; Eliot's, and the dance, 186–87; low and high art combined, 252; as one of Eliot's goals, 103; possible inspiration of d'Annunzio, 122; preference for, 105

Violin and Pitcher (Braque), 134

Virgin Mary reference, 177

Visits to other parts of Europe, 4; Belgium (1914), 147; Italy, 57; London, 52, 147, 284n4, 288n7; museums, 126; Périgueux in Dordogne region,

47, 258; stopover in London, 9, 121; summer trip to Germany, 56–57; Vienna (possible trip 1911), 287n34

Visual arts: avant-garde in Paris, 132–36; Eliot's background, 126; established works of art (London), 130–32; established works of art (Paris), 127–30; overview, 126; zenith of experimentation, 132

Vorticism, 136, 141, 148

Wagner, Richard: Eliot's devotion to, 191; influence on Eliot, 203, 224; influences on, 198, 203; innovation in, 198; *leitmotif,* 199

Wagner, Siegfried, 37, 215

Wagnerian opera, 198–207; influence on Eliot, 207, 278; Munich performances, 56; as music drama, 198; opportunities to attend, 191; *Parsifal,* 293n4; suggestiveness theme, 293n5; Verdenal on, 31, 190–91. *See also Ring des Nibelungen, Der; Tristan und Isolde*

Waste Land, The : allusions to art in contemporary reviews, 140–41; allusion to *Madonna of the Rocks* painting, 128–29; cinematic techniques in, 251, 253; Cubist influence, 139–40, 276; Debussy influence, 49; dissonant modern life in, 255; Fragson influence, 239; gramophone reference, 73; high art and ordinary combined, 129; Hyacinth Girl passage, 200, 201–2; influence of art, 149, 276; influence of avant-garde art, 136–40; influence of ballet, 178, 180, 181, 182, 183, 188–89, 291n1; influence of Beethoven, 214; influence of cafés-concerts, 234; influence of Dostoevsky, 24; influence of Maurras, 45–46, 264; influence of music halls, 243; influence of *Parade* (ballet), 136, 252, 253, 254; influence of popular entertainment, 252–56; influence of Ravel, 197; influence of Stravinsky, 210–11, 222; influence of Wagnerian opera, 196, 198–99, 200, 201–2, 204–6, 278, 293n4; *Le Martyre de Saint Sébastien* as inspiration, 55; on modern love, 201–2; multilayered symbolism, 199; Munich setting, 56; opera quotes, 24; popular dance steps, 248; repetition technique, 199; reviews of, 137; sinister references, 228; sledding episode, 56; stream of consciousness in, 199; street fair influence, 245; structure of *Four Quartets* and, 221; structures of music related, 223–24; Surrealist influence, 139–40

Water symbolism, 194–95

Weather reports, fall term, 34

Index · 323

Nancy Duvall Hargrove is William L. Giles Distinguished Professor Emerita of English at Mississippi State University. She is the author of *Landscape as Symbol in the Poetry of T. S. Eliot* (1978) and *The Journey Toward Ariel: Sylvia Plath's Poems of 1956–1959* (1994) as well as over forty essays on Eliot, Plath, and other literary figures. She is the recipient of numerous teaching and research awards, including four Fulbright lectureships.

CPSIA information can be obtained
at www.ICGtesting.com
Printed in the USA
LVHW082242140622
721311LV00010B/429